ELECTRONIC DISPLAY DEVICES

This book is dedicated to my mother,
Grace Evelyn Walker Perez.
She believed in me when I didn't . . .

ELECTRONIC DISPLAY DEVICES

RICHARD A. PEREZ

TAB Professional and Reference Books

Division of TAB BOOKS Inc.
P.O. Box 40, Blue Ridge Summit, PA

FIRST EDITION

FIRST PRINTING

Printed in the United States of America

Library of Congress Cataloging in Publication Data

Perez, Richard A.
Electronic display devices / by Richard A. Perez.
p. cm.
Includes index.
ISBN 0-8306-2957-2
1. Information display systems. I. Title.
TK7882.I6P46 1987
621.389'7—dc19 87-29030
CIP

Questions regarding the content of this book should be addressed to:

Reader Inquiry Branch
Editorial Department
TAB BOOKS Inc.
Blue Ridge Summit, PA 17294-0214

Contents

Acknowledgments

This book could not have been written without the support of my beautiful and loving wife, Karen. She chopped all the wood, hauled all the water, and pounded all the nails during the some 1,600+ hours this project required. Credit is also due to Karen for proofreading the manuscript, and also for her many helpful comments. Credit goes to the Wizard for his help with the graphs, illustrations, and esoteric physics dilemmas. Thanks to Stan Krute for his computer instruction and for helping me out of many software tight-spots. Thanks goes to John T. Pryor for his inspiration.

I wish to acknowledge the support of the entire electronic display industry. They supplied the information. Of the over 300 manufacturers I corresponded with, there wasn't a sourpuss in the bunch. Thanks!

Introduction

Our lives are filled with information. Much of our time is spent in the communication of information. There are very few of us who don't receive information daily from some sort of electronic display device. It may be the LCD on your wristwatch, the CRT in your computer, the display on your car's dash, and/or the ubiquitous television set. Electronic devices are prime information inputs for just about everyone living in a technologically developed society.

The purpose of this book is to familiarize you with all current forms of electronic display devices. There are many reasons to get better acquainted with electronic displays. The more we understand, the better able we are to use these devices. This book is a technical overview of the electronic display field. An entire book could be written on each individual device. My purpose here is not to delve deeply, but to offer and compare basic information on a wide variety of display types.

Chapter 1 is an introduction to information, electronic display, and the human apparatus we use to perceive the display. Chapter 2 begins the survey of the actual display devices. Included in each chapter is information on how the display works, how it is made, its operating characteristics, strong points, weak points, and sample applications. I have included many more sample applications on the simpler and less costly display devices. I have done this because it is much more probable that these sample applications will be built if they use a $5.00 LED or LCD rather than a $3,000 plasma display. Chapter 10 is a comparison of the display devices surveyed and summarizes the entire field of electronic information display. The emphasis is on finding the right display device for any particular job and on proper application of the display.

Electronic display is a high-tech field. Within this field are technological concepts that range from ultra basic to esoteric beyond belief. I have done my best to render these technologies understandable to anyone familiar with basic science. Over 300 different manufacturers of electronic displays were surveyed to obtain the information presented here. I have assumed only a minimum knowledge of practical electronics. For those not familiar with this information, textbooks on basic physics and/or electronics make excellent companions to this volume.

1

What Is A Display?

A display communicates information. Within this simple, short statement lurks many complex assumptions. Some of these assumptions such as vision, language, and pattern recognition are so much a part of us that we don't even realize we're using them. Other assumptions such as what constitutes information are more consciously made and not as instinctive. This book concentrates on the electronic communication of information using light as the medium. All the display devices in this book, with the exception of analog meters, are light producers or modifiers. This book is the story of information's journey into light and the light's ability to communicate with us.

A display communicates information. This implies that the information is coming from somewhere and that it is going somewhere. In this world of instant electronic communication, the potential sources of information are endless and everywhere. The information's destination is you or me. A display makes knowledge, data, facts, and other information available to our senses. This seemingly simple process is actually a complex mix of physics, physiology, psychology, and information theory.

There are three basic elements in information display. First is the information, from whatever source. Second is the medium which is the device communicating the information. Third, is the user of the information, its destination. If any information display is to work, these three elements must be present. We, as the human participants in the information transfer process, are essential to the success of the entire process. If we don't get the message, the entire process is wasted. An understanding of these three elements enables us to better use the wide array of electronic information communication devices available to us.

A Short History of Electronic Display. Information display started as paintings on cave walls, and probably predates language. We've been drawing pictures much longer than we have been writing words. The techniques of the graphic arts have evolved continually over the last several thousand years. The mediums of information transfer have changed radically during the last century. Instead of paint and rock walls, we now commonly use electricity and light as communications tools.

The earliest purely electronic display is the analog meter. This electromechanical device has been used to measure electricity since the beginning of the 17th Century. While the analog meter is neither a light producer or a light modifier, it is an electronic display that preceeds all others. Its usefulness has been eroded by more modern types, but it is still used in many applications today.

Electronic information display began in this century with the advent of incandescent lighting. A single lightbulb can communicate information by being either on or off. Entire banks of lightbulbs can be lit in a dot matrix fashion to spell out words or draw pictures. Electricity gives us the power to make light or darkness as we wish. Our desire to communicate has led us to use this power to convey information.

The cathode ray tube (CRT) became a widely used display device at the end of the Second World War. This tube was and still is the quintessential display device. It is versatile. It can display pictures, text, numbers, and more. It can even make the image move. Electronic display technology went into high gear with the advent of the CRT. This tube was the device that made television possible. The CRT is used in over 80% of all electronic display devices currently sold. It is everywhere—television sets, computer terminals, games, instruments, home computers...

Electronic display technology is not a static, but a rapidly developing technology. Many new displays are nipping at the heels of the venerable CRT. In most cases they emulate the CRT's manner of information display. We have been spoiled by years of CRT usage. We are not satisfied with any lesser or slower modes of display. The newer display technologies are focusing on reproducing the versatility of the CRT in smaller and lower powered devices. Such devices as liquid crystal displays, electroluminescent displays, and plasma displays were once technical curiosities. Now they are available to anyone who wishes to apply them.

The future holds many display technologies that may replace the CRT. The ability to display three dimensional images is very attractive. Laser holography holds this promise. Flat screen technologies may give us a television set that can be hung on the wall like a picture. One thing is for sure, the displays of the future will convey information faster, with more resolution and color than ever before.

INFORMATION: WHAT IS IT?

The root word of information is inform. Inform means to give form, to shape. Information means giving structure to creative and interpretative processes. It is the organization of knowledge, facts, ideas, and perceptions so that they may be communicated and understood. Information is a response to the purely human need to understand, to know. The form of the information depends on the factors—what the information is, how it is to be communicated, and who (or what) it is to be communicated to. Information may be words, numbers, pictures, sounds, and/or feelings; the list is as endless as our curiosity.

For example, look at a painting by Da Vinci. It communicates with us via our eyes to form an image within our brain, and hopefully informs our consciousness. It is an image, a picture. If you try to tell someone who has not seen it what it means, then you will find that spoken language is unable to communicate the image. The type of information determines the medium necessary to communicate it.

Let's examine several types of information in order to understand the strong points and limitations of each. We should never lose sight of the fact that information is a human concept, and that all these types of information are the work of men. As such, they are organized and limited by our human perceptions and consciousness. This is true of even the most bizarre forms of information that are not directly used by man, like binary information. Some other forms of information have become very "friendly" to us. Consider the words on this page. They are formed of the 26 alphabetical characters that make up the English language. We communicate with these words in both written and spoken forms. They are so familiar to us that we perform communication using them without conscious realization or consideration of their form.

Binary

Binary information is used by computers to process all other types of information. Pictures, words, and numbers are all translated into binary information in order to be processed by computers. Binary information is used directly by very few humans, those who are so deeply into computers that they understand their languages.

Binary language possesses only two elements. *On* or *off*, *1* or *0*, *hot* or *cold*, *high* or *low*. Only two elements are used to represent all types of information. Binary information is based on the sum of integral powers of the number two. Consider the following mathematical equation:

$$N_0 2^0 + N_1 2^1 + N_2 2^2 + N_3 2^3 + N_4 2^4 + N_5 2^5 + N_6 2^6 + N_7 2^7 \ldots$$

Equation 1-1

This equation represents the foundation of binary information. The powers of 2 are multiplied by factors represented by the numbers N_0, N_1, N_2, and so on, which can be either 1 (one) or 0 (zero). No other factors are allowed; they cannot for example be a three, they must be either a one or a zero. The successively larger powers of two are multiplied by these factors to obtain any desired number. Two to the zero power is one, two to the first power is two, two to the second power is four, two to the third power is eight, and so on... By using a factor (either a 1 or a 0) multiplying these powers of two, and by adding the result, we can represent 256 different information states by using eight factors each of which may be either a one or a zero. Now this seems a hopelessly complex way of organizing information. So why bother, when we already have a perfectly good base 10 number system and a serviceable alphabet?

The answer to this question lies in what the information is being used by—the computer. Computers are stupid. They only recognize two states of information, either on or off (1 or 0). The reason for this is that computers "think" with transistor junctions. Each and every junction within a computer (and there are millions of them) can be in only one of two states, either on or off. The computer is incapable of dealing with the myriad forms used in either base 10 numbers or alphabetical characters. It understands only the simplest form of information—digital binary information. It is called binary because it is based on the powers of two, and digital because the information states are nonambiguous. Either one or zero is allowed, but no other states.

Binary information is almost always translated by the computer into numerical, alphabetical, and graphics information for use by the user. This translation is what appears on the computer's display. This translation requires hardware and software to be accomplished. It also requires a fairly complex display device. Some early computers used binary information as their only output to humans. This did away with the necessity for additional hardware. These computers had the binary information encoded into a system of eight lights (LEDs). A lit LED would indicate a one in that position, while an unlit LED indicated zero.

This is the major advantage of the display of binary information. It is very simple. All that is required is a display device that is capable of two states (on or off). One display device is required for each binary digit. Each binary digit is called a bit. Each bit may be represented by an incandescent lamp, an LED, or any other electrically operated bi-state device. Binary information display may be very simple for the computer to implement, but it is very difficult for humans to understand. After all, the binary information system is the native tongue of the computer, but it is as clear as mud to most humans. This is the binary display's greatest disadvantage. Humans don't speak or think in binary. To get over this hurdle, computers now translate their binary information into other forms when communicating with humans.

Analog Information

Analog measurement is the oldest form of information communicated by an electronic display device. It began with the early use of electrical meters. These devices convert electrical parameters, such as current or voltage, into the deflection of a pointer. This pointer is deflected across a printed scale where the measurement is read. This type of readout has certain inherent limitations. The greatest limitation is our inability to visually read the meter's scale to a high degree of accuracy. Let's pursue this further through an analogy.

For example, let's consider measuring a person's height with a tape measure. Stand the person up against the wall, make a mark on the wall, and measure the distance with the tape. Sounds easy and it is. But it is not very accurate. When the measuring tape is placed against the wall, there are certain to be inaccuracies in measuring the distance against the tape's scale. We could say that the person is 6 feet, 1/2 inch tall. But in reality, the person may actually be 6 feet, 17/32 inch tall. We may not be able to read the 1/32 of an inch difference accurately on the ruler's scale. All analog information has some degree of inaccuracy. It is, by its nature, approximate. The degree of ambiguity that analog information possesses is called its resolution. In analog information, the higher the resolution is, the higher its accuracy is.

Analog information may be represented by a wide variety of electronic displays. For example, consider the LED. Binary information can only be displayed by an LED that is either lit or not lit. There is no middle ground with binary. However, analog information can and always does possess an infinite number of interim states between on and off. In conveying analog information, the LED may be either lit or not lit, or any in between state of illumination. Consider an LED that is used to indicate the volume level of a record player. The louder the record player's audio volume is turned up, the brighter the LED becomes. This LED displays audio intensity by its brightness. The information is certainly ambiguous, but it does effectively communicate in an application where binary information would be virtually useless. A single binary indicator can only tell us if this record player was on or off. It is incapable of giving us relative information like the level of the audio.

Digital Information

Digital information has been processed using at least one binary information translation. Consider this example. We are using a digital multimeter to measure the voltage of a car battery. The digital meter reads out in numbers, not in pointer deflection as does the analog meter. The battery's voltage is measured as 12.62 volts. This certainly appears nonambiguous and accurate, but is it really?

The "guts" of the meter have made an analog measurement of the battery's voltage, converted this analog measurement into digital information and then displayed it in the form of numbers. The initial measurement is analog. In this measurement and its conversion to digital information, inherent inaccuracies creep in. The first inaccuracy is due to the imprecise nature of any analog measurement. The second inaccuracy is caused by the measurement's conversion from analog to digital data. Since digital information is nonambiguous, how can it possibly convey the ambiguous analog measurement without inaccuracy. It can't. The actual voltage of the battery may be 12.62307911838 volts, but the meter's analog to digital converter is only capable of resolving the first four digits, and produces 12.62

volts as its reading. The display used in the meter has four digits because it is matched to the four digit analog to digital converter. The display offers only four digits of data, and the information conveyed is limited to these four digits.

This discussion may appear trival, but it points out the often neglected fact that digitally presented information can be approximate. Because digital information is displayed in a nonambiguous fashion does not mean that it is entirely accurate. Any information that contains a single analog step in its processing is certainly inaccurate. This must always be kept in mind when reading information from digital displays.

Digital numerical data is certainly very useful, and its use does eliminate the inaccuracies caused in reading the display. Consider this example, it is very difficult to read the scale of an analog meter to the nearest hundredth of a volt, but it is simple when the measurement is read out in numbers. Digital displays have eliminated the errors introduced when a human eye reads the display. The only remaining inaccuracies are due to the analog measurement, and to the conversion to digital information. As such, the digital readout is more accurate.

There are a wide variety of electronic displays suited for the display of digital data. Many displays are constructed exclusively for the display of digital numbers. The seven-segment display is such a numbers only type. Computer displays, such as the CRT, display numbers, but are not limited to them.

Alphabetical Information

Alphabetical information is nonambiguous. A letter is either an A or a B, there is no letter between A or B. As such, it is eminently suited to binary processing. Alphabetical information display is common using electronic displays. It would be difficult to imagine an office without computers, and CRTs filled with text.

Most alphabets are formed from distinct characters. These characters can be displayed on a variety of electronic devices. Obviously, single analog devices such as meters or incandescent lamps are not suited to the display of text. However, many other display types can display alphabetical information. CRTs, liquid crystal panels, LED panels, electroluminescent panels, and plasma panels all can do this job. Machines that display text are capable of also displaying both binary and digital information. The quantity of this information that may be displayed at a single time is limited only by the size and resolution of the display.

Some languages are not written with alphabetical characters, but with pictures. Such pictographic languages, such as Chinese and Japanese, cannot be displayed on strictly alphabetical displays, and require the next level of display complexity—graphics displays. This situation is very complex in Japanese which is made up of over 3,000 pictographic symbols.

Graphic Information

Graphics displays convey information in the form of pictures. These pictures are usually composed of many many small dots called pixels. A pixel is the smallest unit of information that can be displayed. A picture on the screen of a CRT, for example, may consist of millions of pixels. A good example of the pixelization of an image is a photograph printed in a newspaper. When viewed through a magnifying glass the individual dots that make up the picture are readily apparent.

Graphics information is the most complex and versatile type we have discussed to this point. Graphics displays are not only capable of displaying pictures, but also alphabetical, numerical and binary information. In many computer display systems, for example, text is treated as graphics. Each letter is considered as a minipicture by the computer. The advantages of this approach are obvious. Differing languages, even pictographic ones, can be displayed by the same electronic display device.

Moving Graphic Information

Moving graphics represents the high point of electronic display. An electronic display that can show a picture and make it appear to move is the most complex and versatile type now generally available. And it is the most common, thanks to the ubiquitous television set. Moving graphic information requires the most performance out of a display. The display must have enough resolution to produce a recognizable image, and enough speed to make it appear to move.

Moving pictures are not actually moving on the screen, but are static pictures that are changed so rapidly that they appear to the human eye as moving. This quick change illusion is similar to moving pictures shown on film. The update rate of the screen is very fast, over 30 frames per second. Refresh rates around 60 frames per second are now commonly employed in modern computer displays.

DISPLAY USE DETERMINED BY INFORMATION TYPE

The information below is quick condensation of what type of display is suited for a particular type of information. Much more detailed information is available under the chapter discussing each particular display device. The displays are listed in order of their complexity and versatility, starting with the simplest first. The more complex types can display all the information types of those preceding them.

Binary Displays

Any two state electronic device that makes itself apparent to the visual sense can be used to display binary information. The most commonly used are the LED and the incandescent lamp. Binary displays are usually broken up into groups of eight indicators. A binary display may consist of many groups of eight indicators. If purely binary information is to be displayed in small quantities, then the LED is really the only choice for the job.

Analog Displays

Analog display is now almost totally limited to meters and bar graphs. Bar graphs are a linear collection of indicators, usually LEDs, that indicate analog information by their position in a string. They are just like a thermometer. Bar graph displays are also made using LCD, VFD, and plasma technologies.

Numerical Displays

Numerical displays are available in LED, LCD, VFD, and Plasma technologies. Their forms vary widely, with the seven segment type being overwhelmingly the most commonly used. These numerical displays are available in single digits, or in a collection of digits. These displays are available in a large range of sizes to fit any numerical display need.

Alphabetical Displays

Alphabetical displays are usually of the dot matrix type, although some are of the segmented type. Display technologies commonly used to display text are CRTs, LEDs, LCDs, VFDs, electroluminescent displays, and plasma displays. The dot matrix types are much more versatile and complex than the segmented types.

Graphics Displays

The range of technologies that can display graphics is the most limited. For years, the CRT has been the preferred display for graphics. Challengers for this job are the LCD, electroluminescent displays, and the plasma panels. Display characteristics such as resolution and screen size are critical in the performance of graphics displays.

Moving Graphics Displays

Moving graphics displays almost exclusively use cathode ray tube technology. Liquid crystal displays have very recently been employed in this service, but screen size and resolution are barely up to the job. The CRT is now, and will remain for some time, the only effective electronic device for the display of moving graphics. Both the plasma and electroluminescent technologies hold promise for the video flat panel of the future, but now they are restricted to very few applications.

CHARACTERISTICS SHARED BY ALL DISPLAYS

The characteristics below form the parameters of the world of electronic display. Each characteristic is briefly described to aid you in understanding the detailed information presented later. This discussion is thus very general. Those seeking more specific information will find it under the particular display type. Chapter 10 offers a comparison between all the electronic display technologies on the basis of these various factors.

Power Requirements

All electronic displays require electrical power for operation. Some require high voltage, some need low voltage. Power consumption varies from microwatts to the hundreds of watts for operation. Usually power considerations are not very important if the display is powered from the ac lines. If the display is to be truly portable, then it must carry its own power source in the form of a battery. Power consumption is a critical factor that has excluded many displays from portable operation.

Brightness

Brightness is a subjective measurement of how much light a

display puts out. If a display is to be used outside, then it must be very bright. Indoor use is much less demanding. The displays detailed in this book vary from the LCD, which does not produce its own light but modifies ambient light, to the super bright plasma panels. Science has developed several systems and units for the quantification of light output. This subject is called photometry and is a complex branch of physics with its own terminology. Appendix B offers a primer on photometry for those who wish to delve deeper.

Resolution—Visual and Informational

Resolution comes in two forms with regard to electronic displays. The first is visual resolution and the second is informational. Visual resolution is measured by a pixel's size and by the pixel density offered by a display technology. This situation is similar to the size and density of the dots that make up a newspaper photograph. The smaller each dot is and the closer they are packed together, the more life-like the image is. High resolution means lots of dots packed into a small area. Modern displays offer resolutions that are so fine and detailed that a picture shown on them is finer than the resolving power of the human eye. Such a display is commonly called "seamless."

Resolution in computer displays is becoming more critical as users come to accept pictographic operating environments. For example, consider the newer forms of computers that use small pictures called icons in conjunction with a mouse. This system makes the screen of the display the primary input and output device for the computer. As such, high resolution is essential for such machines to communicate effectively with their users.

In some display technologies, like the CRT, resolution is more a function of information encoding and the driving electronics than it is a function of the actual cathode ray tube. Other technologies, like LCDs and plasma panels, have individual cells which make up the display. The size and density of these individual cells determines the resolution of the display.

Informational resolution is a function of the type of information being displayed. Remember the earlier discussion of measuring a battery's voltage with a digital meter. This is a very good example of informational resolution. Any electronic display is merely a visual representation of information. The display is limited by the resolution of the data being presented to it. Nonambiguous data, such as binary or text, offers infinite informational resolution. Other type of information starts out as approximations long before they reach the actual display. Pictures, moving graphics, and analog measures are examples of essentially ambiguous information.

Speed

Speed is a measurement of the display's capability to change the information it conveys. In most cases, speed is not a prime requirement in a display. It is only when presenting moving graphics that a display must be very fast. Some limitation of speed is inherent in every display technology. For example, it takes a finite time to warm the filament in an incandescent lamp enough to make it glow. Other speed limitations are not due to the actual display device, but to the manner in which it is used. For example, a high resolution picture must have its elements computed and this information transferred to display by its electronic drivers. All this takes time and limits the speed of the entire display package.

Color

The use of color in electronic displays is becoming much more common. Color enables the display to more effectively communicate with the user. Most display technologies offer some form of color. Only a few are capable of displaying full color moving images. Most full color display systems use the synthesis of the three primary colors to produce a full color image.

Operating and Storage Temperatures

Every electronic display device has a range of temperatures within which it will properly function. If this range is exceeded, then the display will cease to function, in some cases permanently. These limitations are forced on the display by the physical technology used within it. Similar temperature limitations are present when the display is inactive, simply being stored. In general, the storage temperature range is much wider than the operating temperature range.

While this factor may not be of much concern to those using displays in controlled indoor environments, it is critical to displays that are used outside or that are portable. In some cases, storage of the display within a car in the hot sun or below freezing temperatures can permanently ruin the display. A good rule of thumb is to look at the physical state of the materials used within the display. In general, solid state displays have the widest operating and storage range, with gas phase displays next, and liquid phase displays offering the narrowest ranges.

Reliability and Mechanical Ruggedness

Mechanical ruggedness is a function of the display's basic material construction, and the physical effects employed to produce light. Mechanical ruggedness is a measure of how much vibration and acceleration the display will withstand before it ceases to function. Some devices, like incandescent lamps, are quite delicate, while others, like the LED, are very rugged. In general, solid state displays are the most rugged, while liquid and gas phase type are more delicate.

Size

Some display technologies have inherent limitations on the size of the screen that can be made. In other technologies, the size limitations are caused by the driving requirements of the display rather than by the actual display device. It is a matter of understanding the limitations involved and selecting the appropriate display device.

Visual Angle

The visual angle rating of a display is a measurement of its limitations with regard to visual angle. It means how far to the side of the display you can view it, and still receive an acceptable image. Electronic displays vary from being viewable at almost 170° from their face, to requiring viewing from directly in front of their screen. Most displays that offer narrow viewing angles are limited by the geometry that went into their construction. Viewing angle is only critical in displays that must be viewed by many people at the same time, or from anywhere in a room. In most cases, we simply sit in front of the display and the image is perfectly readable.

DISPLAY PERIPHERALS AND INTERFACING

An electronic display device is more complex than just the screen where we watch the image. There are many devices behind the scenes. The situation is similar to a movie. We see the actors on the screen, but we don't see the cameramen, directors, set dressers, costume designers, and soundmen that are essential to the production of the movie. Every electronic display contains components, other than the display per se, that are essential to its operation. In some case, the limitations involved in the components form the limits of the actual display. Let's look at some of the behind the screen players involved in electronic display technology.

Display Power Supplies

Every electronic display requires a power supply. In some cases, like the LED, the power supply can be as simple as a battery and a resistor. In others, like the CRT, the supply is more complex, and may employ transformers, diodes, transistors, and regulators. The function of all power supplies in display devices is the same. The power supply takes one form of input energy and converts it into the type of energy required for the display's operation. In some displays, like the CRT, several differing voltages are required for operation. The power supply is responsible for providing all the different forms and quantities of energy required to make the display function.

Some display technologies like ELDs and plasma panels have very complex and strict power requirements, like symmetrical square waves of over 200 volts. These displays may require operation in vehicles with only 12 or 24 volts dc available, and this further complicates the power supply. Fortunately, if a display requires some form of nonstandard power, the manufacturer usually supplies a power converter that accepts a common form of power as input.

Display Drivers and Controllers

Display drivers are the electronic components that actually activate the individual light producing elements that make up the display's screen. They must perform this task with great speed and accuracy. Display systems, like the CRT, require simple drivers, while the modern flat panel displays use complex driving electronics. Plasma panels have very complex high voltage waveforms passing through their drivers. Plasma drivers are semiconductor switches which can withstand the high voltages involved. These drivers have evolved into ICs specifically constructed just for this purpose. Plasma drivers are expensive. The cost of the driving electronics makes up better than half of the completed plasma display's cost. Other types, such as the low-voltage LED, have simple driving requirements and can be driven with just about any standard transistor. Driving the LED displays is both simple and inexpensive.

Some display functions are so standardized and repetitive that specialized controllers have been developed to do the job. One good example of this is the CRT controllers. The operation of the CRT consists of rapid and repetitive scanning of the phosphor screen by an electron beam. This is basically the same operation over and over again. Entire families of specialized ICs have been developed just for this function in CRTs.

Currently, the speed limitations found in most displays are a function of their electronic drivers rather than the actual display itself. This is especially true in high resolution displays which must update millions of pixels within 1/60th of a second. The driving electronics of such displays have to be capable of handling high voltage switching with frequencies in excess of 100 MHz. This is not a simple task even for state-of-the-art electronics. Much research is being conducted on the development of faster, high voltage, driving electronics.

Display Logic and Information Storage

The image we see on an electronic display doesn't appear on the screen by itself. Every element of the image must be computed before it can be transferred to the drivers which, in turn, put the image on the screen. The computation of the image's parameters is of critical importance, and occupies a substantial portion of the entire display's time. Modern high resolution display systems have resolutions in the millions of pixels. Each image of over a million pixels must be completely updated by the computer processor in less than 1/60th of a second. This is a prodigious amount of high speed processing, and only the fastest and largest CPUs are up to the task.

In order to make the CPU's processing job easier, most hi-res displays employ a look-up-table (LUT) in RAM for storage of image parameters. Modern systems may require over 16 megabytes of RAM just for the LUT alone. A hi-res system is far more than just the actual display. It is composed of many electronic components that perform image processing and storage chores. In most hi-res displays, the cost of the actual display device is a small fraction of the "behind the scenes" electronic processing.

LIGHT

Light is the medium through which electronic displays communicate with us. A rudimentary understanding of light, what it is, and how it behaves is essential to understanding visual displays. This introduction to the physics of light is very basic and only contains information selected with light producing electronic displays in mind.

Those desiring more detailed information should consult a basic physics book.

Light is a form of radiant electromagnetic energy which an observer is aware of through the visual sense. Light is only a very narrow band within the entire spectrum of electromagnetic energy. Figure 1-1 illustrates a section of this electromagnetic spectrum, and light's place upon it. The electromagnetic spectrum encompasses many types of energy. All these types have certain characteristics in common. All are radiant forms of energy. The speed of all radiant energy is limited to the speed of light. The frequency of the radiant energy is inversely proportional to its wavelength. Mathematically this can be stated by:

$$c = \lambda f \qquad \textbf{Equation 1-2.}$$

c = the speed of light in meters per second ($\approx 3. \times 10^8$ m/sec.)
λ = the wavelength of the energy in meters.
f = the frequency of the energy in cycles per second (Hz.)

This description of electromagnetic energy is founded on the assumption that this energy is wavelike in its behavior. In many cases it is. Light exhibits many of the characteristics of a wave. The basic properties of the propagation of energy via waves are as follows: rectilinear propagation within a uniform medium; reflection from a surface or boundary; refraction, or bending, when changing speed;

Fig. 1-1. The electromagnetic spectrum

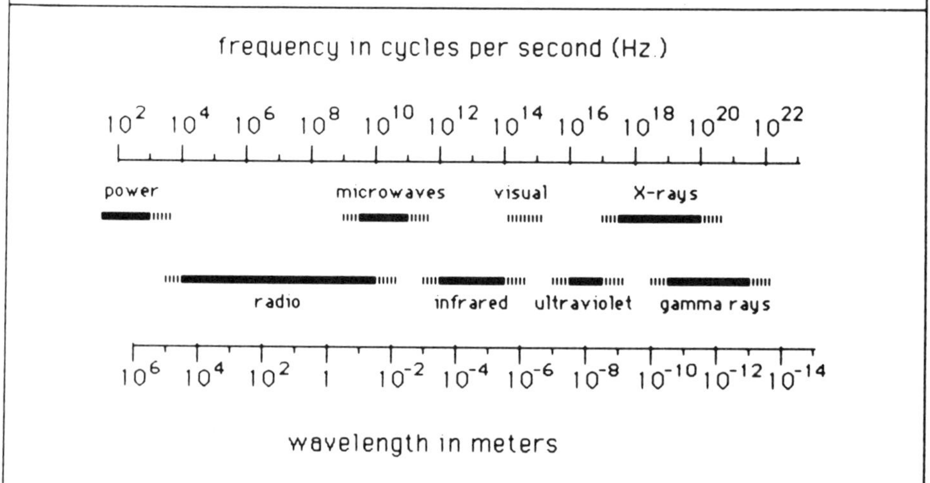

Fig. 1-2. Reflection

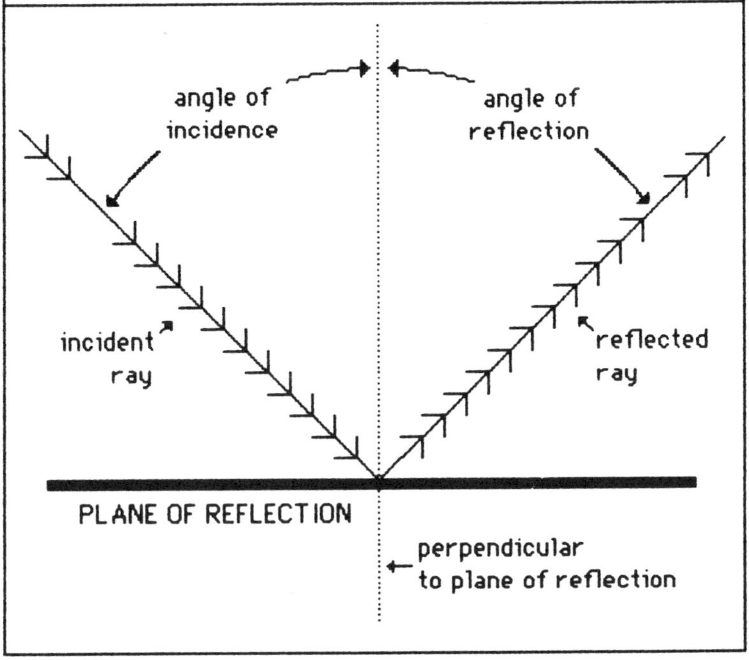

interference when two or more waves are superimposed; diffraction, or bending around corners, when the wave passes the edge of an object. Light exhibits all these wavelike properties.

Of all these properties, only two are critical in electronic displays, reflection and refraction. Reflection is the bouncing off of light waves from the boundary of a medium. Light strikes a surface and some of it is turned back from the boundary and does not enter the new medium. The ray of light striking the boundary is called the incident ray, while the ray bouncing off is called the reflected ray. The angle of the incident ray to a perpendicular to the surface is equal to the angle of the reflected ray to the same perpendicular. Simply stated, the angle of incidence equals the angle of reflection. This is expressed graphically in Fig. 1-2. For a practical example of reflection in display use, consider the reflections created on a CRT screen by ambient lighting.

Refraction is the bending of light rays as they pass through differing mediums. This characteristic describes what happens to the light rays which are not reflected from a boundary, but pass through it. The speed of light is changed as it passes from one material to another. Light is fastest in a vacuum, i.e., the absence of all matter. When light passes through matter, it slows down. The degree which light slows down in a material is called the materials "optical density." The greater the differences in optical density across the boundary, the greater the light is slowed, and the higher the refraction. The ratio of the speed of light in a vacuum to its speed within a material is called a material's "index of refraction". Refraction can be summarized by three basic principles. One, all the rays involved, the incident ray and the refracted ray, are in the same plane. Two, the index of refraction of a material is constant, and does not depend on the angle of incidence. Three, when a ray of light passes obliquely into an optically denser medium it is bent towards the perpendicular. It bends away from the perpendicular when passing into a medium of lesser optical density. Figure 1-3 illustrates this situation. Refraction is of critical importance to the operation of all displays that pass light through a variety of mediums as most do. LEDs, LCDs, plasma panels, and CRTs are but a few examples of devices that must operate by passing light through mediums of different optical density.

All this discussion on light so far assumes light to be a wave. However, in some cases light behaves like it is composed of particles, not waves. Examples of such behavior are the photoelectric effect, and the light emitting diode. Particles of light are called "photons." The study of radiant energy as a particle is called "quantum mechanics." Quantum mechanics tells us that the energy of a photon is proportional to its frequency. This was first mathematically described by the great physicist Max Planck in 1901 as:

$$E = h f$$ **Equation 1-3.**

E = the energy of the particle expressed in joules
h = Planck's constant (6.62×10^{-34} joule-seconds)
f = frequency of the particle in cycles per second (Hz)

If light behaved like a wave, then the LED would not function as it does. Since the LED works, then light must be a particle. Actually, the question of the wave/particle quality of light has yet to be answered. In some situations light is best described as a wave, and in others as a particle. We choose the approach that best describes a particular situation. Electronic displays take advantage of both approaches.

Since light does sometimes behave like a particle, then we should

Fig. 1-3. Refraction

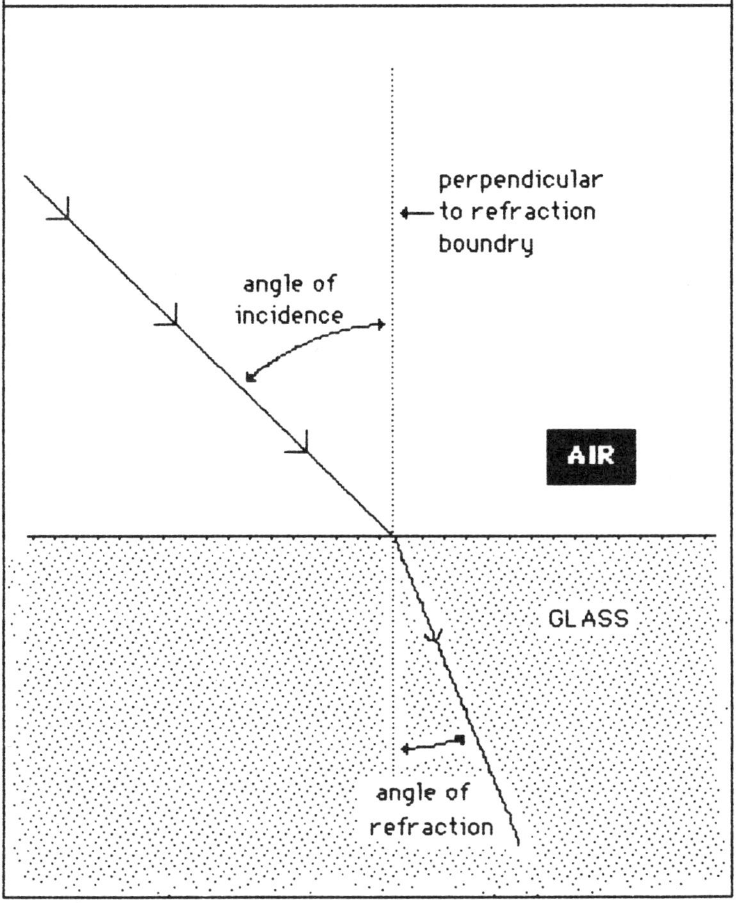

be able to measure the force of its impact on objects. This radiation pressure is infinitesimally small. The pressure of all sunlight striking the Earth is about 4 trillion times smaller than the pressure of the atmosphere on our skin (about 15 psi). But, light does have enough energy to activate our supersensitive light detectors—our eyes.

Science has made a study of measuring light. This science is called photometry and is so important to our understanding of electronic displays that I've located this material in Appendix B. I've done this so you can refer to this material easily from anywhere in this book. If you're not familiar with photometry, then now is a good time to read Appendix B.

HUMANS AND DISPLAYS

A display communicates information. We are concerned with electronic displays that communicate information through the medium of light. We have discussed the effect that information type has on the display. We have discussed the type of display. Now it is time to examine the all important third portion of the information transfer process, the information's destination—human perception.

The journey of the light from the display to perception is a long one. The light is sensed by the eyes which encode its information. This information is then sent to the brain, via neural signals, where it is processed. This processed information is then perceived by consciousness as a visual image. Quite a long series of processes are involved in the perception of visual information. Each process takes place in specialized organs, each with its limitations. This collection of information is finally evaluated by consciousness.

Human Eyes and Displays

The human eye is a marvelous and versatile sensor that we take for granted. It does its job and we are unaware of its many limitations. Electronic displays must work within these limitations. In some cases, electronic displays actually use the limitations of the eye to their advantage, as in the case of simulating motion in an image. In other cases, the display is limited by the human eye, as in the case of color. If we can understand the nature and limitations of the eye, then we can better employ electronic display devices.

The eye is an incredibly wonderful and complex device. We are going to concern ourselves here with its visual characteristics that directly relate to the display of information using light. The characteristics such as light sensitivity, color perception and sensitivity, and motion sensitivity are germane to electronic information display. The eye senses light photons colliding with its retina. The retina is a coating of highly specialized cells on the inside surface of the eyeball. These cells change the light photons falling on them into visual information that is communicated to the brain. Modern theory holds that the retina evolved from the brain, and is actually brain tissue.

The retina is composed of two different types of light receptors. They are called the "cones" and the "rods". There are some 130 million of these sensors within a single human retina. These two types of sensors have evolved into cells which react differently to light's impact. The cones are relatively insensitive to light compared to the rods, but the cones can perceive color. The rods see only in black and white, but are over 6 times more sensitive to light than the cones. The cones are distributed throughout the retina, but are most concentrated in the center of the retina at an area called the "fovea". The fovea is used by the eye for close or detailed work. The rods, however, are more numerous around the periphery of the retina, with very few found in the fovea. Overall, the rods are about 18 times more numerous in the retina than are the cones. When we examine an electronic display, we are primarily using the area of the fovea with its cones.

One of the eye's greatest achievements is the perception of color. Color is our ability to distinguish between light photons of differing wavelengths. Our eyes can distinguish between the longer wavelength red photons, and the shorter wavelengths of blue photons. Color perception focuses our attention on the area of the eye that is most sensitive to color, and least sensitive to overall light input—the cone rich fovea. Figure 1-4 illustrates the sensitivity of the rods and cones to light of various frequencies. Note that the cones are not uniformly sensitive to differing wavelengths of light. The cones are much more sensitive to light of the yellow-green wavelengths than to other wavelengths. This is of critical importance in utilizing color for information display. For two colors to appear of the same luminous intensity on a display's screen, they must actually be produced in differing intensities by the display. For example, consider

Fig. 1-4.

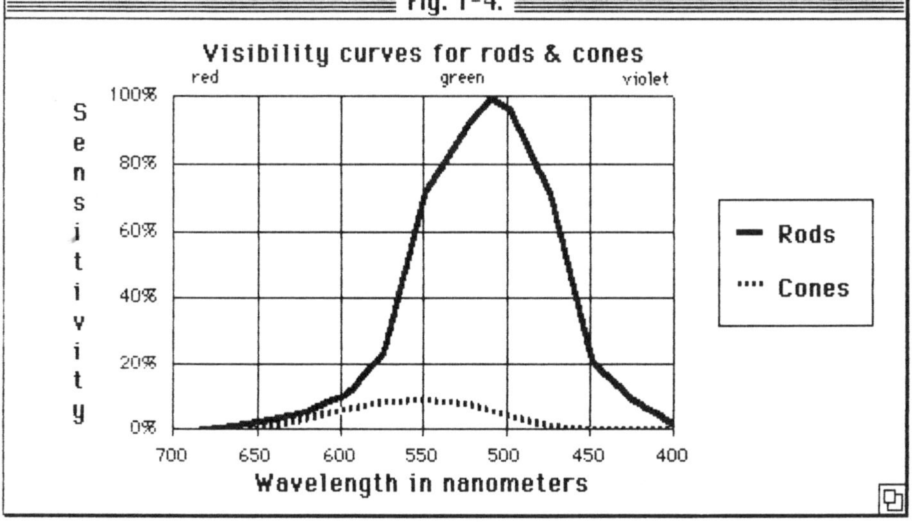

a red rectangle displayed beside a green rectangle of the same size. Because the eye is more sensitive to green light, the display must produce more red light than green if the two rectangles are to appear to the eye as having the same luminosity. The same situation occurs in the use of LEDs, red ones must have more light output to appear as bright as green ones. This is built into the way our eyes perceive color, and electronic displays must compensate for the eye's color bias.

The rods are incredibly sensitive to light. As few as six visual photons falling on the rods will produce an image within the eye. This translates into about 60 photons falling on the surface of the eye's outside surface. The eye is not very efficient, losing about 90% of the incoming light to scattering and internal absorption. The rods of the eye are sensitive enough to distinguish a candle flame at a distance of 17 miles under ideal conditions. While the rods only pass black and white information to the brain, they do have an inherent wavelength bias as shown in Fig. 1-4. The rods are most sensitive to light in the blue-green region.

The overall sensitivity of the eye to light depends on both the rods and cones. In terms of a general average the eye has a sensitivity curve as shown in Fig. 1-5. This chart is called a CIE curve, and represents a standard observer curve. It represents the light response of a ''standard eyeball''. Note that the eye is most sensitive to light with a wavelength of 555 nanometers, or yellow-

Fig. 1-5.

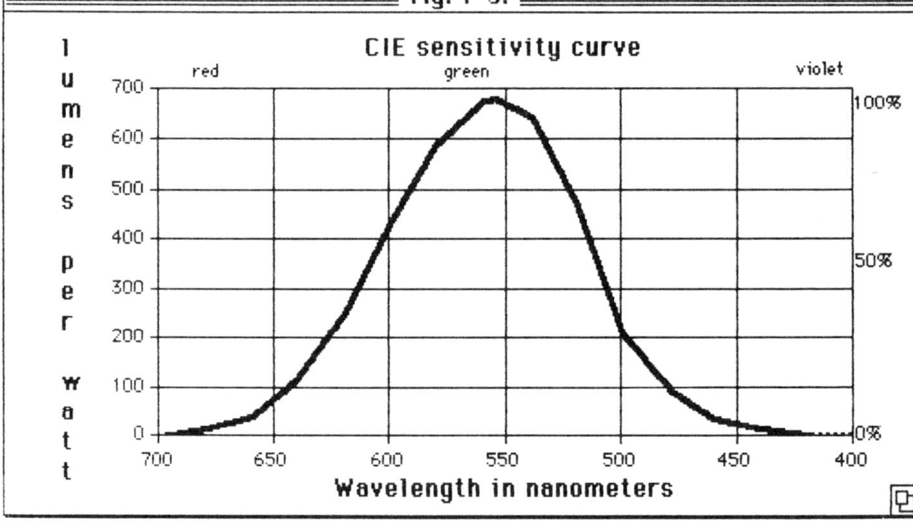

green light. The left-hand y-axis of this graph is calibrated in lumens per watt. This scale is an indication of the eye's efficiency in conversion of photons to neural information. The right-hand y-axis is calibrated in percent.

The eye also has limitations on its' perception of light in relation to time. There is a time lag between the entrance of light into an eyeball and the perception of that light. It takes the eye about 0.1 second to convert photons to neural signals, to relay these signals to the brain, and for the brain to organize these signals into perception. In a visual sense, we live in the past. All our senses have a built-in time lag. Light pulses of too short a duration are not perceived by the eye. And most importantly for electronic displays, the eye holds an image for a short period of time after light has stopped impacting the retina. This is called persistence of vision and is very important in electronic information display. Persistence of vision makes possible such electronic wonders as television.

Consider a flashing light. If the light is turned on and off slowly, say once every second, then our eyes detect it flashing. If the light is turned off and on more quickly, about 50 to 60 times per second, then our eye no longer perceives the light's flicker. It appears to be continuously illuminated. The point at which the eye cannot perceive rapid light changes is called "critical fusion frequency". This critical fusion frequency varies widely from person to person. It also varies with the intensity of the light source. Brighter lights must flash faster than dim ones to attain the critical fusion frequency.

Persistence of vision enables an electronic display to show a sequence of static images without allowing the eye enough time to detect the transition between them. The rate that the static images are changed is faster than the critical fusion frequency. The result is that the image appears to move. This technique is used by video displays which run 30 to 60 images per second. The rate of change of the images is said to be below the eye's "flicker rate". This method of fooling the eye into perceiving motion is used by TV, movies, computer displays, and flat-panel displays.

The rods have a higher critical fusion frequency than do the cones (up to 70 Hz in some people). This means that flicker and movement are more easily detected by the outside of the retina than by the central area, or the fovea. The cones have a lower critical frequency and generally do not detect flicker at rates above 32 Hz. This is to the advantage of electronic display devices as it allows them slower refresh rates. The actual critical fusion frequency varies greatly from person to person and from rod to cone. You can check your individual flicker rate by this simple experiment. Try looking at a TV set out of the side of your eye. To many people the flicker becomes apparent when attention is directed to rod detected visual information. This TV set is flickering at about 30 Hz. If you can see this flicker from the side of your eye (the rods), then your critical fusion frequency is above 30 Hz.

Those wishing to communicate with electronic display devices and those making these devices need to be aware of the limitations of the human eye. Its inherent speed and color bias must be allowed for in successful display application. Not all the sensory limitations are in the actual eye. The eye is only part of the signal chain. It relays neural information to the brain.

Human Brains and Displays

The eye's portion of the visual process is to encode light information into neural impulses. These impulses travel along the optic nerves to the brain. Visual neural information is processed by both hemispheres of the brain, but there is a crossover of this information. The left eye communicates with the right hemisphere of the brain. The right eye's information is processed by the left hemisphere of the brain.

It is the brain's job to make sense of the eye's neural information. This complex process is, even now, not fully understood. It appears as if the information supplied by the eyes is evaluated with consideration of all the other visual information the brain has ever received. Vision is a learned process. The total visual experience of a person affects how the brain interprets any particular packet of neural information from the eye. This learned response is used by many displays to draw from our visual experience information to enhance the display's illusion.

The brain wants to make coherent images of the eye's information. The brain will supply information for imaging that is not actually conveyed by the eye's information. Visual perception is greatly affected by the brain's tendency to see what it expects to see. Simple examples of this very complex process can be seen in several graphic illusions. Figure 1-6 is such an illusion; it is a two dimensional line drawing. It is really only a collection of lines, but our brain interprets it as a three dimensional object, a cube. Not only does it appear three dimensional, but the orientation of the cube changes if we look at it long enough. The eye relays neural information describing a collection of lines to the brain. The brain

Fig. 1-6. A cube?

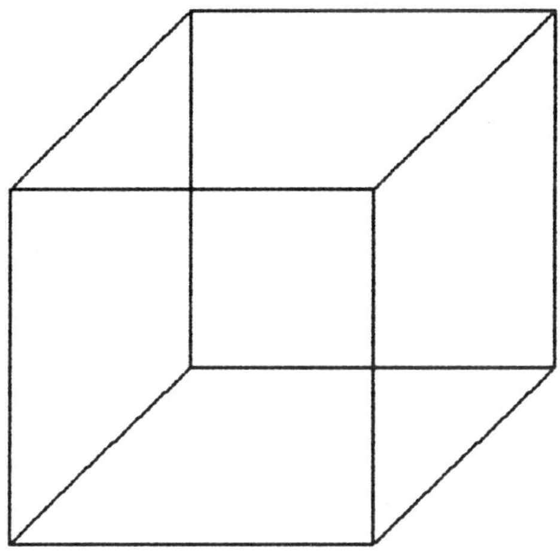

interprets this information on the basis of its visual experience. Another illusion is seen in Fig. 1-7. The vertical lines in this illustration are in fact straight, even though the brain perceives them as curves. Once again, the brain does its best to interpret data based on its experience as as well visual information from the eyes.

Each hemisphere of the brain, and each eye, has evolved to perceive information differently. Science has discovered that the right hemisphere of the brain, which accepts information from the left eye, is responsible for processing images. The right section of the brain seems to be more adept at functions like understanding, imagination, and creativity. The left hemisphere, through the right eye, processes more abstract visual information such as written language. The left hemisphere is more adept at analytical functions such as language, mathematics, and symbolic logic.

When the brain receives visual information, it is processed by both halves of the brain. Information is transferred from hemisphere to hemisphere within the brain. How this information is synthesized

Fig. 1-7. Straight lines?

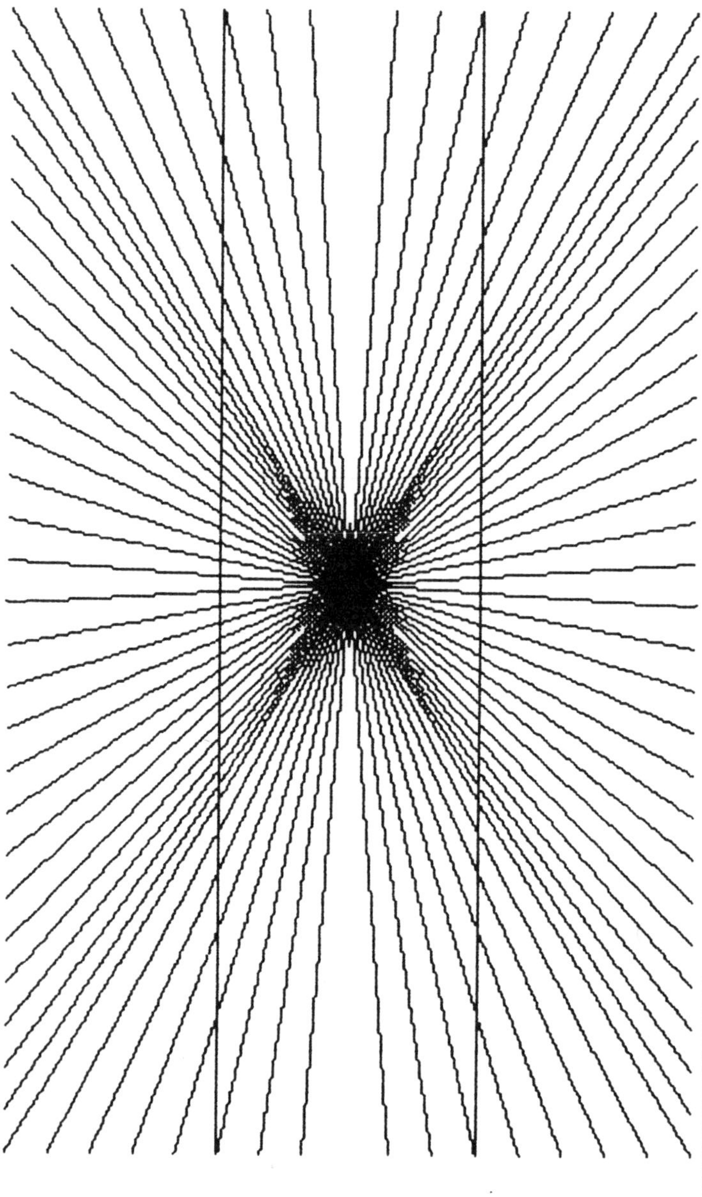

in a coherent image is not known. What is known is that the process more closely resembles a committee meeting than a dictatorial decree. Each hemisphere evaluates information from a different viewpoint. The final visual perception uses information from both hemispheres, in addition to data from memory and imagination. In this way, vision is a dynamic process that is continually being updated by experience.

Human Ideas and Displays

Displays communicate information. The destination of this information is the human consciousness. The media for communi-

Fig. 1-8.

cation must suit the information, and its recipient. For example, describe a cube in a language such as English. Now describe it in terms of mathematical language, and finally graphically in the form of a line drawing. Each of these "languages" is capable of communicating the idea of "cube". But not all languages convey the idea with the same facility. English is hard put to accurately describe the cube. Math can accurately describe the cube, but the graphic image of the cube best conveys the idea.

Those using electronic displays are finding that some information is better communicated in the form of images, rather than by text or other abstract symbols. Color images are becoming a preferred mode of communicating with computers. They are easier for the user to understand, and they cut across written language barriers. The use of images rather than symbols for communication may have additional advantages. Images are processed by the more imaginative and creative sections of the brain. Communication with these sections of the brain can only increase productivity and foster new ideas. Right brain processing will increase the sphere of nonverbal communication. Such visual information processing takes place much faster than analytical left brain forms. Nonsymbolic image information more closely resembles information storage in human memory. As such, images are easier and faster for us to remember than a string of text.

The use of realistic images for communication is sweeping the computer display field. Programs are more graphic than ever before. Color computer monitors, with very high resolution, are being used in applications that previously used only text for communication. Examine the uses you intend for your electronic display. If the information can be communicated in a more graphic fashion, then it is to your advantage to do so. As an example of the use of graphics over text for information transfer, I offer Fig. 1-8. Since a picture is worth a thousand words, I'll let it be its own comment.

2

Incandescent Lamps

Incandescent lamps are among the oldest types of electronic display device still in use today. Only the analog meter has been around longer. The incandescent lamps used in electronic displays have only minor differences in their construction from the common lightbulb used in home lighting. The principles behind the lamps used in display service and lighting service are identical.

In recent years, the electronic display of information has tended toward the use of solid state display devices. While the incandescent lamp can be technically classified as a solid state device, its use has generally been replaced with LEDs in most applications. The remaining hi-tech versions of the incandescent lamps still in display service represent the very best that can be expected from this relatively old technology.

HOW INCANDESCENT LAMPS WORK

The physics behind incandescent technology is the simplest of any type of electronic display discussed in this book. Basically, resistance produced heat is converted into light by the incandescent lamp. The technology used in incandescent lamps has been refined, but it remains virtually unchanged since Thomas Edison invented the first lightbulb.

When materials are sufficiently heated, they give off light. This physical effect is called incandescence. Any other form of light emission is called luminescence. The incandescent lamp uses this incandescent effect to turn electrical current into heat, and heat into visual photons. A thin wire of metal is suspended between electrical contacts, and enclosed in an evacuated glass envelope. Figure 2-1 illustrates the construction of an incandescent lamp. This illustration is symbolic and does not refer to any particular lamp. Electrical current is passed through a thin wire, which is called a filament. The filament has electrical resistance, and gets very hot as electrons are forced to flow through it. When the filament reaches a sufficiently high temperature, it emits visible photons in addition to photons below the visual range. At temperatures below the incandescent

Fig. 2-1. An incandescent lamp

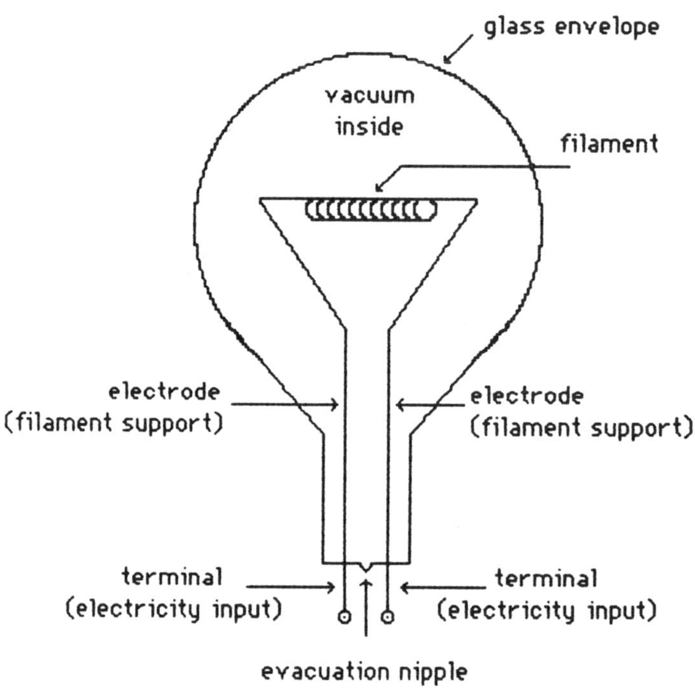

point, the filament emits only infrared photons (heat).

The exact temperature at which a material becomes incandescent varies from material to material. Tungsten is the most commonly used material in incandescent lamp filaments. Tungsten is chosen because it can sustain prolonged heating to the incandescent point without destruction. Tungsten begins incandescence at about 1,000° K and continues getting brighter up until its temperature reaches 3,655° K when it melts. This is very hot. In fact, over 90% of the input energy to an incandescent lamp is wasted in the form of heat. The remaining less than 10% is radiated as visible light. This relatively low energy efficiency is one of the biggest problems associated with incandescent lamp technology. Common household light bulbs have a luminous efficacy around 10 to 20 lumens per watt of input energy. In terms of the wide spectrum of electronic display devices now offered, the incandescent lamp rates last in efficiency.

The incandescent lamp is a very hot item—as anyone who has attempted to change a bulb that is in operation will realize. The interior of the filament of a common, household lightbulb is operating in the neighborhood of 3,000° K. In terms of the Fahrenheit scale, this is around 5,000° F. For those not familiar with the scientific temperature scale of Kelvin degrees (°K), the Kelvin scale has the same degree increments as the Centigrade scale, but the Kelvin scale begins at absolute zero (−459.67° F or −273.15° C or 0° K).

The color of the light output of an incandescent device depends on its filament temperature. At the lowest temperature point of incandescence, the light appears as visible photons in the red region. As the temperature of the incandescent material is raised, additional photons of higher energy (shorter wavelength, and higher frequency) are produced. Most incandescent devices are operated at temperatures high enough so that their light output is a balanced presentation of the combination of light wavelengths that we commonly call "white light".

If the technology of incandescent devices were as simple as just heating them up, incandescent lamps would have been developed and used long before they actually were. There are many other problems associated with getting a material hot enough to glow and still survive. It is manufacturing technology that tamed the super-hot filament into a household device.

HOW INCANDESCENT LAMPS ARE MADE

Thomas Edison tried over 900 different designs before he actually produced a practical, working lightbulb. In part, this high number of attempts reflects Edison's "hit and miss" approach to scientific investigation, and in part, it is due to some very real problems associated with very hot materials. The problems he faced are the same that modern manufacturers of incandescent devices face.

The first problem is the oxidation of the filament material. When a material gets as hot as 5,000° F it will oxidize (burn) in the presence of the slightest amount of oxygen. All incandescent lamps either work in a hard vacuum or in a halogen atmosphere. More on halogen operating environments later, but let's look at the hard vacuum types first. This hard vacuum is necessary to prevent oxidation. A hard vacuum means that the inside of the light bulb has all gasses pumped out of it, and then it is sealed. The "hardness" of the vacuum reflects how much of the gas material the manufacturer can pump out of the bulb before it is sealed. The harder the vacuum, the longer the filament will incandesce before it oxidizes and burns. Anyone who has broken the glass envelope of a lightbulb is familiar with the very short time (in milliseconds) that it will function once oxygen is available to the filament.

The second problem associated with incandescent devices is the loss of material from the filament. At incandescent temperatures, filament molecules boil off the filament; they actually vaporize and leave the filament in the form of a gas. The filament gradually loses material until it breaks. The higher the temperature, the faster matter boils off the filament. You may have noticed that the glass envelopes of your lightbulbs gradually darken as they age. This darkening is due to the impact of the gaseous filament molecules boiling off the filament. As molecules boil off the filament, they actually make the filament thinner, which increases its resistance at the boil off point. This increase in resistance increases the filament's temperature, which in turn again increases the boil off rate. This is a classical case of thermal runaway. If you have observed the operation of your lightbulbs, you may have noticed that they are at their brightest just before they burn out. This effect is due to the loss of material from the filament.

The boil off effect is called "notching" by lightbulb manufacturers because it is usually localized at a specific point on the filament due to its runaway nature. Incandescent device manufacturers classify this notching effect into two types. The first type is caused by the migration of the filament's atoms from a specific point, and is much more prevalent in dc application than it is in ac use. The other form of notching is caused by temperature gradients across the length of the filament, and is caused by the attachment of the ends of the filament to its electrodes. This second form of notching is called the Sorret effect after its discoverer. The point at which the filament is attached to its electrode is cooler than the rest of the filament because the filament is heatsunk at its connection points to the electrodes. Thus, the Sorret effect is inherent in the concept of an incandescent filament. In general, the filament material loss from the first type of notching is about 10 times greater than the loss associated with the Sorret effect.

In recent years, a refinement of incandescent technology has led to the reduction in the rate that material boils off of the filament. Instead of using a very hard vacuum within the lamp's envelope, halogen gas is used instead. The halogen gas vapor (such as iodine) combines chemically with the tungsten molecules boiling off the filament. The tungsten/halogen compound continually redeposits itself back onto the filament, thus increasing the filament's life. The use of a halogen operating atmosphere does not eliminate the Sorret effect, but it does extend the life of the lamp's filament by as much as ten times. The use of halogen gas also greatly reduces the darkening of the glass envelope surrounding the lamp.

Halogen lamps require higher operating temperatures to make use of this redepositing effect which does not occur at lower temperatures. Care must be taken to operate halogen lamps at their rated temperatures if their additional longevity potential is to be realized. Bulb temperatures of halogen lamps should be at least 250° C at the outside surface of the glass envelope if this redeposition effect is to work. The glass envelope of these halogen lamps are constructed of special quartz glass to withstand their higher operating temperatures. Such lamps are commonly called "quartz-halogen" lamps. Quartz-halogen lamps are brighter and more efficient than the more common hard vacuum types. Use only lamp sockets that are designed to withstand the additional heat of the quartz-halogen lamps.

INCANDESCENT LAMP CHARACTERISTICS

Incandescent lamps offer a wide variety of operating characteristics depending on their type and size. The information below is a generalized summary of incandescent technology. It is specific only where a radical difference in operating characteristics is present between differing types of lamps.

Power Requirements

The input power requirements of incandescent lamps are very strict. Incandescent lamps are voltage operated devices. If the manufacturers recommended voltage is not supplies by the user, then the lamp's operating characteristics are drastically altered. *Input voltage is the most critical factor that must be considered when operating incandescent lamps.*

If the input voltage is too low, the lamp's filament will not reach its proper temperature. In this case, the lamp will emit a dimmer and redder light. Luminous efficacy is also greatly reduced by operation at voltages lower than recommended. If the manufacturer's recommended operating voltage is exceeded, then the lamp will be brighter, but very short lived. Stay as close as possible to the manufacturer's recommended input voltage if you want the lamp to deliver its full potential light and longevity.

The current consumption of an incandescent lamp is a function of its input voltage. Figure 2-2 illustrates the relationship between input voltage and current consumption. This graph is normalized into percentage figures rather than absolute figures so that it applies to all types and sizes of hard vacuum incandescent lamps. Note that a reduction of 5% in input voltage reduces the current consumed by the lamp by about 3%. And an increase of 10% in operating voltage increases current consumption by over 5%. This points out the essentially resistive nature of the incandescent lamp. In fact,

Fig. 2-2.

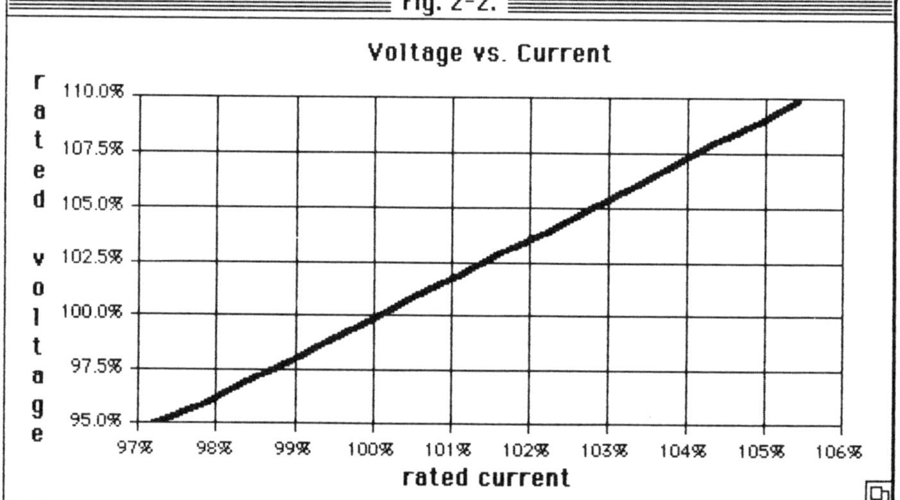

Fig. 2-3.

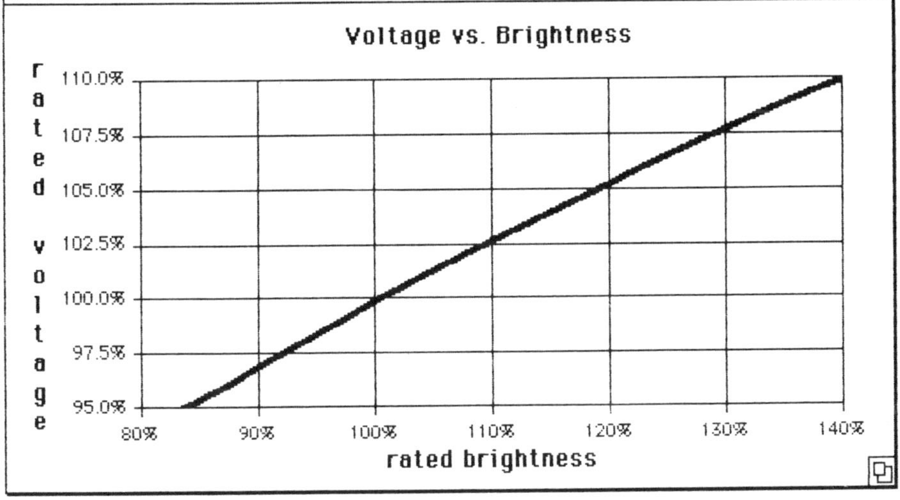

electrically, the incandescent lamp is treated as a resistor in design calculations.

In an absolute sense, incandescent lamps are made with voltage inputs anywhere between 1.0 volts to well over 200 volts, either dc or ac. The incandescent lamp will function on either ac or dc voltages, and it is unique in this respect. No other display device is available in such a wide range of input voltages and waveforms. Current consumption of incandescent lamps varies from as little as 0.01 amperes to well over 10 amperes. Wattages vary from microwatts to thousands of watts. The variety of electrical sizes offered by incandescent technology is staggering.

Brightness

The brightness of any incandescent lamp is a function of its input voltage. Figure 2-3 illustrates this relationship and is normalized into percentages so as to be widely applicable to just about any hard vacuum type of incandescent lamp. Note that a reduction of the input voltage by as little as 5% results in a brightness loss of almost 17%. An increase of just 10% over the recommended input voltage will increase the lamps light output by a whopping 40%. The lesson to be learned here is that pushing the lamp to higher voltages to get more light does, in fact, radically increase its light output, but this increased output greatly reduces the longevity of the filament. If you require more light output from an incandescent lamp, then use a higher output lamp rather than increasing the input voltage supplied to a smaller lamp. More on this in the section on incandescent lamp longevity.

Manufacturers rate the brightness of their lamps in many basic units. Candelas, foot-Lamberts, lumens, and mean spherical candle power (MSCP) are all units that are used to quantify the incandescent lamp's light output. Measurements made in foot-Lamberts are more ambiguous and less able to be verified than other types of measurement, while the candela system more accurately represents what the eye actually sees. If you are reading incandescent specifications and are not familiar with these terms, consult Appendix B. Appendix B is a primer on photometry that defines these terms and their interrelationships. A thorough understanding of these differing types of light measuring systems is essential for making sense out of any manufacturer's brightness ratings for their products. In conversational terms, incandescent lamps are available in brightnesses that range from very dim to absolutely blinding. No other display technology offers such a wide range of brightnesses as does the incandescent lamps, especially at the high end.

Speed

The incandescent lamp is a very slow electronic display device. This is inherent in using the incandescent effect to produce visible light. The filament of the lamp must warm up to the incandescent temperature point before it will emit light. It must also cool down before it will cease emitting light. The response time of incandescent displays is in substantial fractions of a second. This is far too slow to be useful in the display of rapidly changing information such as moving graphics. Incandescent lamps are best for displaying of the slowest changing types of information.

Size

Incandescent lamps are available in a very large range of physical sizes and base configurations. Let's examine the smaller sizes first. Figure 2-4 illustrates some of the myriad types of miniature lamp bases. These different base configurations are available in a range of six difference sizes. These sizes are named in the same fashion as LEDs, T-½, T-¾, T-1, T-1¾, and so on. The base configurations remain the same, but the physical size, light output, and power consumption grows with the lamp size. Some miniature lamps are

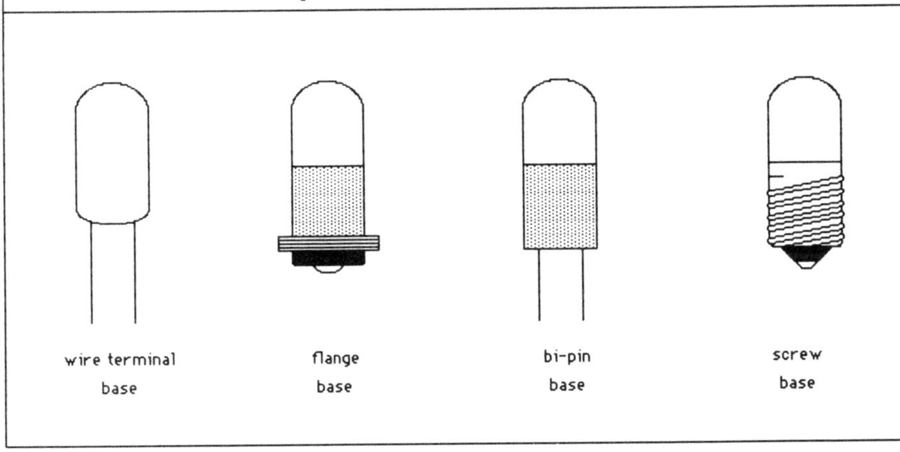

Fig. 2-4. Miniature lamp bases

equipped with axial wire leads, others have wedge bases. The wedge base type are now very common in automotive instrumentation. Some miniature lamps are made in housings that look just like the common tubular cartridge fuse. Miniature lamps are also available with insulated wire leads, such types are called "flying lead" lamps.

In the larger lamp sizes, the use of screw and bayonet base configurations are the most common. Once again, there are a large number of differing sizes. A survey of incandescent lamps has shown that there are in excess of 60 different types of bases and sizes available, far to many to be specific here. If you are looking for a replacement for a burned out incandescent lamp, be sure to take the old one with you. Without the burned out lamp as an example, it is virtually impossible to find the correct replacement.

A new development in incandescent lamp packaging is the seven segment and sixteen segment lamp packages. These packages mimic the seven and sixteen segment LED and LCD packages used as numerical readouts. These incandescent packages have been developed for military uses that require super-high brightnesses not obtainable with LEDs.

Colors

An incandescent lamp that is properly run within its rated temperature operating range produces a very balanced combination of colors that are perceived by the eye as white light. It is very simple to turn the lamps output into a single color by passing it through a colored optical filter. As such, the incandescent lamp can be made to appear as any color desired. A common example of this approach can be found in automotive dash instrumentation. The use of a filter does, however, reduce the overall light output of the lamp. Lamps used in filter service are commonly specified with higher brightness to compensate for losses with the filter.

Longevity

Incandescent lamps have never been known for their long life. They are the shortest lived of all electronic display devices. The longevity of an incandescent lamp is a direct function of its input voltage. Figure 2-5 illustrates the relationship between input voltage and lamp longevity. The information on this graph is normalized into percentages so as to be universally applicable to all types of hard vacuum lamps. Note than an input voltage increase of as little as 5% will reduce the lamps longevity by almost 50%. Input voltage increases of 10% over the manufacturer's ratings will decrease the lamps longevity by almost 70%. This information points out the critical nature of input voltage to incandescent devices. Too high a voltage greatly reduces lamp longevity.

Figure 2-5 also illustrates the increase in lamp longevity that can be realized by reduction of the input voltage. Reduction of input voltage by as little as 5% can increase the lamps life to 185% of

Fig. 2-5.

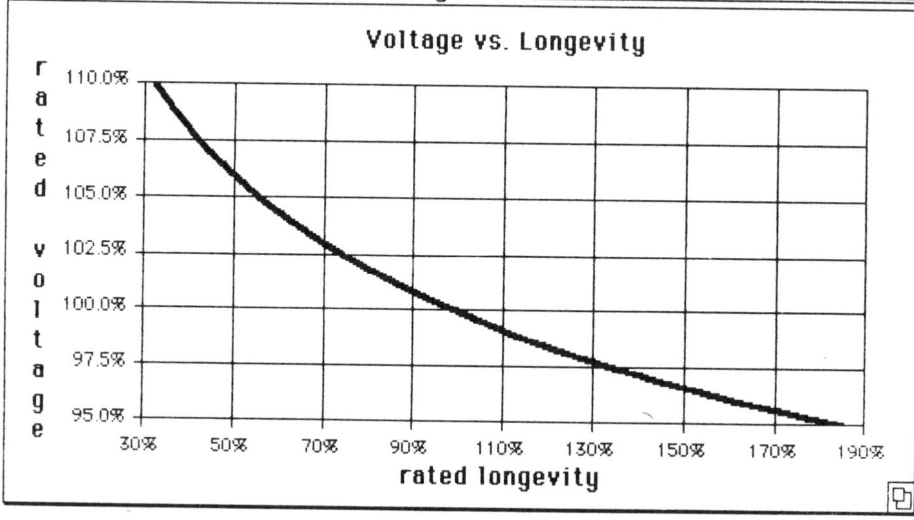

its rated life. Since the incandescent lamp is a voltage operated device and essentially a resistor, voltage reduction is simple. In dc or ac service, a resistor may be inserted in series with the lamp to reduce its input voltage. In dc service, a forward biased diode may be inserted in series with the lamp to obtain a uniform voltage decrease of about 0.75 to 1 volt. While these techniques do reduce the lamps light output, they also greatly increase the lamps longevity. A practical application of this information is the use of the rheostat dimmer provided for automotive dash instrumentation dimming. Keeping this rheostat set for the minimum acceptable light output of the dash display will greatly extend the life of these hard to replace lamps.

In general, the longevity of an incandescent lamp is directly related to its brightness. The brighter the lamp, the shorter its lifetime. Super bright lamps used in projectors, for example, have lifetimes in the range of 20 hours. The upper range for incandescent lamp longevity is in the range of 5,000 to 7,000 hours of operation.

ADVANTAGES

The major advantages of the incandescent lamp are its high brightness and simplicity of use. Among electronic displays there are none brighter than the incandescent type. This is very important in displays used in vehicles and other outside applications. The incandescent lamp's major competitor is the LED, which has poor sunlight readability. The incandescent lamp is very simple to use. It needs only to be attached to a power source of the proper voltage through its two electrical leads. No special driving electronics are required.

DISADVANTAGES

The major disadvantages of the incandescent lamp are its very low energy efficiency and short lifetime. The energy efficiency picture for these lamps is very grim. They convert less than 10% of their input energy into useable light. The common household lightbulb has an efficiency of less than 6%. This reduces the range of applications for which they are suited to those with substantial amounts of power to waste. In terms of longevity, the incandescent lamp is the shortest lived electronic display device discussed in this book. This factor alone has led to its replacement with the super long lived LED which can function for over 100,000 hours of continuous service.

SAMPLE APPLICATION

Application of the incandescent lamp is very simple. Figure 2-6 illustrates the use of an incandescent lamp as an on or off indicator for any type of load. The use of the appropriate lightbulb for the power supply voltage is the only real decision that needs to be made. This schematic is applicable to all forms of power from low voltage dc to standard ac household voltages. If satisfactory longevity is desired from the lamp, be sure to use the smallest size (in terms of light output) that will meet your need.

Fig. 2-6. A lamp on/off indicator

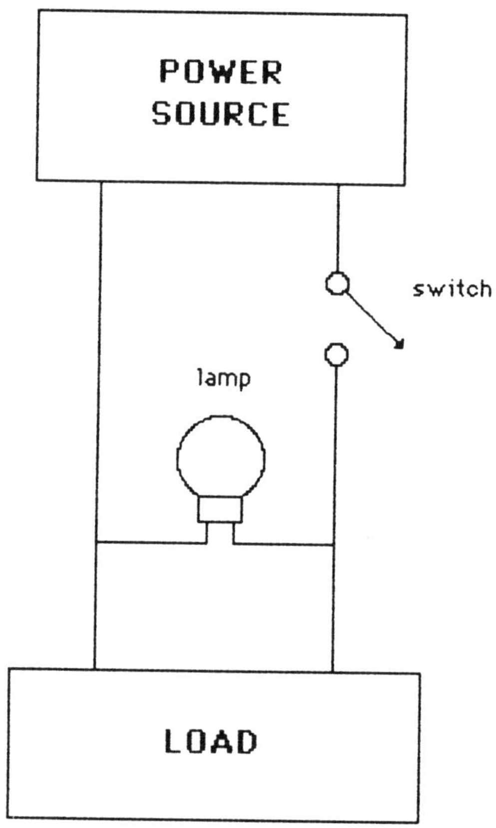

COST

The cost of incandescent lamps vary widely with size and light output. Cost is generally a factor of how widespread the usage of a particular lamp is. For example, a sub-miniature lamp may cost several times what a household lightbulb costs. This is a function of the number made and how the lamps are distributed. In general, incandescent lamps cost between $0.25 to well over $20.00 for the more esoteric types.

If you are considering the use of incandescent devices for display, choose lamps that are readily available from common sources such as hardware or automotive stores. The use of specialized lamps can greatly increase the display's cost and make finding replacement lamps difficult.

LISTING OF MANUFACTURERS

The following manufactures of incandescent devices have contributed information to this chapter. A full listing of their addresses and telephone numbers is found in Appendix A—The Electronic Display Devices Manufacturers.

Info-Lite Corporation
JKL Components Corporation
Leecraft Manufacturing Co. Inc.
Visual Communications Co.
Wamco Technical Sales Inc.

3

Analog Meters

Analog meters measure electrical parameters. They display quantitative information regarding electrical current and electrical voltage. As such, they are very specialized display devices. They measure current flow and that's all. They are obviously unsuited to the display of text or graphics images. Even though analog meters are the least versatile electronic display device discussed in this book, they have survived the test of time, and many are still used today. Considering their age and restricted use, their continued usage points out their suitability for many specific applications. Analog meters are locked into competition with the all electronic digital metering systems, and are generally losing this battle.

Analog meters are the oldest form of electronic display device. These meters use the link between the flow of electrical current and the magnetic field that is produced by this flow of electrons. Credit for this discovery goes to the Danish physicist Hans Christian Oersted. In 1819, Oersted noticed that a compass needle was deflected when placed near a wire carrying electrical current. Oersted speculated that the deflection of the compass needle was caused by a magnetic field surrounding the current carrying wire. This assumption was correct and provided the first experimental proof of the link between electricity and magnetism. This discovery also made possible the earliest technology for measuring electrical current and voltage—the analog meter. The physical basis of analog meter operation has been refined over the centuries, but its essence remains true to Oersted's speculations.

Oersted's work is so important that a description of his experiment is useful in helping us understand the operation of analog electrical meters. Oersted's experiment was actually very simple. He used only four components—a battery, a switch, a wire, and a small hand held compass. The configuration of this circuit is shown in Fig. 3-1. Oersted first placed the wire over the top of the compass, with the wire passing directly over the compass' pivot point. This section of wire was orientated so that it pointed north, and, of course the compass pointed north. The switch was left open so that no current was flowing through the wire. Section A of Fig. 3-1 illustrates this configuration. Next, Oersted closed the switch and allowed electrons to flow through the wire. This resulted in the compass needle being deflected to the left, i.e., the north point of the needle was deflected to the west. This configuration is shown in section B of Fig. 3-1. Then, Oersted reversed the polarity of the battery and once again closed the switch. Reversal of the battery's polarity caused the electrons to flow through the wire in the opposite direction. This resulted in the compass needle being deflected to the right. The north point of the compass needle moved toward the east. This third configuration is shown in section C of Fig. 3-1. From this experiment, Oersted deduced two things. One, the direction (polarity) of the magnetic field depended on the direction of electron

Fig. 3-1 Oersted's experiment

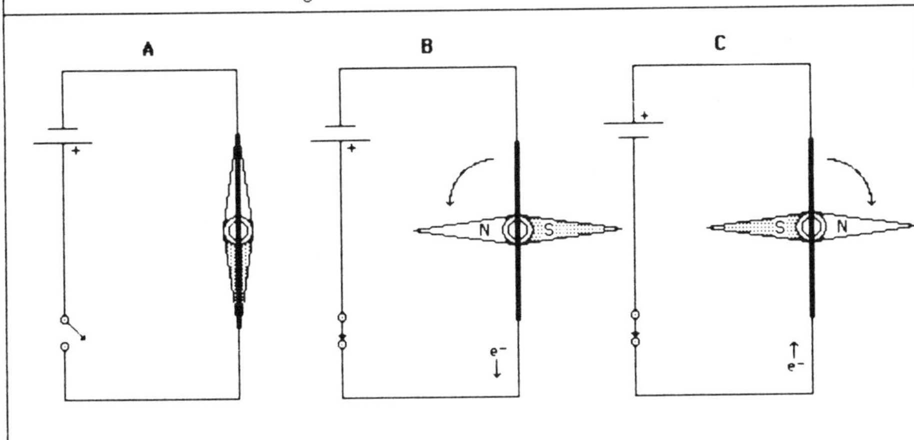

flow within the wire. And two, that the intensity of the magnetic field was related to the distance between the wire and the compass needle. Oersted performed the same experiment again, but he placed the wire underneath the compass rather than above it. The results were the same with one difference, the direction of the deflection of the compass needle was reversed. This early experiment into the relationships between electronic motion and magnetism was very important. It enabled physical pioneers to measure electronic motion by its magnetic effects, and is the birthplace of all analog meter technology. Try this experiment for yourself. While it is very simple physically to do this experiment, consider the scientific intuition and curiosity that led Oersted to his discoveries some 170 years ago.

HOW ANALOG METERS WORK

Oersted's discoveries eventually led to the development of the first analog meter called the "galvanoscope". The galvanoscope is essentially the same device that Oersted used, but instead of a single

Fig. 3-2. A galvanoscope

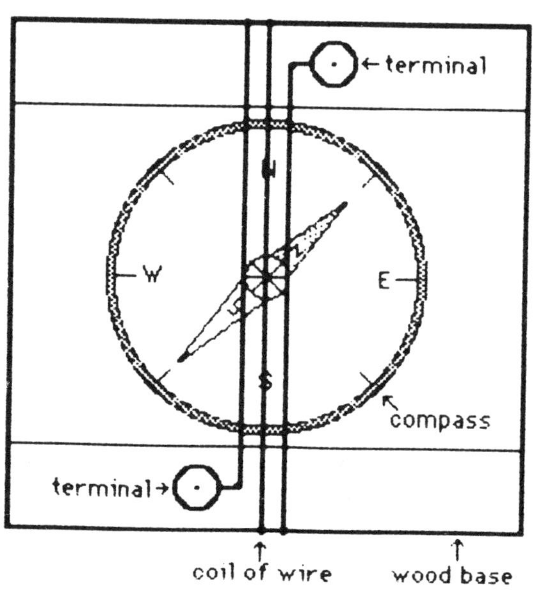

Fig. 3-3. A galvanometer (moving coil meter)

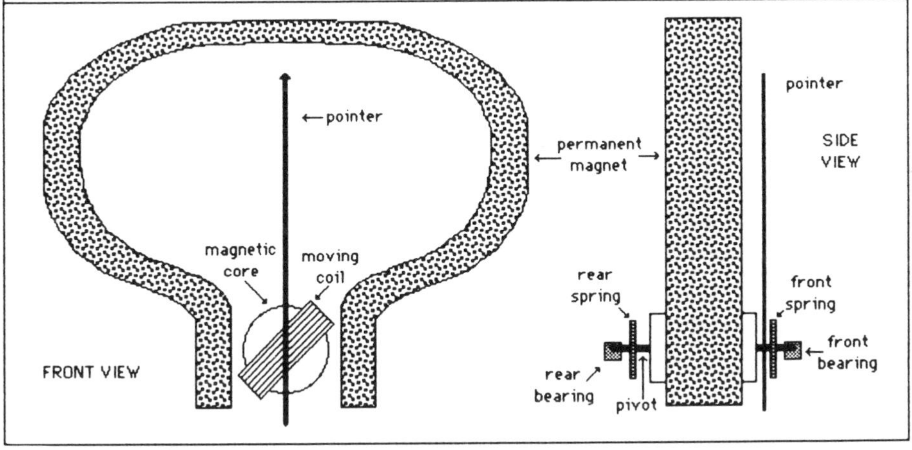

wire crossing the compass, a coil of wire is used. Figure 3-2 illustrates the early form of the galvanoscope. The French physicist Andrè Marie Ampère was responsible for the use of the coil of wire in place of the linear conductor. Ampère also formulated the early equations that mathematically describe the relationship between electrical current and its magnetic field. For these discoveries Ampère has had the basic unit of electrical current named after him. Basically, the galvanoscope is a more sensitive refinement of Oersted's original meter.

After the principles involved in the galvanoscope were more thoroughly understood, a more versatile and sensitive form of analog meter was developed. It is called the galvanometer. The galvanometer contains all the basic elements used in the construction of modern analog meters. The physical form of the galvanometer is shown in Fig. 3-3. In the galvanometer, a coil of wire is suspended between the poles of a permanent magnet. This coil is suspended by an axle that rides on two jeweled bearings, one at each end of the axle. This coil of wire becomes an electromagnet whenever electrical current passes through it. The galvanometer uses two magnets (one a permanent magnet and the other an electromagnet) instead of one permanent magnet (the compass needle) as the galvanoscope does. The use of two magnets greatly increases the sensitivity of the galvanometer over the more primitive galvanoscope. The moving coil is often wound around a magnetic core in order to further increase the galvanometer's sensitivity.

In the galvanometer, the permanent magnet is fixed in its position, while the electromagnet (the coil of wire) is free to rotate on its jeweled bearings. The electrical current is supplied to the wire coil by two small coil springs. The galvanometer is adjusted so that the pointer on the moving coil reads zero on the scale when no electrical current is flowing through the coil. In many galvanometers the zero position of the pointer is often placed in the middle of the scale. Such a meter is said to be "zero center reading".

When an electrical current is passed through the moving coil, it becomes an electromagnet. This electromagnet magnetically interacts with the fixed permanent magnet. The moving electromagnetic coil is either attracted or repelled depending on the direction of the current flow through the moving coil. The net effect is that the moving coil rotates in attempt to align its magnetic field with the magnetic field of the fixed permanent magnet. As the moving coil rotates, it opposes the force of the two springs that hold its axle in position. In scientific terms, the moving electromagnet exerts "torque" on its springs, it actually does "work" on these springs. The moving coil's final resting place is determined by two factors—the amount of electronic flow through the coil, and the springs' force impeding its motion. Since the forces exerted by the springs are relatively constant, the amount of needle deflection in the galvanometer is directly proportional to the amount of current passing through the coil.

The actual amount of deflection produced in the coil, per unit of current flowing through the coil, is called the meter's current sensitivity. If an analog meter is to be actually useful, then its deflection must be accurately related to an absolute amount of current. Current sensitivity is usually expressed in terms of microamperes (or milliamperes) per unit of scale division. Current sensitivity is abbreviated using the letter k. The mathematical relationship between coil deflection and coil current is expressed as:

$$k = \frac{i}{s}$$ **Equation 3-1**

k = meter current sensitivity in microamperes per scale division
i = coil current in microamperes
s = amount of coil deflection expressed in meter pointer movement

The moving coil of the galvanometer has an appreciable amount of electrical resistance. Ohm's law tells us that a potential (voltage) difference occurs across the coil as current moves through it. It is from this voltage drop across the meter's moving coil that the second critical meter parameter is established. This second parameter is called the voltage sensitivity of the meter. Voltage sensitivity is the product of the meter's resistance and the current sensitivity. Voltage sensitivity is calculated by the following equation and is expressed in microvolts per scale division:

$$\text{Voltage sensitivity} = k\,R_m \qquad \textbf{Equation 3-2}$$

k = meter current sensitivity in microamperes per scale division

R_m = resistance of the meter movement in ohms (Ω)

Both the voltage and current sensitivity are essential pieces of information necessary to properly use any meter. The voltage sensitivity factor is inherently related to the meter's coil resistance. Meters can be fabricated with the same current sensitivity, but with differing voltage sensitivities. Let's look ahead to the ways that this basic meter movement is applied in its modern forms.

Pivot and Jewel Movements

The pivot and jewel type of meter movement bears the closest resemblence to the ancient galvanometer type we have discussed to this point. Its physical configuration is the same as the galvanometer's pictured in Fig. 3-3. All meter movements using a rotating coil within a fixed magnet are often called d'Arsonval meters after their developer. Pivot and jewel meter movements offer good accuracy and ruggedness. Since their moving coil is suspended on two jeweled bearings, they are relatively immune to ambient vibration that may cause pointer oscillation. This factor is critical on many applications like machinery and moving vehicles.

The pivot and jewel arrangement works on magnetic repulsion and/or attraction of elements that rotate only. These elements do not move in relation to each other than in a radial fashion. This configuration yields a meter movement with linear current sensitivity. As such, the scale of the pivot and jewel movements have linear scales. This is not true of other types of meters, like the iron vane movement which has a logarithmic scale.

One of the major disadvantages of the pivot and jewel type is that it is effected by ambient magnetic fields and/or ferromagnetic materials. Placing a pivot and jewel meter movement in a panel that is made of a magnetic material, such as steel, will affect its accuracy.

To overcome this problem, many manufacturers will adjust their pivot and jewel movements to compensate for the presence of magnetic materials. Some pivot and jewel types have the heart of their movement magnetically shielded to prevent their interaction with ambient magnetic fields and materials.

Pivot and jewel movements have certain inaccuracies inherent in their design. For example, there must be some mechanical clearance between the axle and the jeweled bearings to prevent binding and to allow free movement of the coil's axle. This clearance results in inherent inaccuracies known as "fallover error." Fallover error is most prevalent in meters where the coil's axle is operated in the horizontal position. Another inherent inaccuracy is introduced by the friction present between the pivots and the jewels. This is called "friction error" and is built into the design. One more inaccuracy is introduced by the pivot rolling up the side of the jewel instead of remaining in the jewel's valley. This is called "roll-in-jewel factor" and can be eliminated by gently tapping the meter to settle the pivot. All these inaccuracies are due to the mechanical construction of the pivot and jewel meter movement.

Taut Band Movements

The taut band meter movements are essentially the same as the pivot and jewel types except for the method of suspending the moving coil. Instead of an axle supported by two jeweled bearings, the taut band movements suspend the moving coil with torsion bars. This suspension system is very similar to torsion bars used in some automotive wheel suspensions. The axle of the coil has two torsion springs at each end. These torsion springs are the only support for the moving coil.

The use of torsion springs eliminates the problems of fallover error, bearing friction error, and roll-in-jewel factor error. The taut band movement is a frictionless movement, and offers greater accuracy than the pivot and jewel types. As with most developments in electronics, the taut band movement involves compromises. The taut band movement is very sensitive to vibrations. For example, consider a meter movement used in a piece of electronic gear equipped with a cooling fan. The cooling fan introduces vibration into the equipment. This vibration is mechanically coupled to the meter through the equipment's enclosure. This vibration will affect the meter's accuracy. For this reason, taut band meter movements are only suitable in low or no vibration environments. The taut band movement is not suited for applications like moving vehicles. The taut band movements have the same sensitivity as the pivot and jewel types to stray magnetic field and/or magnetic fields. The taut band movements must be either shielded or compensated for magnetic effects if mounted in panels constructed of ferromagnetic materials.

Iron Vane Movements

The iron vane movement is a special type designed for use with ac rather than dc electricity. Consider running ac current through the coil of a pivot and jewel movement. Since the current is constantly changing direction in an ac waveform, the direction of the magnetic field within the coil will also be changing polarity in time with the current. This results in a reading of zero in the pivot and jewel movement, regardless of the current flowing through the coil. In order to overcome this problem, a special set of meter movements was developed specifically for ac operation—the iron vane meter movement.

The physics of the iron vane meter movement is very simple. If two similar iron bars are subjected to a common magnetic field, a repulsive force is developed between the two bars. In the iron vane meters, one of the iron vanes is held captive within a coil of wire. This coil of wire is called the actuating coil, and is fed the ac waveform which it converts into a magnetic field. The other iron vane is also within the coil, but it is suspended on a pivot and jewel arrangement so that it is free to rotate. The magnetic field produced within the coil repels the moving iron vane. It does this without regard for the polarity or either the driving current or the magnetic field. Figure 3-4 illustrates the internal construction of an iron vane meter movement.

The iron vane meter functions by magnetic repulsion of the two iron vanes within the movement. As such, the two vanes move apart. Since the distance between the two vanes increases with deflection, this meter movement is inherently non-linear in its operation. The magnetic fields within the meter operate at varying distances between the two vanes. The inverse square law of field energy applies to these two vanes because the distance between them changes. This results in non-linear operation. Compare this to the dc pivot and jewel movements where all deflection is strictly radial in nature—resulting in linear operation. Iron vane meters always have their scale's calibrated in logarithmic fashion, i.e., the intervals of equal current are compressed on the low end of the scale and expanded

Fig. 3-4. An iron vane meter movement

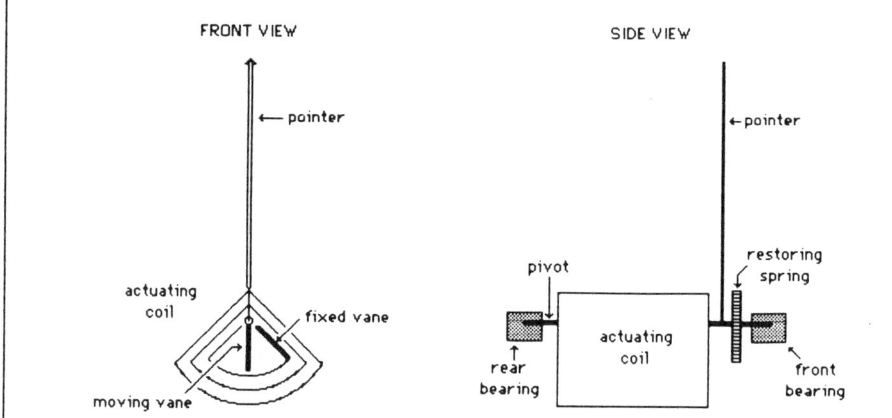

on the upper end of the scale. Iron vane meters can be recognized at a glance by their characteristic logarithmic scale.

Electrodynamo Meter Movements

The electrodynamo meter is another movement that bears strong similarities to the basic dc galvanometer. The electrodynamo movement can be operated by either ac or dc currents. The basic difference here is that the electrodynamo types do not use permanent magnets, but only electromagnets. Both the static and moving coil of the electrodynamo meters are operated from the ac input current. As such, both these coils maintain a constant magnetic phase relationship, allowing basic galvanoscope techniques to be applied on ac current.

The electrodynamo movement uses three coils. The one moving coil is suspended on a pivot and jewel arrangement between two other fixed coils. Figure 3-5 illustrates the physical configuration of the electrodynamo movement. The moving coil is deflected by the magnetic field created by the two fixed coils. The two fixed coils may be considered electrically as a single coil with a separation in the middle. Both the moving coil and the fixed coils are fed from the same ac waveform. The ac waveform produces alternating polarity magnetic fields within all the coils. Since all the coils are fed from the same source, the resulting magnetic fields stay in phase. This phase identity produces unidirectional pointer motion with either ac or dc current input.

Fig. 3-5. An electrodynamo meter movement

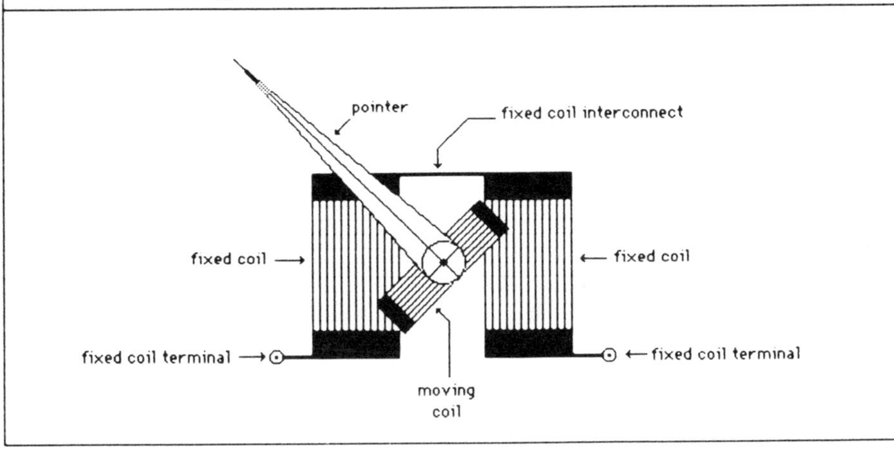

The electrodynamo meter movement may be wired up to measure a variety of electrical parameters. This versatility, coupled with the ability to use both ac or dc current as input, is responsible for the electrodynamo movement's popularity. Figure 3-6 illustrates three different coil connections for this movement. Note that the same electrodynamo meter movement may be used to measure voltage, current, or wattage. All that is necessary is to rewire the meter and provide the proper programming resistors.

Fig. 3-6. Electrodynamo coil schematics

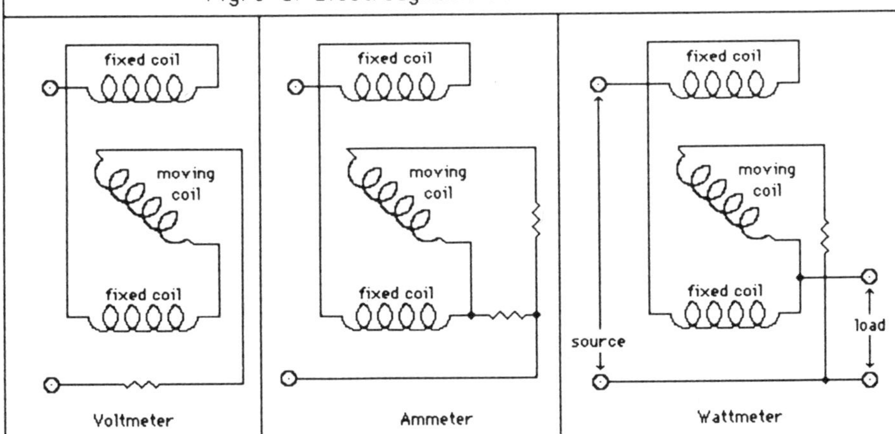

The electrodynamo meter is difficult to manufacture. As such, it is expensive. The usage of this meter is restricted to high end applications. By far, most of the meters employed in strictly ac service are of the iron vane type.

HOW ANALOG METERS ARE MADE

All analog meters are constructed in basically the same manner. The differences in price between meter movements is due to the degree of mechanical and electrical tolerances used in the meter. Precision and high accuracy meters are more difficult to manufacture and cost more. The moving coils are wound of very fine copper wire by a coil winding machine. The moving coil is then attached to its axle (pivot), which already has its return springs in place. The bearings that hold the pivot are V shaped and usually constructed from man-made sapphire. Sapphire is very hard and can be polished to the high degree necessary to reduce pivot and jewel friction to an absolute minimum. If a permanent magnet is used in the meter, then it is made from modern magnetic alloys such as ALNICO. The development of these very strong magnetic materials has led to a shrinking of both the meters inherent size and cost. Taut band movements are suspended by strips of gold foil which are stretched tight to suspend the coil's axle.

The basic meter movement is placed in a case constructed usually of styrene, phenolic, or polycarbonate plastic. In some cases, the meter's enclosure is made of non-magnetic metallic material. Some meters use steel for a case material, and the movement must be especially designed to operate with a ferromagnetic enclosure. The prime advantage of a steel case is that it shields the meter from stray magnetic effects. The front of the meter's case is constructed from transparent plastic, such as polystyrene or Plexiglas. In some cases glass is employed as a cover.

Most manufacturers offer their most accurate movements in "ruggedized" versions. The ruggedized versions are usually self shielded by their metal cases against stray magnetic fields and ferromagnetic panels. They are also sealed against environmental hazards such as moisture, temperature extremes, and vibration. In many cases, the ruggedized meters are filled with nitrogen gas to eliminate oxidation within the movement. The cases of ruggedized meters are sealed units employing "O" rings and many screws. Don't open these meter cases to rescale them. If the ruggedized meter is opened, it is very likely that it cannot be resealed effectively by anyone other than the manufacturer.

ANALOG METER CHARACTERISTICS

Analog meters vary quite widely in their operating characteristics. It is basically a matter of the price of the meter. The less expensive meters offer less accuracy and reliability. The information presented here represents a survey of analog meter technology, from the cheapest to the most expensive. The primary aim of this section is to define the terms and methods used by manufacturers to rate and describe their meters. An understanding of these terms and characteristics will enable us to decide on the best meter for any particular application.

Power Requirements

The analog meter has one very big advantage in terms of power requirements—it is almost always powered by the circuit that it is measuring. As such, it has no external power requirements, and needs no power supply or battery for its power source.

Dc meters are current operated. This is true whether the meter is used to actually measure current or voltage. The current rating of the meter is not of critical importance. A meter can be fooled into measuring more current than its basic movement will accept. This can be done by the use of shunts. In the case of voltage measurement, series resistance can be added to expand the meter's range of operation. The situation is the same for most ac types of analog meters.

In terms of current, meters are very sensitive. Analog movements can be made that will accurately measure as little as a microampere of current. Through the use of shunts (either internal or external), this current range can be expanded to thousands of amperes. Standard models with internal shunts are made by most manufacturers in the following current ranges—0 to 10 μA, 0 to 20 μA, 0 to 50 μA, 0 to 100 μA, 0 to 200 μA, 0 to 500 μA. The input ranges of the milliampere versions follow the same ranges, as do the models designed to read in amperes.

The resistance of the basic meter movement roughly follows the current rating of the meter. The less current it takes to drive the meter to full scale deflection, the greater the resistance of the movement. For example, a meter that measures 0 to 50 A will have an internal resistance of around 2200 Ω, while one that measures 0 to 500 μA will have an internal resistance of about 300 Ω. In the case of a meter measuring from 0 to 500 mA, the internal resistance of the movement may be as low as 0.2 Ω. Meters that measure current in the range of several amperes usually require an external shunt. This is done to keep the heat generated by the shunt out of the meter's case. Since the meter is a mechanical device, heat within the meter's case can greatly affect the basic accuracy of the movement. The exact resistance of the meter's movement is one of many factors that are determined by the meter's construction. First among these is the length and gauge of the wire used to wind the meter's coil. Later, we will discuss a method of determining the exact electrical resistance of a meter's movement.

The power dissipated across a meter movement can be easily calculated by using Ohm's law. Simply treat the meter as a resistor. From Ohm's law we can calculate power as equal to I^2R. Square the amount of current flowing through the meter and multiply this by the meter's internal resistance. For example, the 50 μA movement discussed earlier will dissipate 5.5 microwatts, and the 500 mA meter will dissipate 50 milliwatts. This is a very small amount of energy and points to the very great efficiency of analog meters.

Analog meters are used in many applications just because of their power requirements. They are very efficient and do not require external power sources for operation. These facts alone are responsible for the use of analog movements in many applications where electronic digital metering may have been used. This power factor is very important, and is responsible to the continued usage of a very old, mechanical technology in this age of total electronic solutions to measuring problems.

Resolution

Resolution in an analog meter simply means how well we can read the scale of the meter. Resolution is defined here as how small of a change in the meter's reading can be accurately read from the meter's face. For example, consider an application where we wish to measure a current that varies from 0 to 100 milliamperes. We could employ a meter with a full-scale deflection of either 100, 200, or 500 mA. In the case of the 500 mA movement, we would only use the lower ⅕ of the meter's scale. This would result in a decrease of the actual resolution by a factor of five. If the maximum resolution is desired from a meter, then it should be sized properly.

Use a meter with a full-scale deflection that is nearest to the maximum amount of current to be measured. The use of oversized meters reduces the effective resolution, and thereby the accuracy, of the meter.

Many meters employ an arc of reflective material underneath the meter's scale. Such meters are said to have a "mirrored scale." This mirror is used to eliminate parallax errors when reading the meter. Its use is simple, align your eye so that the reflection of the pointer coincides with its reflection on the mirror. A mirrored scale increases the effective resolution and accuracy of any meter movement because it enables us to read the meter's scale more accurately.

Scale Size

Scale size greatly affects how well we can read a meter. Scale size means the length of the calibrated area that the meter's pointer traverses. Scale size has nothing to do with the electrical size of the meter, but is related to the physical size of the meter. The larger the meter's scale is, the easier the meter is to read. Larger sized scales mean more effective resolution and greater accuracy.

Meters are made in a variety of scale sizes. The scale size is directly proportional to the meter's case size. For example, a meter whose case is a 1.5 inch square contains a scale that is an arc 1.31 inches long. A meter with a 3.5 inch square case contains a scale that is an arc 3.33 inches long. The larger meter has about 3 times the scale size of the smaller. As such, the larger meter offers about 3 times the effective resolution of the smaller meter. Use the larger size of meter if you require greater resolution and effective accuracy. While the larger meter has the same inherent (and rated) accuracy of the smaller, the larger is simply easier to read accurately.

Zero Starting Scales

The majority of the meters made have their scales starting at zero. This is adequate for most uses, but in some specialized applications this can decrease the effective resolution of the meter. Expanded scales are commonly used in voltage measurement. Consider a meter used in a 12-volt battery system. A discharged 12-volt lead-acid battery will have a voltage around 11 volts. When undergoing recharging, the battery's voltage may rise to about 16 volts. If we wish to measure the battery's voltage with an analog meter we have several choices. Consider a 0 to 20 Vdc analog meter. Since the battery's voltage never goes below 11 volts, the lower ½ of the meter's scale is never used. Since the battery's voltage never rises over 16 volts the top ⅕ of the meters's scale is also never used. This results in a loss of effective resolution.

The same situation exists in an ac voltmeter used to measure line voltage. Line voltage may vary from about 105 volts (maybe less in brownouts) to about 125 volts. If a meter is employed that reads from 0 to 150 volts, then over 80% of the meter's scale is wasted. Again, there is a loss of effective resolution. The answer is to expand the meter's scale. This means that the meter is configured electrically so that it starts its deflection at a voltage higher than zero. Expanding a meter's scale makes the entire length of the meter's scale more effectively employed in measurement.

Expanded Scales

Even though a meter may electrically have zero as a starting point, it is possible to fool the meter electrically to expand its scale. An example of this is completely discussed later in this chapter. The expansion of the meter scale in the 12-volt battery voltmeter example means that we start the scale at 11 volts. Full-scale deflection is accomplished at 16 volts in the expanded scale version. The expansion of the meter's scale enables us to effectively use the entire scale.

Many manufacturers offer expanded scale versions for specific uses such as the two examples previously mentioned. These meters are certainly worth the extra cost. The expanded scale offers greater effective resolution, and thereby increased accuracy. If a manufacturer does not make the expanded scale that you need, then you can make it yourself using the techniques described later in this chapter. Expansion of the meter's scale is accomplished electrically outside the meter, and does not require any modification of the meter's delicate, precision mechanical movement.

Speed

The analog meter is an electromechanical device which is relatively slow. Most manufacturers rate their meters with a response time of about 2 seconds maximum. Response time is defined as the time required after an abrupt change in the quantity of energy being measured until the meter's pointer accurately reflects the new quantity being measured. This response time factor represents the worst case scenario for the meter, and in practice the meter is usually somewhat quicker. Analog meters are the slowest measurement device discussed in this book.

Speed is certainly not the analog meter's strong point, but meters are quick to display small changes in input energy. In fact, the analog meter is faster at displaying small changes in energy than are their digital counterparts. This is due to the sample and hold techniques employed in the analog to digital conversion of the digital meters. Digital meters sample and convert their readings in about ⅓ to ½ seconds. Analog meters can display the same change in less than one third of the time. Digital meter manufacturers are now putting fast acting bar graphs in their digital meters' LCDs to make them read changes faster. In some cases, there are as many as 30 elements in this fast acting bar graph. Once again, the digital meters are narrowing the range of the analog meter's applications.

Accuracy

Accuracy is the limit, usually expressed as a percentage of rated full-scale value, which the errors inherent in a meter will not exceed. The conditions used to rate accuracy are specifically defined as to temperature, vibration, and other environmental parameters. Accuracy is rated with tapped readings. This means that the meter movement is gently tapped with the finger to settle the pivot and jewel and eliminate the roll-in-jewel factor.

Accuracy varies slightly from meter type to meter type, and greatly from manufacturer to manufacturer. In general, the more expensive the meter, the more accurate it is. Pivot and jewel types have accuracies of $\pm 2\%$ of full scale, with $\pm 5\%$ being the least accuracy of any manufacturer. Taut band types have accuracies of $\pm 2\%$ of full scale. Ac rectifier types (i.e., dc types used with a series diode) have accuracies in the neighborhood of $\pm 3\%$ of full scale. Iron vane types have accuracies of about $\pm 2\%$ to $\pm 5\%$ of full scale. Accuracy is rated at 23° C in a nonvibrating environment.

Repeatability

Repeatability is the ability of a meter to repeat its readings taken when deflecting the pointer upscale, compared to the readings taken when deflecting downscale. Repeatability is expressed in a percentage of full scale. Repeatability includes the following errors—friction error, roll-in-jewel error, fallover error, and magnetic hysteresis. Basically, repeatability is a measure of the consistency of the meter's measurement.

The pivot and jewel type of meter offers repeatability in the range of 2%. Taut band movements are much more consistant. They have a repeatability of less than 0.2%. This points out the inaccuracies introduced by the use of pivot and jewel suspension over the use of torsion suspension. Ac rectified types exhibit the repeatability of the dc movement used to make them, 2% for pivot and jewel and <0.2% for taut band types. Iron vane meters have repeatability ratings of 2%. These figures represent the minimum repeatability error figures, and many less expensive meters have repeatability errors over twice as great.

Temperature Effects

Temperature influence is defined as the percentage of change (of full scale value) in the indication of the meter that is caused purely by the effect of temperature changes. Temperature affects both the tension on the return springs of the meter and the magnetic fields produced by permanent magnets. Temperature also affects the resistance of the moving coil, and of any electromagnets in the meter.

Pivot and jewel types have temperature inaccuracies of about 0.02% per degree Centigrade. Taut band types exhibit inaccuracies in the range of 0.01% per degree Centigrade. Ac iron vane meters have temperature inaccuracies of 0.02% per degree Centigrade. As can be seen from these figures, temperature has only a very small effect on the analog meter's accuracy in comparison to other sources of inaccuracy.

One of the strong points of the analog meter is its ability to perform over a wide range of temperatures. Well made (i.e., expensive) analog meters will operate over a temperature range of −20° C to 50° C. Less expensive types have a temperature operating range of 0° C to 40° C.

DC METERS

The majority of the meter movements employed today are dc types. This versatile type of meter can be used to measure a variety of electrical parameters, depending on how it is wired into the circuit. Either a pivot and jewel or taut band movement can be used. Let's see how a basic dc galvanometer movement can be used to either measure dc current or dc voltage.

DC Meter Circuits

The most basic dc meter circuit is the ammeter. Ammeters are used to measure electrical current. Figure 3-7 illustrates the schematic of a dc ammeter. Note that the ammeter is used in series with the load. This is the case of all ammeters. This circuit can be used whether the shunt resistance is internal or external to the dc ammeter. A small portion of the current flows through the actual meter movement, while the bulk of the current flows through the shunt. This arrangement allows the use of sensitive meters with low current ratings in the measurement of higher amounts of current. In Fig. 3-7, R_m is the internal resistance of the actual meter movement, R_s is the resistance of the shunt, I_m is the current passing through the meter movement, and I_s is the current passing through the shunt. The total amount of current passing through the entire circuit is represented by I_t. I_t is the current that is under measurement and which is indicated by the meter. The following equation describes the current flow through the circuit:

$$I_t = I_s + I_m \qquad \textbf{Equation 3-3}$$

Since the two resistances, R_m and R_s are in parallel the following mathematical relationship is also true:

$$I_m R_m = I_s R_s \qquad \textbf{Equation 3-4}$$

Fig. 3-7. DC ammeter

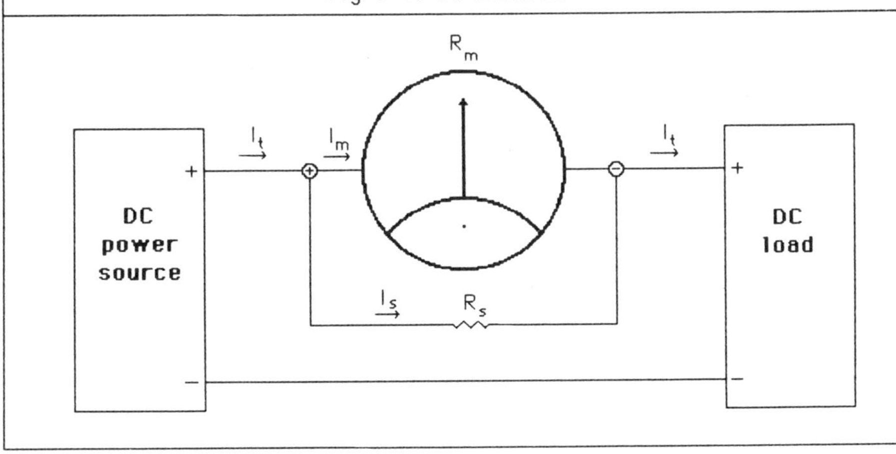

A combination of these two equations results in:

$$R_s = I_m R_m \div (I_t - I_m) \qquad \textbf{Equation 3-5}$$

R_s = the resistance of the shunt in ohms (Ω)
I_m = the current flowing through the meter in amperes
R_m = the meter's resistance in ohms (Ω)
I_t = the total current to be measured in amperes

This relationship allows us to calculate the appropriate shunt resistance for any particular meter movement that is required to indicate any particular amount of current. With this equation, we can work minor marvels in dc current measurement. For example, a meter that reads 1 mA of current full scale, can be employed to measure a current of 1 ampere, 10 amperes, or even 100 amperes with the appropriate shunt. In fact, the shunt need not even be an actual resistor. It can be a piece of copper wire. Use the Copper Wire Table to determine the resistance per unit length of any piece of copper wire. Simply measure out the correct length of a particular wire gauge for the proper resistance, and use this wire shunt in place of the shunt resistor. The possibilities of expanding the current range of ammeters are endless.

The next circuit uses a dc ammeter to measure dc voltage. In fact, this circuit represents all analog dc voltmeters, since they all employ the basic galvanometer which measures current. Figure 3-8 illustrates the schematic of the dc voltmeter circuit. Note that the dc voltmeter is connected in parallel with the power source. The resistor, in this case, is connected in series with the meter movement, rather than in parallel as in the ammeter. This resistor is called a multiplier. In this illustration E represents the dc voltage being measured, I_m is the current flowing through the meter, R_m is the meter movement's resistance, and R_s is the resistance of the multiplier resistor. The following equation describes this circuit:

$$E = I_m R_m + I_m R_s \qquad \textbf{Equation 3-6}$$

This equation when solved for the resistance of the multiplier yields:

$$R_s = (E \div I_m) - R_m \qquad \textbf{Equation 3-7}$$

R_s = the resistance of the multiplier resistor in ohms (Ω)

Fig. 3-8. DC voltmeter

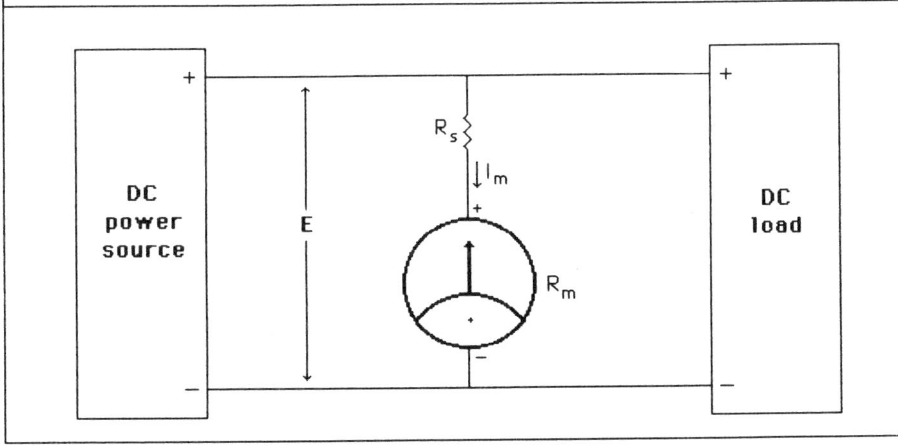

E = the voltage under measurement in volts
I_m = the meter's current rating in amperes
R_m = the meter's resistance in ohms (Ω)

This equation allows us to convert a dc current meter into a dc voltmeter that will read any particular dc voltage we may require. All we need to know is the current rating of the dc ammeter (this is easy—just look at the meters scale), the meter's resistance, and the maximum voltage we intend to measure. Once again, the dc galvanometer is used to do a job for which it was not originally intended. One should not assume that these techniques of adapting the basic dc movement sacrifice accuracy in any way. These are the same techniques used by the meter's manufacturer to make the range and variety of the meters they produce.

These "meter fooling" techniques are only some examples of what may be done with the versatile dc movement. If you understand the essence of what is being done to the dc movement, you can construct a meter that will exactly fit your needs. You need not sacrifice any accuracy in the process. The only potentially sticky factor is the exact value of the meter's resistance. This chapter will show how to empirically and exactly calculate the resistance of any dc meter movement.

Dc Meter Cost

Basic dc meter movements are available in a wide range of costs.

On the low end, we find smaller pivot and jewel movements with accuracies around 5% costing between $8.00 to $16.00. Larger pivot and jewel meters, with accuracies in the 2% range, cost between $26.00 to well over $60.00 depending on size. Taut band meters cost between $30.00 to over $90.00 depending on size and accuracy. In general, the taut band types are not made in the less expensive and less accurate versions. Size and accuracy are the main factors affecting an analog meter's cost. The bigger and more accurate it is, the more it is going to cost.

From the prices mentioned above, it is easy to see why the analog meter is finding it very difficult to compete with the digital types. Digital meters with accuracies in the 0.7% range can now be purchased for less than $40.00. More of this accuracy is actually realized by using digital readout systems. A collection of numbers is less ambiguous than reading an approximation of a meter's scale.

The real bargain for analog meter users is found in the surplus markets. Many analog meters now in service are being replaced by digital types. These "pull-outs" are available as surplus for a fraction of their original cost. In many cases these surplus meters are of the highest quality and accuracy. Electronics manufacturers generally do not use surplus meters. A meter requires quite a bit of panel space, and the panel cutout varies from meter to meter. When an electronics manufacturer considers analog metering, he wants repeatability and standardization. Surplus meters are a now you see it, now you don't, type of proposition. The supply is simply not reliable enough to interest major electronics manufacturers. So this leaves the surplus meter market to the home builder and experimenter.

AC METERS

Most ac meter applications actually employ dc movements. Diodes are used in series and/or parallel with the dc meter. As such, the information is essentially the same as previously discussed under dc meter circuits. In some cases, especially when measuring ac voltages, special circuits are employed to read either the peak or average voltage of the ac waveform.

Ac Meter Circuits

Figure 3-9 illustrates two circuits used to measure the average voltage of an ac waveform. Both circuits employ a dc ammeter as the basic meter movement. Processing is done to the input signal

Fig. 3-9. Average reading ac voltmeter circuits

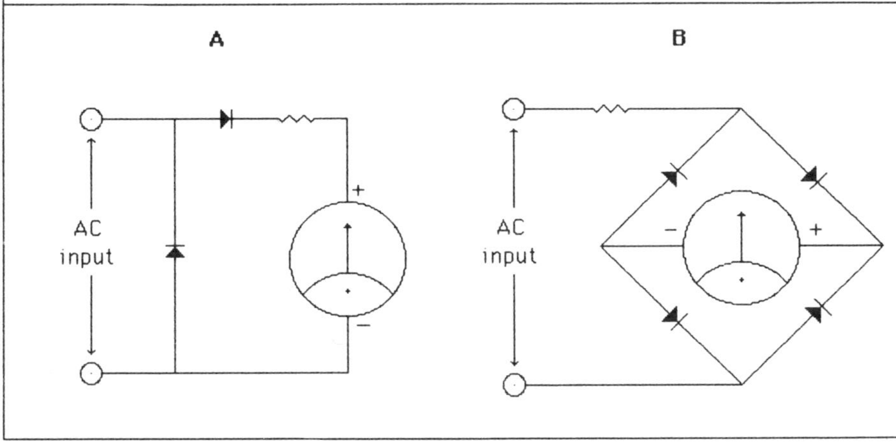

with passive components. Section A of Fig. 3-9 is a circuit that uses half wave rectification, while section B shows the full wave rectification version. In section A, the diode in series with the meter actually provides the rectified pulsating dc to the meter. The reverse bias diode in parallel with the meter provides a low impedance dc current path for the negative half wave of the input ac signal. The resistor in series with the meter is the multiplier. It determines the amount of voltage that will actually drive the meter to full scale deflection. This situation is identical for the full wave version. Since both these circuits offer dc current to the meter after the diode(s), the equations in the dc circuit section may be applied.

Peak reading ac voltmeters can be made with the circuit shown in Fig. 3-10. Once again, the actual meter movement is a dc type. The meter is coupled to the ac input signal with a capacitor. In this circuit, the time constant of the combination of the two resistors and the capacitor is critical. This circuit works most accurately when the capacitor holds the peak voltage of the ac input signal during the entire period of the ac waveform. This is accomplished by having the time constant of the resistor and capacitor network being over 20 times longer than the period of the ac input signal. The actual value of the capacitor is determined by the value of the resistors, which in turn are determined by the full scale rating and resistance of the meter movement.

Ac current is best measured by using an iron vane type movement. This movement is connected in series with the ac load.

Fig. 3-10 Peak reading ac voltmeter

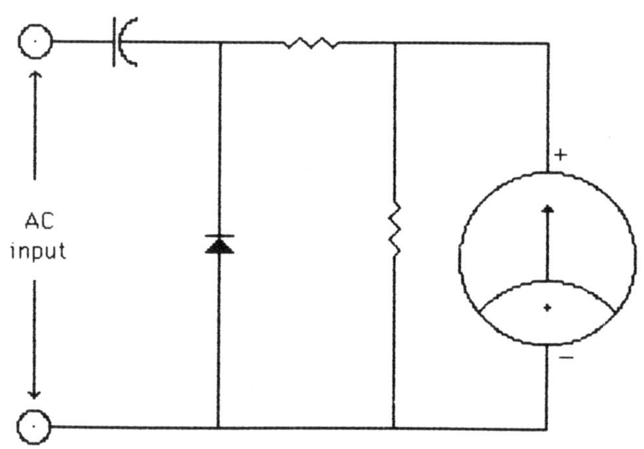

Shunt resistors may be used with the iron vane ac ammeter in the same manner as dc types. Figure 3-7 illustrates this hookup. Iron vane meters can be used to measure ac voltage directly without the circuits mentioned above. The main problem with using the iron vane types as ac voltmeters is that they will not accurately measure ac waveforms with frequencies much over 100 Hz. Their use at power frequencies of 60 Hz is quite accurate and universal.

Ac Meter Cost

Costs of the ac meters that use dc movements are the same as the dc types with slight increases for the additional diode(s). Ac iron vane meters cost in the range of $35.00 to $90.00 depending on size and accuracy. In general, iron vane movements are not made in the less expensive models.

USING ANALOG METERS EFFECTIVELY

This section gives two techniques that can make the usage of dc meters more accurate and increase resolution. The first is a method of exactly determining the meter's dc resistance. The second deals with a very accurate shunt circuit that expands the scale of a dc voltmeter.

Determining the Exact Resistance of a Dc Meter

Most dc meters come with their resistance marked on them by the meter's manufacturer. Note that in some cases, this figure is followed by "±5%" to "±10%". This means that the meter's resistance value, supplied by the manufacturer, is an average rating. The resistance of the actual meter you have may vary by as much as ±10% of this value. If you use the manufacturer's rated meter resistance in calculations involving the meter's resistance, then the eventual accuracy of your completed meter circuit can be in error by as much as ±10%. You can determine the exact value of the meter's resistance simply, and make your measuring circuit much more accurate.

The process is really a very simple application of Ohm's law. Figure 3-11 illustrates a schematic of the circuit used to accurately measure the meter's resistance. This technique does have several requirements if it is to be accurate. An accurate (less than 1% error) multimeter is required. Use the digital variety if you can. The power source showing in the schematic must be stable. If you don't have a regulated dc power supply that goes as low as 1.5 volts, then use a fresh alkaline D sized dry cell battery. The potentiometer used must be of the ten turn type in order to have sufficient adjustability.

The actual measuring process is as follows. Adjust the wiper

Fig. 3-11. Measuring a meter's resistance

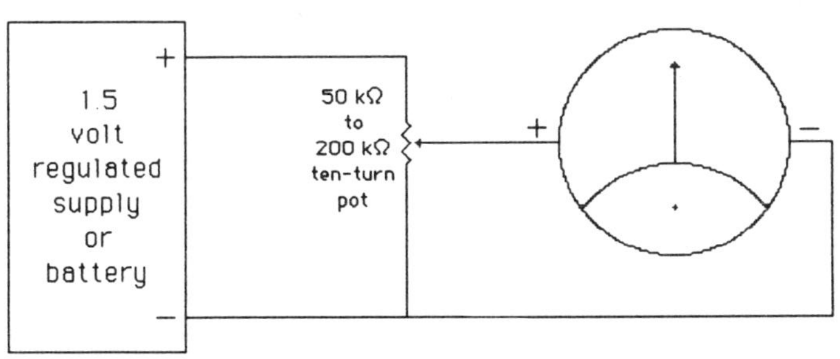

of the potentiometer to ground. Connect the line from the pot's wiper to the anode of the meter. Gradually raise the wiper of the potentiometer above ground until the meter reads full scale. Measure the dc voltage across the meter at this point. Next measure the current through the meter when it is deflected full scale. If you wish, you can read the current flowing through the meter under test right from its own scale. Using the same meter to measure both the voltage across the meter and the current flowing through it increases the accuracy of this process by eliminating any differences between the two meters. Ohm's law tells us that the meter's full scale resistance is its full scale voltage divided by its full scale amperage. So divide the voltage by the amperage and get the actual resistance of the meter movement.

If you perform this process over the entire meter's scale, you will notice that the actual resistance of the meter movement varies with its deflection. This is totally normal and inherent in the mechanical nature of analog meters. You may wish to use the resistance value of the meter at the point on its scale where you desire the greatest accuracy. Or you may wish to take readings at 25%, 50%, 75%, and 100% of full scale deflection and average the values. Whatever approach you use, this method will make any circuit employing the meter more accurate by using the actual value of the meter's resistance rather than its rated value.

Expanding the Scale of Dc Voltmeters

Figure 3-12 shows the schematic of a circuit that uses a dc microammeter as a precision expanded scale voltmeter. This particular version is configured for 12-volt battery systems, such as an automobile, an RV, or an alternative energy system. The meter begins reading at 11 volts dc, and is fully deflected at 16-volts dc. This circuit uses a precision shunt regulator IC, the TL 431 made by Texas Instruments. The TL 431 is available in an 8 pin DIP case, and contains a temperature compensated voltage reference. By changing the values of the resistors programming the meter and the shunt regulator this circuit can be used to expand the meter's scale anywhere in the region of 1.5 to 32 volts dc.

This circuit uses a 100-microampere full scale dc ammeter. The circuit functions by elevating this meter's ground to 11 volts. The 11 volts are measured at the test point on the schematic. Simply adjust the 5 kΩ potentiometer (VR2) programming the TL 431 until

Fig. 3-12. Expanded scale voltmeter

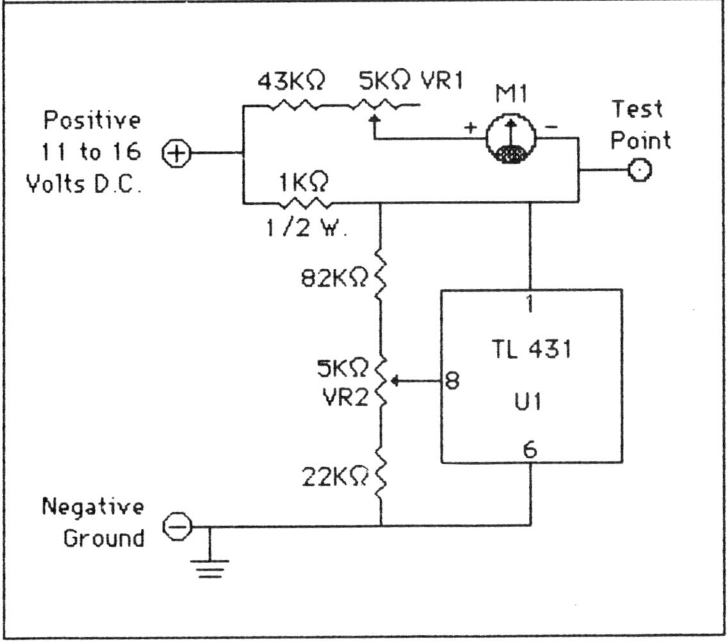

exactly 11 volts are measured at the test point. Use an accurate DMM for this measurement. The TL 431 will keep this test point (and the meter's cathode) at 11 volts, regardless of changes in the input voltage. Next adjust the 5 kΩ potentiometer (VR1) that is in series with the anode of the meter until the meter reads correctly. For example, at 11 volts input to the circuit the meter reads zero, at 12 Vdc input the meter reads 20 μA, at 13 Vdc input the meter reads 40 μA, and so forth.

Dc current meters other than 100 μA movements may be used in this circuit. Simply change the programming resistors in series with the meter's anode to suit the particular meter you have. The TL 431 is capable of handling the current of movements up to 10 mA full scale. No change is required in the shunt regulator portion of the circuit. This circuit can be as accurate a ±0.1 Vdc if a 2% meter movement is used.

The big advantage of this circuit is that it is very accurate even down to input voltages as low as 11 Vdc. Expanded scale circuits using series zener processing do not offer anywhere near this accuracy at the meter's low end. This is due to the nonlinearity of zener diode's voltage drop at low currents. The high accuracy of this circuit is due to the use of a shunt regulator configuration. This assures high accuracy at the low end of the meter's scale.

4

Cathode Ray Tubes (CRTs)

The cathode ray tube is the most popular electronic display device in existence. It is also one of the oldest, being invented in 1878 by an Englishman named Crookes. Over 80% of the electronic displays used worldwide are CRTs. There are very few people in technologically developed countries that don't spend some time watching a CRT daily. The CRT is most common as the device that displays television pictures, and this usage accounts for the majority of CRTs manufactured. The CRT is also the preferred display for computers. It offers large screen size, fast speed, and full color. While other display technologies challenge the venerable CRT, it still remains the king of the electronic display devices.

In this chapter we will primarily discuss the CRT itself and the various techniques used to encode information for it. The CRT has been in use for so long that a large number of different methods have been developed to display information on it. These methods are radically different approaches to differing display requirements. While the methods of displaying information on the CRT are diverse, the CRT technology used remains fairly constant. A thorough understanding of the basic physical operation of the basic CRT will enable us to better understand the differing encoding techniques used.

HOW CRTs WORK

The cathode ray tube is a specialized type of vacuum tube. It uses the same principles in its operation as do other vacuum tubes. If you are not familiar with the physical principles used in vacuum tubes, please seek this information in a basic text on electron tube operation. All vacuum tubes are essentially electron accelerators. They use electrostatic charges to manipulate the motion of electrons through a vacuum. In the case of the CRT, the beam of accelerated electrons is directed at a phosphor covered screen. When the electron beam impacts the phosphor coating, it stimulates the phosphors into emitting the light which displays the information on the CRT's screen. If a material emits light when under bombardment or stimulation by high energy electrons, it is said to fluoresce, while the after-glow that remains after the electron beam is shut off is called phosphorescence. It is from this effect that the phosphors get their name.

Figure 4-1 illustrates schematically the physical construction of a typical cathode ray tube. This illustration is simplified for our use as a sample of CRT operation, and it is not drawn to scale. Let's look at the CRT system by starting at the end of the tube's neck. The first element of the CRT is the source of the electrons and is called the cathode. The cathode is located at the extreme opposite end of the CRT from the display screen. Most CRTs use an indirectly heated cathode. This means that the actual electron emitter is heated by a separate filament called a heater. This heater is constructed

Fig. 4-1. Basic CRT physical construction

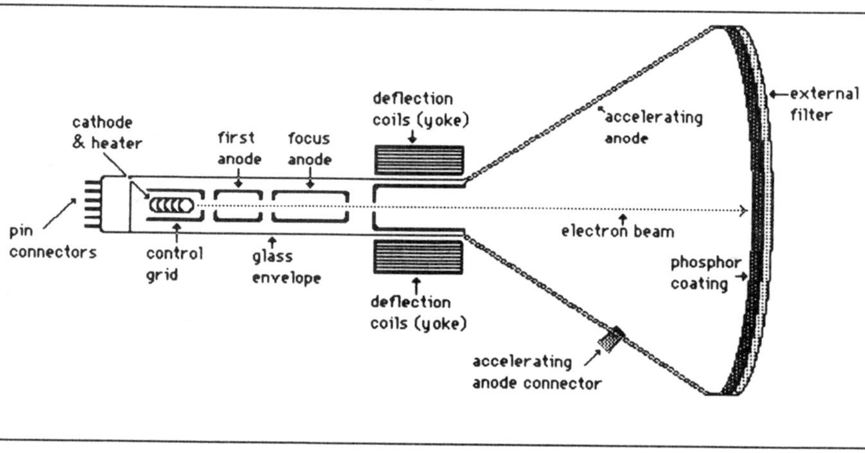

of thoriated tungsten which is heated by the passage of low voltage electrons through it. The cathodes of CRTs are heated to the temperature range of 800° C. The higher the temperature of the cathode, the more electrons it emits per unit time. Regulation of this temperature is critical to the tube's operating characteristics and longevity. Cathode temperature is regulated by the amount of electrical energy flowing through the filament of the heater. This entire cathode assembly of cathode and heater is the source of the electrons that will be manipulated to form the eventual display on the CRT's screen.

The next element of the CRT is the control grid. The control grid has the function of controlling the number of electrons per unit time entering the accelerator section of the tube's neck. The control grid acts as an electron valve, and determines the levels between the display of illumination and non-illumination on the CRT's face. The control grid is charged with a variable, small amount of positive charge. This charge draws the electrons from the cathode into the rest of the tube by electrostatic attraction. When this charge is above a certain level, the electrons are allowed into the accelerator section for processing and eventually illuminate an area on the screen. When the charge on the control grid is below a certain level, the electrons are not sufficiently attracted to enter the accelerator portion of the tube and this results in an unilluminated (black) area displayed on the CRT's screen. The control grid controls the level of luminosity displayed on the CRT's screen, which may be either black, white, or any grey level in between. In color CRTs, the control grid controls the luminosity of the individual colors displayed on the screen. The video luminosity information is coupled to the control grid by the video amplifiers of the display.

The third element of the CRT is called the "first anode." This anode may be either constantly positively charged at the same voltage, or the charge on it may be varied (modulated) to aid the control grid with luminosity control. The first anode's job in the CRT scheme of things is to assist the control grid in controlling the luminosity of the display. The use of a first anode allows the voltage on the control grid to be reduced while still retaining control of the CRT's luminosity. This reduction of the control grid's voltage allows the usage of less expensive, faster video amplifiers to drive the control grid. In some less expensive CRT designs, the first anode is deleted entirely and all luminosity control is handled by the control grid.

The third element of the CRT is the "focus anode." In the focus section the electron beam is accelerated and focused into as tight a beam as possible. There are three methods of focusing the electron beam. These are high voltage electrostatic, low voltage electrostatic, and electromagnetic. The high voltage electrostatic type of focus offers the best performance and is used in virtually all CRTs. It delivers the smallest spot on the screen, and more consistent uniformity of the spot's size everywhere on the screen. The high voltage electrostatic technique uses a tubular anode within the neck of the tube. This type of construction allows the finished CRT to be shorter than other focusing methods.

The fourth active element of the CRT is usually simply called the "anode." It is actually the last in a series of anodes. In this text we will refer to it as the "accelerating anode," as its function is to rapidly accelerate the electron beam on its way to collision with the screen's phosphors. The accelerating anode is located at the end of the neck where it joins the bell shaped section of the tube. This anode is physically present through the inside of the CRT's bell. This entire section of the CRT is part of the accelerating anode and is held at the same high voltage. The acceleration of the electron beam imparts kinetic energy to the electrons that make up the beam. This kinetic energy is translated into light by collision with the phosphors on the CRT's screen. The amount of voltage on the accelerating anode determines how much the beam is accelerated. The absolute luminosity of the CRT display is a direct function of the voltage of the accelerating anode. The higher this voltage is, the brighter the phosphors on the screen will glow when they are struck by the electron beam.

After the electron beam is accelerated, there remains only one more step to perform before it impacts the phosphors. The beam must be directed to the location on the screen that is desired to be illuminated. This job actually requires very little energy; the mass of an electron is about 10^{-27} grams and very little power is required to affect the electron's motion. The process of directing the electron beam to the proper location is called "deflection." Deflection is accomplished in two manners, electrostatic and electromagnetic.

In the electrostatic approach, another two sets of anodes are added within the tube's neck. One anode set is orientated vertically while the other is placed horizontally. These deflection anodes are oriented so that a varying charge applied to them will deflect the beam to the proper position on the CRT's screen. The electron beam has already been accelerated by the accelerating anode and is moving very quickly through the electrostatic field generated by the deflection anodes. The electron beam is within the electrostatic field of the deflection anodes for a very short time. This limits the amount of deflection that may be obtained by the deflection anodes. Electrostatic deflection is used exclusively in small CRT's where only small angles of deflection are required. The electrostatic technique offers faster response than the electromagnetic method. This faster response is offset by the decreased resolution of the electron beam, particularly when it is deflected to the edges of the display. The spot appears mushy, larger, and out of shape at the edges of the screen when the electrostatic deflection technique is used. Electrostatic deflection is used almost exclusively in CRTs designed for oscilloscope and vector scanning service.

Electromagnetic deflection is the preferred method for almost all CRTs currently being manufactured. In this technique, a "yoke" is placed around the neck of the CRT. This yoke is actually two coils of wire, one coil producing magnetic field vertically, the other horizontally. These coils are positioned coaxially to the electron beam. This yoke is external to the CRT's envelope; it is not located inside the tube as are the electrostatic deflection anodes. This yoke controls the position of the electron beam by establishing a variable magnetic field through which the beam must pass. The electron beam is deflected by magnetic interaction with the yoke's field. The electromagnetic approach to deflection offers the highest resolution of the electron beam. This yields a small, consistent spot anywhere on the screen. Electromagnetic deflections also offers the maximum deflection angle possible, making it suitable for large screen CRTs. Electromagnetic deflection is the type used exclusively in CRTs designed for TV and computer service. This form of deflection is suited to either vector or raster scanning techniques. The electromagnetic characteristics and physical positioning of the yoke are critical to the overall functioning of the CRT. Since the yoke is a current operated device, it is far simpler to implement than the voltage operated electrostatic technique requiring thousands of volts on the deflection anodes. The use of current rather than voltage to control spot position greatly simplifies the deflection amplifiers that drive the yoke.

After all stages of processing, the electron beam meets its intended destiny and collides with the phosphor coating on the screen. The result is light. Not just any light, but light of the correct intensity, correct duration, and in the correct place. The electron beam flys across the screen so quickly (over 650 meters per second) that the net effect is an image updated so rapidly that it is flicker-free and appears to move. The actual physical principles used in the CRT are very simple, just a highly controlled, high energy, electron beam crashing into light emitting phosphors. The triumph of CRT video lies in the manner that the CRT is used. While the basic operation of the CRT is simple, the methods of encoding and reproducing data for display on the CRT are very diverse and complex. The real intelligence resides in the effective use of the CRT and not in the technology that produces the actual tube. Figure 4-2 illustrates the different stages of processing that the electron beam undergoes on its journey to the screen. This block diagram shows the most common type of CRT in use, one with electromagnetic deflection and high voltage electrostatic focusing. The different methods of employing the actual CRT in practice are fully covered under that particular method of CRT use.

HOW CRTs ARE MADE

CRTs are a specialized type of vacuum tube, and as such, much of the manufacturing procedures used to make them are the same as other vacuum tubes. The use of filaments, grids, anodes, and electrostatic charges to control electronic motion is not new and many old tried and true techniques are used in CRT construction. Here we will concentrate on the differences between the CRT and other types of vacuum tubes.

The CRT has been adapted specifically for display service. Its job as a vacuum tube is not to amplify, oscillate, or rectify as most vacuum tubes do, but to display information. All the electronic processing within the CRT's envelope is dedicated to this task. The

Fig. 4-2. CRT block diagram

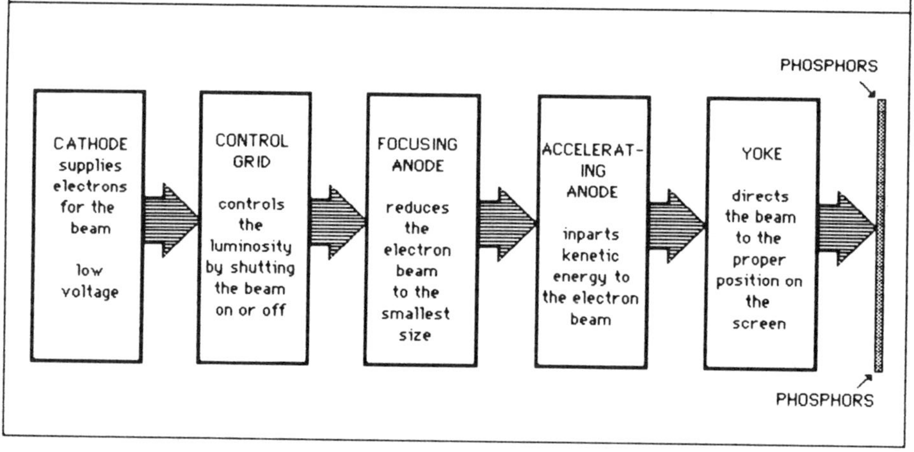

problems faced in CRT design and manufacture are those of spot size, linearity, luminosity, resolution, and speed.

The Glass Envelope and Within

The glass envelope that encloses the CRT is called the "bulb". It is constructed of a specialized glass that remains relatively clear under sustained electron bombardment. Ordinary glass compounds gradually become dark and opaque under high voltage electronic impact. The bulb is fabricated by conventional glass manufacturing techniques, but with much higher quality control and standards. The CRT envelope must enclose a hard vacuum, and must withstand implosion. Care should be taken whenever working with or around an exposed CRT tube. Breakage of a CRT can result from a sharp blow in the neck area. The tube can implode and shoot off dangerous flying glass shards. CRTs are usually strengthened by adding a metal tensioning band around the periphery of the CRT's screen. This tension band also allows mechanical mounting of the heavy CRT within the display device, while protecting the tube from implosion.

The shape of the CRT's bulb is determined by several factors, among which are the size of the screen, and the deflection angle of the beam. The overall length of the CRT is a function of the deflection angle. In general, smaller deflection angles result in smaller spot size, better linearity, and greater resolution on the screen. Smaller deflection angles also require less deflection power, simplifying deflection amplifier design. Simple geometry shows us that for the same sized screen, greater deflection angles result in shorter overall tube lengths. Figure 4-3 illustrates the geometrical relationship between overall CRT length, deflection angle, and screen size. The physical shape of the CRT is a trade-off between several conflicting physical factors. CRT manufacturers desire the highest resolution and performance possible, but the CRT is a bulky item and every attempt is being made to shrink its overall length while maintaining a large screen size. The modern trend is toward shorter CRTs with greater deflection angles. Currently manufactured CRTs for TV use have deflection angles between 90° and 120°. Resolution and linearity are maintained by more accurate and complex deflection driving electronics.

The diameter of the neck of the CRT has become somewhat standardized at 36 mm (1.4375 in). Standardization has allowed mass production of cathodes, grids, anodes, and deflection yokes. There is a movement by high resolution CRT manufacturers to reduce the

Fig. 4-3. CRT geometry

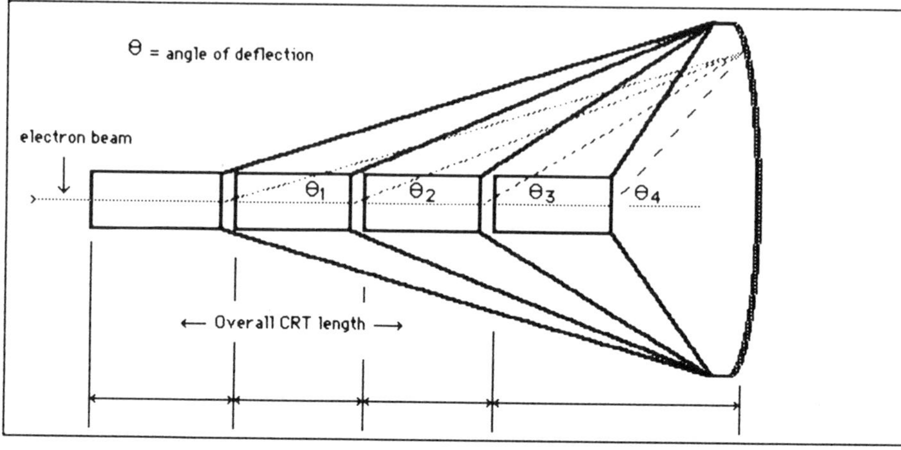

diameter of the tube's neck in order to decrease deflection power and increase resolution. Some smaller neck sizes being used now are 28 mm (1.125 in) and 22 mm (0.875 in). The relationship between deflection power and neck size is based on electromagnetic or electrostatic fields, which are mathematically described by the inverse square law of electric and magnetic fields. For example, when the neck of a CRT is reduced in diameter from 36 mm to 22 mm, the power necessary for the same amount of deflection is cut in half. Reduction in neck size, however, requires greater alignment precision between the various electrodes contained in the neck. Once again, another compromise must be made between divergent factors in CRT design and manufacture.

The length of the CRT's neck is directly related to the diameter of the neck. Generally, the neck of a 36 mm in diameter CRT is between 18 and 23 cm long. As the diameter of the neck is reduced to say, 28 mm then the neck's length shrinks to between 10 to 13 cm. Since everyone is trying to reduce overall CRT length, we can look forward to CRT's with smaller necks both in diameter and length. Once again, advancements in the electronics that drive the CRT make it possible to make the tube shorter without reducing resolution or increasing power consumption.

The phosphor coating is attached to the inside of the CRTs screen. In the case of color CRTs, a mask or grid is placed over the phosphors. The use of this mask is discussed later under the various CRT scanning techniques. The accelerating anode is a metalized conductive coating that is thinly and evenly spread over the entire inside of the CRT's bell. The accelerating anode stops just at it enters the neck of the CRT. The electrodes and their associated wiring are installed in the tube's neck. The tube is then evacuated and sealed at the very tip of the neck. The electrical connector for the tube's electrodes is added and the CRT is ready for testing.

Many CRT manufacturers apply a conductive coating to the outside of the bell of the tube. This coating is grounded and electrically dc isolated from the accelerating anode coating inside the bulb. The net effect is a very inexpensive, high capacitance, filter capacitor for the accelerating anode. The glass envelope plays the role of the capacitor's dielectric. This external conductive coating must be physically separated from the anode connector passing through the CRT's bell or arcing will result. The external conductive coating capacitor is primarily used in entertainment TV CRTs. The high resolution CRTs forego this technique because it creates varying electrostatic fields within the tube which decreases resolution.

CRT Phosphors

The subject of the phosphors used to coat the inside of the CRT's screen is of critical importance and the subject of much research and innovation. There are in excess of 150 different chemical compounds used in current CRT phosphor manufacture. They all have one thing in common, they emit light in the visual wavelengths when bombarded by high energy electrons. Other than this one common factor, they offer widely differing operating characteristics. Differing physical characteristics include chemical composition and phosphor particle size. The operating characteristics we will discuss for CRT phosphors are color, luminous efficiency, and persistence. Phosphor compounds are designated by "P" numbers which are registered with the Joint Electron Devices Engineering Council (JEDEC) of the Electronic Industry Association (EIA).

Ideally, any phosphor used in CRT manufacture should emit light in a very narrow bandwidth, that is, its light output would have very high color purity. For example, the reds would be very red with no trace of orange or purple. Unfortunately, this degree of color purity is very difficult to obtain, and compromises must be made. In full color systems, the primary colors of red, blue, and green are mixed to obtain all the other colors. This primary color mixing requires very pure primary colors if the resulting hues are to appear true.

As a group, most phosphors used in CRT manufacture are oxides of inorganic crystalline materials which have minute amounts of impurities added. These impurities are called "activators" and are added to increase the phosphor's luminosity and to modify its color. There is currently much research being done on the use of rare earth compounds, such as neodymium, gadolinium, and yttrium, for CRT phosphors. Table 4-1 lists some commonly used phosphors, their peak light wavelength in nanometers (nm) and their chemical composition. Note that many of the compounds are sulfides and oxides containing rare earth metallic elements. The size of the phosphor is related to its chemical composition and crystalline structure. Phosphor size varies from a few microns in diameter to over 30 microns. Screen resolution is directly tied to phosphor size, and high resolution CRTs use the smallest sized phosphors to attain small spot sizes.

The JEDEC of the EIA uses what is known as a "Kelly Chart" to classify the color of phosphor's light output. The Kelly chart is a standardized method of defining the color of lighting and phosphors. This chromaticity diagram uses rectangular coordinates to exactly define a phosphors apparent color and hue. Figure 4-4 illustrates

Table 4-1. CRT Phosphors, Their Chemical Composition, and Peak Wavelength.

Phosphor No.	Chemical Composition	Peak Wavelength (nm)
P1	Zn_2S10:Mn	525
P4	ZnS:Ag	460
P4	ZnCd:Ag	560
P4	CaO:MgO:SiO_2:Ti	420
P4	ZnOBeOSiO_2:Mn	550
P11	Zn:Ag	460
P16	CaMgSiO_3:Ce	385
P22 (red)	various compounds	630
P22 (green)	various compounds	516
P22 (blue)	ZnS:Ag	450
P24	ZnO:Zn	510
P31	ZnS:Cu	522
P37	ZnS:AgNi	470
P43	Gd_2O_2S:Tb	540
P45	Y_2O_2S:Tb	420-540
P47	Y_2SiO_5:Ce	400

Fig. 4-4. Kelly chart

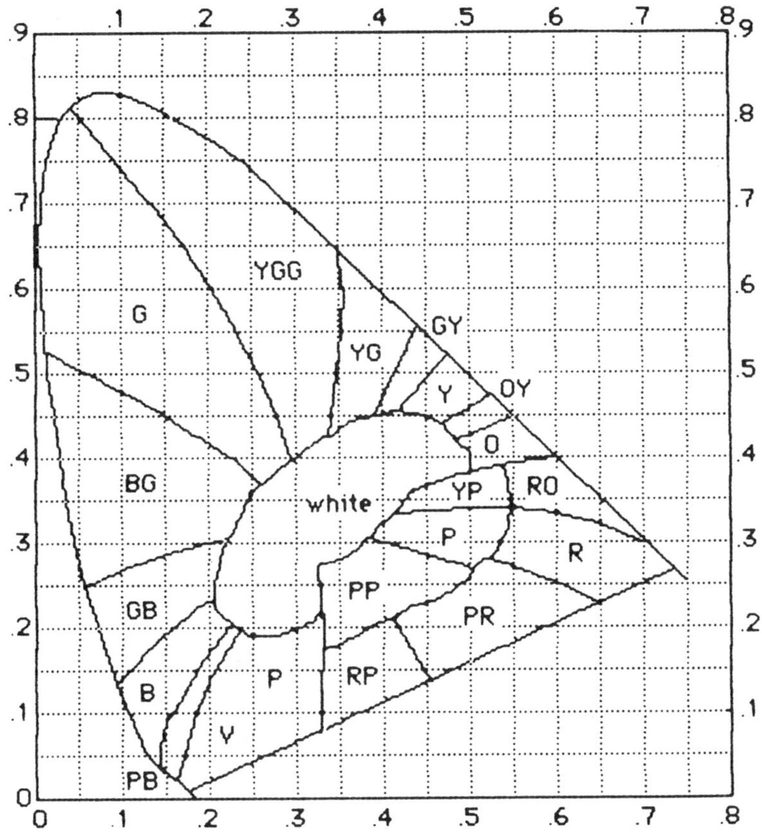

R = red
RO = reddish orange
O = orange
OY = orange yellow
Y = yellow
GY = greenish yellow
YG = yellow green
YGG = yellowish green
G = green
BG = bluish green
GB = greenish blue
B = blue
PB = purplish blue
V = violet
P = purple
RP = reddish purple
PR = purplish red
PP = purplish pink
P = pink
YP = yellowish pink

a Kelly Chart with the colors marked upon it. Figure 4-5 is a Kelly Chart with several of the more commonly used CRT phosphors' colors designated on it. In this manner an accurate terminology for the color of phosphors has been developed. In many CRT applications, the exact color of the phosphor is not important, but in a CRT designed for color entertainment television the color hues and intensities are critical. The most commonly used phosphors in color TV CRTs are the family designated as P22, which come in three varieties, red, green, and blue.

The phosphors still glow for short periods of time after the electrons cease to bombard them. This characteristic is called "per-

Fig. 4-5. Phosphor colors

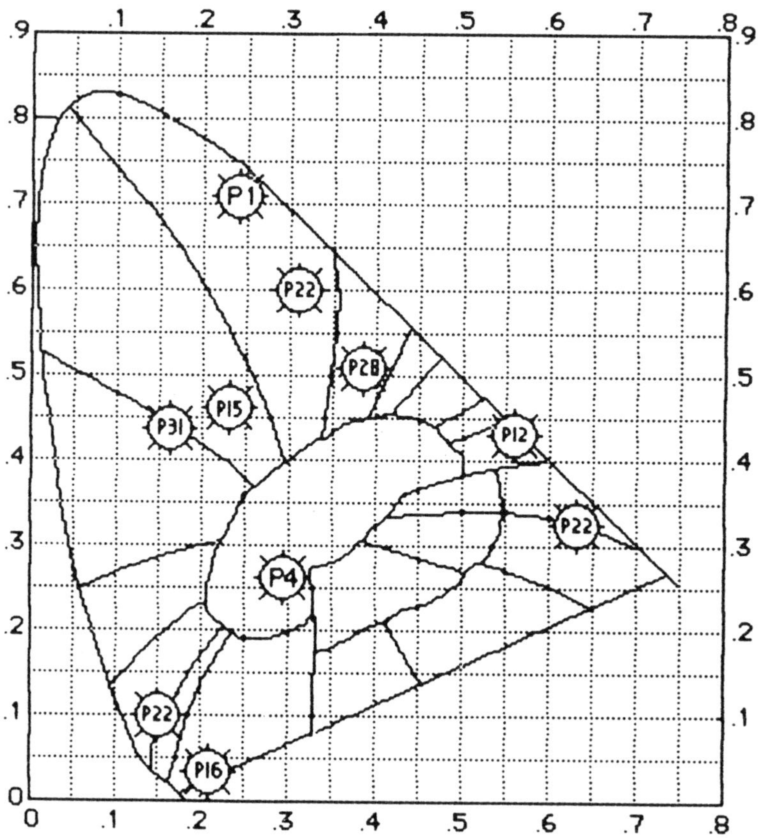

sistence'' and is critical in CRT design. Persistence and scan rate are inseparably connected. In common terms, the faster a phosphor decays, the more often it must be impacted by the electron beam to obtain a flicker-free image. Table 4-2 lists the decay time ranges of a phosphor and its persistence classification. Without some persistence in the phosphors, the CRT would appear to flicker. These persistence classifications are based on the time it takes the phosphor's light output to fade to 10% of its steady state (i.e., under electron bombardment) luminosity. Many types of long persistence phosphors are based on fluoride compounds. While they offer long persistence, they can be easily and permanently damaged by high beam currents. Such damage is called ''burning'' and results in permanent phosphor discoloration and loss of luminous efficiency. Figure 4-6 illustrates graphically the persistence of several commonly used CRT phosphors. Note that the decay time axis is logarithmic. Note, also, the wide range of decay times available to meet a wide range of CRT uses.

Table 4-3 lists many commonly used CRT phosphors, their steady state color, their decay color, their decay times, their Kelly coordinates, and their relative luminous efficiency. This table is only a partial listing of the vast armada of CRT phosphors available to the CRT designer and manufacturer. The steady state color of a phosphor is measured when the phosphor is under excitation by the electronic beam.

The luminous efficiency of a phosphor is based on the P4 phosphor's luminous efficiency and is a normalized measurement of how well a phosphor converts kinetic electronic energy into visible light. The P4 phosphor emits white light. It has long been the most commonly used phosphor in the manufacture of black and white CRTs for entertainment television use. The P4 phosphor used for a standard is raster scanned at a beam intensity of 0.015 μA per square cm and an anode voltage of 12 kilovolts. The luminous efficiency of

Table 4-2. Phosphor Decay Time and Persistence Classification.

Decay Time to 10%	Classification
1 sec or longer	Very Long
100 ms to 1 sec	Long
1 ms to 100 ms	Medium
10 μs to 1 ms	Medium Short
1 μs to 10 μs	Short
less than 1 μs	Very Short

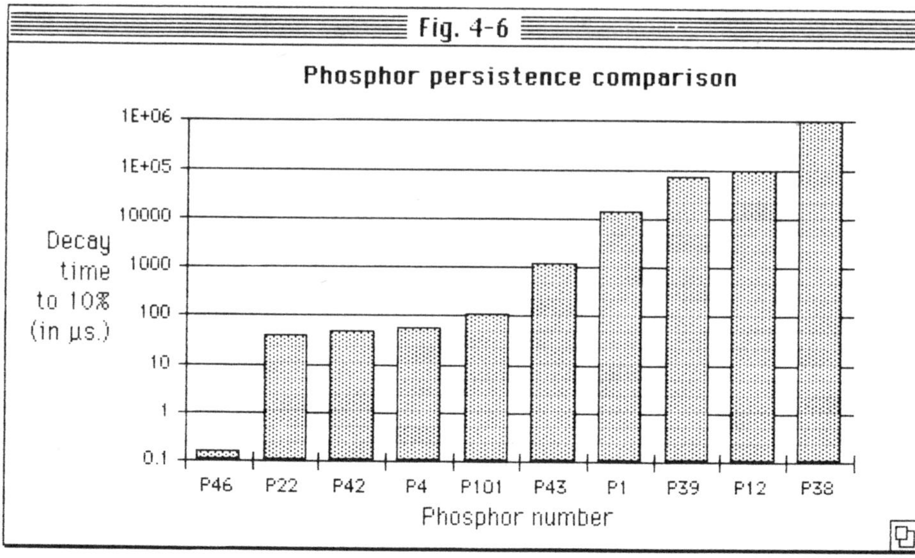

any phosphor is absolutely expressed in terms of lumens per watt of input energy.

The luminous efficiency is also a function of the amount of electronic kinetic energy which is a function of the accelerating anode voltage used in the CRT. Figure 4-7 is a graph that shows the

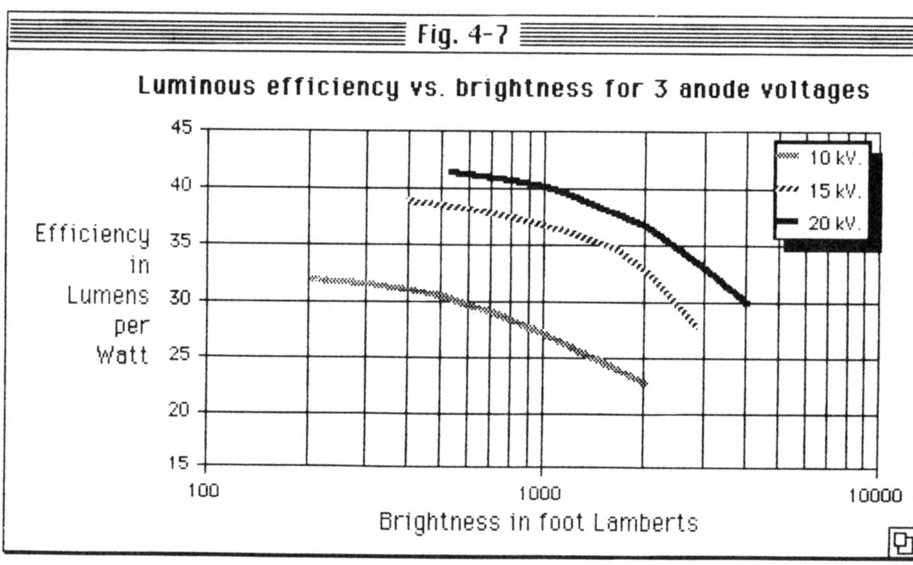

Table 4-3. CRT Phosphor Characteristics.

P No.	Steady State Color	Decay Color	Decay Time to: 10% Level	1% Level	Kelly Coord. X	Y	% Efficiency
P1	yellowish green	yellowish green	14 ms	45 ms	.240	.710	75
P2	yellowish green	yellowish green	75 μs		.270	.545	
P4	white	white	60 μs	380 μs	.265	.300	100 (standard)
P7	white	yellowish green	60 μs	400 μs	.197	.181	59
P11	blue	blue	60 μs	350 μs	.149	.144	48
P12	orange	orange	95 ms	325 ms	.544	.451	35
P16	violet	violet			.199	.016	1
P19	orange	orange	175 μs	225 ms	.580	.415	32
P22	red	red	1 ms		.655	.335	200
P22	green	green	40 μs	300 μs	.346	.604	195
P22	blue	blue	40 μs		.070	.155	180
P25	orange	orange	45 ms		.445	.555	
P26	orange	orange	175 μs	225 ms	.580	.415	32
P28	yellow green	yellow green	45 μs	550 μs	.368	.513	66
P31	yellowish green	yellowish green	70 μs	380 μs	.282	.545	150
P38	orange	orange	1.0 s	4.5 s	.561	.436	33
P39	yellowish green	yellowish green	70 ms	900 ms	.220	.720	85
P40	white	yellowish green	45 μs	300 μs	.255	.330	76
P42	yellowish green	yellowish green	50 μs	450 μs	.270	.560	110
P43	yellowish green	yellowish green	1.2 ms	2.5 ms	.350	.540	115
P45	white	white	1.6 ms	3.7 ms	.255	.320	60
P46	yellowish green	yellowish green	<160 ns		.405	.555	25
P55	blue	blue	60 μs	350 μs	.148	.060	22
P56	red	red	2.25 ms	5.2 ms	.645	.345	50
P101	yellowish green	yellowish green	110 μs	17 ms	.208	.644	67
P104	white	white	60 μs	380 μs	.280	.312	127
P105	white	yellowish green	50 μs	600 μs	.198	.200	47
P106	orange	orange	240 μs	1.25 ms	.585	.395	58
P109	yellowish green	yellowish green	70 μs	380 μs	.300	.600	165
P115	white	white	60 μs	380 μs	.322	.362	125
P116	yellow	yellowish green	140 ms	1.1 s	.224	.719	60
P118	white	white	60 μs	380 μs	.260	.280	84
P124	yellow green	yellow green	60 μs	380 μs	.435	.540	188
P134	orange	orange	30 ms	85 ms	.552	.445	65
P154	yellowish orange	yellowish orange	60 μs	9 ms	.540	.455	70
P158	yellow	yellow	65 ms	805 ms	.475	.510	33
P160	yellowish green	yellowish green	60 μs	450 μs	.280	.570	160
P162	yellowish green	yellowish green	80 μs	4.5 ms	.240	.660	100
P164	white	yellowish green	70 μs	16 ms	.265	.290	60
P167	white	white	65 μs	380 μs	.365	.400	140
P168	yellowish green	yellowish green	60 μs	300 μs	.305	.610	195
P169	yellow	yellow	1.3 ms	3.25 ms	.470	.470	85
P171	white	yellow green	200 μs	30 ms	.365	.400	55
P175	red	red	600 μs	1.6 ms	.645	.345	45
P177	green	green	90 μs	25 ms	.230	.695	95
P178	yellowish green	yellowish green	70 μs	380 μs	.282	.545	120
P179	white	white	1 ms	2.4 ms	.360	.365	115
P180	yellowish orange	yellowish orange	60 μs	1.5 ms	.480	.425	57

luminous efficiency (expressed in lumens per watt) of a typical phosphor versus its brightness (expressed in foot-Lamberts) for three levels of anode voltage, 10, 15, and 20 kilovolts. Since both higher luminous efficiency and smaller spot size are produced by higher anode voltages, the modern tendency is to increase the anode voltage as high as practically possible. This is usually in excess of 20 kilovolts. Care must be taken when working on an exposed functioning CRT, the high anode voltages can deliver a very nasty shock to the unwary.

An interesting phosphor technique is applied in color CRTs that do not require precise shades and hues to be displayed. This technique is called "beam penetration" color, and uses variations of the anode's voltage to reach differing colored phosphors that are layered in the CRT's screen. Its primary advantage is the simplicity of the

Fig. 4-8. Beam penetration CRT

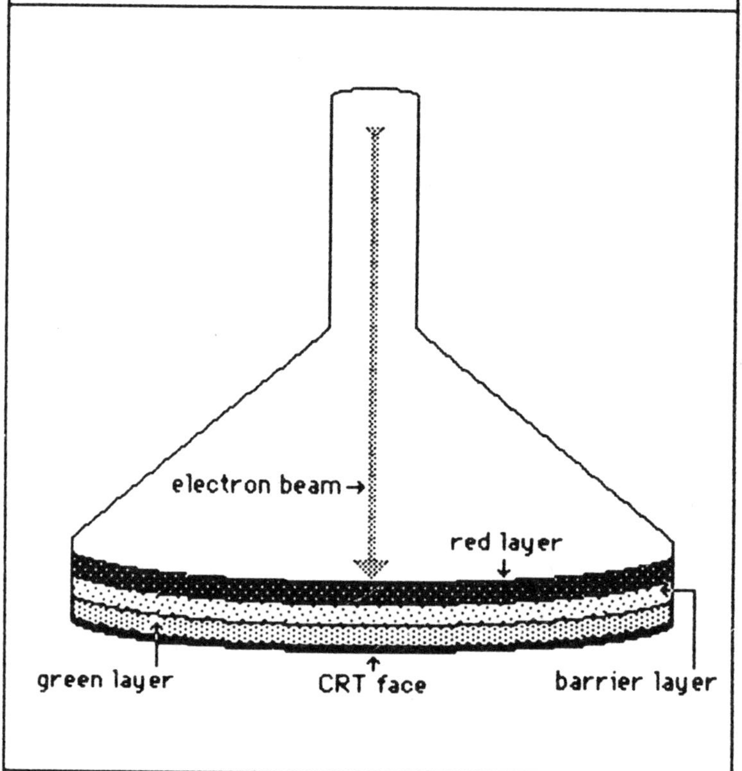

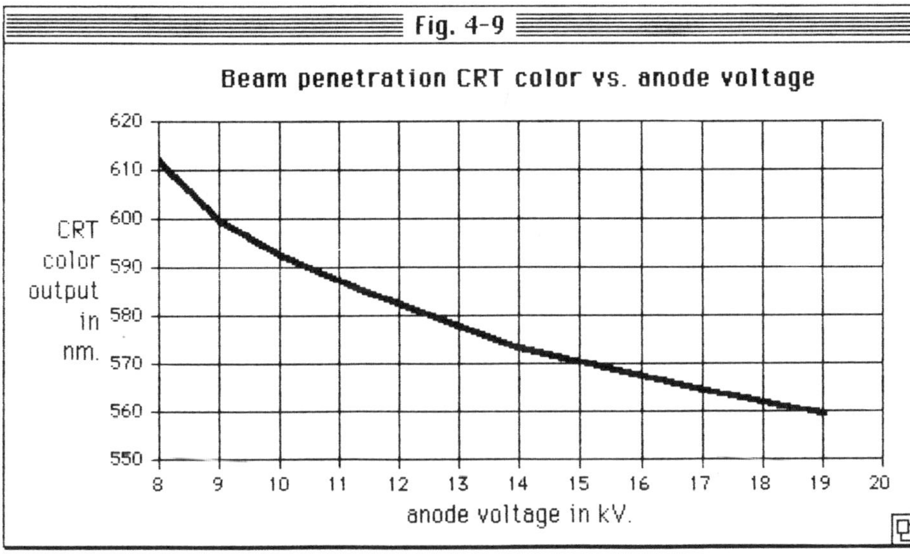

CRT used. Most color CRT systems use at least three electron guns to achieve color, while this system uses only one. For example, consider a CRT that has a green phosphor residing on the tube's screen. A nonfluorescent barrier coating is deposited over the green phosphors and then a layer of red phosphors is deposited over the barrier layer. Figure 4-8 illustrates the layering of the phosphors in a beam penetration CRT. The electron beam scanning the screen hits the red phosphors first. If the energy of the beam is low enough, then it will impact only the red phosphors without penetrating through the barrier and exciting the green phosphors. The result is a red color on the screen. If the anode voltage is raised, it will impart more energy to the electron beam. This increased energy causes the beam to penetrate the barrier layer and excite the green phosphors in addition to the red ones. Due to the eye's inherent green color bias, and the location of the green phosphors closer to the CRT's screen, the displayed image will appear to be green.

The relationship between anode voltage and the displayed color's wavelength is graphically shown in Fig. 4-9. Notice that a change of anode voltage from kV to 19 kV results in the displayed color changing from red to yellowish green. Any color in between can be obtained by using the correct anode voltage. In this example, 11.5 kV will produce an orange color, and 14 kV will produce a yellow color. This technique of beam penetration color is used to increase readability in industrial and military CRTs where exact full color renderings are not required. Beam penetration techniques allow the use of color for emphasis in a CRT display without the additional complexity and cost of multiple electron guns. In this example four distinct colors, red, orange, yellow, and green are displayed by a single electron gun. Examples of special phosphors used in beam penetration CRTs are phosphors numbered P51, P52, P111, and P133.

Another beam penetration technique does not use layering of the differing phosphors. Instead one of the phosphors, usually green, is uniformly coated with the barrier layer. The red and green phosphors are then mixed and applied to the CRT's screen in a single homogeneous layer. The barrier coating over each green phosphor makes it respond only to electron beams of higher intensity. This approach to beam penetration color is called the "pseudo-onionskin" technique. A variation of this method coats the green phosphors with red phosphors. The same net effect is realized, the color displayed on the screen is a function of the accelerating anode's voltage. While beam penetration techniques can generate some degree of color in a CRT display, they do however, extract a price. The anode voltage is a major factor interacting with focus voltage, and deflection power to produce a small reliable spot on the screen, i.e., high resolution. If the anode voltage is widely varied, then the focus and deflection supplies must be made to track the variation in the anode's voltage. This will result in a minimum loss of resolution due to the modulation of the accelerating anode's voltage. The technique compensating for variations in focus due to changes in beam energy is called dynamic focusing.

CRT Contrast Enhancement Filters

The ambient light environment surrounding any type of display will affect the display's readability. Many CRTs use an optical filter or coating placed in front of the screen to minimize the effects of ambient lighting. These filters and other contrast enhancement techniques are used to reduce the glare and reflections from ambient light sources on the CRT's screen.

The simplest and most common method of reducing the glare is to simply etch the face of the CRT with hydrofluoric acid. The etching process removes the shiny polished glass surface from the screen's face. Etching leaves a matte surface that diffuses the reflected images. This etching technique reduces the coherence of reflected images by over five times. The reflections appear as areas of light rather than coherent images. In some cases, a transparent matte material is bonded to the front of the unetched screen. The use of any second coating over the screen introduces additional refraction and other losses, and usually is restricted to actual neutral density filter materials.

A neutral density filter may be bonded to the face of the CRT to increase the contrast of the display. The idea here is that the ambient light must pass through the filter twice, while the CRT's light must only pass through it once. The most commonly used filter is a 30% grey filter, which means that 30% of the light passing through the filter is absorbed by it. This filter will increase a black and white CRTs contrast some 50% by reducing ambient lighting reflections over six times. The greater the density of the filter, the greater the increase in contrast. However, the light being emitted by the CRT must also pass through the filter. This effectively puts an upper limit on the density of the filter at about 70%. The higher density filters are most often used in an area with high levels of ambient light.

In the case of single color CRTs, the filter is color matched to be highly transmissive only in the range of the phosphor's light output. It is this combination that offers the best performance in high ambient light situations. For an example of colored filter use, consider the phosphor P43, which emits light in a very narrow bandwidth centered around 545 nm. The use of a filter matched to this wavelength can increase the effective contrast of a CRT using the P43 phosphor in high light environments by over 2.5 times. This approach is taken in many industrial and military CRT displays.

CRT CHARACTERISTICS

All the many and diverse CRT displays rely on the operation of the same device—the cathode ray tube. The basic operations of accelerating and directing a high energy beam of electrons into collision with a screen of phosphors remains the same for all types of CRTs. Beyond this most basic shared characteristic, many variations of CRT are made. The most common variation on the single gun monochrome CRT is the color CRT. Many types of CRTs, for everything from color entertainment TV to high resolution computer displays, have been developed. Confusion between these myriad displays can be eliminated by recalling the basic one gun CRT's design—all other types are merely more complicated variations. It is important to also remember that the scan method used in a CRT is a function of the encoding scheme and its associated electronics. The same CRT can be used for interlaced raster scanning or noninterlaced sequential scanning or even vector scanning. The method of scanning is not determined by the type of CRT itself, but by the manner in which it is used. This basic versatility is one of the CRT's best selling points.

Basic CRT Types

The most basic type of CRT contains only single color phosphors and a single electron gun assembly. It is mainly used for the display of black and white entertainment television. This basic type is illustrated in the diagrams earlier in this chapter. The monochromatic, one gun, CRT is the basic building block of the more complex CRT types. First, let's consider a CRT designed for full color entertainment TV service.

The full color CRT contains not one but usually three guns. Each one of these three guns is aimed only at a specific colored phosphor. One gun for each of the primary colors—red, blue, and green. Each gun produces a distinct electron beam which can range over the entire screen. All three electron beams are scanned across the screen together. Each gun is, however, directed so that it can only illuminate a single colored phosphor, regardless of its location on the screen. Each pixel on the color CRTs screen is composed of a three phosphor set, one red, one blue, and one green. If a pixel is required to display red, then the red phosphor of that pixel, and only the red phosphor of that pixel, is impacted exclusively by the red gun's electron beam. Colors other than the primary three are produced by mixing the primary colors. For example, if a pixel is required to be yellow then both the red and green phosphors at that pixel's location are activated by simultaneous operation of both the red and green guns. The resulting mixture of red and green creates a yellow spot on the screen. Each of the three guns has its own cathode, control grid, and focusing anode, but all three guns share the same accelerating anode and deflection yokes. Color is controlled in intensity by applying three analog chrominance waveforms to the individual control grids of the three guns.

The three electron guns used in color CRTs are arranged in two configurations, triangular and in-line. The triangular arrangement is called a ''delta'' configuration. Figure 4-10 illustrates both the delta and in-line gun arrangements. Precise alignment of the three guns,

Fig. 4-10. Color CRT gun configurations

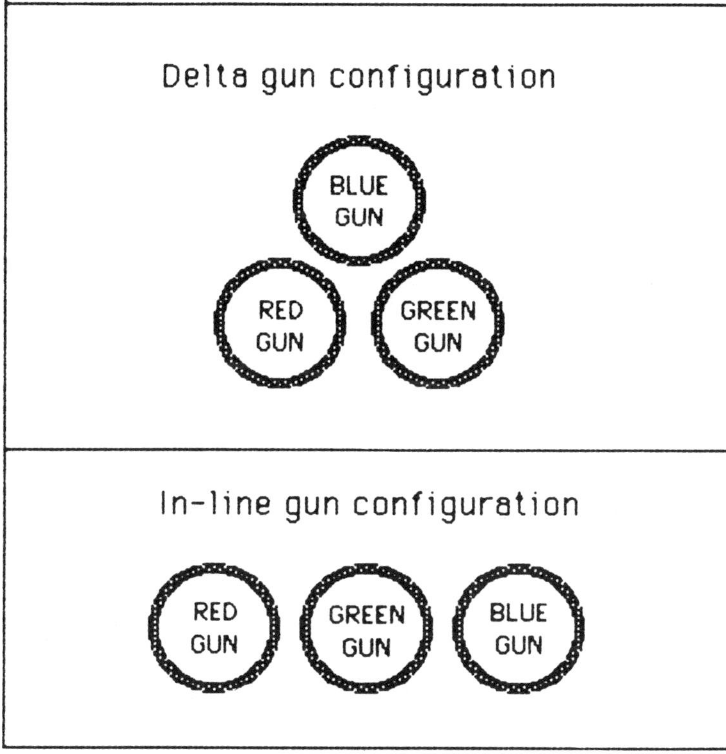

both physically and electronically, is critical regardless of their configuration. Poor alignment of the individual guns will produce impure coloration and colored halos around displayed images. The in-line arrangement is easier to physically align, to electronically align, and maintains its alignment longer than the delta configuration. The in-line type is also less expensive to manufacture, and is more commonly found on CRTs smaller than 19 inches in diagonal measurement.

The delta gun configuration offers greater resolution than the in-line type. This characteristic is built into the geometry of phosphors on the screen. A delta gun scans phosphors which are also arranged in a triangular configuration. The in-line gun scans phosphors which are arranged in-line, as either rows of vertical dots or as vertical stripes. The striped configuration is gaining in popularity as it is easier and cheaper to manufacture. The phosphors are the same size and three (red, blue, and green) phosphors are necessary to complete a single pixel. If the three phosphors that make up a pixel are arranged in a triangle they occupy less space than if they are placed in-line. The result is a smaller, rounder pixel. Figure 4-11 illustrates the geometry of this situation. The delta configuration has inherently better resolution if all other factors are equal. The delta configuration is usually used in CRTs over 19 inches in diagonal measurement, or in applications demanding the ultimate resolution of a full colored image.

The major problem encountered in all types of full color CRTs is the improper activation of adjacent phosphors. The electron guns cannot be directed precisely enough to obtain pure colors at all locations on the screen. There is always some amount of spillover which illuminates phosphors which should remain dark. In order to solve this problem almost all full color CRTs use a "mask" placed over the inside of the screen. The mask is a metallic grid that absorbs some of the electrons from the beam and prevents their reaching the boundary areas between the phosphors. The mask provides a matrix for the electron beams to scan through. The mask enables a beam to strike an individually colored phosphor within a pixel without striking any of its neighboring phosphors. The result is increased color resolution and purity. Next time you view a color CRT, get up very close to the screen and the matrix will be apparent as a black grid lying over the entire screen.

The mask is configured in two patterns. One is the delta pattern and it is used with the delta gun and delta phosphor configuration.

Fig. 4-11. Color CRT phosphor configurations

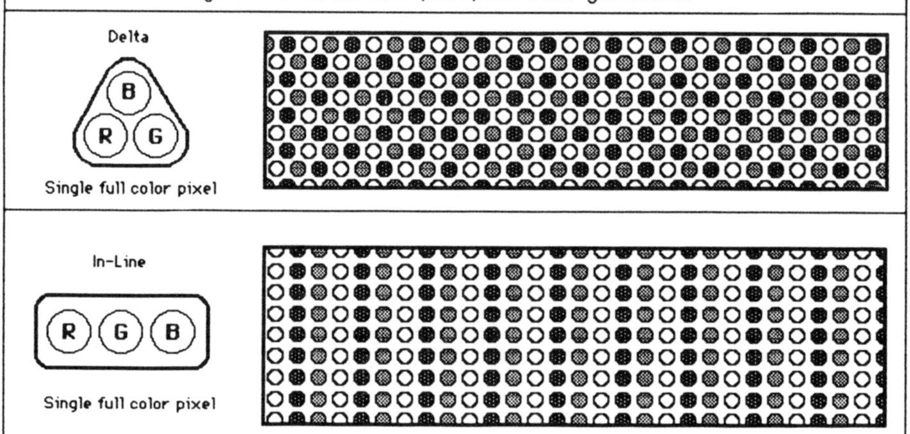

Fig. 4-12. Color CRT mask configurations

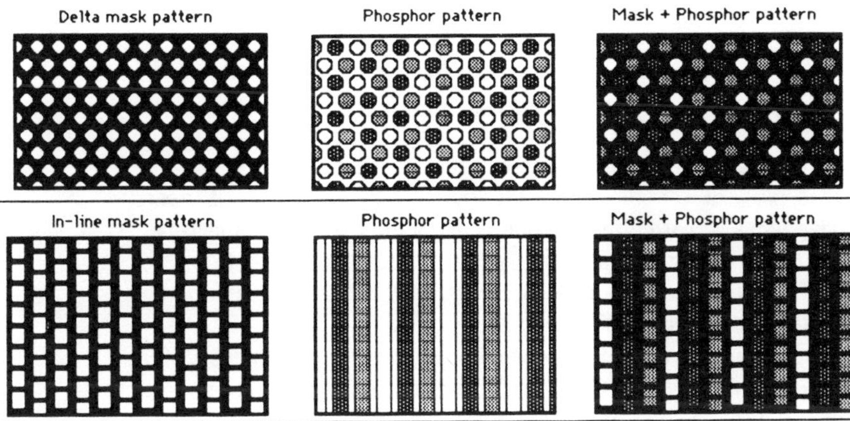

There is also a form of linear mask used for in-line gun and phosphor systems. Figure 4-12 illustrates these two types of color CRT masks, the phosphor patterns they are used with, and a combined drawing of the mask and the phosphors. The use of masks can increase the color clarity of a CRT, but the technique is not without drawbacks. Some of the electrons emitted by the guns are absorbed by the mask. Some types of very high resolution delta masks can absorb over 80% of the electrons emitted by the guns. The in-line mask, due to its rectangular configuration, absorbs less electrons than the delta type. The slotted mask absorbs only 50% of the electrons directed at the screen's phosphors. The absorption of the beam electrons by the mask reduces the overall luminance of the CRT. This reduction is usually compensated for by raising the accelerating anode's voltage and thereby the beams' current.

The resolution of the mask becomes the overall limiting factor for the CRT. As the apertures of the mask's grid are made smaller, the physical framework of the mask becomes a greater portion of the mask's overall area. The higher the resolution of the mask, the smaller its apertures must be, and this inherently leads to high beam electron absorption by the mask. Masks in high resolution CRTs are a very fine, lacy, network of what appears to be black wires. This wire grid must be able to survive intense, high energy, electronic bombardment without deforming or overheating. The minimum amount of physical structure that can accomplish this has now become the limiting factor in full color CRT resolution. Modern masks feature pixel apertures as small as 0.5 mm. It is interesting to note that high resolution, monochrome CRTs which do not use a mask are currently displaying almost twice the resolution of color CRTs using a mask.

Power Requirements

CRTs, since they are vacuum tubes, require multiple power sources, several of which are high voltage supplies. Each of these supplies must be within the specifications of the CRT's manufacturer if the tube is to perform as intended. Spot size and, ultimately, the CRT's resolution is greatly effected by voltages present on the CRT's various active components.

The heater of the CRT is usually fed with low voltage dc between 6.3 to 12.6 volts. Current consumption of the heater ranges from 200 mA to 700 mA, depending on tube size. The overall performance of the CRT is closely tied to cathode temperature which is in turn determined by the heater's power consumption. High performance CRTs often have their heater's voltage regulated to within 1%, while entertainment type CRTs obtain satisfactory performance with heater regulation between 5% to 10%.

The control grid of the CRT is responsible for determining the luminance of the display at any given point in time. The control grid is powered by 40 to 70 Vdc. The higher 70 Vdc figure will offer smaller spot sizes and better resolution, but places additional power demands on the video amplifiers that control the tube's luminosity. Entertainment type CRTs usually power the control grid with around 40 Vdc to minimize the expense of the luminosity amplifiers.

The first anode of the CRT is powered by 200 to 500 Vdc. This level of voltage initially accelerates the electron beam into the focus section of the CRT. The focus section is usually powered at between 20% and 30% of the accelerating anode voltage. The accelerating anode is usually supplied a voltage excess of 20 kV, which results in a focus anode voltage of 5 kV. This relationship between focus and accelerating anode voltage assures small spot size, and helps minimize the overall size of the CRT. The current involved in the first anode and the focusing anode are very low in a properly functioning CRT, usually less than 5 μA.

The accelerating anode's voltage is a critical factor in determining the CRT's overall performance. Accelerating anodes are powered at between 20 and 30 kV, with currents in the range of 100 to 400 μA. The overall luminosity of the CRT is directly proportional to the accelerating anode's voltage and current. The easiest way to increase the luminosity of any CRT is to increase its accelerating anode's voltage. The anode voltage also varies with the size of the CRT. The larger the CRT's screen, the greater the accelerating anode's voltage must be in order to obtain a constant luminosity to area ratio. There are, however, limitations placed on raising the anode's voltage. Increased voltage will darken the glass face of the CRT at greatly increased rates. The other problem associated with high accelerating anode voltage is X-rays.

The impact of high energy electrons with metallic elements generates X-rays. There is a practical upper limit to the anode's voltage determined by the acceptable level of X-ray radiation. The U.S. Federal government has set the upper limit of X-ray radiation acceptable from CRTs at 0.5 milliRoentgens per hour. This amount of radiation is very small, about .05% of the radiation of a dental X-ray. On the down side, 0.5 milliRoentgens/hr. is about 40 times the hard radiation received when standing outside in the sunshine. If you're sitting in front of a CRT for 40 hours weekly, you receive a cumulative X-ray dosage roughly equivalent to a single dental X-ray every five years. In most CRT designs, 0.5 milliRoentgens per hour translates to anode voltages in the neighborhood of 35 kV. Many manufacturers include metallic shielding around the tube to reduce X-ray radiation, and to allow the anode voltage to be higher than 35 kV. However, this shielding is metallic and opaque; it cannot be employed over the faceplate of the CRT. Figure 4-13 illustrates the relationship between the accelerating anode's voltage and the intensity of the X-ray radiation produced. All CRTs produce some amount of X-ray radiation. It is prudent not to sit any closer to the display than necessary. After all, there is no minimum daily requirement for hard radiation like X-rays. The worst X-ray producers are large screen, high resolution, color CRTs which use delta masks. These types employ the highest accelerating anode voltages of any type, and care should be taken not to sit closer than necessary.

The overall power consumption of a CRT display is related to two factors—screen size and the presence of color. The power consumption of a CRT is directly proportional to the screen's area. For example, consider a square CRT with a 5-inch edge measurement, and a resulting screen area of 25 square inches. This CRT will consume approximately one quarter the power of a square

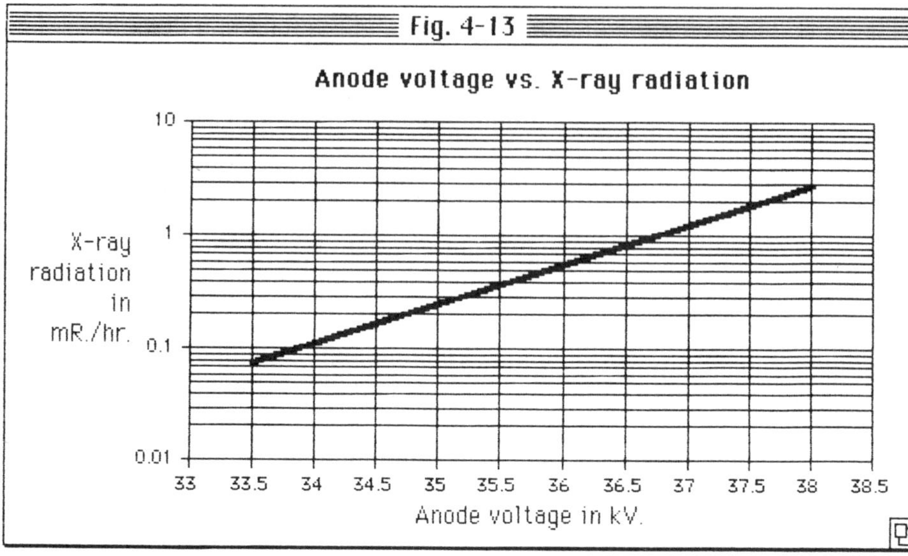

CRT with a screen area of 100 square inches, or an edge dimension of 10 inches. This relationship holds true for all CRTs, either monochrome or color. The larger the CRT's screen, the larger its power consumption becomes. This situation is compounded by color CRTs. Most color CRTs use three electron guns instead of one. As such, they often consume almost 3 times as much power as a monochrome CRT of the same size. The electronics that drive the CRT consume a very small amount of the power used by the display. Most of the power consumed in a CRT display is used by the actual CRT itself. Figure 4-14 is a graph relating the overall power consumption of various sizes and types of CRTs. If power consumption is a factor in CRT service, then use the smallest sized tube that will do the job.

Brightness

The brightness of a CRT is termed its "screen luminance". The screen luminance of a CRT can be measured in two manners—area brightness or line (spot) brightness. In general, area brightness is used to rate the luminosity of most CRTs, while line brightness measurements are only performed on high resolution CRTs.

The unit used in the measurement of area brightness is Candelas per square meter (Cd/m^2). This measurement is taken under standardized raster scanning and with the spot of the CRT focused to its minimum size. The measuring instrument used is an area integrating photometer. Most monochrome CRTs are capable of area brightnesses in excess of 300 Cd/m^2. This is a very large amount of light; the CRT is one of the brightest display devices now available. To experience the brightness of a CRT yourself, try this simple experiment. Within a darkened room, tube a television set to an unused channel (this produces an all white screen on the CRT). Walk behind the CRT to a position where the screen is not directly visible. Observe the illumination of the room by the light coming from the CRT's screen. A fully illuminated (white picture) 19″ CRT produces more light than a 60 watt incandescent lightbulb.

Line brightness measurement is taken only on very specialized CRTs used in dot or stroke writing techniques, or in vector scan service. As accurate line brightness measurement is complex and tedious, it is usually not undertaken for low cost CRTs. In line brightness measurement, a pattern of widely spaced lines are displayed on the screen. This display has tightly controlled scanning speed and repetition rate. A specialized photometer, called a slit photometer, is used to measure the luminous intensity at every point on the screen. The slit photometer has a very small aperture and the ability to measure brightness of a very small area, less than 0.5 mm^2. Line luminosity measurement details the luminosity of the spot at all positions on the CRTs screen, and is very different from the averaging techniques used in the area brightness measurement.

Fig. 4-14

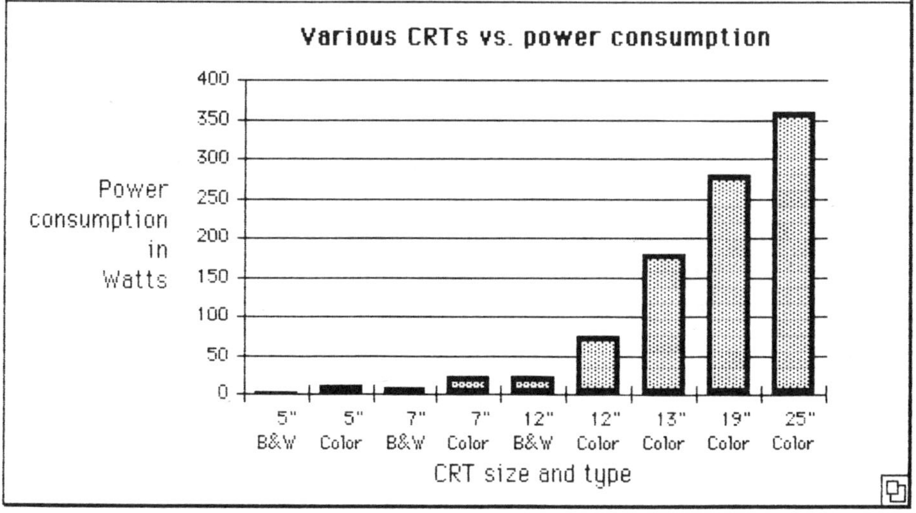

It is the extra effort that goes into measuring the luminosity of all the possible spot positions on the screen that makes line brightness measurement so expensive, and restricts its use to the higher priced CRTs. A CRT that has been line brightness measured will possess a record and chart of the line luminosity values at all positions on the screen.

No matter what method is used to measure the brightness of a CRT, the measurement is taken at a specified value of the CRT's anode voltage. Since anode voltage has such a great effect on luminosity and spot size, it must be at a standard voltage for the particular CRT before any brightness measurement is meaningful. If the brightness measurement is to reflect actual operation of the CRT, then the spot must be focused to its smallest size before the measurement is taken.

Resolution

Resolution in CRTs are measured in three differing manners, the "shrinking raster" method, the "spot-size" method, and the "modulation transfer function" (MTF) method. The method used depends on the type and cost of the CRT being measured. Resolution in a CRT basically means how close can we place the smallest light area to the smallest dark area on the screen and still maintain an acceptable luminosity difference between the two areas. In plain English, how small can we make an image and still have it recognizable. Regardless of the method used to measure resolution, the CRT under measurement should be set at its working luminosity. Resolution measurements taken with a CRT at less than working luminance will be high and misleading.

The shrinking raster method of measuring resolution is usually employed on entertainment type and low cost CRTs. The shrinking raster method tells us the maximum number of horizontal lines it is possible to display on the CRT. Its measurements are expressed in the number of lines per inch or lines per mm. It indicates the number of lines that may be displayed on the CRT before the lines begin to merge and become indistinct. In this method, a raster pattern which contains a known and set number of horizontal lines is displayed on the CRT's screen. The raster generator is a special type that allows for adjustment of the vertical height of the picture. With the brightness set at its operating level, the vertical of the raster is reduced until the lines begin to merge. The judgement of when this happens is done by eye through a 10 to 50 power microscope. The height of the raster at this point is divided by the number of lines and a measurement in terms of lines per inch or mm results. The shrinking raster method of determining resolution is the simplest and most common way of rating CRT resolution. It does, however, have some inherent inaccuracies. One is that the determination of exactly when the lines on the screen merge is highly subjective and varies from person to person. Another is that instability in the raster's driving electronics may produce false, but distinct, lines on the screen long after the lines have appeared to merge. This effect is called "raster jitter", and represents uncontrollable noise rather than real resolution.

The spot size method of determining resolution is closely linked with line brightness measurement; they both use the same techniques and equipment. In this method of measuring resolution, a slit photometer is moved across a tightly focused spot on the screen. The slit on the photometer is very small in relation to the spot's size. As the slit on the photometer is gradually moved off the spot the luminosity drops. The distance at which the spot's brightness (determined by the photometer) is reduced to 50% determines the spot's size, and thereby the CRT's resolution. From the spot's size we are able to compute the maximum number of picture elements (pixels) in both the vertical and horizontal dimensions. The spot size method offers a far more accurate and objective way to determine CRT resolution than the shrinking raster method. Resolution determined by the spot size method measures the entire screen, pixel by pixel, and data comparing the edges of the screen to the center is available from this method. The spot's size is one method commonly used to rate high resolution CRTs. High resolution CRTs now display dots of less than 0.5 square mm.

The third method of determining resolution is the most complex and accurate. The techniques used in the modulation transfer function (MTF) method comes closest to actual CRT usage, and as such, they provide the most reliable information. In the MTF method, a sine or a square wave is used to modulate the electron beam as it scans every line. The line appears as a linear series of alternating light and dark areas on the screen. The screen's luminous response to the frequency of the beam's driving waveform is measured by a slit photometer. Numerically speaking, the MTF number is the definite integral of the CRTs luminosity from dark to light with respect to the frequency of the beam's driving waveform. Since the

MTF process of resolution measurement requires taking hundreds of thousands of data points, it is reserved for the most expensive high resolution CRTs.

The issue of CRT resolution has been clouded by differing methods of measurement, and a mania by users for ever increasing resolution. How much resolution is enough? The fact of the matter is that most users can barely see a single pixel of a modern 1280 × 1240 pixel, high resolution, 13-inch diagonal CRT. The difference between a dot on the screen that is 0.26 mm and one which is 0.21 mm is beyond the distinction of most untrained human eyes. CRT resolution is already so good that screens are likely to become larger, rather than increasing their resolution. At this point in time, the CRT offers greater resolution, both in monochrome or in color, than any other electronic display device.

Speed

The CRT display is a device that consists of not only a display tube, but also the electronic circuits which drive the tube. In terms of speed, the actual cathode ray tube is very fast, potentially much quicker than the electronics that drive it. The electron beam used in the CRT has negligible mass, and as such, it can be manipulated very quickly. There are many methods of classifying the speed of various functions that the CRT must perform in order to display an image. In some cases, these functions are described in terms of time; others are expressed in terms of frequency (operations per second). It is first necessary to define these functions so that their quantification becomes meaningful. These terms and times are defined in terms of raster scanned CRTs.

The electron beam scans the screen horizontally beginning at the upper left hand corner of the screen. It scans one horizontal line to the right edge of the screen and then it returns to the left side to begin scanning the next line in exactly the same fashion. While the beam returns from the right edge to the left, its intensity is suppressed and no image is displayed during this time. This is called the "horizontal blanking interval" and is abbreviated t_{HB}. The time it takes the beam to scan a single horizontal line is called the "horizontal scanning frequency" (f_H) and is expressed in kilohertz, or lines scanned per second. The horizontal scanning frequency is the reciprocal of the time it takes the electron beam to complete a single cycle from the left of the screen to the right and back again to the left. The horizontal frequency measurement includes the horizontal blanking time. The horizontal scanning frequency of modern CRTs varies from 15.75 kHz to over 64 kHz, with horizontal blanking times from 12 μs to less than 3.5 μs.

After the electron beam completes a single screen full of horizontal lines, it must return from the bottom of the screen to the top and begin the next series of lines. During this bottom to top return process, the beam's intensity is suppressed and no image is displayed. The time it takes the suppressed beam to complete this process is called the "vertical blanking interval" and is abbreviated t_{VB}. The time it takes for the beam to scan an entire series of horizontal lines and return to the top to begin again is called the "vertical scanning frequency" (f_V) and is expressed in Hz. The vertical scanning frequency is the reciprocal of the time it takes the CRT to perform a single complete series of horizontal lines and return to begin the process again. The vertical scanning frequency measurement includes the vertical blanking time. Today's CRTs have vertical scanning frequencies from 40 Hz to over 70 Hz, with vertical blanking times from 1 ms to 0.5 ms. The use of a 60 Hz vertical scanning frequency is very common and is a defacto standard for CRTs made and used in the US. This vertical scanning frequency is used as it is just beyond the flicker rate for the average human eye, and presents minimal interaction with the 60 Hz ac voltage used to power the CRT.

Figure 4-15 graphically illustrates these various functions and intervals. This illustration uses only a few lines scanned across an imaginary CRT for demonstration purposes. In reality there are more than 500 lines scanned across the CRT, far too many to be effective in an illustration showing their interrelationships. The bottom line is that a modern CRT can display a horizontal line in less than 16 μs, and a complete vertical cycle (an entire screen full of horizontal lines) in less than 17 ms.

Another CRT function that is time quantified is the response of the electron beam to being turned on or off and is abbreviated t_{EB}. This period determines how fast the CRT can go from an illuminated dot on the screen to one which is dark. This figure is called rise and fall time, and is usually less than 20 nanoseconds (ns), which is an incredibly short time. The rise and fall times of a CRT are much quicker than the electronic processing that drives the CRT. Currently, the limit of the mass produced silicon based electronic processing driving the tube is about 100 ns. This is 5 times slower than the CRT's ability to switch from light to dark. The use of gallium arsinide electronic junctions for CRT processing promises to catch

Fig. 4-15. CRT time parameters

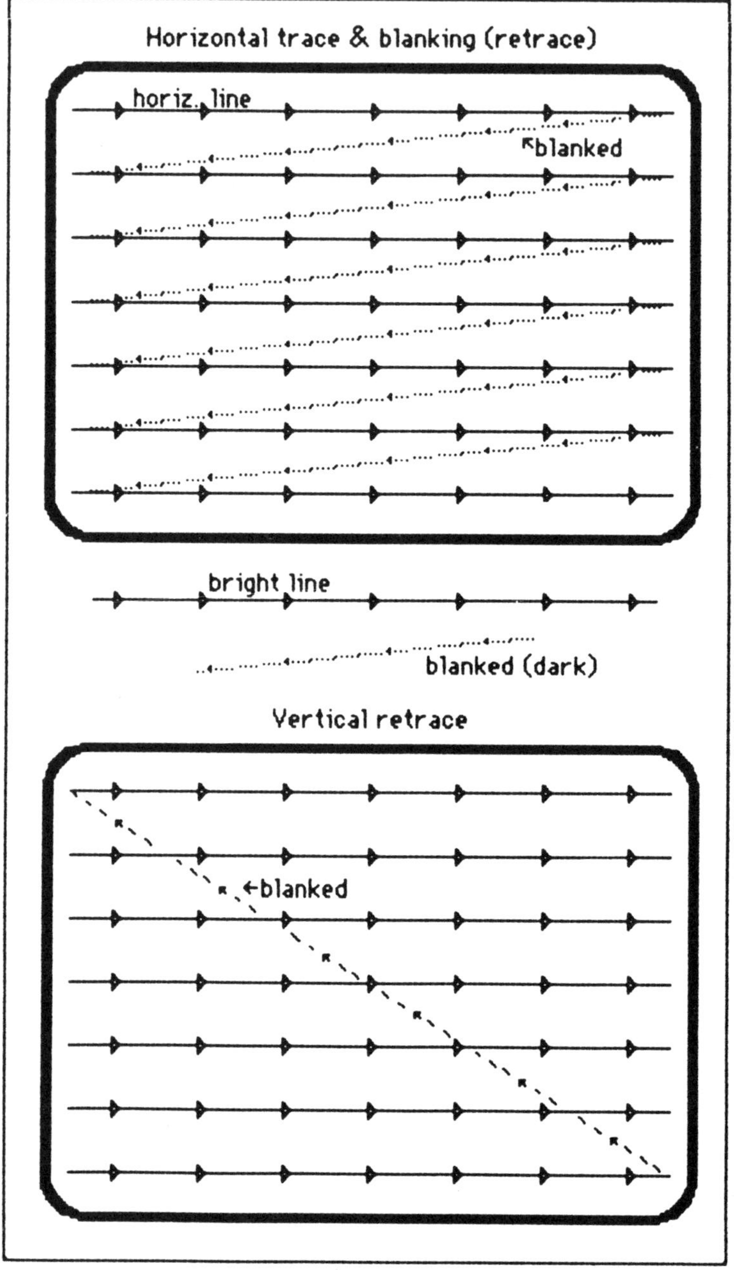

up with the CRT's inherently fast response times. Another method of increasing speed is the use of multiple guns scanning more than one line at a time. This parallel approach is just now being implemented in CRT displays of the highest resolution.

Video Bandwidth

All CRT functions, such as the vertical and scanning frequencies and rise/fall times, affect how much information the tube can display per unit time. All these factors are rolled into a single parameter that describes the CRT's time related performance. This parameter is called the "video bandwidth" of the CRT. Video bandwidth is a measure of how much information the CRT can display per unit time, and is usually expressed in MHz. Video bandwidth indicates the maximum number of adjacent light and dark areas that may be displayed on a particular CRT per second. For example, a standard raster scanned TV picture contains 525 lines. These lines are divided equally into two fields, each of which is scanned in 1/60th of a second. A complete picture consists of both fields, or all 525 lines scanned in 1/30th of a second. This video scheme, along with the CRT time parameters, translates to a video bandwidth of about 4 MHz. Each of these lines consists of light and dark areas. A video bandwidth of 4 MHz, using a conventional TV raster scan, means that approximately 256 light/dark transitions can be displayed per line, or over 120,000 light/dark areas per screen. In other words, the video bandwidth not only gives an idea of the speed of the CRT's operation, but also its effective operating resolution. The higher the video bandwidth is, the greater the resolution of the CRT display.

High resolution CRTs display more information per unit time than do the lower resolution TV types. Modern hi-res CRTs possess video bandwidths from 40 MHz to 125 MHz. Video signals with a bandwidth in these areas are very fast. In fact, the video signal is in the vhf rf range. If the CRT's time parameters are known, then the video bandwidth can be computed by the equation shown in Fig. 4-16. In this equation all frequencies are expressed in hertz (cycles per second), while all times are expressed in seconds.

Size

CRT size is usually measured by diagonal screen measurement. This measurement is dependent on the relationship between the CRT's screen height to its screen width. This quantity is known as the CRT's "aspect ratio." Aspect ratio is not necessarily an

Fig. 4-16. Video bandwidth

$$VB = \frac{[1-(f_V T_{VB})][1-(f_H T_{HB})]}{T_{EB}}$$

VB = Video bandwidth

f_V = Vertical scanning frequency

T_{VB} = Vertical blanking time

f_H = Horizontal scanning frequency

T_{HB} = Horizontal blanking time

T_{EB} = Beam on/off time

inherent quantity in the CRT, but also a function of the scanning method, or how the CRT is used. CRTs used in TV service have an aspect ratio of 3 to 4. This means that the vertical height of the CRT's screen is 3 units while the horizontal width is 4 units. The same ratio holds for the dimensions of each pixel displayed on the screen. A TV picture is a rectangle that is wider than it is tall. The pixels in this service are also rectangular, not square. Figure 4-17 illustrates the relationship between screen diagonal size, vertical height, horizontal width, and aspect ratio for a CRT used in TV service. Modern computer displays tend toward a 1:1 aspect ratio, and square pixels. This makes their use in engineering graphics much simpler.

The CRT is available in a wide variety of sizes. Very small round CRTs are being manufactured for military use with screen diameters as small as 25 mm. These tubes are small enough to be used inside a helmet. Direct view color CRTs for TV service are commercially available with diagonal measurements from 2 inches to 35 inches, and just about every size in between. In general, no matter what the scanning method, the smaller the CRT, the greater definition it can display. For example, consider a CRT used in standard TV service. A standard TV signal allows 525 horizontal lines. If these lines are displayed on a 5-in CRT then each line must be narrower than if they are displayed on a larger, say 21-in, CRT. This means that the smaller CRTs display images that appear better defined than those displayed on larger CRTs. This is also a function of how close to the CRT the viewer is. Try this simple experiment. Turn on a monochrome TV set that does not use a mask and sit directly in front of it. The lines on the screen are very apparent if you put your nose directly on the screen, but as you back away from the tube the actual lines become indistinct and merge into a "seamless" picture. The size CRT required for any particular application is a function of how close it is to be viewed. The closer you are to the CRT, the smaller it should be in order for the individual lines to merge into a seamless picture. A good rule of thumb is to view a CRT from a minimum distance of about one foot for every inch of diagonal screen measurement. If you've got a 5-in screen, then view it from a distance of 5 feet from the screen. If you've a 19-in screen, then

Fig. 4-17. Screen size and CRT aspect ratio

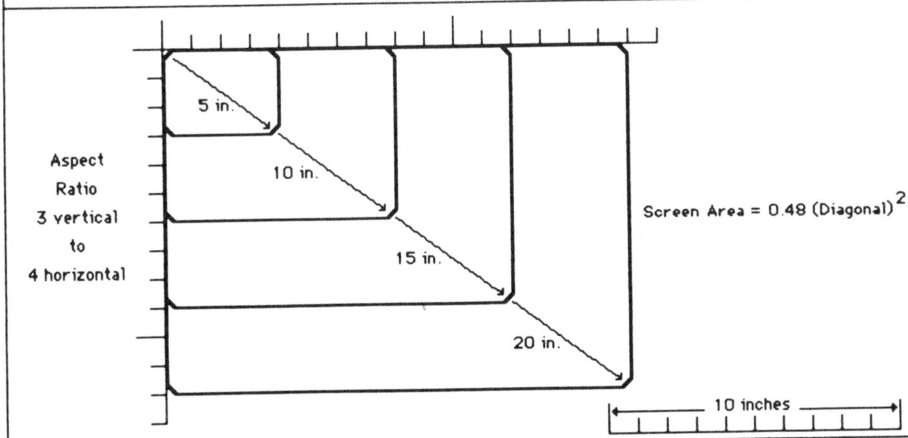

view it from 19 feet away. This assures a seamless picture without the individual lines becoming apparent.

The overall size of the CRT is one of its biggest problems. If you examine a TV set or a computer using a CRT, you will see that the majority of the space is occupied by the CRT itself. Every effort is being made to shrink the overall length of the CRT while maintaining the same sized screen. The problems associated with shorter necked CRTs are reduced resolution, reduced linearity and greatly increased deflection power requirements. All these problems are a function of the increased deflection angles necessary to implement the shorter necked tubes while maintaining their screen areas.

Operating Characteristics

All CRTs use an electron beam to scan the screen's phosphors. As such, they share a great many operating characteristics. The differences between the various specialized types of CRTs are in the area of video bandwidth, resolution, size, and video signal encoding techniques. The CRT is a very plastic display device. Its basic operating characteristics allow a wide range of video signal encoding techniques to be used on any given CRT. This versatility of the CRT is unique among display devices, and is the primary reason for its popularity and longevity among electronic display designers.

Visual Angle

A CRT can be viewed from very wide angles. In fact, the CRT offers the widest viewing angle of any two dimensional electronic display devices. The outer limit of its viewing angle approaches 180°. However, a CRT is best viewed within 60° of a perpendicular to the screen's face. This yields a total optimum viewing angle of up to 120°. Ambient lighting is one external factor that can limit the CRT's viewing angle. Since the CRT has a nearly flat screen, any ambient light source can create distracting reflections and glare. Most CRTs are equipped with anti-glare and anti-reflective coatings over the screen's face to minimize these problems. No matter how effective these coatings are, they cannot totally eliminate the problem. The effect of reflections and glare can be very simply eliminated by the proper position of ambient light in the area where the CRT is being used. It is up to the actual user of the display to arrange his viewing environment to eliminate reflections. This is easily accomplished by locating ambient light sources behind the CRT's face rather than in front of it. If a CRT is used in a room lit by sunlight through windows, then the CRT should be located facing North so that sunlight does not fall directly on its screen.

Memory

The CRT has inherent and essential memory built into the phosphors that make up its screen. The persistence of these phosphors is essential to the flicker-free operation of the CRT. The electron beam can only strike the screen at one location at a time. The ability of the phosphors to continue emitting light after the electron beam has moved on is the only factor that creates a flicker-free image from the rapidly moving electron beam scanning the screen. This persistence of the phosphors represents the memory of the CRT's screen. Research into the persistence characteristics of CRT phosphors is intense. Many differing types have been developed to meet a variety of requirements. Very fast phosphors have decay times around 160 ns, while phosphors with decay times as long as 10 seconds have been developed. It is essential that a designer or user of a particular CRT secure the phosphor coating that suits the decay times of his particular application.

Operating Temperature Range

The CRT has a very wide range of operating temperatures. In fact, a display using a CRT is limited by the temperature operating characteristics of the driving electronics and power supply; not by the tube itself. Most manufacturers rate their CRT based displays to operate between 0° C and 50° C. These limits represent the entire display device, and not the CRT itself. The actual CRT itself is capable of functioning over a temperature range of −50° C to 100° C.

All displays using CRTs should be provided with adequate ventilation to ensure cooling and to prevent overheating. While the CRT itself does not create a large amount of heat, the electronics that drive and power it do. CRT displays are equipped with cooling slots that enable air to circulate through the display and carry the heat away. Do not operate a CRT display with these cooling slots obstructed as overheating of the driving electronics and power supplies will result. If a CRT display is operated in environments with temperatures over 40° C, then it is a very good idea to put an exhaust fan on the top of the display's cabinet to increase air flow. Even a small fan moving as little as 30 cubic feet of air per minute can make a big difference in the CRT display's overall temperature.

CRT Longevity

A CRT has an effective lifetime in the neighborhood of 10,000 hours if operated at maximum brightness. After this period of time, the screen's phosphors gradually become dimmer and the tube must be replaced if full brightness is required. The average operating brightness of the tube affects its longevity. The brighter the tube is run, the shorter its full brightness longevity becomes. If you desire more longevity from your CRT display, then simply reduce its brightness to the minimum acceptable level. CRTs that are run at reduced brightness will last over 20,000 hours before becoming dim enough to require replacement.

RASTER SCAN CRTs

Raster scanning techniques are used in the overwhelming majority of CRT displays. Raster scanning is a technique for using the CRT, not a specific type or form of the CRT itself. Television uses raster scanning, as do almost all high resolution computer CRT displays. Raster scanning is a generic term that refers to a repetitive sequence of lines scanned across the screen. Not all raster scanning techniques are the same, in fact, except for TV standards, there are wide variations between different raster scanning techniques. The basic idea is the same, but the time constants and interlacing techniques used to produce an image vary widely. Any type of CRT can be used in raster scan service, but the magnetic deflection type are by far the most popular.

The information in this section on raster scanning primarily refers to the technique used in U.S. commercial television. This is the most common type and accounts for the majority of the CRTs implemented in displays. High resolution raster scanning is covered under the section on high resolution displays.

How It Works

Let's follow the journey of the electron beam across the screen of a common, everyday television set. The electron beam starts at the upper left hand corner of the screen and scans the first line all the way across to the right side. The beam is then blanked during its return journey back to the left edge of the screen. Here it begins to scan the next line. This next line is not the second line of the image, but the third. The beam scans the third line and returns to the left to scan the fifth line. The process continues until all the odd numbered lines of the image are scanned onto the screen. This screen full of odd lines is called a field. In this case, since only the odd lines are scanned, it is called the odd field.

After the first field of odd lines is scanned, the beam is blanked during its journey from the bottom of the screen back to the top. Here it begins scanning the even lines of the image. This process continues in the same fashion until the complete even field is scanned. The beam is then blanked until it reaches the top of the screen and the entire process begins again. The two fields, the odd field and the even field combined, comprise a complete image and are called a frame. This technique of first scanning the odd lines and then the even lines of an image in separate fields is called interlacing. Figure 4-18 illustrates this technique. The illustration is greatly magnified and shows the process symbolically. In actual practice, a TV field consists of hundreds of lines, not just the few used in the illustration.

It takes the CRT ⅙₀th of a second to scan a single field. The two fields comprising a complete frame take ⅓₀th of a second to scan. This is just below the 25 to 30 Hz flicker rate detectable by the human eye, and is the reason for the time relationships chosen for the TV raster scanning. The persistence characteristics of the phosphors are essential in maintaining a flicker-free display using this or any other raster scanning technique.

Fig. 4-18. TV raster scanning technique

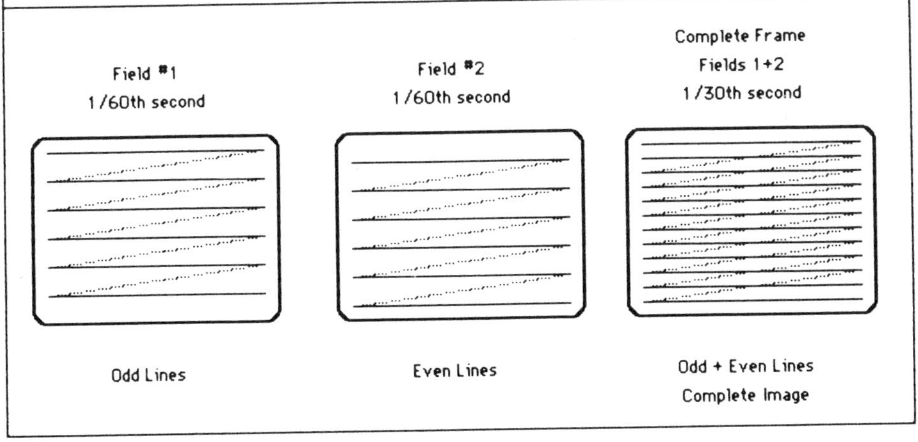

This electronic signal used to encode television raster scan video was developed in the 1940's, and represents the best that could then be done. Limitations within this encoding method are due to the relatively slow electronics then available to drive the CRT. A basic understanding of the way the TV video signal is put together will give us a better understanding of how the CRT is implemented in this application. The entire TV signal's waveform occupies a space of 6 MHz. This includes both the audio and visual (video) portions of the information. Figure 4-19 illustrates the frequency distribution of a U.S. standard television signal. The video information is amplitude modulated, with its carrier frequency located 1.25 MHz above the lower boundary of the TV channel. The audio is frequency modulated, with its carrier located 4.5 MHz above the video carrier. The chrominance information is encoded on a sub-carrier located 3.579545 MHz above the visual carrier. All this information is included within the 6 MHz wide TV channel.

The video portion of the signal carries all the luminosity information, the horizontal syncronizing and blanking pulses for each line, the vertical syncronizing and blanking pulses for each field, and in the case of color, all the chrominance information for each line. This signal provides all the information necessary to display an image on the CRT, and is called a "composite video" signal. Figure 4-20 illustrates a composite video signal used in standard U.S. television. The illustration is symbolic and is not drawn to scale, but is greatly compressed along the time axis. This illustration shows two complete

Fig. 4-19. Frequency distribution of a standard US TV signal

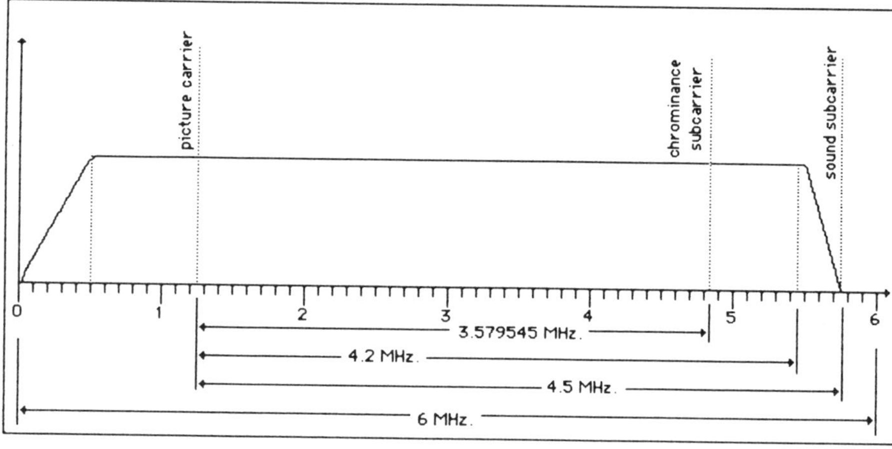

Fig. 4-20. Standard US composite video TV signal

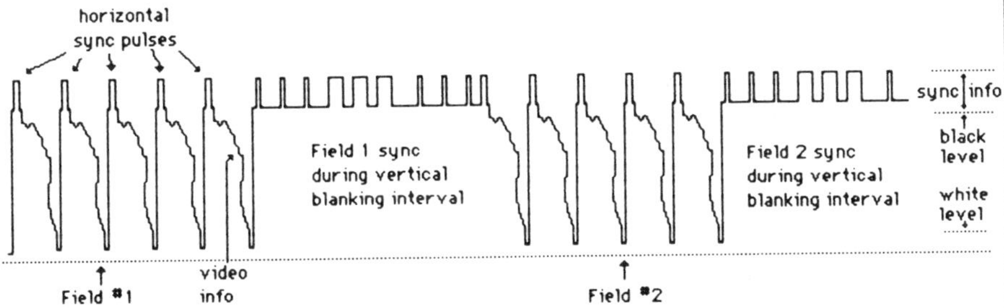

Note: not drawn to scale; actual fields contain hundreds of lines.

fields that make a single frame. The illustration shows only a few lines of video information, when in actual practice there are hundreds of lines per field. The syncronizing pulses are placed at voltage levels higher than the luminosity information. The region is called the "blacker than black" region, and represents the maximum voltage excursion of the video carrier. Pulses occurring in this region are said to be above the blanking level. Both the horizontal and vertical syncronization pulses are used by the CRT display to keep exactly in step with the picture information. They are responsible for keeping each and every line and each and every field exactly where it should be on the screen. Without these synchronizing pulses the picture would dissolve into meaningless noise on the screen. These pulses require very fast rise and fall times, i.e., their waveforms have vertical leading and trailing edges. This is essential for the consistent and properly placed display of luminosity information on the CRT's screen.

Figure 4-21 is a more detailed diagram of a composite video signal. This illustration concentrates on the syncronizing pulses present during the vertical blanking interval between fields and ignores most of the luminosity information that both preceeds and follows these pulses. The unit H, used to define a time constant, is the time it takes the CRT to scan a single, complete, horizontal line. In standard U.S. TV raster service, H is 63.5 μs. Note that all the synchronizing pulses are based on H or multiples of it. Figure 4-22 is an enlargement of the waveform as it directs the CRT to begin

Fig. 4-21. TV composite video sync region

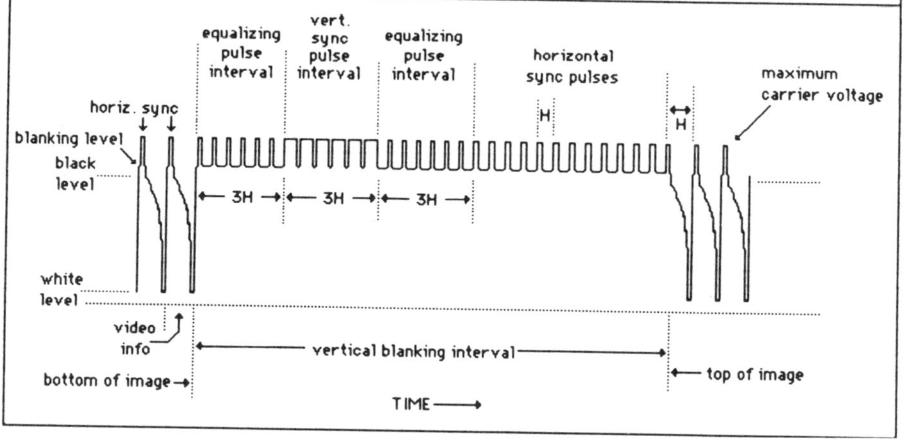

the first line in a field. Illustrated here are the last horizontal sync pulse and the beginning of the luminosity information for first line of a field. Note that the actual luminosity information is amplitude modulated between each of the horizontal sync pulses that separate each line. The more voltage the analog luminosity signal has, the darker that particular area on the screen is. The video luminosity signal is modulated from 12.5% (white) to 75% (black) of the blanking level. The sync information is present only above (100% to 120+%) the blanking level.

Fig. 4-22. TV composite video luminosity encoding

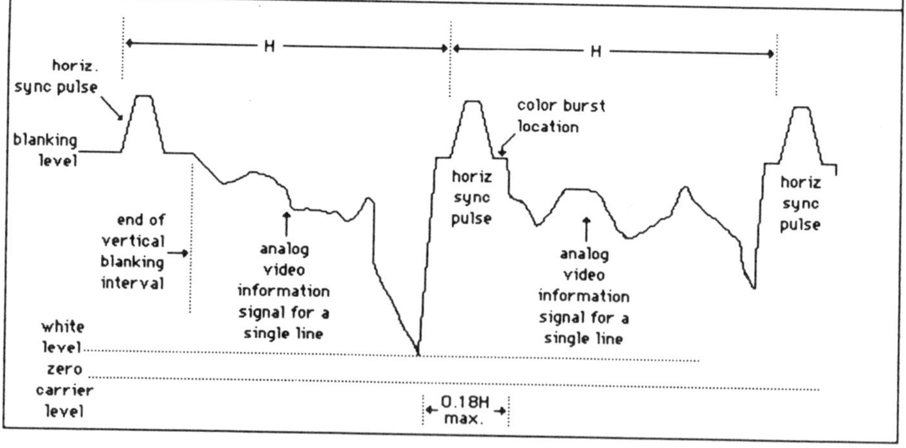

Fig. 4-23. TV horizontal sync pulse

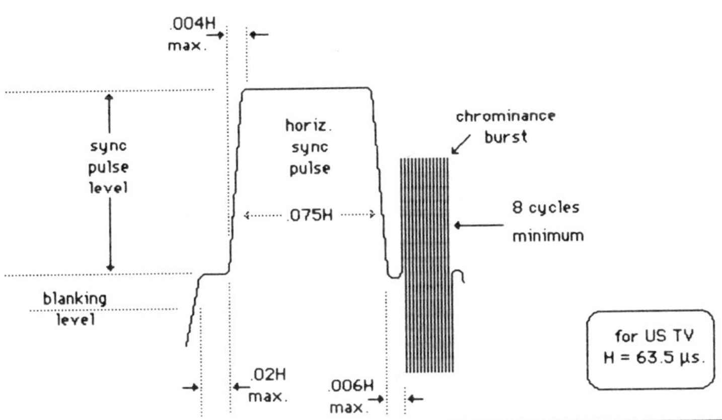

Figure 4-23 shows a representative horizontal synchronizing pulse. Note that the 3.579545 MHz burst that controls the color of the particular line is included at the end of each horizontal sync pulse. One of these color bursts occurs for each and every line displayed on the CRT. The position and type of encoding used for chrominance information reflects the retrofit nature of color TV. This segment of the signal was added to the basic TV waveform some 10 years after it was first developed. The basic idea is to include color information in a signal that would also be compatible with the current monochrome TV technology. As such, compromises were necessary so that a color signal remained compatible with the millions of black and white TVs already in existence.

Advantages

The major advantage of raster scanning is the relative simplicity of the electronics and the signals driving the CRT. The interlaced raster scanning method used in television can be implemented in the display with electronics that are relatively slow in comparison with other video encoding techniques. The sync pulses in this method are quasi-digital and offer a fair amount of noise immunity, which is essential for video signals broadcast over the air. The frequency modulation method used in television audio offers very good fidelity with its bandwidth of 25 kHz. The FM audio signal also gives superior noise immunity to any amplitude modulation technique.

Another advantage of the TV raster scanning technique is its standardization. The composite video encoding techniques discussed here are held to rigid standards by the National Television Systems Committee (NTSC), and the method is, in fact, called "NTSC composite video." This technique is used in over 130 million TV receivers in the U.S. alone. There is a large amount of video equipment available for this system due to its popularity. Every terrestrial television transmitter, every video cassette recorder, and every TV monitor used in commercial U.S. TV systems all employ the standardized NTSC TV raster methods outlined here. This level of standardization is necessary to ensure compatibility in broadcast television reception.

It is wrong to assume that NTSC composite video is the only technique used for encoding television signals. NTSC is the standard in the U.S. and other countries such as Japan, but other methods do exist and are used elsewhere in the world. In fact, there are 13 over-the-air TV broadcast standards currently in use worldwide. For example, in Germany and Great Britain, a standard called PAL is used. The PAL standard uses 625 lines, a vertical scan rate of 50 Hz, and an 8 MHz video bandwidth. In France, the TV system used is called SECAM and uses a system similar to Great Britain's but the audio is amplitude modulated. The increased number of lines in both these non-NTSC-standard systems results in greater resolution of the TV picture. The lower scan rates also result in increased flicker that is objectionable to some viewers. In any case, TV equipment constructed for use in these various systems will not display images unless used with the video encoding of that system. None of these systems are compatible, but each are a world unto itself. Information encoded in one system is not portable to any other. All TV pictures may look about the same on the screen, but the methods used to produce the image differ and are not compatible.

Disadvantages

The biggest disadvantage to NTSC video is its age. It represents the very finest of 1940's technology and lags far behind what it is possible to accomplish in video imagery with today's fast and sophisticated electronics. Every change, such as color, that has been added to the NTSC system has had to be compatible with everything that has gone before. This approach greatly limits the development of the TV image. Basically, the TV pictures we are watching now are not very much better in resolution than they were 30 years ago.

Non-NTSC video techniques used in high resolution computer monitors can produce images with over 4 times the resolution of a standard NTSC TV image. These systems are not compatible with the millions of NTSC TV sets already in use and are not adopted for on-the-air use for this reason.

The particular disadvantages of NTSC video are many. It should be remembered that all these complaints represent a case of 20/20 hindsight. NTSC video is almost 50 years old, and considering when it was developed, it represents a great technical achievement. This does not, however, mean that it is perfect. Far from it. The number of lines scanned in NTSC video is 525. With current technology, we could easily be displaying twice this number. In fact, one of the current methods to increase broadcast TV's resolution is to double the number of lines in a fashion that would be compatible with regular NTSC receivers.

The luminosity information of NTSC video is amplitude modulated, which makes the picture very susceptible to noise. All natural and man-made electrical noise can be considered amplitude modulated. Every time noise occurs, such as thunderstorms, bad electrical motors, and solar flares, it produces interference with AM video. If the video was FM encoded, like the current satellite TV transmission methods, then the noise immunity of the signal would be many times greater. When NTSC video was conceived, the technology to frequency modulate the large bandwidths required for TV images was not commercially possible. FM video is now possible, and cheap to accomplish with modern fast electronics. Color was added to NTSC video long after the standard was developed, and as such, it represents a great compromise in color image quality. Once again, non-NTSC video is capable of much greater color fidelity, but these systems are not compatible with all the existing NTSC TV sets.

Sample Application—A Television Set

The TV set is the most common application of raster scanned video in CRTs. Figure 4-24 illustrates the block diagram of a typical television receiver. The NTSC TV signal is modulated onto an rf carrier for broadcasting by a television station. This rf TV signal is intercepted by the receiving antenna, amplified, and tuned by the TV set's tuner. The tuner selects the frequency (channel) desired for viewing. The signal is then heterodyned down in frequency within the i-f stages of the TV set. Some TVs use a single i-f stage, while

Fig. 4-24. TV receiver block diagram

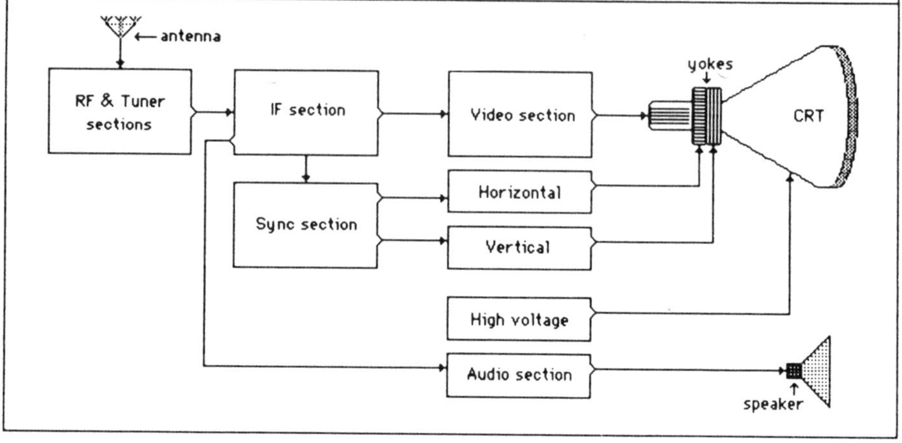

others use several. In all cases, the signal is again amplified in the i-f stage(s). The AM video and the FM audio are then separated. The audio is detected and amplified and sent to the speaker. The video is separated into the sync and the luminosity components. The sync pulses are amplified and applied to the CRTs magnetic deflection yokes, while the luminosity information is amplified and applied to the control grids of the CRT. This block diagram is greatly simplified. Actually the common TV set is a very complex piece of electronic wizardry. It is easily the most complex piece of electronic hardware present in the average American home. Computers are considered by most to be the epitome of electronic technology, but in fact, the lowly TV set employs a greater variety and complexity of circuits than does any computer. Next time you look at a TV, take a moment to appreciate the incredible electronic magic necessary to bring moving and talking images into our homes. Those interested in more detailed information of broadcast TV are referred to the wonderful book *Television from Analog to Digital* (TAB #1972) by Stan Prentiss. This work is very complete and well written.

Cost

The TV set is a very common piece of electronic hardware. It would be difficult to find a more mass produced display device. Due to this level of mass production and marketing, the cost is very low. Monochrome TV sets can be purchased for well under $100. Color TV sets cost somewhat more but can be found for under $200. As with all CRT displays, the cost is proportional to the size of the screen. Sets with screen sizes between 7 and 15 inches are the least expensive, while those smaller or larger are more expensive. At these prices the common TV receiver is an incredible bargain.

VECTOR SCAN CRTs

Vector scan CRT displays use a radically different approach to positioning the electron beam on the screen. The raster scan displays use a regular set pattern of lines scanned across the screen. The vector scan method allows the electron beam to range over the screen without any predefined pattern of scanning. The beam can be thought of as a "flying spot" that may be positioned at any point on the screen.

Figure 4-25 illustrates both vector scanning and raster scanning in action. Note that the raster scanned beam covers the entire screen to produce the triangle used as a sample image. The raster beam is blanked when an area is not required to be illuminated. The vector scanned beam is much more direct in its approach to displaying the triangular image on the screen. The beam is not blanked, but left active throughout its scan. Vector scanning systems blank the beam only when it crosses an area of the screen that is not supposed to be illuminated. The vector scanned beam simply traces the outline of the image directly on the screen. Vector scanning CRT displays are also called "X-Y" CRT displays. While any type of CRT may be used for vector scanning service, the CRT employing electrostatic deflection are most commonly used in this type of encoding method.

Fig. 4-25. Raster vs. vector scanning

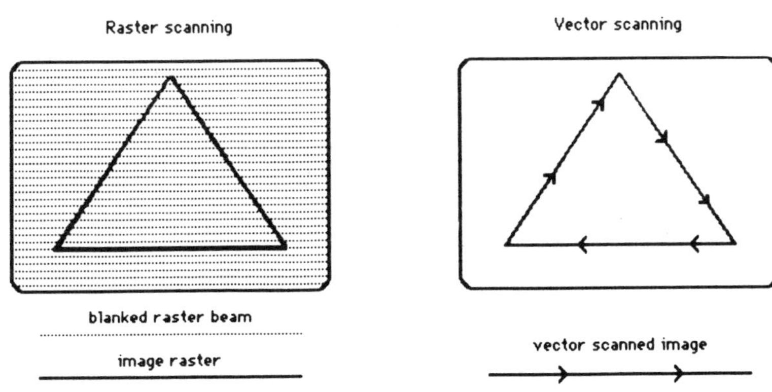

How It Works

The electron beam is directed across the screen's phosphors by a set of voltages present on the deflection anodes within the CRT's neck. There are two sets of deflection anodes, one is oriented vertically and controls the vertical deflection of the beam. The other is oriented horizontally and controls the horizontal position of the beam. The vertical plates are called the "Y" anode, while the horizontal plates are called the "X" anode. Figure 4-26 illustrates the internal construction of the electrostatically deflected type of CRT most commonly used in vector scan service.

The actual amount of voltage present on the deflection anodes varies with the size of the CRT screen. The CRT screens used in vector service are commonly round, and not the rectangular screens found in raster service. An electrostatic CRT with a screen diameter of 90 mm will require about 25 volts per cm of beam movement from the screen's center. As the CRTs grows larger, then the deflection voltages increase. A CRT with a screen diameter of 280 mm requires deflection anode voltages around 75 volts per cm.

In general, vector scanned and electrostatically deflected CRTs have smaller screens than magnetically deflected raster scanned CRTs. The vector scanned tubes are also much longer. This is due to the greater difficulty of producing large deflection angles (over 75°) using the electrostatic deflection method. Instead of a set of raster pulses used to coordinate the beam's horizontal motion, the vector scan CRT display uses an internal timebase or an analog volt-

Fig. 4-26. Electrostatic deflection CRT construction

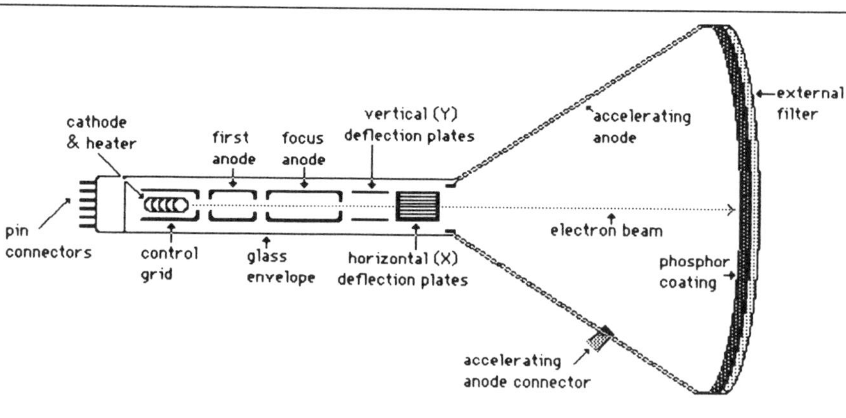

age. The timing ranges of the internal timebase are determined by the type of service and image the CRT is required to display.

Advantages

The major advantage of vector scanning is speed. This encoding method does not require the beam to repeatedly traverse the entire screen to produce an image. The beam need only trace the image on the screen. As such, time consuming actions such as horizontal retrace blanking and vertical retrace blanking are not required. This results in faster image production. In general, the vector scanning method can reproduce a simple image on the CRT over 8 times faster than the raster scanning methods. This increase in speed is only realized in simple, linear images. If the image is as complex as a TV picture, then the raster method is faster than the vector method. In keeping with their higher speeds, vector type CRT displays are equipped with phosphors with very short persistence times.

Due to the relatively small size of vector scanned CRTs, the power consumption using this method is much lower than raster methods. The anode voltages of this type of CRT display are commonly below 15 kV, much lower than the larger raster types. The electronics that drive the deflection plates are totally analog and much simpler than those used in raster scanning methods. All these factors combine to give vector type CRT displays lower power consumption than any other type of CRT based displays.

Disadvantages

The vector scanned CRT display cannot display relatively complex images as well as the raster type. The amount of signal encoding necessary to produce a complex image, like a moving TV picture, is enormous, many times greater than raster types. The use of a raster method removes the burden of retrace and blanking information from the actual video signal. In raster service the signal must only ensure that the display is synchronized with the information. In vector type encoding, all the blanking and retrace information must be included constantly in the encoding signal. This is due to the vector systems lack of standardized and repetitive beam motion.

Sample Application—An Oscilloscope

Vector scanning is most commonly used in oscilloscopes and equipment which displays voltage versus time images. Electronic test equipment, medical monitors, and industrial process control equipment are the most common users of the vector scanning method. Figure 4-27 illustrates the block diagram of an electrostatically deflected CRT implemented as an oscilloscope. Note that the x-axis of the display is driven by an adjustable time base. The signal to be displayed is amplified and fed to the y-axis deflection plates. This block diagram is greatly simplified. In actual practice, additional circuits are used to trigger and adjust the CRT trace. In a display of this type, many of the CRTs functions such as beam intensity, X and Y no-signal beam position, and beam focus are user adjustable from the front panel. This is in keeping with the professional service that the vector type display receives.

HIGH RESOLUTION CRT DISPLAYS

High resolution CRT displays are not becoming quite common in computer applications. The rapid growth and increased demand for better video displays for computers and CAD/CAE terminals has produced many types of increased resolution CRT displays. These modern displays have one thing in common—they can display more detailed information faster than conventional NTSC CRT displays. These hi-res units are the hot rods of the CRT displays.

These displays are commonly raster scanned, with a non-interlaced scanning method. Non-interlaced scanning means that each line of the display is scanned in numerical order. A complete image is reproduced in a single frame consisting of only a single field. Non-

Fig. 4-27. Oscilloscope block diagram

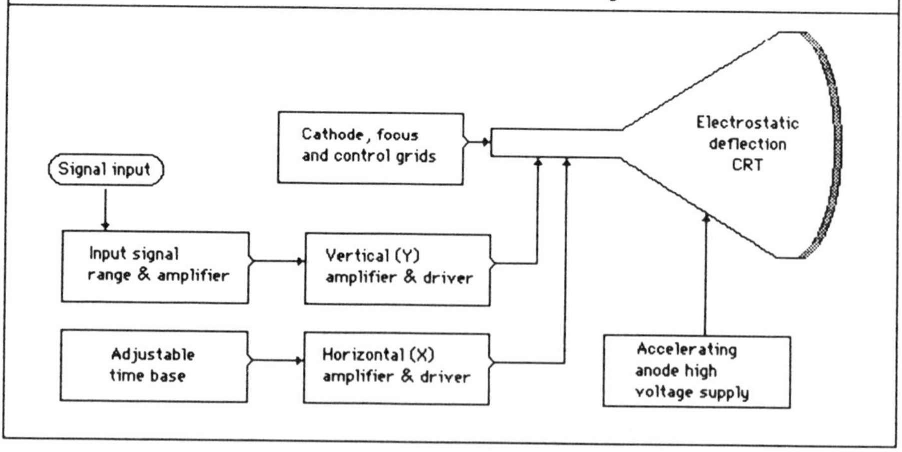

interlaced scanning is also called sequential scanning. High resolution CRT displays generally have a 1:1 aspect ratio, and square pixels. This approach simplifies their use in engineering and graphics applications such as typesetting and medical imaging.

The exact definition of what constitutes a high resolution CRT display is far from clear. Even the manufacturers of these displays cannot agree on what exactly is high resolution. In fact, the term "high resolution" is more an advertising slogan, than a specific scientific standard. As a generic concept, high resolution means that the display reproduces an image that is subjectively sharp in its detail. In general, any CRT display with a total pixel count of over 512 by 512 pixels can be and is called high resolution. Such a display can produce an image with over twice the number of discrete elements as a conventional television image. In general, these displays have very small spot sizes, advanced electronics, and increased speed.

The actual CRTs used in most high resolution displays do not differ greatly from those in standard TV service. The difference is in how the CRT is used, and in the vastly faster electronic processing that encodes the information for display. Faster electronic processing is necessary for the hi-res system to display greater amounts of information while still maintaining a screen image that does not appear to flicker.

How It Works

The high resolution displays are pixelized. Each line displayed on the screen is divided into a discrete number of pixels. Instead of analog signal encoding for the CRT's electron beam luminosity and motion, the signals used in hi-res displays are commonly digital. Digital image processing is necessary to assure image stability coupled with very high speed. After the signals are digitally processed, they are converted into analog forms and amplified. This is then sent to the actual CRT. It is the recent advances in high speed digital electronics that make high resolution CRT displays possible and affordable. The use of digital image processing also interfaces more simply with the digital computers that drive these displays.

High resolution CRT displays now commonly have pixel counts of 1024 by 1024 pixels. Some reach pixel densities of over 2048 by 2048 pixels. This amounts to over 4 million discrete picture elements displayed on the screen. The video refresh rates on high resolution CRT displays are 60 Hz, or greater, i.e., the CRT displays 60 complete images per second. The video bandwidth of the signal necessary to drive these displays without flicker can be in excess of 200 MHz. This places incredible demands on the design and speed of the electronic processing driving the CRT.

The central processing unit (CPU) of the computer driving these high resolution displays must be time shared between two tasks. The first is the computation that generates and stores the parameters of the image. The second is the relaying of these computed parameters to the CRT which displays the image. The image processing, RAM refreshing, and other chores are usually carried on during the vertical retrace blanking period and, in some very fast CPUs, during the horizontal retrace interval. A modern 8 MHz CPU can perform over a thousand operations during the vertical blanking interval. Some types of specialized and more expensive high resolution CRT displays actually use two CPUs, one for image processing and another for CRT control.

The CPU generates the image's parameters and stores them in a look up table (LUT). The LUT is a section of the computer's memory reserved specifically for the information that defines the image to be displayed. In a high resolution display this area of memory may be very large, over 4 megabytes (MBs) reserved for the LUT is common in CAD applications. The CPU then transfers this information in the LUT to a digital to analog converter (DAC). The DAC converts the digital image information, usually one line at at time, into an analog signal which is amplified and sent to the CRT's electron beam. The CPU is free to perform additional image computation and refresh the RAM and LUT during the blanking intervals. A video controller IC is used in many high resolution display systems to reduce the processing requirements placed on the CPU. The video controller is itself controlled by the CPU on a high level. The video controller then takes care of such mundane chores as sync and blanking. Figure 4-28 illustrates the block diagram of this process. Most computer CPUs are now capable of performing in excess of 4 million operations per second, and every bit of this speed is necessary in high resolution CRT displays.

In contrast to regular CRT displays, the hi-res types are using digital processing for all video functions up to the final amplifiers that drive the actual CRT. The digital signals are converted to analog at the last possible moment. The analog signal is then amplified by very fast electronics to power levels suitable to run the CRT. Analog circuitry does not possess the temperature stability and accuracy to process video images at the speeds required by modern high-resolution CRT displays.

Fig. 4-28. Hi-Res computer CRT display block diagram

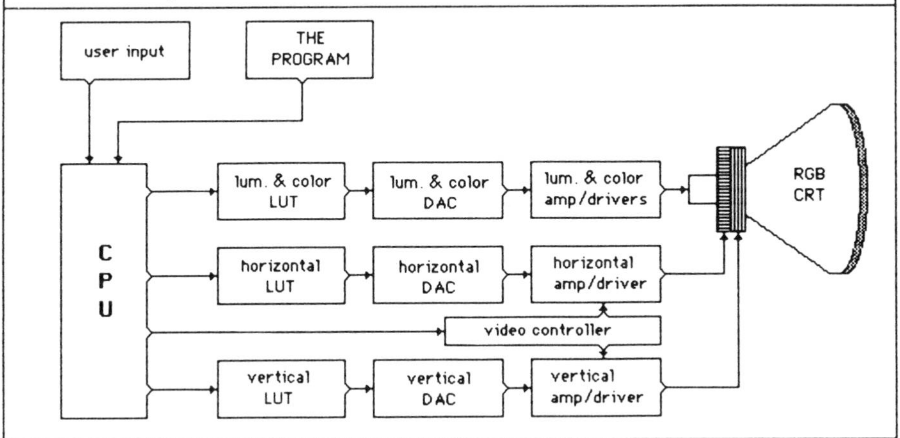

Advantages

The main advantage of increased screen resolution is subjective. An image displayed on a high resolution CRT is simply more pleasant to look at. There is no doubt that it is more pleasant to work with a fine grained image on a CRT rather than a coarse one. Operator fatigue is greatly reduced by higher resolution. It is also possible to display some types of information more efficiently using distinct images rather than text. This use of images or "icons" is becoming popular in computer systems now, and is made possible by the high resolution of the CRT displays being used. Some applications such as medical imaging, military satellite imaging, and industrial imaging require higher resolution of visual pictures than is possible using NTSC or other video encoding techniques.

The use of non-interlaced scanning on hi-res CRTs offers an improvement in the area of speed. Since a single frame comprises a complete image, one of the vertical retrace blanking periods is eliminated in relation to interlaced scanning. This increases speed.

Disadvantages

The disadvantage of high resolution CRT displays is not subjective—cost. Every component that goes into the display must be made to a higher precision than in a normal CRT display. This means higher cost. The electronics used in processing the video image, and in amplifying and coupling to the CRT, must be very much faster than those used in normal CRTs. Again, this increases cost. The higher resolution of the display requires more time and space within the CPU and the computer's memory. In many cases, a video PC card carrying additional circuitry to help out the CPU and expand memory, is used to implement a high-resolution display in a computer.

Sample Application—A Computer with 512 × 512 CRT

Let's consider a high resolution, color CRT displaying 512 × 512 pixels. Let's say this CRT is used as a display for a 16 bit microcomputer. This display has a 1:1 aspect ratio and is raster scanned at 60 Hz in a noninterlaced fashion. This example is typical of many RGB monitors used in small computer applications. If 512 is multiplied by 512, then we see that the display has a total of 262,144 individual pixels. The video monitor has an operating vertical retrace interval of 0.9 ms and an operating horizontal retrace interval of 7.6 μs. These retrace intervals are based on the CRT manufacturer's recommended operating parameters.

Figure 4-29 illustrates the time periods involved in putting the image on the screen. This illustration shows three basic time periods, display time period, vertical blanking period, and horizontal blanking period. During the display period, a rapid stream of image data is sent to the CRT. The CRT spends a very short time at each pixel's location, about 45.2 ns. This stream of data is carried on at 22 +MHz, over five times faster than the 4 MHz NTSC video. Each

Fig. 4-29. Time parameters for a 512 X 512 Hi-Res. CRT display

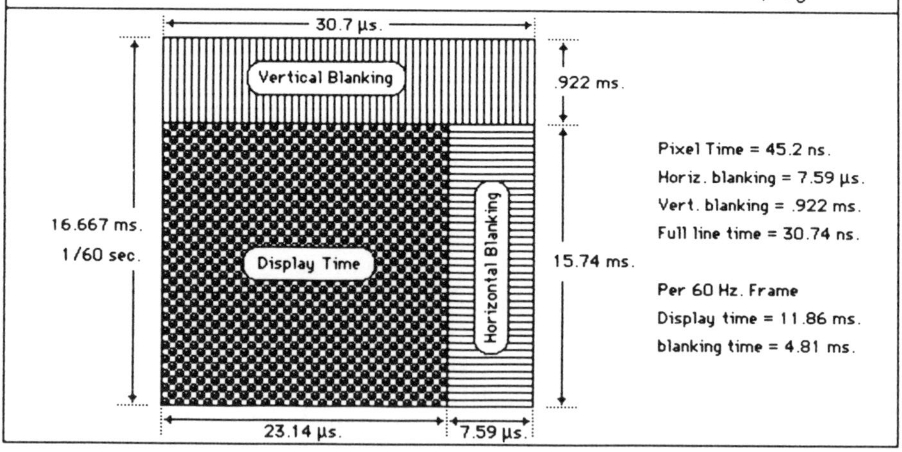

Fig. 4-30.

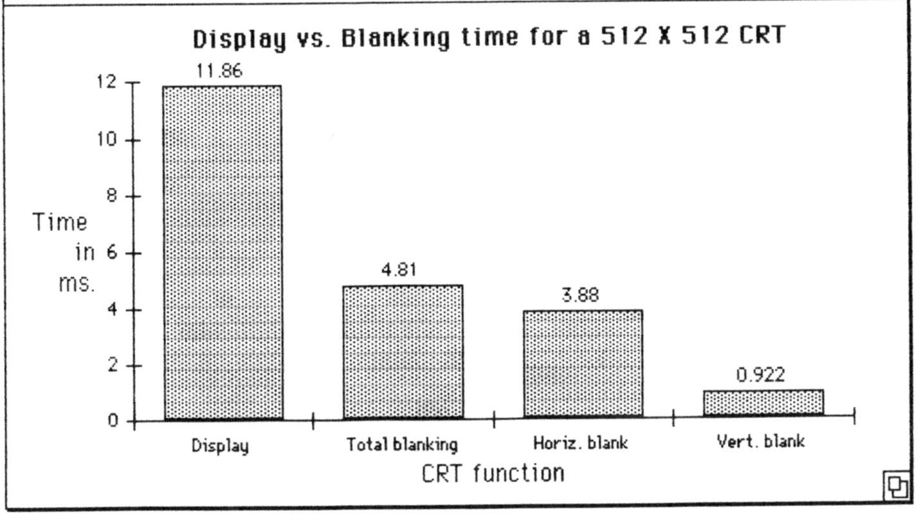

line of the display takes 23.1 μs to write on the screen. After a line is written, it takes 7.59 μs for the CRT to return in position to write the next line—the horizontal retrace interval. A combination of both the horizontal line's write and retrace times is 30.7 μs. After a complete screen of 512 horizontal lines is scanned the vertical blanking interval of 0.922 ms occurs as the beam returns to the top of the screen.

Using this data, let's examine how the time is proportioned between the CRT's activities necessary for image production. All this information is for a single frame of 512 lines by 512 pixels per line, and represents scanning 512 lines, with 512 horizontal blankings, and 1 vertical blanking. The display time period is 11.86 ms. The vertical retrace period is 0.922 ms. The total horizontal retrace period is 3.88 ms. The amount of time spent in blanking, both horizontal (512 times) and vertical (1 time) is 4.81 ms. The sum of both display time and blanking time is the period it takes to display a complete frame, and is 16.67 ms (1/60 or 60 Hz) in this application. Blanking takes up 28.86% of the time, while actual display accounts for 71.16% of a complete frame's period. Figure 4-30 illustrates this information graphically.

The method of encoding the video data for this type of display is digital and elegant. This example display uses an RGB color encoding system. Each group of four pixels on the screen is assigned a single computer word of 16 bits. Bits 0 to 3 describe the luminosity of the pixels, bits 4 to 7 describe the blue content of the pixels, bits 8 to 11 describe the red contents, and bits 12 to 15 describe the green contents. Figure 4-31 illustrates the complete word describing 4 pixels. Each individual pixel is described by 4 parameters, luminosity, red, blue, and green. Each parameter is described by 1 bit of information. This gives 8 levels of color and 2 levels of luminosity for each pixel. Each pixel is capable of 15 (2 to the 4th power minus 1) different combinations. An entire screen is described by 1,048,576 bits (2 to the 20th power), or 65,536 16-bit bytes of information. A screen can contain up to 15 raised to the 262,144th power differing combinations, which is a number too big to even think about, much less write down. Get an idea now of why these displays are called high resolution and why they require a computer to process their image parameters? It takes a massive amount of electronic processing to get this amount of information onto a screen in 1/60th of a second. Only a digital computer is capable of this feat.

Figure 4-32 illustrates a simplified block diagram of the circuitry feeding the video data to 512 × 512 CRT. The CPU in this block diagram is assisted in the video chores by two other ICs, the horizontal controller and the vertical controller. These two devices are linked to the same video clock and control the movement parameters of the CRT's electron beam. A RAM controller coordinates the storage of the image's parameters (LUTs) in RAM. The video controllers send synchronizing signals to the RAM

Fig. 4-31. Pixel Data Structure

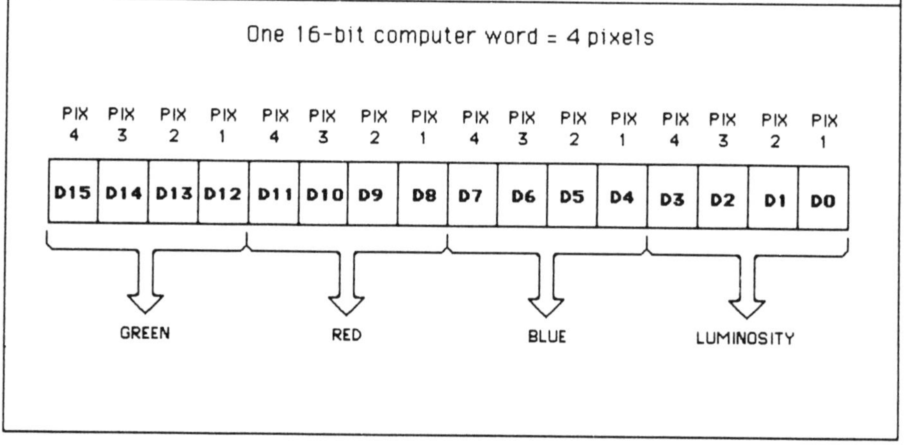

Fig. 4-32. Hi-res processing block diagram

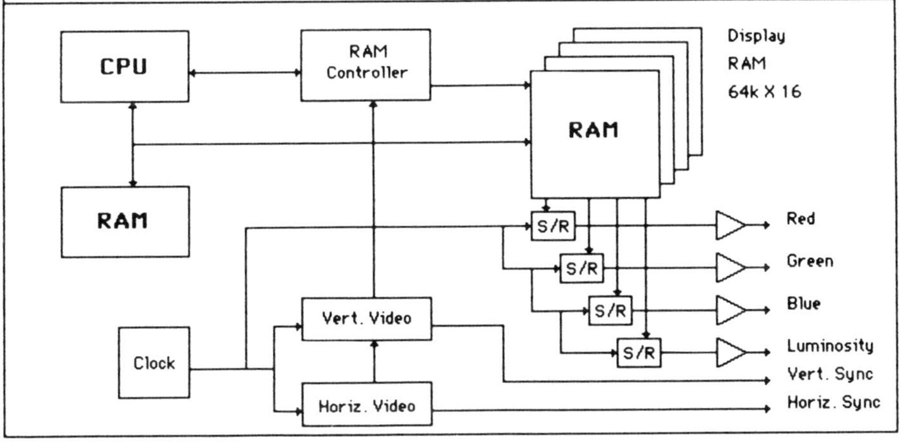

controller. These signals assure that the portions of the RAM used for the display LUTs are not refreshed while transferring information to the display. The video controllers tell the RAM controller when the electron beam is in either vertical or horizontal blanking, and the RAM controller enables the CPU to refresh the data in the display LUTs. This prevents display flicker.

The portion of the RAM set aside for data that describes the image is 1024k and is arranged as an array of 16 @ 64k RAM chips. This is a lot of RAM, but it is the minimum required to store a complete frame in this video system. The screen contains an array of 512 × 512 pixels, and each pixel is allowed 4 bits of information, the product of these numbers is 1,048,576. The RAM is grouped into blocks of four which are connected to shift registers. There are four shift registers, one for each color and one for luminosity. The shift registers receive the data from the RAM and generate the stream of serial digital data on its way to the CRT. This data stream must first be converted from a digital signal to an analog signal, and then amplified before it actually drives the CRT.

Cost

The high-resolution CRT monitors cost in proportion to their resolution and size. A small 512 × 512 color monitor costs between $300 and $450. A larger 1024 × 1024 color monitor will cost between $900 to well over $2,000. These prices do not reflect the additional electronic circuitry necessary to apply these hi-res monitors in actual computer service. Electronic processing can add between 15% to 75% to the cost of the actual monitor.

CHOOSING THE RIGHT CRT FOR THE JOB

Let's assume that of all the various display technologies available to us, we have decided that a CRT is right for our particular application. The question is which CRT from the myriad types available. The information here is designed to lead the potential customer through the morass of manufacturer's claims to the display that works best for him. Performance is a criteria as well as cost. Let's start with the common garden variety TV receiver.

TV receivers are mass produced and costs vary widely. Make your choice on the performance of the display first, and then go looking for that particular unit at the lowest price. First, it is necessary to choose the size of the screen. Keep it as small as practical. If you plan on viewing the CRT from a close distance, say under 10 feet, then a 7- to 12-inch diagonal screen is sufficient. Using a larger screen will result in less apparent resolution, higher power consumption, and higher cost. If color is chosen, ask about the configuration of the CRT's electron gun. The delta gun models have higher resolution and price than the in-line types. Anyone buying a TV receiver should consider one with a NTSC composite video input in addition to the stock rf channel tuners. Many video devices such as VCRs and satellite receivers have composite video outputs. The use of composite video rather than rf through an rf modulator gives much better picture quality and lessens video noise. It also simplifies switching and hook-up chores between video sources and the display.

Choosing a monitor for a non-NTSC video display is more complex than selecting one for TV service. For one thing, there are about as many different video encoding systems as there are computers. Be sure that the monitor you are considering is compatible with the video techniques used in your computer. Also check to see that the video processing electronics that interface between the computer and the monitor are available and compatible. Consider only monitors which have met the above compatibility requirements. Interfacing a monitor with a computer can be as simple as plugging things in. But it can be a complex and expensive nightmare if the computer and monitor do not agree on the system of video encoding.

Now that all incompatible monitors have been eliminated, the next choice is resolution. Decide how much resolution is required. In most cases, the lower range of high-resolution monitors is sufficient. A 512 × 512 pixel monitor offers fantastic resolution when compared to a NTSC monitor. Consider not only the added expense, but also the added memory and processing requirements of the higher resolution displays. If you don't need the increased resolution, then it is not efficient to use it. Using a display with too much resolution only increases the cost of both the monitor and the electronic processing necessary to implement it. The CPU is required to process an excess of screen information—this wastes the CPU's time and slows the computer down. Massive amounts of processing are required to provide the data for a high resolution display. Be sure you actually need the increased resolution before spending your money and your computer's time on it.

If you decide that high resolution is for you, then examine the manufacturer's specifications carefully. Check to see that the resolution of a particular CRT is rated at its full luminosity. If not, then derate the manufacturer's resolution claims. Check to see what methods used to test the CRT's resolution. The MTF is the best method, but is usually only employed in high end units. The dot pitch ratio is a good specification to use as a rule of thumb. Consider dot pitches in the neighborhood of 0.26 mm to 0.31 mm, which are commonly available today. Keep the screen size to a minimum. If the dot pitch is constant, then the larger the screen, the more information it carries. Larger screens are going to use more of the computer's memory and slow down its operation.

In some cases, it may come to a choice between high resolution and color. This choice may be prompted by financial and memory considerations. This choice also depends on the use of the monitor. In general office work, and most business usage, high resolution is preferable to color in the display. Professionals can spend many hours in front of the CRT; high resolution graphics and characters minimize eye fatigue. If a hi-res monochrome display is decided upon, then consider a phosphor that is either green or amber. The use of these colors, to which the eye is very sensitive, means higher readability with lower levels of CRT luminosity. This means the CRT will last longer and is more cost effective.

If a color hi-res monitor is decided on, then it should pass the test for resolution first. The next thing to consider is misconvergence, the inability of the various electron guns, one for each color, to come together at the same point on the screen.

Misconvergence should be rated at the CRT's maximum luminosity, and should be specified at both the center and edges of the screen. Consider a center misconvergence of 0.5 mm to be the maximum allowable. Misconvergence less than 0.2 mm is barely detectable by the human eye. Misconvergence is acceptable if below 0.75 mm at the edges of the screen. Some manufacturers include electronic processing to correct for the CRT's misconvergence. These circuits are certainly worth the money if you require consistently high resolution over all portions of the screen.

Many manufacturers of high resolution CRT displays bundle the electronics hardware necessary for processing the image with the display. This is a very good way to ensure compatibility. If the processing is not up to the speed of the CRT, then its resolution is wasted. With video bandwidths in the neighborhood of 100 MHz, it is important to pay as much attention to the video processing as the actual monitor.

LISTING OF CRT DISPLAY MANUFACTURERS

This is a list of all CRT display manufacturers contributing information to this chapter. Their addresses and telephone numbers are available from the Electronic Display Device Manufacturers Data Base in Appendix A.

ADAC Corp.
Ampex Corp.
Ann Arbor Terminals Inc.
Calcomp/Sanders Inc.
Centronic Ltd.
Clinton Electronics Corp.
Colorgraphic Communications Corp.
Dage MTI Corp.
Datacopy Corp.
Dipix Inc.
Enterprise Systems Corp.
Gigatek Ltd.
Graftek Inc.
Hoppmann Corp.
Hughes Aircraft Corp.
Ikegami Electronics USA Inc.
Industrial Data Terminals Corp.
Infodex Inc.
International Imaging Systems Inc.
ITT Information Systems Inc.
Kanematsu Electronics Ltd.
Leader Instruments Corp.
Litton Industries Inc.
Lundy Electronics & Systems Inc.
Metheus Corp.
Mitsubishi Electronics America Inc.
MPB Corp.
New Media Graphics Corp.
Ocean Technology Inc.
Princeton Graphic System Inc.
Ramtek Corp.
Raytheon Corp.

RCA Corp.
Robot Research Inc.
Spectragraphics Corp.
Sperry Univac Corp.
Tektronix Inc.
Telex Computer Products Inc.
Thomas Electronics Inc.
TRW Corp.
VG Systems Inc.
Vidco Inc.
Visual Technology Inc.
XKD Corp.

5

Light Emitting Diodes (LED)

The light emitting diodes are the small red, green, or yellow indicators we see on many electronic devices. The LED may be a single light (called a lamp), a numerical display (called a seven-segment display), or a group of dots showing alphabetical characters (called a dot-matrix display). They seem to be everywhere. These LEDs are among the most common forms of display devices that convert electricity into light. They are also among the easiest to use and most reliable display devices.

The LEDs are rapidly replacing incandescent lights as panel indicators. The reasons for this are cost, reliability, and most importantly, power consumption. The lowly LED is a real power sipper, consuming some 90% less power than an incandescent lamp of the same light output.

HOW LEDs WORK

The LED is a diode. It is a very specialized diode designed to produce light. It is a semiconductor, and its operation is best described in terms of quantum mechanics. Physicists began speculating at the turn of the century that certain semiconductor junctions could emit light. It was not until 1963 that semiconductor technology was sufficiently advanced to produce commercially available LED devices.

The LED junction does indeed work; it emits light of very discrete color, but our understanding of its actual operation is still theoretical. The most current theory used to describe the effect is the Semiconductor Energy Band Theory.

If a voltage is applied to forward bias a pn junction, then the majority carriers (electrons) will migrate from the N-side Conduction Band to the P-side Valence Band. The electrons are said to migrate across the semiconductor's "energy gap" (E_g). this energy gap is measured in electron volts (eV), and represents allowable energy states which an electron can attain. The electrons are excited to cross the energy gap by the electric field of the applied forward voltage. During this migration, the electrons lose a discrete amount of energy which is radiated as light and heat. It is this lost energy that we see radiated through the LED's clear plastic case. The LED is unique in that the energy lost within the junction is what we use. In most diodes, the useful energy is that which is passed through the junction, and we try to minimize junctions's loss. Just the opposite is true in the LED, where we try to lose the maximum amount of energy within the junction by converting it to light.

All semiconductor materials have different and discrete energy gaps. The wavelength (i.e., color) of the emitted light is determined by the quantity of energy the electrons lose while crossing the diode's energy gap. Semiconductors with smaller energy gaps produce light of lower frequency and longer wavelength. Conversely, semiconductors with larger energy gaps emit light of higher frequencies and shorter wavelengths. The mathematical relationship between the wavelength of the emitted light and the semiconductor's energy gap is:

$$\lambda = \frac{12380}{E_g} \qquad \textbf{Equation 5-1}$$

λ = peak wavelength of light emission expressed in angstroms (A).

E_g = semiconductor energy band-gap expressed in electron volts (eV).

LED junctions are designed to emit light within the visual range of our eyes' perception. As such, the energy gaps of their junctions fall within a very narrow range. Outside this range, diode junctions still emit light energy, but it is too low in frequency to be visible to the human eye. Gallium compounds are most commonly used in

LED construction, because their junctions emit lost energy within the visual spectrum. Table 5-1 shows the relationship between several gallium compounds, their energy gaps, the wavelengths, and colors of their emitted light. Gallium compounds have several advantages in semiconducting junctions. They have low reverse bias leakage, low inherent noise, high speed, and their electron mobility is high. Most importantly, they emit light in the visible spectrum.

The intensity of the light emitted by the LED junction is a function of the number of electrons passing through the junction per unit time. In other words, the brightness of an LED depends on the amount of current flowing through it. LEDs, being diodes, are current operated devices. The more current that passes through the LED's junction, the brighter it becomes. There is an upper limit to the amount of current that a junction can transfer. If this limit is exceeded, the junction may be destroyed by heat.

The LED junction may be powered by a wide range of voltages. If an LED is operated from a constant voltage power source, then some form of current limitation through the diode junction is necessary. Omission of this current limitation will result in thermal runaway and destruction of the junction. Figure 5-1 illustrates the basic LED circuit employing a resistor for current limitation. The amount of resistance needed is a function of three factors, and can be expressed by:

$$R_L = \frac{Vcc - V_f}{I_f} \qquad \textbf{Equation 5-2}$$

Table 5-1. Band-Gap Data for Gallium Compounds.

Material	Band gap Eg in eV.	Wave-length λ_o in A	Color
GaAs:Zn	1.375	9000	infrared
$GaAsP_{.4}$	1.876	6600	red
$GaAsP_{.5}$	2.029	6100	amber
$GaAsP_{.85}$:N	2.098	5900	yellow
GaP:N	2.211	5600	green

$$\lambda = \frac{12380}{E_g}$$

Fig. 5-1. Basic LED circuit using current limitation

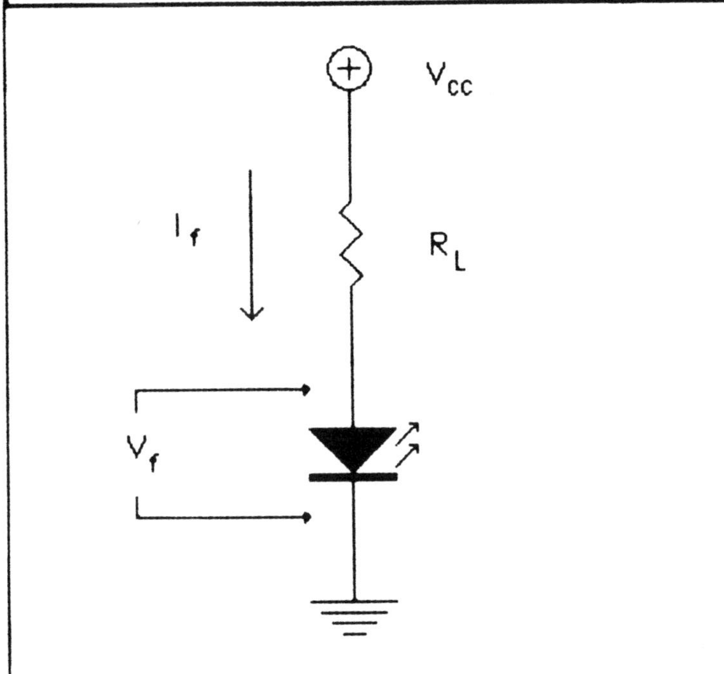

$$R_L = \frac{V_{cc} - V_f}{I_f}$$

R_L = amount of resistance expressed in ohms (Ω).
VCC = supply voltage expressed in volts (Vdc).
V_f = diode forward voltage drop expressed in volts (Vdc).
I_f = diode forward current expressed in amperes (A).

The diode's forward voltage drop and forward current limit are available from the manufacturer's specifications. Use the nearest value standard resistor that is higher than the computed value in Equation 5-2. The forward voltage drop of LED junctions are commonly between 1.5 and 2.6 volts. This is a function of the range of energy band gaps that emit light. The forward current limit of an LED is a function of junction size, purity, and physical configuration, in addition to external physical factors such as temperature.

HOW LEDs ARE MADE

The actual chip where the LED junction resides is constructed in much the same manner as many transistors and integrated circuits. The materials used are highly pure, up to one part in over ten million, semiconductor compounds. The N side of the gallium junction is diffused with dopants such as arsenic (As), phosphorus (P), or aluminum (Al). This diffusion is accomplished by ion implantation in a vacuum chamber, creating a diode junction of the proper energy gap.

The LED chip is then attached to a cathode post which forms the cathode of the diode. In high output models, a reflector is often placed under the chip to reflect more light to the front of the LED. This reflector is "coined" into the LED's cathode post. The LED chip is attached to the cathode post by a conductive epoxy. The anode of the LED chip is then wired with very fine wire to the anode post of the diode. These posts are made of lead which is plated with a coating of copper about 0.001 mm thick, and then plated again with 0.003 mm of silver. This assures low resistance connections with the actual LED chip in addition to easy soldering when the LED is installed in a device.

The LED chip, with anode and cathode posts attached, is then encapsulated in an epoxy case. In most applications, this case has a lens cast into its front to focus the light forward. The shape of this lens determines the visual viewing angle of the finished LED. Many of the epoxy cases are tinted with dyes to obtain some variation of the LED junction's inherent color. Figure 5-2 illustrates the internal mechanical construction of a typical T 1-¾ LED lamp. Note that the mounting rim of the case is flattened next to the cathode lead. The cathode lead is also shorter than the anode lead., This is done to aid in recognition of the cathode lead during the end use of the device.

LEDs are assembled into many different types of packages, differing in physical construction. No matter what form the LEDs take, all of their junctions are basically the same. It is the light output of the chip that is used and arranged differently. Each of the different

Fig. 5-2. Internal construction of T-1 3/4 plastic LED lamp

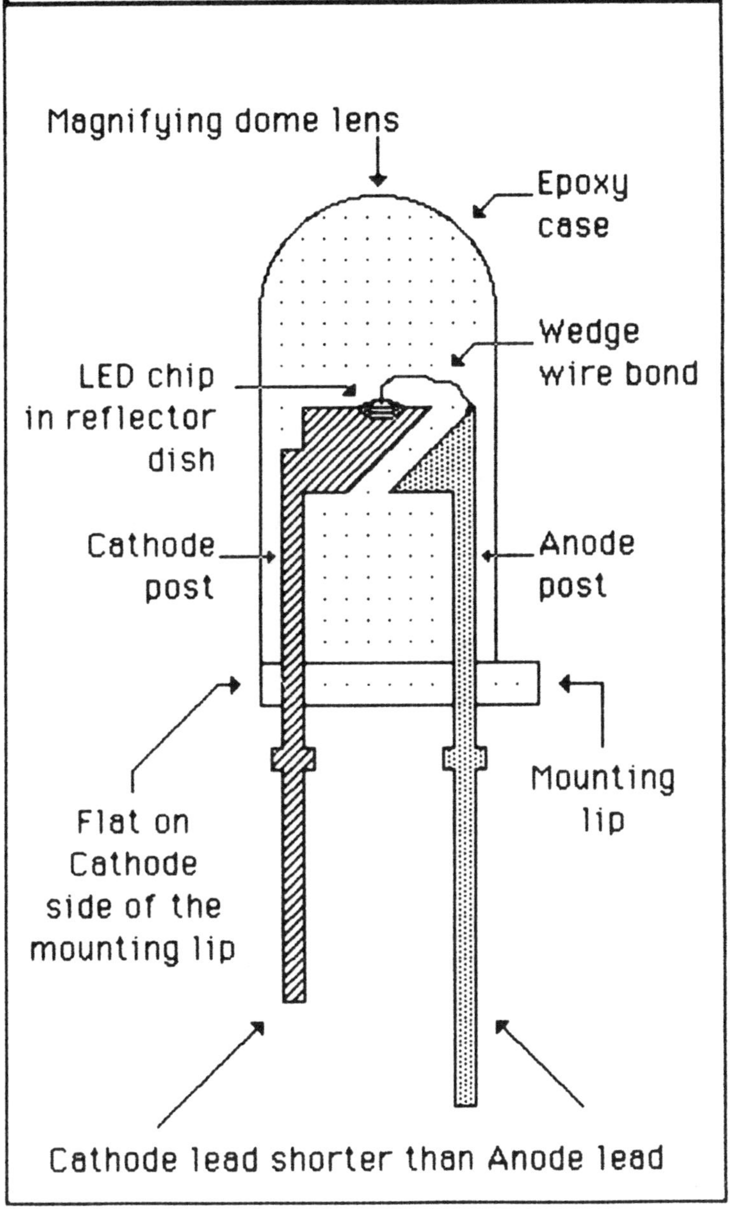

physical forms of LEDs is discussed later under its respective type. LED manufacturing is a highly automated procedure, carried on by machines which produce thousands of completed LEDs and LED displays daily. It is mass production that gives the LED its inexpensive price.

LED CHARACTERISTICS

A thorough understanding of the characteristics of the LED junction and its many forms will better enable us to apply these devices in practice. The LED is a wonderful display device, but it requires proper application in order to be a successful display. The information in this section is oriented to the single LED lamp, but the details apply to any LED junction regardless of its package.

Junction Design

LED junctions are constructed from a wide variety of gallium compounds. Gallium is a metallic element with an atomic number of 31. It is found in nature as a trace element in a variety of minerals including bauxite and coal. The gallium used in semiconductor manufacture is hyper-pure (99.99999+%), and costs about $1.00 per gram. Red and yellow LEDs are available with two basic junction materials, gallium arsenide phosphide (GaAsP), or gallium aluminum arsenide (GaAlAs), deposited on a base of gallium phosphide (GaP). Green LEDs are usually fabricated using doped gallium phosphide (GaP) vapor deposited on gallium phosphide (GaP).

One of the more recent advances in LED technology is the usage of GaAlAs on GaAlAs junctions. This junction technology is producing red LEDs with about twice the light output of previous types, while consuming the same amount of current. This newer technology is difficult to mass produce. The major problem has been attaining sufficient junction layer thickness.

You might have noticed the lack of blue LEDs. This is because the junctions are very difficult and expensive to make. They also have very low light output, about 200 times less than red. This inefficiency is built-into the quantum mechanics of the blue junction. The development of blue junctions is a high priority as it would add another primary color to the LED family. This is highly desirable in producing controlled color displays as the primary colors can be mixed to obtain other colors. Some of the materials being used in blue junction fabrication are silicon carbide, zinc, selenide, and gallium nitride. The experimental silicon carbide junctions have light outputs of about 6.0 millicandles (mcd) at a wavelength of 480 nanometers (nm). Current consumption is about 20 mA with a junction forward drop around 4 volts. The increased power dissipation across the junction is another design problem with the elusive blue LED.

The trend of modern LED designers is to reduce the power consumed by the junction, no matter what its type. LEDs that were commonly run on 20 mA years ago are now being run on 1 to 10 mA. This lowering of the LED's consumption makes them directly compatible with modern CMOS circuitry. Most companies now offer commercial junctions which emit 2.0 mcd of light for as little as 2 mA of forward current. Usage of these low current, highly efficient, LEDs is very common in computer equipment.

Power Requirements

The LED is a current operated semiconductor device. As such, it will operate over an incredibly wide range of input voltages, provided the current through the junction is limited. Figure 5-1 illustrates usage of a resistor to limit the current through the LED junction. It is necessary to provide enough voltage to forward bias the LED junction, thereby overcoming the energy gap. This is a small amount of voltage, typically 1.6 to 2.8 volts dc depending on the LED's color. LED junctions can be powered directly by TTL sources, which attain 5 volts in their high states (be sure to use the proper amount of current limitation for the particular LED you are using). CMOS sources are also capable of driving LED junctions, provided that they have sufficient current output to adequately drive the LEDs junction.

The LED is a small consumer of power. Some junctions can be powered by as little as 2 milliamperes of current, or about 4 milliwatts of power. These super-efficient LEDs are capable of being driven directly by CMOS or MOS logic with no transistor buffering. Even in the case of very large LED junctions, the input power is less than 650 milliwatts, or about 125 milliamperes of dc current. These high-output junctions are used for panel illumination and other large illumination jobs.

Reverse bias voltage is limited on LED junctions much in the same manner as all other semiconductor junctions. If this reverse bias voltage is exceeded, the LED's junction will be permanently destroyed. Reverse bias voltage is rated at between 4 and 25 volts by most LED manufacturers. Reverse bias is seldom a problem in dc circuits. But if you are dealing with ac or pulsed dc into reactive loads, then be sure that the reverse voltage remains below the manufacturer's absolute ratings. One technique is bypassing the LED with another diode. LEDs constructed with gallium junctions have reverse bias current leakage that is an order of magnitude smaller than regular silicon junctions.

Since the LED is a current operated device, the only real decision facing a designer in a dc circuit is how much resistance to add to limit the junction's current. Figure 5-3 illustrates using an LED with an active-low drive circuit using an NPN transistor. In this circuit, the LED is illuminated when the transistor is conducting (i.e. on). The amount of resistance needed can be calculated by:

$$R_L = \frac{VCC - V_f - V_{ce}}{I_f} \qquad \textbf{Equation 5-3}$$

R_L = amount of resistance expressed in Ohms (Ω).
VCC = supply voltage expressed in volts (Vdc).
V_f = LED forward voltage drop expressed in volts (Vdc).
V_{ce} = saturated forward voltage drop of the transistor in volts.
I_f = LED forward current expressed in amperes (A).

The LED may be powered from an active high circuit as illustrated in Figure 5-4. In this case, use Equation 5-2 to calculate the value of the current limiting resistor needed. This circuit lights the LED when the transistor is not conducting, or in the high state. This circuit assumes that the transistor has a V_{ce} of 0.4 volts when conducting.

The LED's junction may also be operated on ac voltages. Figure 5-5 illustrates the operation of an LED from an alternating current power source. Since the LED should only be operated in the forward bias mode, a 1N914 diode is used to provide reverse bias protection for the LED junction. In this circuit, the LED will light only when the current is flowing in one direction. Since the frequency of the ac line is at 60 cycles per second, the flashing of the LED will be too fast for most people to detect. The LED will appear to be continuously illuminated. A variation on this circuit is pictured in Fig-5-6 which uses the ac waveform to drive two LEDs located "back to back." This circuit eliminates the necessity of the 1N914 diode, which consumes power while providing no visual indication. It also provides LED indication for the current in both directions. In both these illustrations, Equation 5-2 provides the necessary value for

Fig. 5-3. LED active-low drive circuit

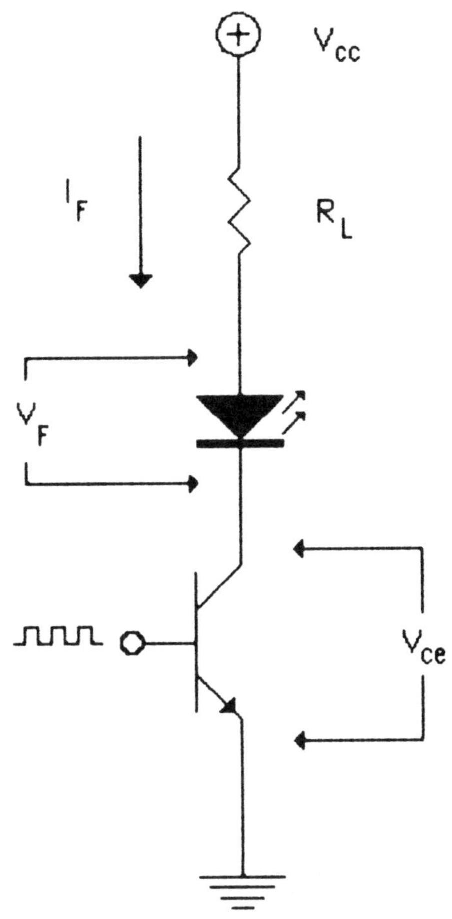

$$R_L = \frac{V_{cc} - V_F - V_{ce}}{I_F}$$

Fig. 5-4. LED active-high drive circuit

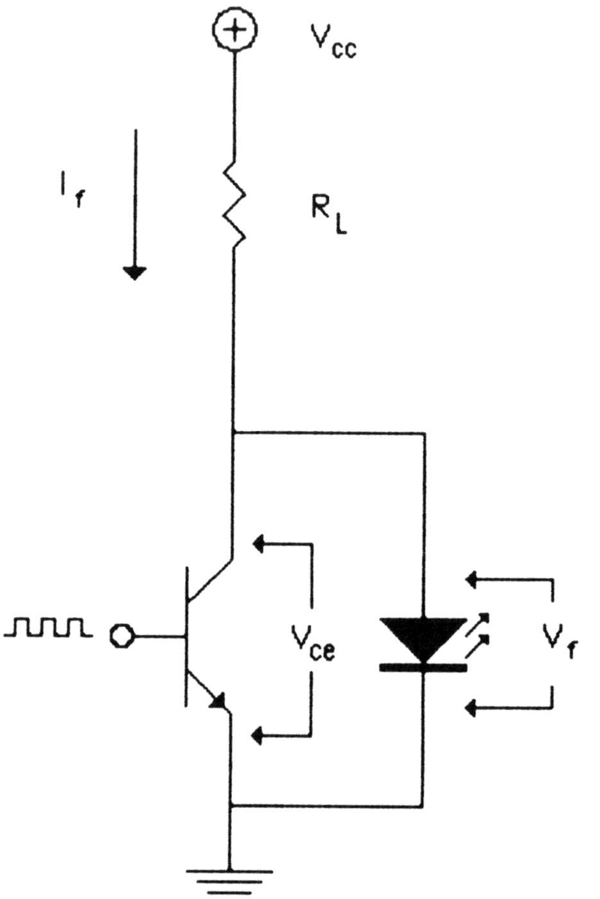

$$R_L = \frac{V_{cc} - V_f}{I_f}$$

Fig.5-5. LED operation on ac.

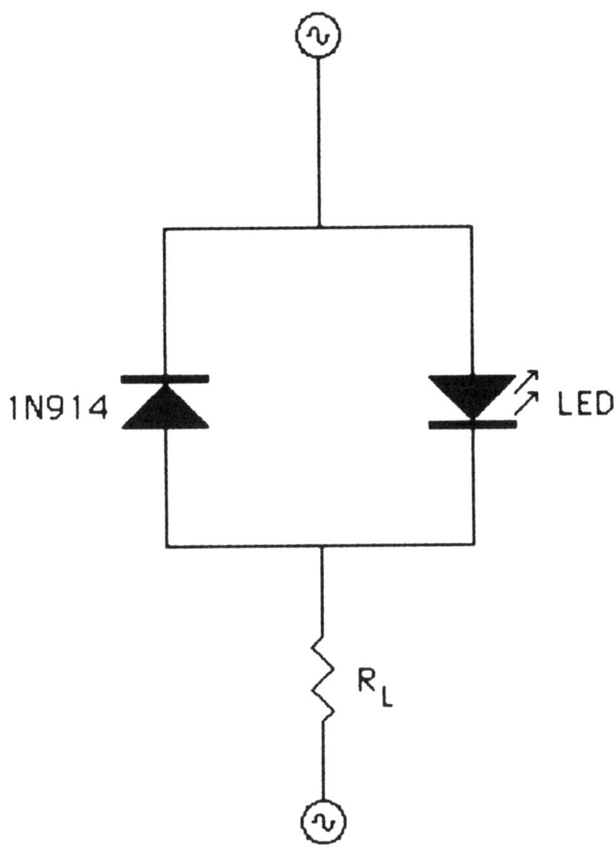

$$R_L = \frac{V_{pep} - V_f}{I_f}$$

Fig. 5-6. LED operation on ac.

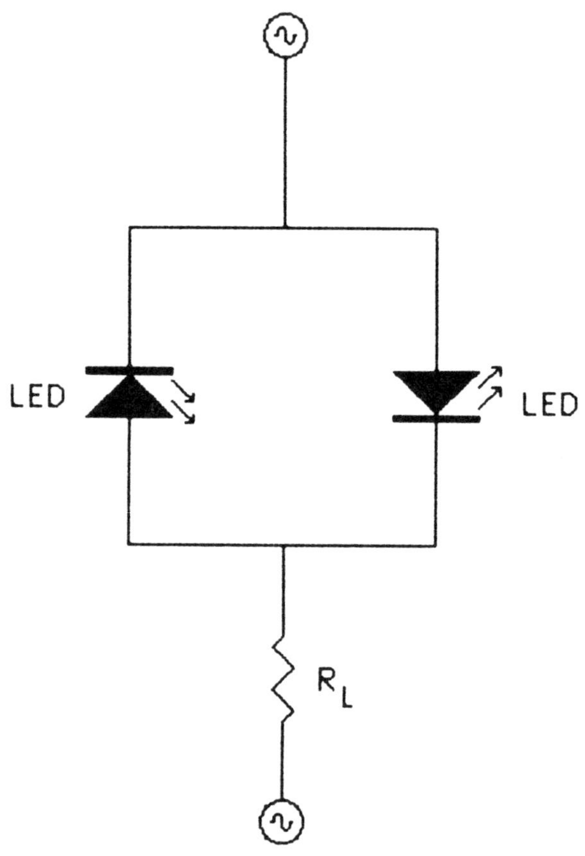

$$R_L = \frac{V_{pep} - V_f}{I_f}$$

the current limiting resistor. Use the peak voltage value of the ac waveform to ensure that the LED junction is not overdriven. Since the 60 cycle ac waveform is sinusoidal and relatively slow, use the dc current limit as a guide. 60 cycle sinusoidal power is too slow to be considered "pulse operation", which refers to operation at around 1 kHz. using a square wave.

In both ac and dc operation, the LED's junction dissipates about the same amount of power. The actual amount of power is a function of junction size and how hard the junction is being driven. For example, consider a red LED which has a forward voltage drop of 1.8 volts. This LED has a dc maximum forward current of 25 milliamperes. From the equation for power ($P = IE$), we can calculate that the junction is dissipating 45 milliwatts. The maximum power rating on this sample LED is listed as 135 milliwatts by the manufacturer. Notice that the supply voltage is not a factor in this calculation. If the entire circuit is considered, including the current limiting resistor, then power consumption is greater and the supply voltage must be considered. If you wish to power the LED in this example from a 12 Vdc supply, then Equation 5-2 gives a value of 408 Ω for the current limiting resistor. The equation for power ($P = I^2R$) shows the resistor's power dissipation to be 250 milliwatts and a ¼ watt resistor is required. Note that the resistor's consumption is about 5.5 times the energy dissipated by the actual LED junction. The entire LED circuit is consuming the sum of both the LED's and the resistor's power dissipation or 295 milliwatts.

When using voltages above 5 volts to power the LED, most of the energy is being consumed by the current limiting resistor. One way to minimize this consumption is to use very efficient LEDs which draw currents under 2 milliamperes for full illumination. Minimizing the current through the LED, and thereby through its current limiting resistor, assures low power consumption in the entire circuit. This is especially important when using voltages above 12 volts. If the example LED is powered by 48 volts dc, then the resistor would consume 1.15 watts or 25 times the power of the LED's junction. The LED, with its current limiter, is best suited and most efficient at voltages under 16 volts.

LEDs are semiconductor devices, and their power handling capabilities are effected by temperature. The LED junction's temperature is the sum of ambient temperature, and the temperature rise above ambient within the actual junction. Since it is difficult to measure the actual temperature of the junction, LEDs are commonly derated as a function of ambient temperature. Figure 5-7 illustrates

Fig. 5-7.

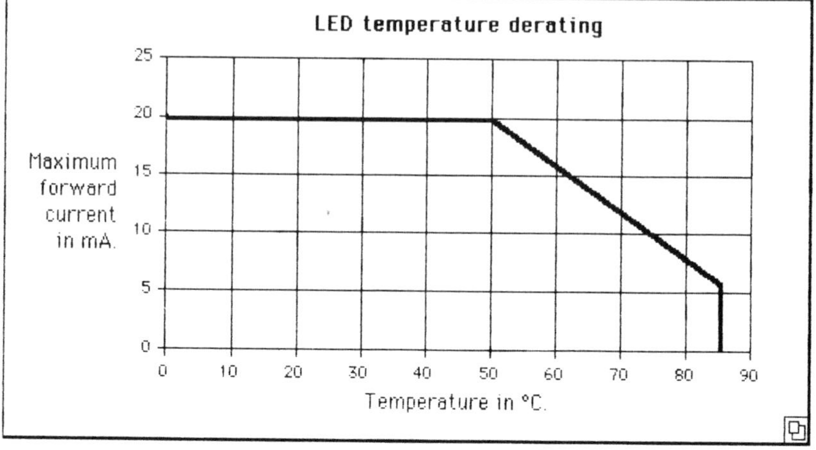

the relationship between maximum allowable junction current and ambient temperature for the typical red LED. Red and green LEDs are derated about 0.5 milliamperes for each centigrade degree above 50° C, or 1.8 milliwatts per centigrade degree above 25° C. Yellow LEDs are derated about 0.2 milliamperes for each centigrade degree above 50° C, or 1.6 milliwatts per centigrade degree above 50° C. Derating is necessary if an LED is to survive in hot environments. Heatsinking is a factor determining how well the LED is able to lose its heat to its surroundings. The cathode post is the primary path for heat transfer from the LED since it is physically attached to the chip. Leave cathode leads long for maximum heat dissipation.

When an LED is operated from a dc or low frequency (under 100 Hz) ac power source, junction temperature is a linear function of junction current. This junction temperature is called "average junction temperature". In order to squeeze more light out an LED with lower power consumption and temperature, the LED is often "pulsed." This means that the LED is fed pulsating, short duration, square-wave dc at frequencies over 1 kHz. In the pulsed case, it is the peak junction temperature that is the effective limit, not the average temperature.

Higher light output can be obtained from the LED by pulsing the current flowing through its junction. Such pulses are very short in duration (between 1 an 1,000 μ seconds) and of low duty cycle (between 0.1% and 25%). This technique allows the junction's current and peak light output to be increased by a factor of between 3 and 6 times. The value of the current limiting resistor is decreased to allow for the increased current. For example, the sample LED we discussed earlier was consuming some 25 milliamperes of current. In a pulsed mode, this same LED can be driven at 75 milliamperes, while maintaining acceptable peak junction temperature. Figure 5-8 shows the relationship between maximum tolerable peak current and pulse duration. The y axis of this graph is the ratio of the maximum operating peak current to the temperature derated maximum dc current ($I_{p\,max}/I_{dc\,max}$). The x axis of the graph is the duration of the pulse in microseconds (μs). Three curves are shown for refresh rates of 10 kHz, 3 kHz, and 1 kHz.

Circuits that pulse LEDs are simple to build, very effective, and more efficient than dc operation. Figure 5-9 illustrates a circuit to pulse an LED using a NE 555 integrated circuit timer. This circuit is designed to use 12 Vdc as a power input. Note that the value of the current limiting resistor R2 has been reduced to 120 Ω to allow for increased current flow through the LED junction. The potentiometer R1 allows the duty cycle of the LED pulse circuit to be varied from 4% to 96%. The circuit oscillates with a period of approximately 2,500 Hz. Varying the timing capacitor on the NE 555 timer will change the period of the waveform; the more capacitance, the slower the period of the oscillation. LEDs which are pulsed by circuits such as this appear to be brighter to the average observer. Due to the very high refresh rate, the display appears continuous.

Fig. 5-8.

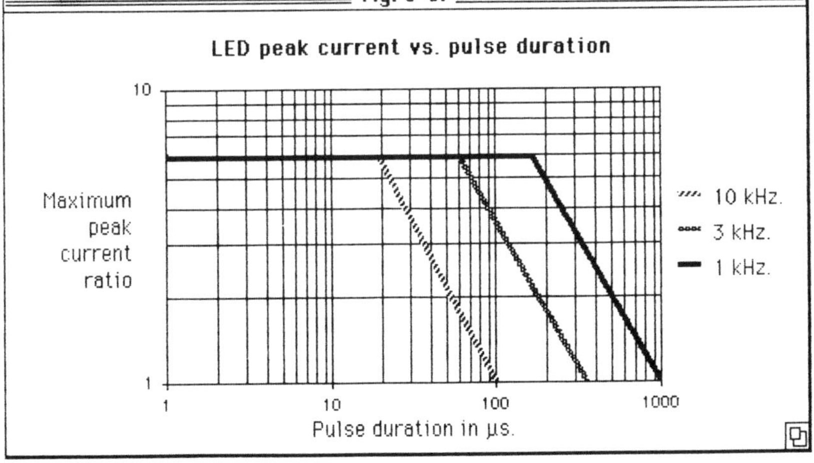

Fig. 5-9. NE 555 LED pulse circuit

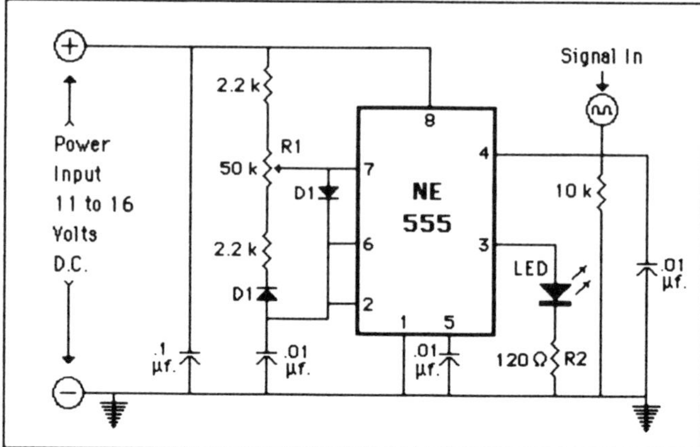

D1 - 1N914 diode

Use R1 to adjust duty cycle of LED indicator.

Signal In will turn on LED when it is over 3 volts d.c.

Approx. frequency of the pulse train is 2.5 kHz.

Adjust R2 to suit the particular LED in use.

Pulsing the LED is also more efficient, as more of the energy is dissipated in light and much less in the current limiting resistor. Since the advent of very low current LEDs (less than 2mA), the use of pulse circuitry is becoming much less common among commercial designers.

The amount of forward voltage loss (V_f) through an LED junction is a function of the amount of dc forward current (I_f) flowing through the junction. The LED shares this characteristic with all semiconductors. Figure 5-10 is a graph that shows this relationship for a common T-1¾ red LED which has a maximum average forward current rating of 25 mA. This graph is very useful in finding the forward voltage loss of diodes when they are pulsed and running high dc forward current.

Some types of LEDs have their current limiting resistor contained within their package. This simplifies the printed circuit board as no external current limiting resistor is required. These "integrated resistor LED lamps" are commonly available for use on either 5 or 12 Vdc. While the integrated resistor lamps do simplify construction, they produce more heat within their cases than regular LED lamps. The increased heat is due to the power being dissipated by the resistor within the LED's package. This increased heat leads to premature junction weakening or failure.

Light Output

LED junctions come in many different sizes. Some are small,

drawing low current and outputting less light than larger junctions which consume more current. To further complicate measuring and classifying light output, most LEDs have a lens cast into their cases. These lenses focus the light output in beams. The luminous intensity of LEDs are measured by the manufacturers within the len's focused output. These factors affect the scientific measurement of exactly how much light the junction is radiating, and where it is being radiated. Since the LED is viewed by the human eye, subjective factors such as color, and ambient light level must also be considered. Let's first examine the scientific measurement of the junction's light output.

LEDs can be had with visible light outputs from 0.1 to over 1,000 millicandles (mcd). The average for most bright T-1¾ LEDs is around 150 mcd. Considering how little power the LEDs consume, this is a very high light output. Remember, millicandle is a general scientific unit for light output, and does not consider the inherent biases of the human eye. For example, in low ambient lighting conditions, a T-1¾ LED outputting 150 mcd can be directly front viewed from about 40 feet.

The time averaged light output (I_v) of an LED is proportional to its forward current. The more current through the junction, the more light is radiated. Figure 5-11 illustrates the relationship between the relative luminous intensity (I_v) and the dc forward

Fig. 5-10.

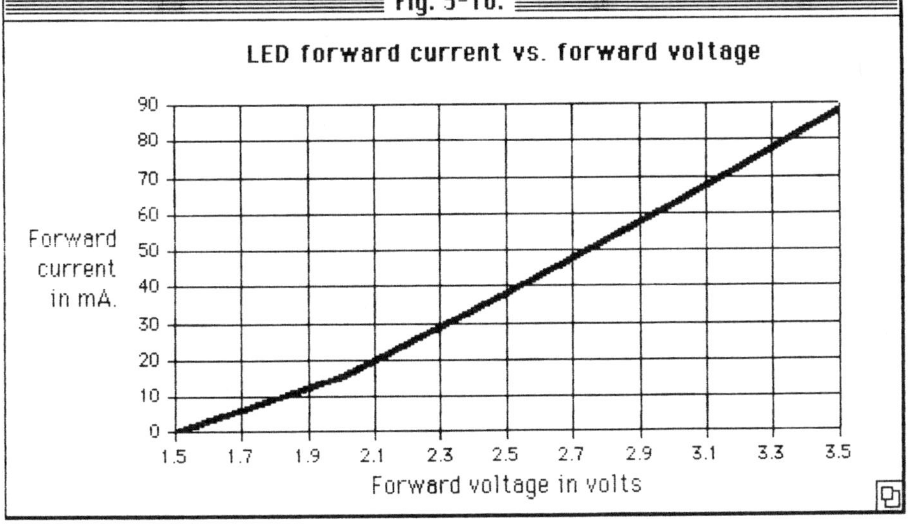

Fig. 5-11.

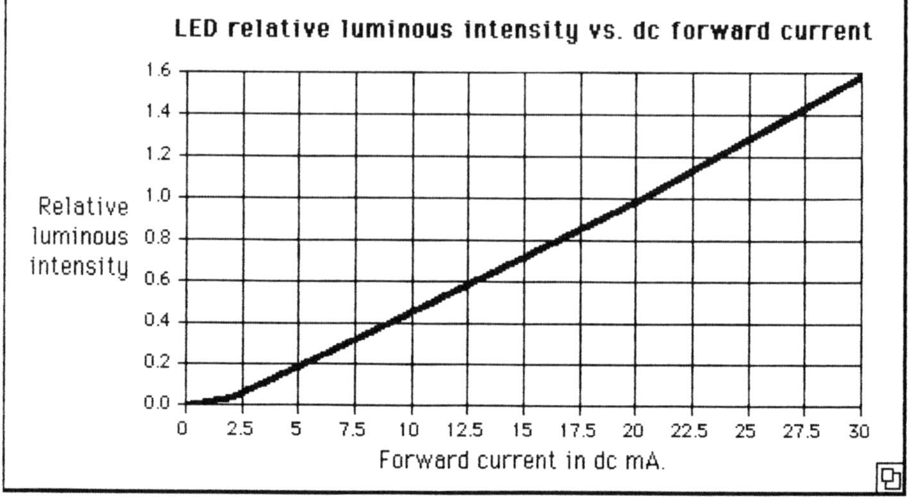

current of a typical red LED junction. The relative luminous intensity is normalized at the standard operating dc forward current of the diode, in this case 20 mA. This graph shows that the relationship between normalized light output and forward junction current is fairly linear.

The luminous intensity of the LED differs in pulsing conditions. Figure 5-12 illustrates the same diode as Figure 5-11 but the LED is being pulsed instead of being fed dc. The x-axis has been changed from dc current to peak current. The y-axis is relative luminous efficiency ($\eta_{I\,peak}$) which is the ratio of the luminous efficacy (η_v) at any current to the luminous efficacy (η_v) at a rated current. Luminous efficacy ($PI\eta_v$) is the ratio of visible light output to power consumption; its unit is lumens/watt. Figure 5-12 shows the relative efficiency of the LED's light conversion process for a sample LED rated at 20 mA. This graph may be used in dc service if the peak forward current is equal to the dc forward current ($I_{p\,max} = I_{dc\,max}$). Notice that the harder we drive the LED, the less efficient it becomes in converting electricity to visible light. Green LEDs are the most efficient ($\approx$600 lumens/watt), then yellow ($\approx$550 lumens/watt), then red ($\approx$150 lumens/watt); all ratings are at a forward current of 20 mA. This is due to the color response characteristics of the human eye, not to any inherent physical characteristics of LED junctions. Remember that the lumen is a unit which considers the eye's color biases.

Derating the LED's junction current for high ambient temperatures produces less light output from the device. This is a necessary evil when dealing with semiconductor devices such as LEDs. Heat is the Number One killer of semiconductors; LEDs are no exception. The LED junction becomes less efficient in converting electricity to light as its temperature rises. An LED will lose 25% of its light output between 22°C and 100°C. If you are using LEDs at temperatures above 50°C and are pushing the LED at near maximum dc forward current, then you must rerate the junction's current. Derating and temperature responses will reduce light output. The solution to high temperature operation is very simple. At high temperatures (over 50°C), use a larger (more output) LED and derate its current. This will result in the required amount of light output without damaging the LED's junction.

The viewing angle of an LED lamp greatly influences its relative light output to a user. This is discussed in the section titled Viewing Angle.

Resolution

The actual junction that produces light within the LED is very small, between 0.01 and 0.1 square mm. As such, the LED junction itself is capable of very high resolution. If only the junction itself is viewed from a distance of about a meter, it appears as a point source.

Fig. 5-12.

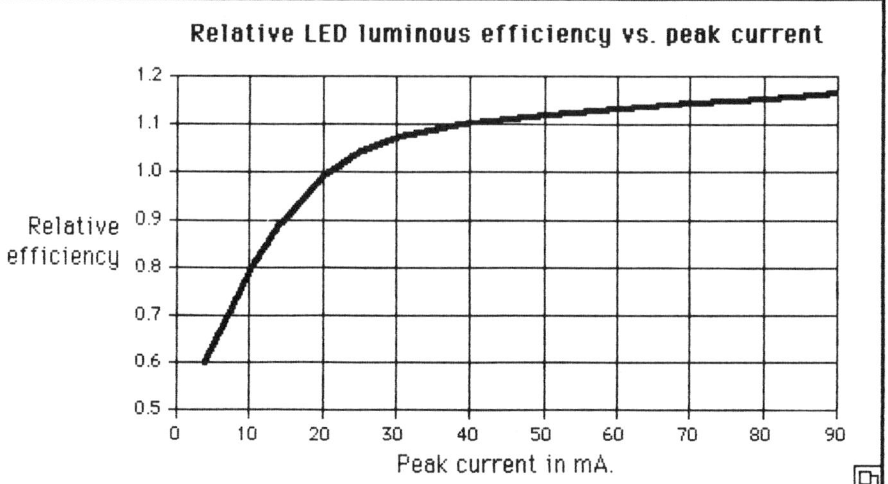

However, the effective resolution of LED lamps is limited by the size of their cases and lenses. If the effect of an LED lens is considered, then the illuminated area is much larger than the junction itself. This, added to the physical size of the epoxy case, makes the LED lamp a low resolution device at close ranges. This is in keeping with the LED lamp's primary function as a panel indicator.

LED junctions are also assembled into dot-matrix packages. Since there are many LED chips within the basic display package, these dot-matrix type displays have much greater effective resolution than the lamps. For example, alphanumeric displays contain as many as 35 LED junctions within an area of 0.52 square cm, or about 1.5 square mm per junction. This demonstrates that the low resolution of most LED displays is a function of choice and not necessity.

Speed

The LED junction is a very fast acting device. Red and yellow LED junctions are capable of response within 50 to 100 nanoseconds (ns) of power application. The green junctions are very much slower at 250 to 500 ns. In general, the LED is capable of turning on or off at about 10,000 times greater speed than the human eye can detect. LED junctions are capable of delivering a "flicker-free" display in either dc or pulsed operation.

Color

LEDs are commercially available in four basic colors—red, high efficiency red, yellow, and green. The elusive blue LED junction is now a reality, albeit a rare and very expensive (over $50 each) reality. These colors are a function of the materials making up the LED's junction. Equation 5-1 gives the basic relationship between the color of the light the LED radiates to its junctions energy band gap (chemical composition). This relationship is very discrete, it is not possible to combine a red junction with a yellow one and produce orange. The inherent color output of the junction is often slightly modified by using a dye mixed in the epoxy case. LEDs with dyed cases are said to be "tinted." Untinted cases are called "water clear."

The color of a LED's output peaks within a very narrow range of wavelengths. The wavelength of the majority of the LED's output is called the "dominant wavelength" (λ_p). This dominant wavelength occurs at the peak of the LED's light output. Figure 5-13 illustrates the relationship between a LED's relative light intensity

Fig. 5-13.

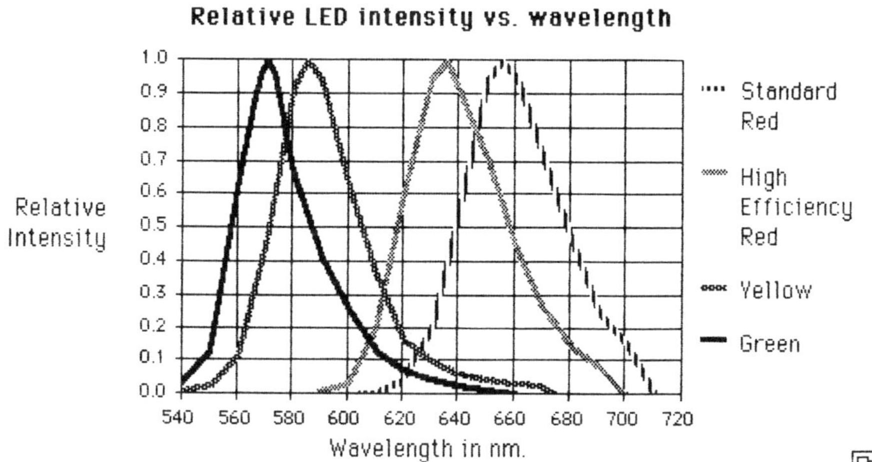

to the wavelength (color) of its output. The y-axis of this graph is normalized so that the amount of light output at the dominant wavelength is 1. The x-axis is the wavelength (color) of the LED's light output measured in nanometers (nm). There are four curves on the graph, one for each of the inherent LED colors. Note the extremely sharp rise and fall of these curves. The LED junction produces only very discrete wavelengths of light. The point on each curve where it crosses 0.5 on the y-axis defines the LED's "spectral line halfwidth" ($\Delta\lambda_{1/2}$). This spectral line halfwidth is very narrow for all LED junctions, less than 40 nm wide. Figure 5-13 illustrates the very monochromatic light output of LED junctions.

LED displays commonly have their light output filtered to increase their contrast with the world around them. The first criteria of any display device is readability. Use of the proper filter can increase the readability of any LED display. Ambient light level and color, and LED color are two factors affecting the choice of filter. There are filters for indoor applications, and those suited to outdoor (sunlight) applications. In addition, the filters are optimized for the wavelengths (colors) of the light they must pass. Figure 5-14 illustrates the usage of a filter on an LED display, and how it works.

In the following examples of filter application, there are three lighting conditions considered—low ambient, medium ambient, and high ambient lighting. In all cases, the filter will absorb some of the

Fig. 5-14. Using a filter to increase LED readability

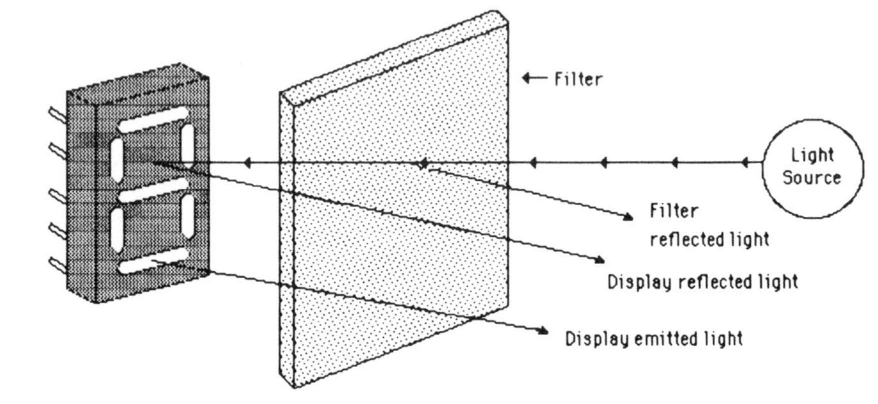

LED output and this light is lost. The amount of light passed by the filter within its spectral range is called "transmittance," and is expressed in percent. The loss within the filter is balanced by the better readability of the display caused by increasing its contrast to its environment.

Standard red LEDs have a dominant wavelength (λ_p) of around 655 nm. In low ambient light conditions, they are filtered using a long wavelength pass red filter with sharp rolloff in the 600 to 630 nm range. This filter absorbs the shorter green, yellow, and blue wavelengths of the ambient light and passes the longer wavelength red of the display. It transmits about 70% of the red LED's light output. This filter saves power by its high transmittance. In medium ambients, use the same filter but with a transmittance of 45%. In higher ambient lights, the standard red LED is filtered by a bronze or neutral density grey filter with a transmittance around 20%. Purple filters are also used on red LED displays under high ambient lights. Purple is a combination of red and blue, which is perceived by most people as a distinct color. The contrast between the purple filter and the red LED is very vivid and pleasing to most observers. This color contrast increases the red LED's visibility in high ambient light levels.

High efficiency red LED junctions have a dominant wavelength (λ_p) around 635 nm. The filter used for them in low ambient lighting levels is a long wavelength pass filter with a cutoff between 570 to

600 nm. The color of an HE red LED through such a filter is a deep reddish orange. Note the lower frequency of this filter's cutoff from the one used in the standard red LED. The LEDs have a very narrow spectral half line width, making it critical to choose the filter with the right wavelength cutoff. Once again, use a bronze/grey filter for medium or high ambient lighting conditions.

Yellow LEDs are a much greater challenge to filter than their red counterparts. This is due to the eye's increased sensitivity to the shorter wavelengths of visible light. In low ambient lighting, yellow LEDs are filtered by a band pass filter which is centered around the LED's λ_p of 583 nm. This filter passes about 30% to 40% of the light output of the yellow LED, and appears dark yellow or amber when viewed in sunlight. In higher ambient levels, use the bronze/grey filter with a transmittance of around 20%.

Green LEDs are the most difficult to filter, as the eye is very sensitive to their color. Green light is also very common in most ambient light situations. This makes it very difficult to filter out ambient lighting within their color range. The green LEDs have a dominant wavelength (λ_p) of around 565 nm. At low ambient levels, they are filtered by a band pass filter centered on their λ_p. Such filters have low transmittance, around 18% to 25%. Green LEDs are not recommended for use in medium or high ambient light environments. If they are to be used, then filter them with a grey filter with a transmittance around 18%. Even though most of the display's light output is absorbed by the filter, its contrast with the environment is greatly increased. The red LED is the best color to use in high ambient light levels.

If there is more than one color LED in a display, then use the neutral density grey filter. While this filter has nearly equal transmission of all wavelengths, it does increase the display's luminous contrast. This contrast is attained by attenuating the ambient light twice, once as it enters the filter and once as it is reflected off the display and leaves the filter, while the LED's output is only attenuated once. The transmittance of this grey filter is around 20%.

LED filters are most commonly made of plastic because it is easy to fabricate and inexpensive. The transmittance of plastic filters is a function of the dyes and their amount used in the filter's manufacture. It is not a function of the thickness of the filter. Glass is also used as a filter material. The glass filters have transmittance that is proportional to their thickness. The thicker the glass filter, the more light it will absorb. In general, the glass filters are more effective at their job than are the plastic filters. They're also very much more expensive, and subject to breakage.

Size

LED lamps are available in a wide variety of sizes, from subminiature to the jumbo T-1¾ case. The larger T-1¾ case is by far the most popular. This size (5 mm in diameter) best duplicates the function of the incandescent panel lamps that the LEDs are replacing. Smaller sized lamps are used as status indicators on printed circuit boards, and in areas where size and power consumption is a problem.

Figure 5-15 illustrates the T-1¾ (5mm) LED package, and gives its dimensions. Figure 5-16 does the same for the T-1¾ Low Profile package, and Figure 5-17 for the T-1 (3mm) package. All dimensions on these three illustrations are in millimeters, with the inch equivalents given in parentheses. Note that two numbers are given for each dimension. These represent the minimum and maximum allowable values. Figure 5-18 shows a typical subminiature LED package. These subminiature LED lamps are used as indicators on the actual printed circuit board, not on panels.

Element Thickness

The LED junction is very thin, less than .01 mm in thickness. Since the LED lamp is intended as a panel indicator, its case is very much thicker, up to 10 mm. The actual limiting factor of the thickness of an LED display is the interconnecting wiring which supplies power to each and every junction. This wiring occupies many times more space than the LED's actual junction.

Minimum and Maximum Display Size

The minimum size of an LED display is limited to about 1.5 square mm. If the wiring and case are considered, this dimension rises to about 5 square mm. The maximum size of an LED display is not limited. The technique in a large LED display is to assemble the display from many individual LED elements. Displays are manufactured using 256 LED junctions packed into a 96 mm square, these squares are stacked both vertically and horizontally to produce a display of unlimited size.

Fig. 5-15. T-1 3/4 LED lamp

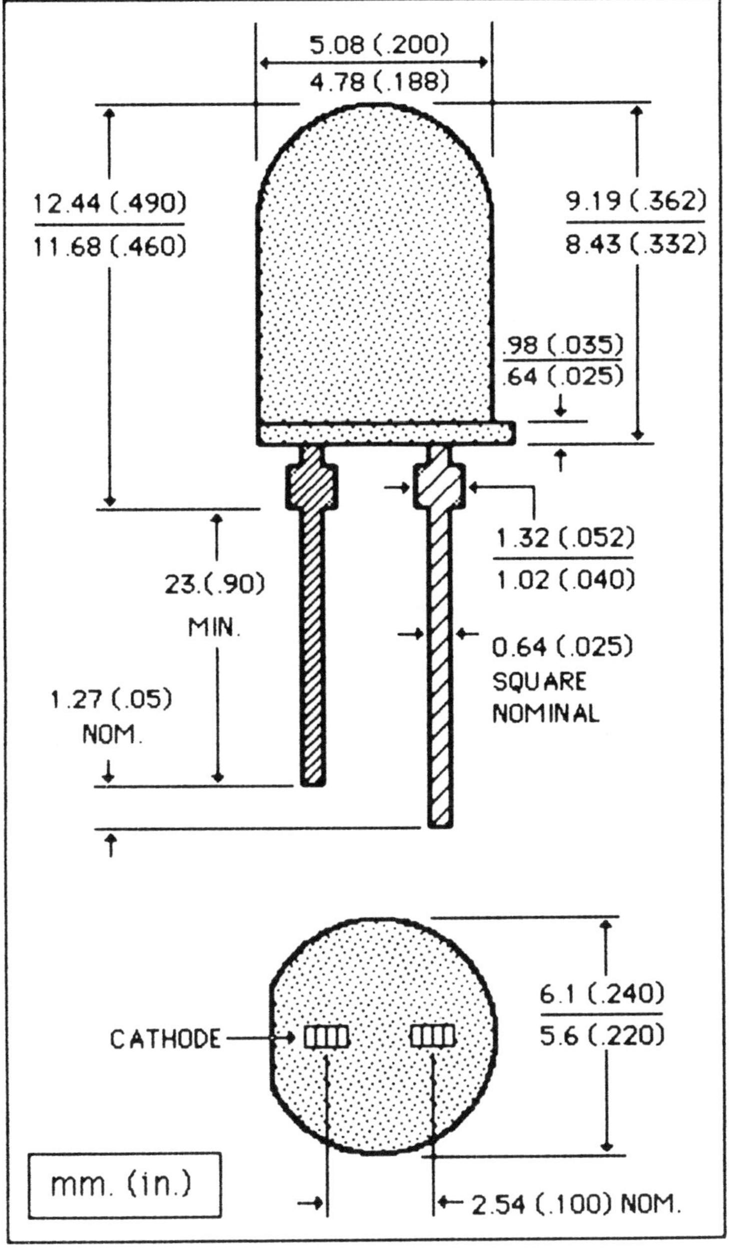

Fig. 5-16. T-1 3/4 Low Profile LED lamp

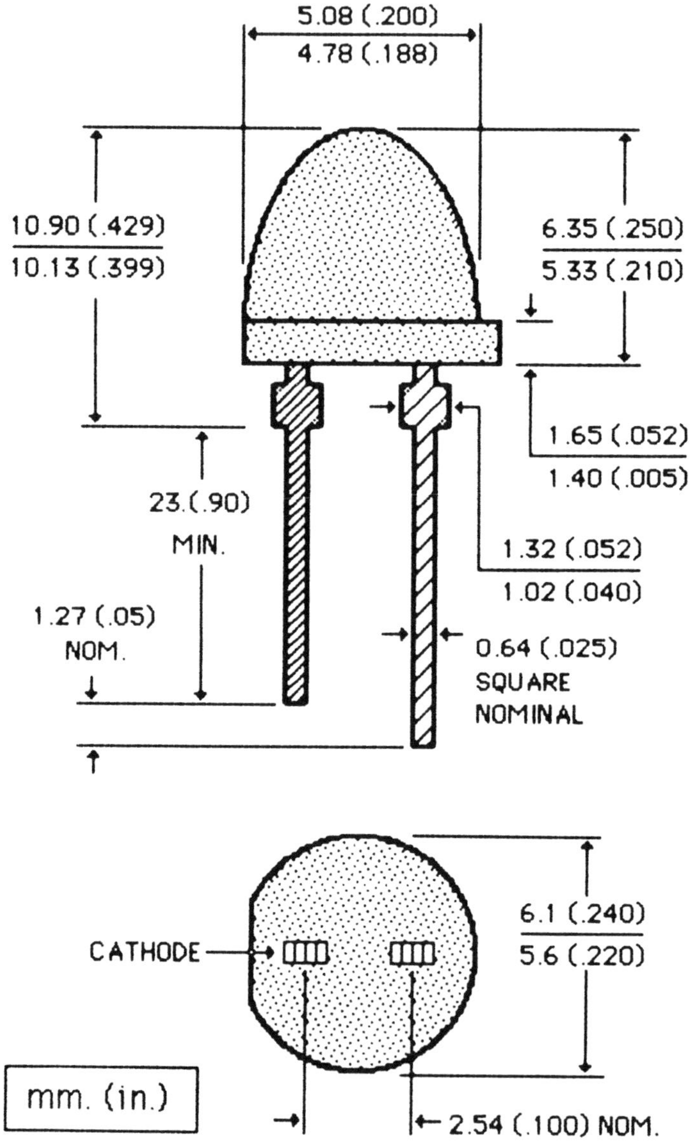

Fig. 5-17. T-1 LED lamp

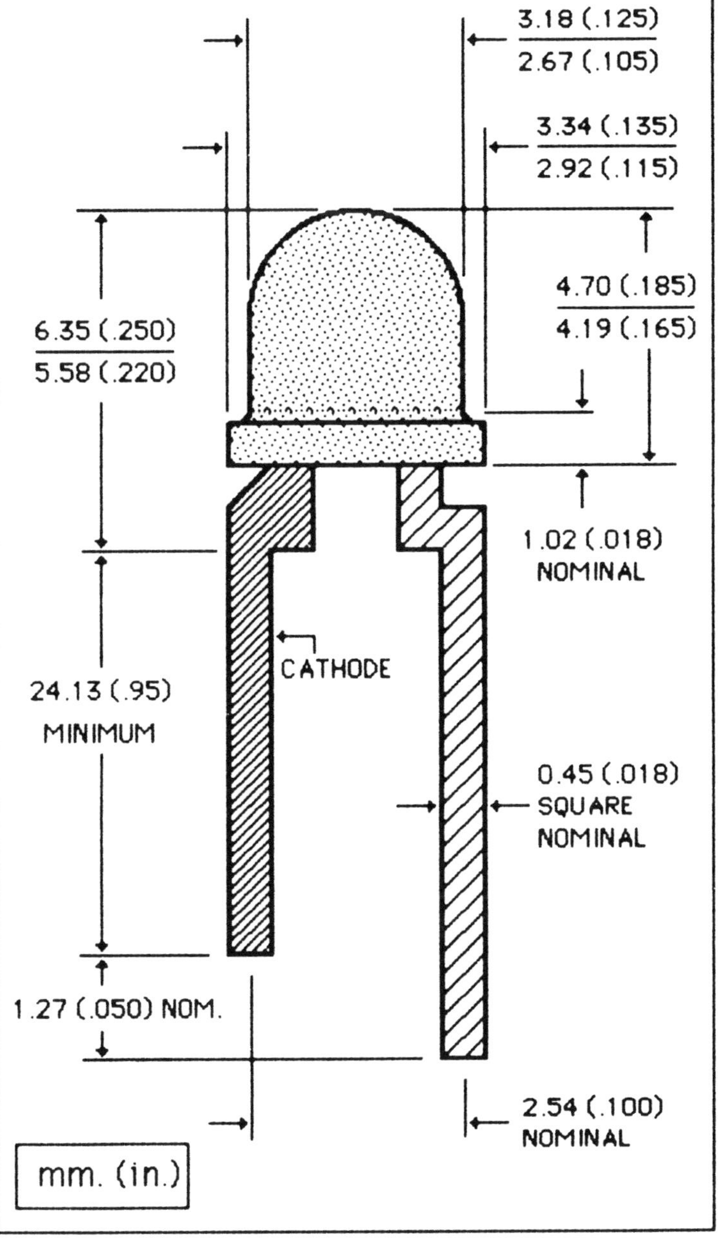

Fig. 5-18. Subminiature LED lamp

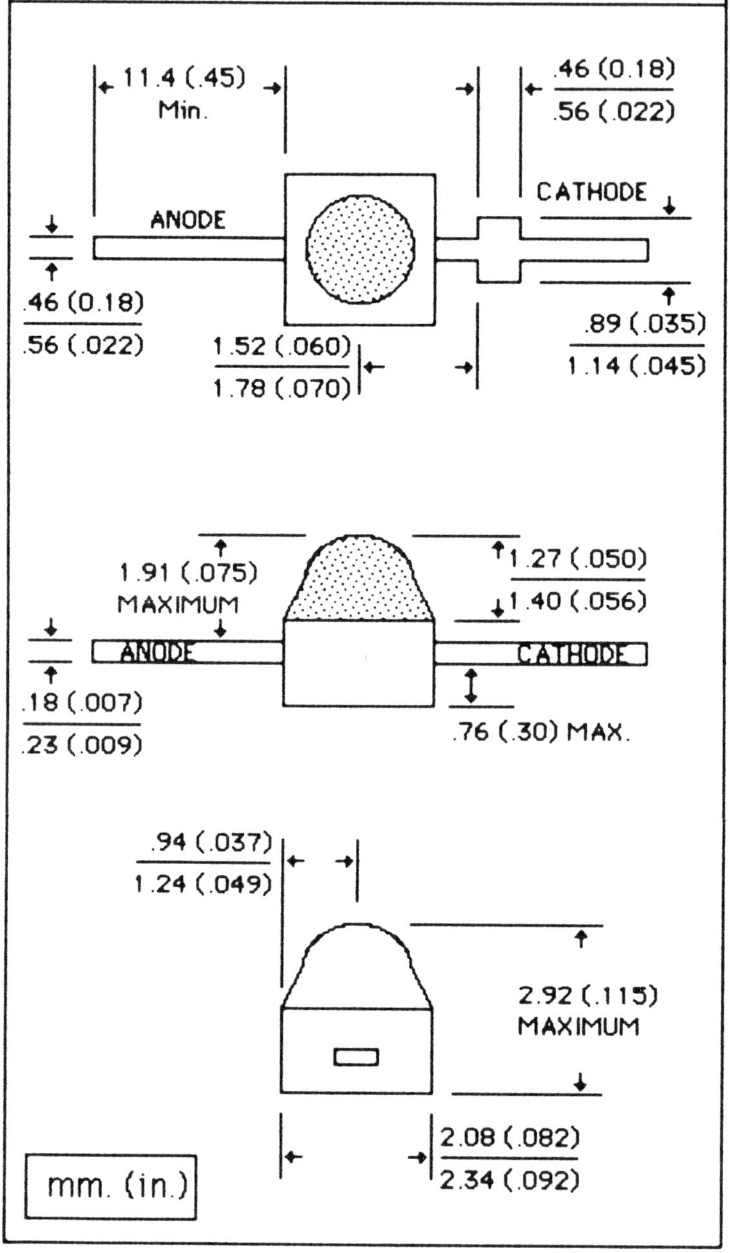

Operating Characteristics

These operating characteristics are specifically aimed at the LED junctions which are packaged in lamp cases. The information on the junctions, however, applies to all LEDs regardless of case style. Attention to details such as viewing angle can make the difference between a highly readable display and one which is hard to read.

Visual Angle

The spatial distribution of an LED lamp's light output is determined by the lens cast into its case. The junction itself radiates light in 360° in all planes, but this light is blocked to the rear by the junction's mounting structure. Since LEDs are viewed from the front, a reflector is used behind the junction to project more of the light out of the front of the case. The lens serves to focus this light into either narrow or wide beams. The types with narrow beams are commonly referred to as "direct view" and those with wider beam widths are called "illuminators." The illuminator LED lamps are used to light up legends printed on translucent plastic, from behind and some have very high (up to 1,000 mcd) light output.

The LED lens's spatial distribution is rated as the total viewing angle between half luminous intensity points, and is called "$2\theta_{1/2}$." It is the off axis angle at which the luminous intensity is half the axial luminous intensity, and its unit is degrees. The "$2\theta_{1/2}$" for LED lamps varies from 22° to 140°. Those with small $2\theta_{1/2}$ are more suited for viewing directly down their axis, while those with larger $2\theta_{1/2}$ spread their light out for wide angle viewing. Figure 5-19 illustrates the relative light intensity of several LED lamps in relation to the spatial distribution (viewing angle). Four LEDs are shown on this graph, having $2\theta_{1/2}$s of 24°, 45°, 75°, and 135°.

In the past, the LED lamps had their output focused into a narrow beam for direct viewing. This was due to the relatively small luminosity available from the older junctions. This narrow viewing angle was a problem in displays used in high ambient light. The only way to see if the LED was on or not was to get directly in front of it. LED luminous intensity in modern lamps is so high that there is a general trend of using the wider viewing angle devices in most panel indicator applications. Modern junctions put out so much light that it can be spread around without sacrificing readability.

Longevity

The LED junction has incredible longevity. Failure in an LED

Fig. 5-19.

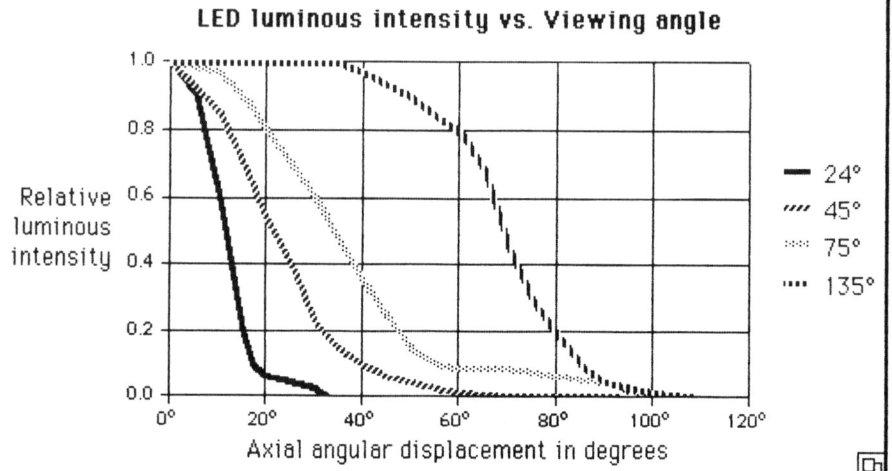

is defined as the inability to perform its intended function. There are two major areas of LED failure. These are catastrophic and parametric failures. Catastrophic failure is when the junction simply goes out and refuses to light. Parametric failure is when the LED still lights, but has its luminance drastically reduced.

Catastrophic failure is usually caused by operation of the LED junction beyond its specifications. Causes of catastrophic failure are too much junction current, too high operating temperature, and too much reverse voltage. These failures are due to incorrect use of the LED within a circuit. Mechanical failures such as defective wire bonds, and junctions lifting from their mounts are examples of failures caused by stressing the LED too greatly.

An LED is much more likely to fail within the first 500 hours of operation than it is for the next 50,000 hours of operation. This "infant mortality" is caused by junctions that were not perfectly made during the manufacturing process. Failure after the "burn-in" period is very much lower. Adult mortality after the burn-in period is truly random, and cannot be alleviated by testing or further burning in of the LEDs.

One way of measuring failure is defined as the "mean time between failures per unit time of operation," and is abbreviated MTBF. MTBF is the reciprocal of failure rate and is expressed in hours. The MTBF for LEDs is a function of the ambient temperature. The higher the junction's temperature, the more likely it is to fail. This is true with all semiconductors, not just LEDs. LEDs operated at room temperature or below (<30° C) have a MTBF of 11,201,000 hours. This is a very long time, over 1,000 years. Obviously, this figure is based on mathematical extrapolation of actual test data, since there are not LEDs which are older than 30 years. If the ambient temperature is above 90° C, then the MTBF drops to 806,000 hours, or around 90 years. The LED is an incredibly long lived display device. Compare this to the MTBFs of 1,000 hours for the incandescent bulbs that the LEDs are replacing.

LED reliability should never be a problem once the infant mortality period is past. The LED will survive if the circuit it is used in does not exceed any of the junction's maximum ratings. This is up to the circuit designer. The LED manufacturer has done his part.

Over a period of time, the LED junction begins to put out less light than when it was new. This intensity degradation is the long term wearout mechanism in LED displays. Parametric failure is defined as an intensity reduction of 50% over a period of time. This 50% reduction in light output is easily visible to most human eyes. Figure 5-20 is a graph which shows the normalized intensity degradation as a function of time in hours. Four curves are pictured for different current levels through the junction. Note that, the higher the current, the more quickly intensity degradation takes place. The logarithmic x-axis represents time, and implies that the rate of intensity degradation decreases as the operating time of the junction

Fig. 5-20.

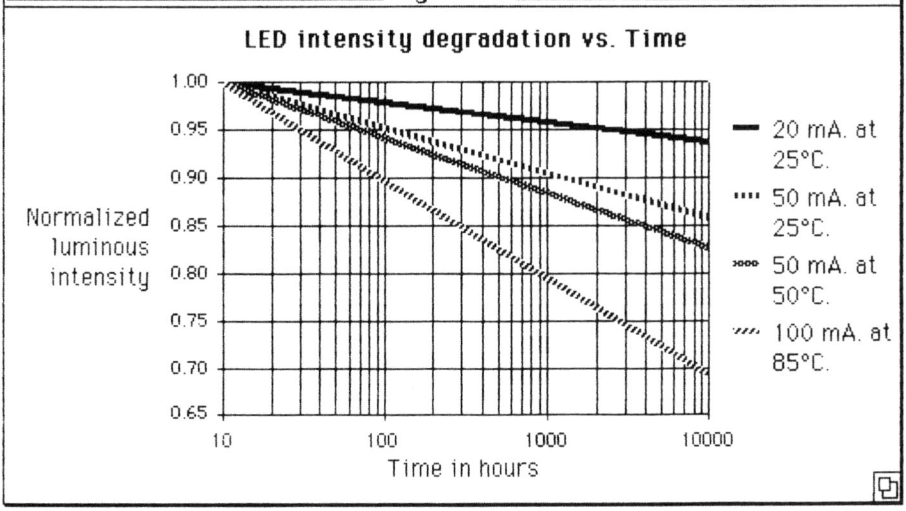

increases. Junction temperature is another factor which increases intensity degradation. Note that the higher current curves on Fig-5-20 are also higher junction temperature curves. An interesting sidelight on LED intensity degradation is that yellow LEDs age about twice as fast as their red or green counterparts.

When more than one LED junction is placed in a single case, the MTBF of the entire display is reduced. Consider a 7-segment LED numerical display. This display actually contains 8 LED junctions, and if any one of these junctions fails then the entire display is useless. As such, the MTBF for a 7-segment display is ⅛ that of a single LED lamp. The more complex the display, the more likely it is that it will fail over a period of time.

Operating Temperature Range

The temperature at which an LED junction is operated is one factor that affects all of the display's parameters. Increased temperature increases junction losses and decreases both luminous output and longevity. High rates of thermal cycling can actually cause mechanical failures within the junction's wire and die connections.

Red and yellow LED lamps are rated to operate within the temperature range between −55° C to 100° C. Green LED lamps are more sensitive to temperature and are operated between −20° C to 100° C.

One of the best methods of keeping the LED's junction at close to ambient temperature is to heatsink the cathode lead of the lamp. The cathode lead is physically attached to the actual LED chip and is capable of transferring heat from it. Simply leave the cathode lead long, or solder it to a PC board pad with enough mass to act as a heatsink.

LED Lamp Mounting Hardware

Mounting LED lamps can be as simple as drilling the appropriately sized hole in the panel, inserting the lamp, and cementing it into place with epoxy. If the hole is properly sized, LEDs can also be press fit into place. However, for those desiring a more finished appearance for their devices, a variety of mounting hardware is available. Some of these devices incorporate the electrical connections for the LED, while others simply hold the LED in place on the panel. Figure 5-21 illustrates several different styles of LED mounting hardware. Some types of LED sockets are push in, with no soldering required. If you are soldering LEDs, be sure to heatsink

Fig. 5-21. LED mounting hardware

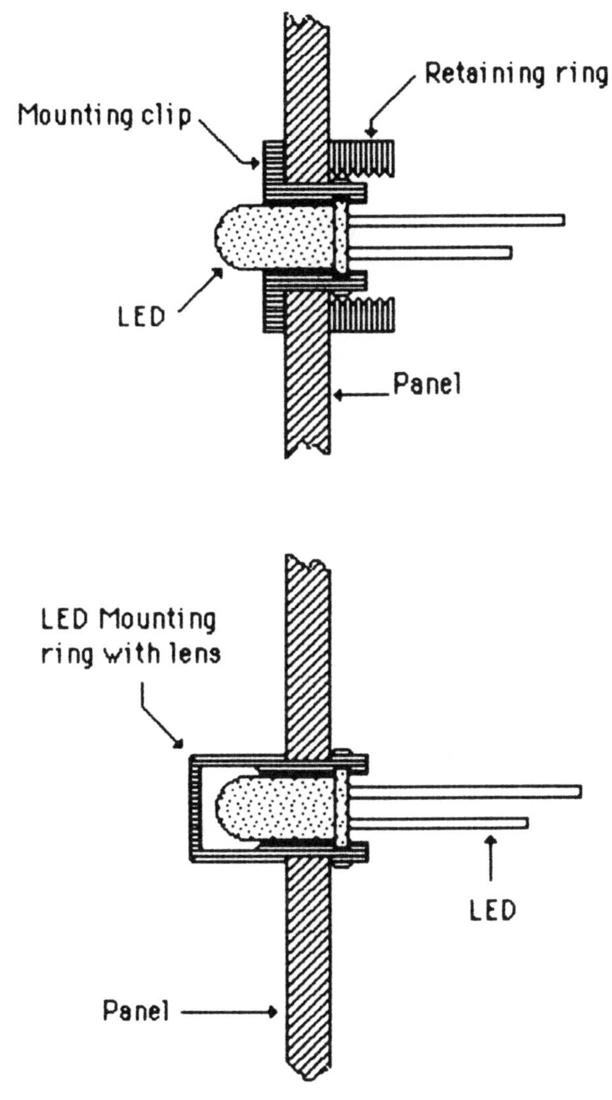

them in the same manner as any semiconductor during the soldering process.

Some LED mounting sockets contain a built-in current limiting resistor. This can simplify wiring and reduce the amount of PC board space required for a device. If these types of sockets are used, be sure that the resistor is the right value for the particular LED in use. Resistor values commonly found in this type of socket vary from 120 Ω to 2.2 kΩ, making them suitable for supply voltages between 5 and 24 volts dc.

It has been demonstrated that bare LEDs on the front of a panel represent a danger to sensitive ICs within the device. These bare LEDs are often located near a switch. When a person operates the switch, static discharge may occur through the LED and its wiring that may damage sensitive CMOS or MOS integrated circuits. A person walking across a carpeted floor can pick up a static electric charge in excess of 7 kV. This may be discharged through the LED lens and into the device's logic. The use of special insulating mounts is recommended for projects containing sensitive ICs. These insulating mounts more than double the amount of static electricity required to arc and cause damage.

LED Lamp Sample Applications

One of the most common uses for the LED lamp is as a panel indicator. An example of this is an LED mounted into a panel that indicates the status of a switch (or relay, transistor, etc.). If the switch is closed (conducting), then the LED lamp is lit. If the switch is open (not conducting), then the LED lamp is not lit. Figure 5-22 illustrates such a circuit. The input power in this example is 12 Vdc from a battery. A quick reference to the manufacturer's specifications for the LED shows that its maximum forward current is 25 mA, while its forward voltage loss is 1.8 volts. Equation 5-2 (in the case of a switch or relay) tells us that a 408 Ω resistor will do the job. Notice that the resistor used in the circuit is 1,000 Ω, or about twice what the equation recommends. This doubling of the current resistor is done for two reasons. First, it is desirable to conserve power, and secondly, the maximum luminous output of the LED is greater than is necessary. In addition, this indicator is designed for a battery system, and the system voltage may be as high as 16 volts during charging conditions. If the 408 Ω resistor is used, and the system voltage were to rise to 16 volts, then the LED junction would pass 35 mA of current. This would exceed the manufacturer's rating.

Fig. 5-22. An LED switch indicator

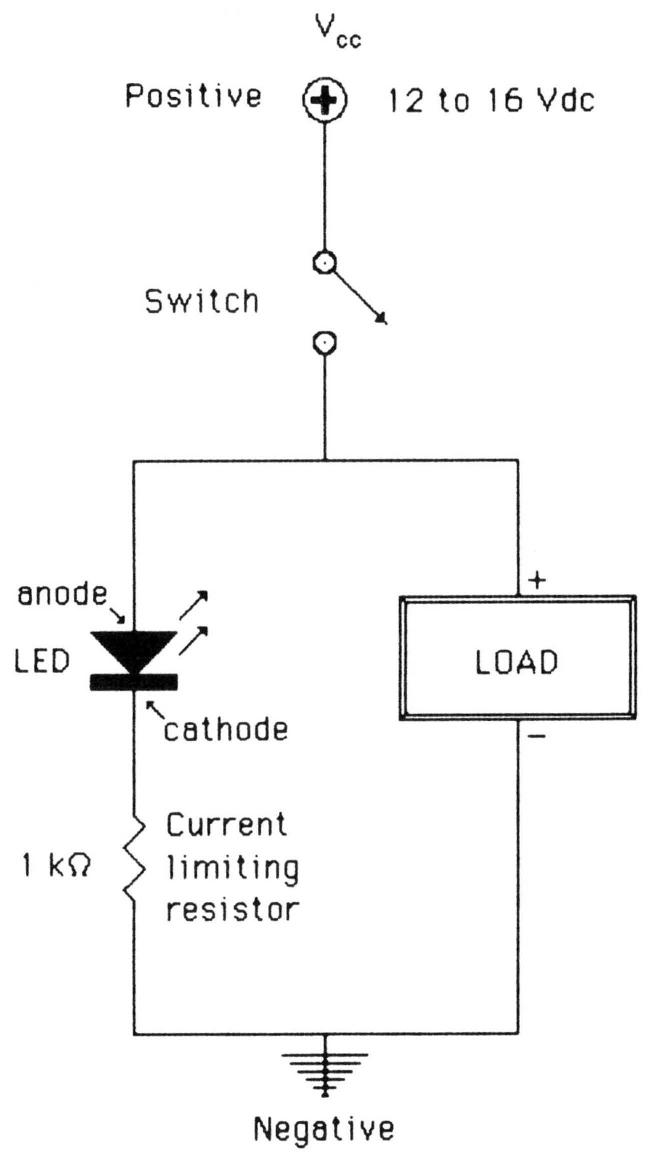

In most applications, LEDs can be used just as effectively by reducing the forward dc current to about half of the manufacturer's maximum specifications. Modern junctions are so bright that the loss of luminous output is usually acceptable. Derating in this fashion reduces power consumption, and ensures longevity. This situation is analogous to the concept that just because your car will go 120 mph, it doesn't mean it is prudent to operate it there. Semiconductors will last much longer if they are not continually pushed to their limits.

In the next sample application, sound information is converted into light, see Fig. 5-23. This application uses a single LM 324 Quad Op amp as a series of active bandpass filters, and to drive three strings of LED lamps. The LM 324 has four op amps on its chip and we are using three. The circuit takes its audio input from a stereo, a radio, or even a preamplified microphone. The version in the illustration is configured for audio input from an 8Ω source. The bandpass filters only amplify the portion of the audio signal that is within their frequency range. In this example, red LEDs are chosen to respond to the lower portion of the audio spectrum, and are filtered by a low pass filter. The yellow LEDs are sensitive to the midrange, and are fed with a band pass filter. The green LEDs are keyed to the higher audio frequencies, and are supplied by a high pass filter. The intensity of the sound is tracked by the LEDs. The louder the sound, the brighter the LEDs become. This sample

Fig. 5-23. LED sound into light display

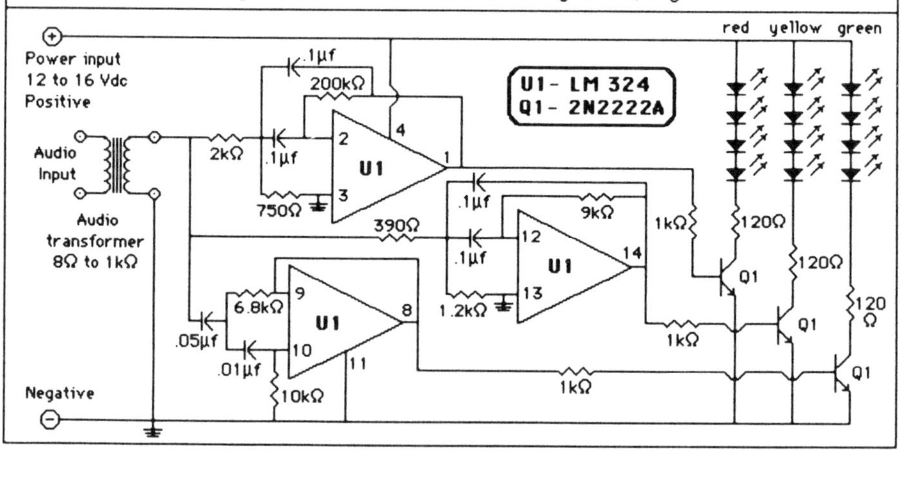

application is an entertainment type display, and it is designed to give as much light output as possible. Note that several LEDs are used in series strings. This technique gives more light for the amount of power consumed by reducing the energy dissipated in the current limiting resistor. Consider four red LEDs all placed in series, as in Fig. 5-23. The voltage drop over these four red junctions is the sum of their individual drops or about 8 volts. If we specify the voltage input to the circuit at 12 volts, the LED current at 25 mA and the driver transistor loss at 1 volt, then Equation 5-3 gives a value around 120Ω for the current limiting resistor. The amount of power dissipated in the resistor is 75 mW, while the power dissipated in the LED string is 200 mW. This represents more efficient conversion of the power into light. This technique of stacking LEDs is useful whenever more light is desired and the supply voltage is over 6 volts dc.

LED lamps are not limited to the classic round shape of the T-1¾ or T-1 packages. LEDs are now made in a variety of shapes to suit any project. The preceeding sample application is a good place to try out some of these highly varied new packages. Figure 5-24 illustrates just some of these newer lamp packages. The shaded areas in the illustration are the areas which are illuminated by the LED junctions. All the types shown have lead centers 0.1 inches apart, so they are stackable in standard integrated circuit spacing. The rectangular shapes are much easier to stack neatly than are the round.

LED Lamp Cost

LED lamps are highly mass produced semiconductor devices, and their low price represents this fact. LED lamps cost between $0.10 and $0.50 each in single units. Considering the LED's long life, this is an outstanding value.

SEVEN SEGMENT LED DISPLAYS

The seven segment LED is used for displaying numbers. That's all it does. It doesn't display text, pictures, or anything but numbers. They are very commonly used in televisions, radios, calculators, clocks, cash registers, scales, test equipment, and home appliances. The colors available in seven segment displays are the same as those in LED lamps. The seven segment display uses eight LED junctions arranged for a single purpose—displaying numbers.

Fig. 5-24. New LED packages

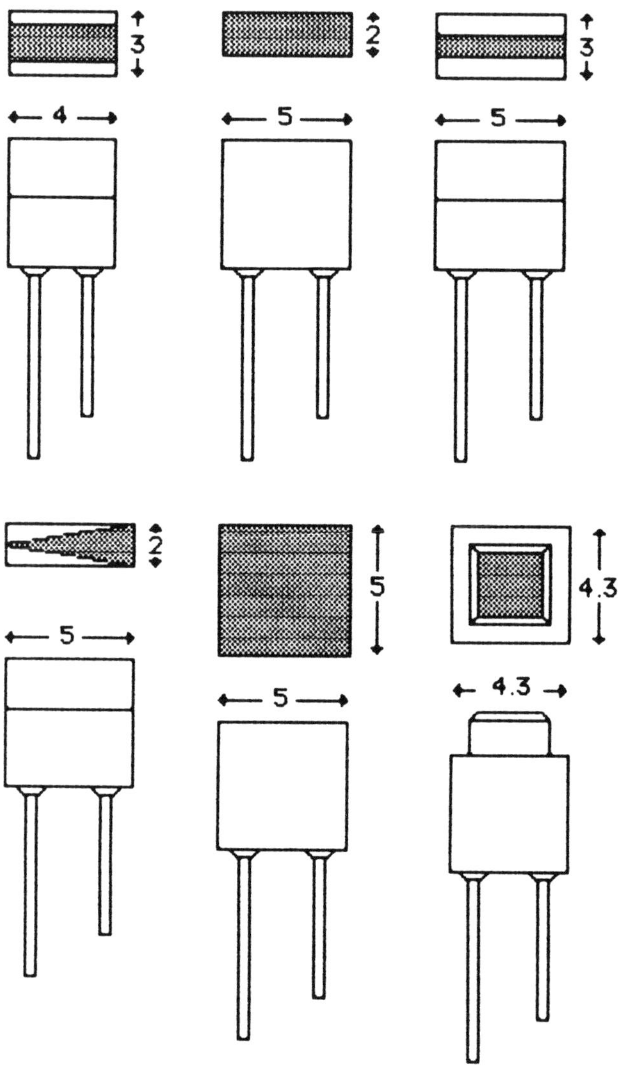

All dimensions are in millimeters (mm.)

How It Works

The seven segment display actually contains eight LED junctions assembled in a single epoxy package. Figure 5-25 illustrates the physical configuration of the LED junctions that make up the seven segment display. Each of these junctions has a light diffusing cavity, which stretches and reflects the LED's light into a rectangular shape. The light diffusing cavities are filled with diffusant loaded epoxy to provide even illumination at the segments.

The actual LED junctions in the seven segment display are supported within the device by a lead frame. The lead frame also acts as a current conductor for each junction. Cone shaped cavities are cast into the epoxy case above each junction. The epoxy case is colored to provide maximum contrast with the illuminated segments of the display.

Seven segment LED displays come in a variety of sizes, from 0.3 to 1.8 inches tall. The larger the package, the more readable

Fig.5-25. LED seven segment display

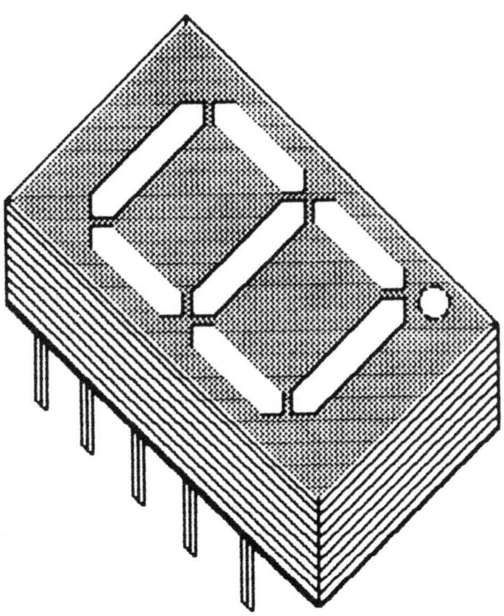

Fig. 5-26. Physical dimensions for a 0.362 seven segment display

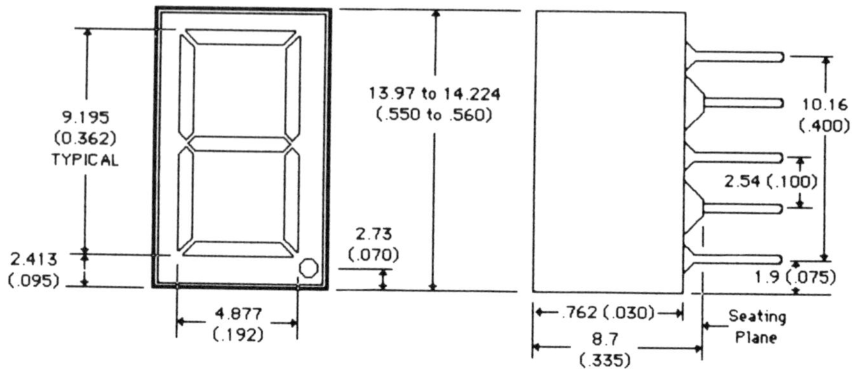

it is at longer distances. the 0.3 inch display is visible from 5 meters, while the 0.56 inch display can be seen from about 7.5 meters. The 0.8 inch display is visible from 9 meters. The size to use is determined by the distance between the viewer and the display. Figure 5-26 shows the physical dimensions of a 0.362 tall seven segment display. Note that the display size dimension refers to the active area of the display and not its case dimensions. The pin out dimensions on most seven segment displays are the standard 0.1 inch integrated circuit spacing. This makes the seven segment display compatible with standard IC sockets.

Types of Seven Segment Displays

Seven segment displays are available in two basic configurations—common anode and common cathode. This refers to which of the leads of the LED junctions are held in common. In the common anode type, all the anodes of all the junctions in the display are directly wired to each other within the display case. The exact opposite is true for the common cathode displays, which have all the LED's cathodes wired together. This common wiring of one side of the LEDs is done to save space and reduce cost by eliminating redundant wiring within the display. The practice also saves space and connections on the printed circuit board where the display is finally soldered.

Each segment of the display is referred to by a letter. The decimal point is called "DP". This standard allows us to relate the individual segments of the display with their respective pins on the bottom of the package. Figure 5-27 shows the reference letter for each segment and the decimal point. This system of reference is standard for all seven segment LED displays, both common anode and common cathode.

The decision of which type of seven-segment display to use is based on several factors. First is the state of the logic that is to switch on the display. Common anode displays are turned on by a low (L) logic state, while common cathode displays are turned on by high (H) logic states. Common anode displays are easier to implement and to drive, especially when high brightness is required. Common cathode displays are easier to multiplex when several digits are required.

Fig. 5-27. Segment reference letters

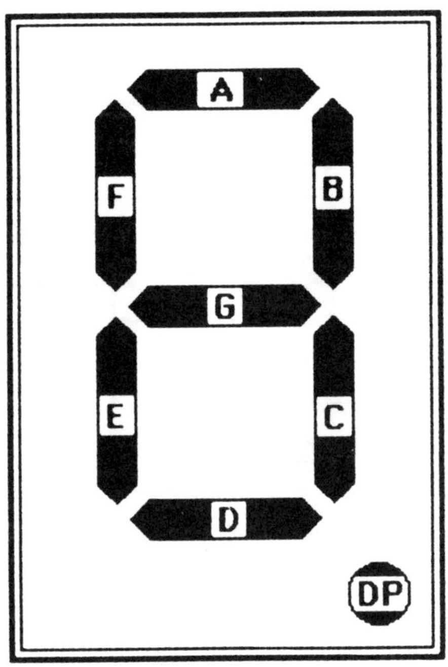

Common Anode

Figure 5-28 illustrates the internal electrical construction of a common anode seven segment display. Note that all the anodes of all eight LED junctions are directly wired to pin 1 of the display. The pin out configuration of LED seven segment display varies from manufacturer to manufacturer, so be sure to check the specifications for the particular display that you re using. In Fig. 5-28, each of the diodes (segments) within the display is coded with its identifying letter.

Common anode seven segment displays require their own special type of decoder/driver chip. This chip interfaces between the data to be displayed and the actual seven segment LED display. One example of such a decoder/driver chip for common anode displays

Fig. 5-28. Schematic of a seven segment common anode display

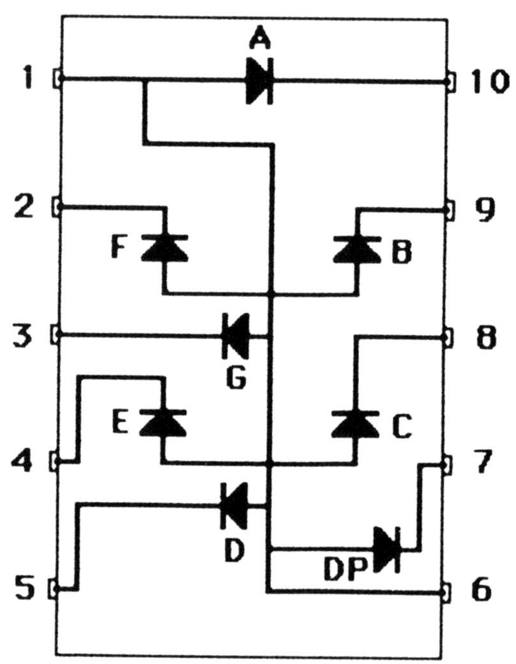

Fig. 5-29. Common anode seven segment display driver (7447)

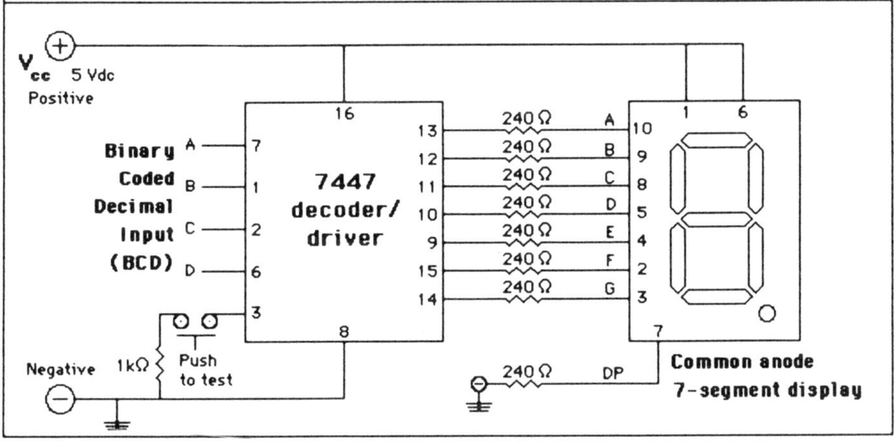

is the 7447. The 7447 takes binary coded decimal (BCD) data from a counter or other source, and drives the appropriate segments on the display to form decimal numbers. It is a 16 pin DIP with open-collector outputs; it can sink up to 40 mA of current for each segment. Its maximum operating voltage is 15 Vdc, with a power consumption maximum of 320 mW. The 7447 requires the addition of external resistors to limit the current through the display's junctions. The use of external current limiting removes most of the heat from the driver chip, and insures greater longevity. Figure 5-29 illustrates the use of the 7447 decoder/driver chip with a common anode seven segment display. The LED segments have their current limited to 12.5 mA each by 240 Ω resistors. The 7447 also features a lamp test mode, by grounding pin 3 of the IC all segments of the display will light. Leading and/or trailing zeros are automatically suppressed by the chip. If the BCD input is zero (LLLL) and pin 5 is also low, then the display is blanked.

Common Cathode

The electrical configuration of the common cathode seven segment display is illustrated in Fig. 5-30. In this case, all the cathodes of all the LEDs are wired in common to pin 1 of the display. Again, not all pin outs are standardized, so be sure to check your particular display. The situation is the exact opposite of the common anode display.

Fig. 5-30. Schematic of a common cathode seven segment LED display

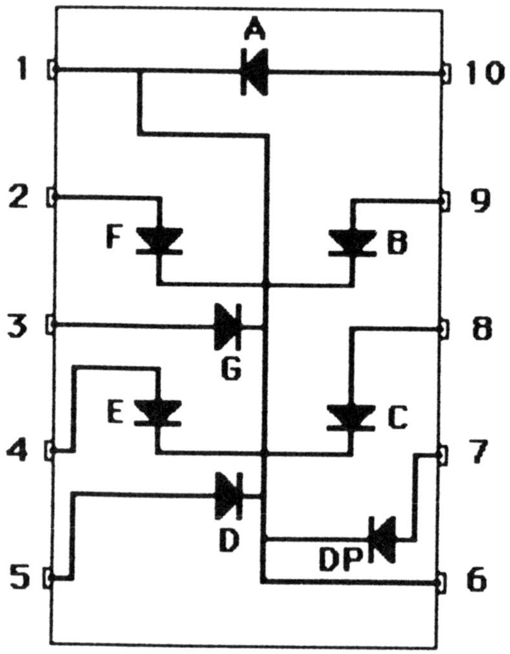

The common cathode seven segment display can be driven by the Fairchild 9368 decoder/driver chip, among others. The 9368 decoder/driver chip uses open emitter output stages which are capable of delivering a constant 15 mA of current to each display segment. Due to the internal current limitation, it is not necessary to add external current limiting resistors to the display. This convenience is had at the expense of limiting the display's brightness, and increased heating within the decoder/driver chip. The 9368 offers zero blanking modes as does its common anode cousin the 7447. Figure 5-31 illustrates a block diagram of the 9368 in action with a common cathode display.

Single Digit

Single digit seven segment displays can be combined to form

larger displays. The problem with this technique is that it is difficult to physically align all the digits evenly. Even small misalignments are very noticeable to the eye. It is also difficult to obtain individual seven segment displays that match each other exactly in luminousity and color. For displaying more than one digit, it is better to use a multiple digit display rather than a collection of single digit packages. In some special cases, this may not be possible. For example, a display may require a "1" always displayed in its most significant digit, and a plus or minus sign may be required to precede this "1." If single digit packages are used, then adding a special seven segment display which displays a "1" with the appropriate sign is not difficult. Figure 5-32 illustrates a "seven segment" LED display package which displays only "±1."

The modern trend in applying seven segment displays is to use multiple digit packages for any display that requires more than one digit. This is due to the simplicity of installing the multiple digit

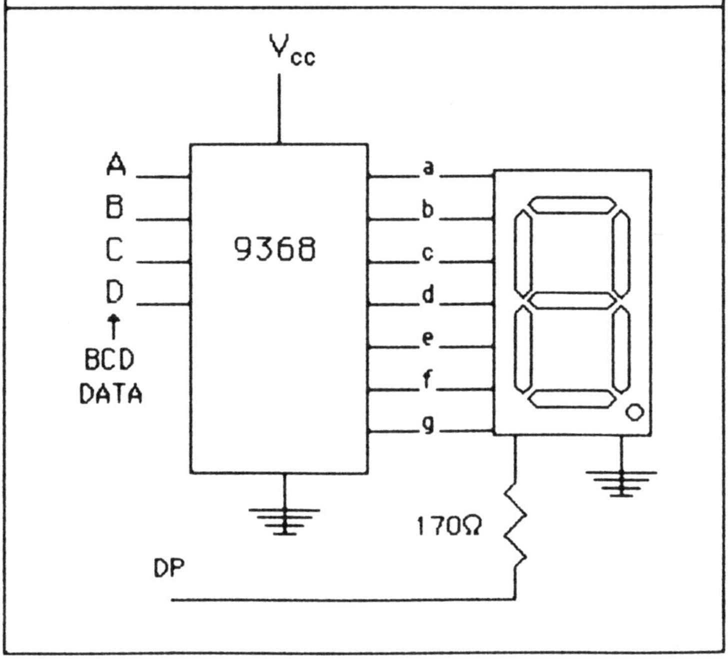

Fig. 5-31. Common cathode seven segment display & decoder/driver

Fig. 5-32. ± 1 LED display

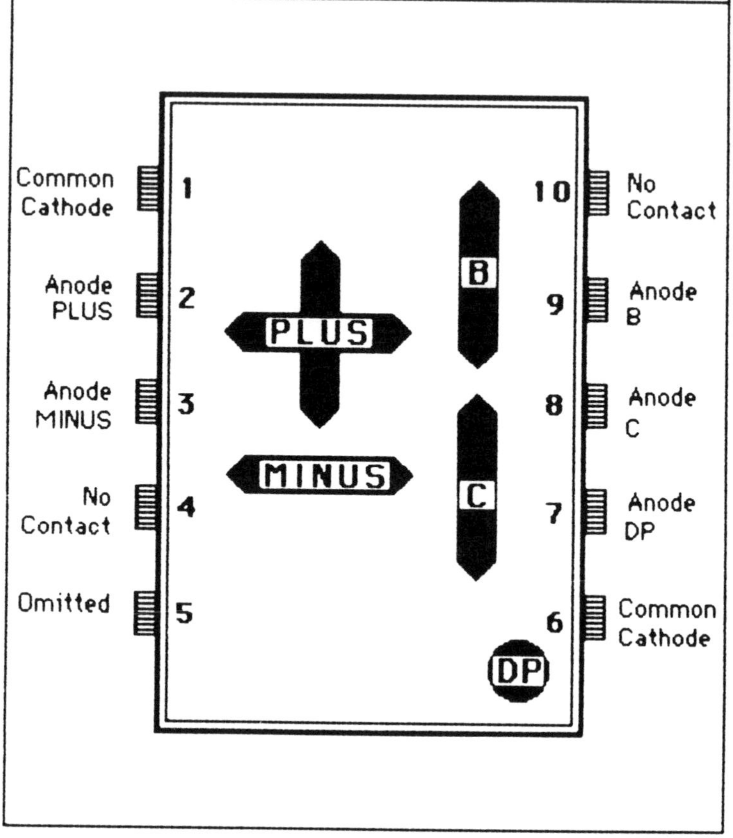

displays, and their inherently perfect alignment and optical characteristics.

Multiple Digit

The majority of seven segment displays used commercially are single packages containing two, four, or more single digits. These multiple digit packages may be either common anode or common cathode. Figure 5-33 illustrates a two digit package which is configured for direct drive. Direct drive means that each segment (LED junction) of each digit has one individual connection which is external to the package. Anodes or cathodes may be held in common, but each diode in the package has one separate line to the outside world. Direct drive LEDs may be driven by standard decoder/driver chips in exactly the same manner as single digit packages.

When the number of digits gets to four, within the display the situation becomes too complex for direct drive. There are simply too many connections to place on the outside of the package. The four digit display is usually "multiplexed". This means that the connections external to the package are held in common by the digits; each LED within the package does not have its own current path to the outside world. Multiplexing is "time-sharing" of the current paths external to the display and the decoder/driver hardware. The technique of multiplexing allows the actual number of connections to the display chip to be held to a minimum, thus simplifying assembly and lowering cost. Figure 5-34 illustrates a four digit display that is intended for multiplex service. Note that the display shown in Fig. 5-34 only uses 12 lines to drive all four digits (35 segments), while the direct drive display in Fig. 5-33 uses 16 lines to drive 2 digits (14 segments). The advantages of multiplexing the lines in large seven segment displays is obvious.

In order to drive a multiplexed, multiple digit display, it is necessary to use specialized decoder/driver ICs designed for the purpose. The multiplex circuit connects all the like segments of each digit in parallel. This forms a matrix of seven segments by N (the number of digits) digits. In actual operation, the decoder/driver logic selects the appropriate segments for each digit in turn. Each digit is illuminated one after another very rapidly, i.e., the display digits

Fig. 5-33 Two digit, seven segment, direct drive LED display

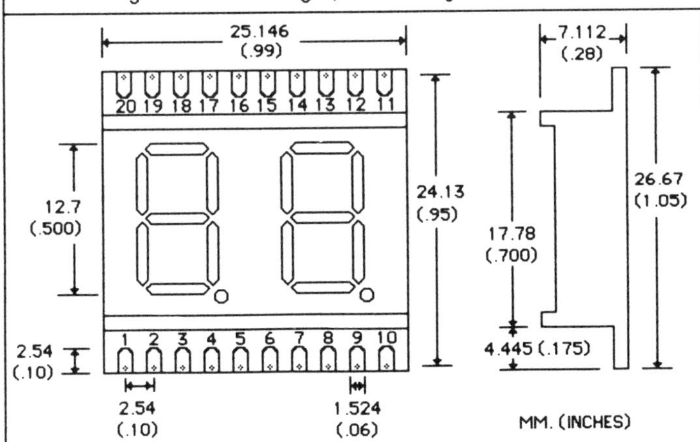

Pin	Function
1	Digit 1 E segment
2	Not used
3	Digit 1 D segment
4	Digit 1 DP segment
5	Digit 1 C segment
6	Digit 2 G segment
7	Digit 2 E segment
8	Digit 2 D segment
9	Digit 2 DP segment
10	Digit 2 C segment
11	Digit 1&2 Common
12	Digit 2 B segment
13	Digit 2 A segment
14	Digit 2 F segment
15	Digit 1 B segment
16	Digit 1 A segment
17	Not used
18	Digit 1 F segment
19	not used
20	Digit 1 G segment

Fig. 5-34. Four digit multiplexed, seven segment, LED display

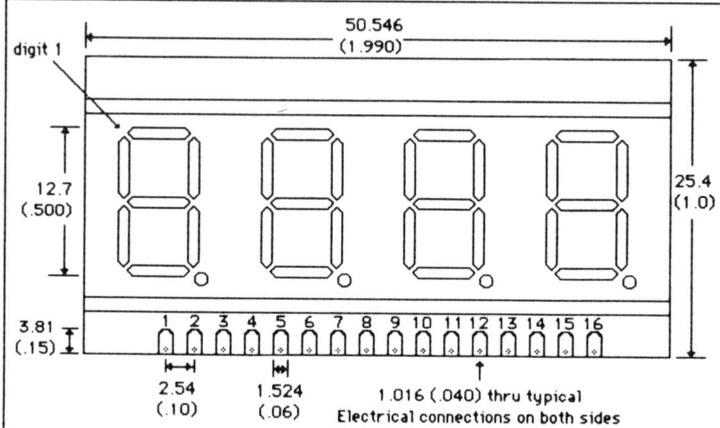

Pin	Connection
1	A segments
2	No connnection
3	D segments
4	Digit 1 common
5	No connection
6	No connection
7	Digit 2 common
8	C segments
9	No contact
10	Digit 3 common
11	B segments
12	F segments
13	E segments
14	Digit 4 common
15	DP segments
16	G segments

MM. (INCHES)

are sequentially strobed. The rate of the strobing is so rapid (over 100 Hz per digit), that the display appears continuous to the eye. Figure 5-35 illustrates a block diagram of a multiplexed five digit, seven segment, common cathode LED display. Note the usage of a clock, divide by five counter, and other multiplexing hardware. The BCD to seven-segment decoder, the seven segment driver, and the current limiting resistors are shared in common by all the digits in the display. The parts count on such a display is far less than that required for a direct drive display of the same number of digits.

Fig. 5-35. Multiplexed, five digit, seven segment, LED display

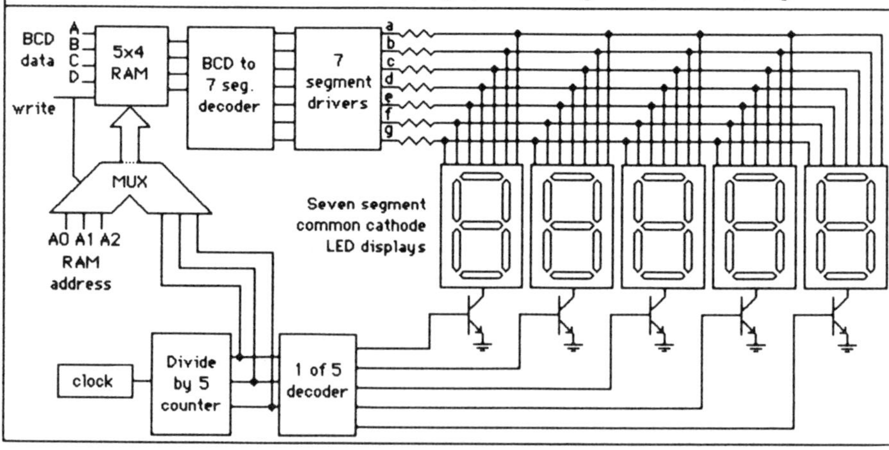

Multiplexing LED seven segment displays requires special attention to the current limiting resistors used for the display segments. Each segment within the display can be characterized by the schematic shown in Fig. 5-36. Note that there are now two transistors which must be conducting for any single segment within the display to light. One transistor junction is for the segment driver and another is for the digit driver. The losses in the extra transistor junction must be allowed for when calculating the value of the current limiting resistor. The value of an individual resistor may be specified by the following:

$$R_L = \frac{VCC - V_{ce(seg)} - V_f - V_{ce(dig)}}{I_f} \qquad \textbf{Equation 5-4}$$

R_L = amount of resistance expressed in ohms (Ω).
VCC = supply voltage expressed in volts (Vdc).
V_f = LED segment forward voltage drop expressed in volts (Vdc).
$V_{ce(seg)}$ = saturated forward voltage drop of the segment driver, expressed in volts at I_{peak}.
$V_{ce(dig)}$ = saturated forward voltage drop of the digit driver, expressed in volts at ($I_{peak} \times 8$).
I_f = LED segment forward current, expressed in amperes (A).

Note that this equation uses the I_{peak} (peak current) to rate the voltage losses within the segment and digit drivers. This value assumes that all the segments within a single digit are lit. It is eight times the current drawn by a single segment. Voltage losses within the segment driver are rated as if all segments within a single digit are lit. The digit driver and its associated transistor are rated at eight times this current because they must pass the combined current from all the segments within a single digit.

Advantages

The seven segment display has much to offer if you are going to display numbers. It is highly readable, capable of being run at logic voltage levels without complex circuitry, and inexpensive. It is also a small consumer of power. It is highly night visible as it provides its own illumination. It is available in a large range of colors and sizes. Seven segment displays can be stacked to display very large numbers. There is no limit to the size of the number to be displayed.

Fig. 5-36. Single segment LED multiplex circuit

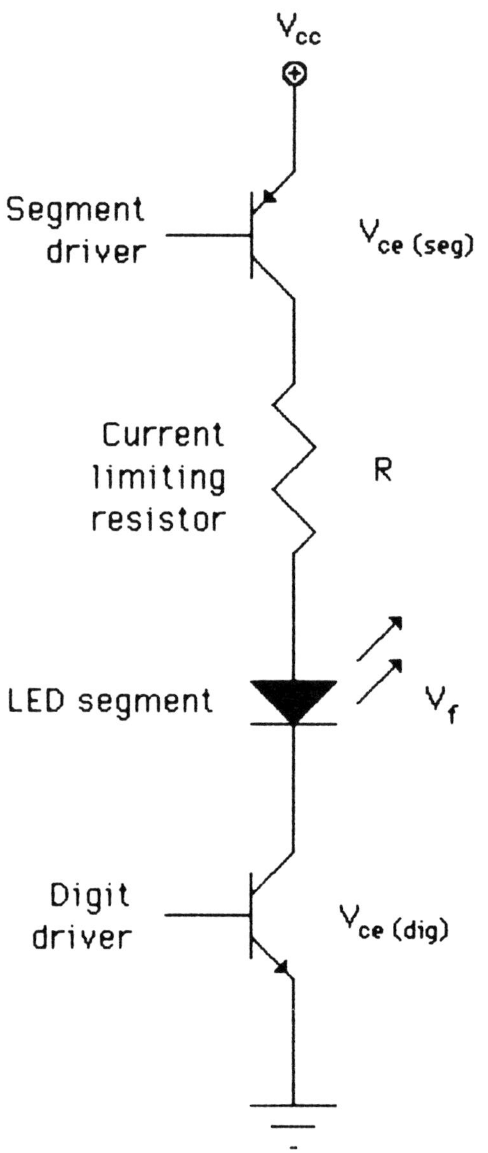

The decoder/driver IC logic needed to implement the seven segment display is very commonly available, simple to use, reliable, and inexpensive. Table 5-2 lists some of the BCD to seven segment decoder/driver chips and their characteristics. The column "Output Structure" refers to the type of element within the IC that is used to actually drive the seven segment display. The column "Active State" refers to the output state of the decoder/driver when the IC is powering the display to illumination. Low active states are used to drive common anode displays, while high is used to drive common cathode displays. The manufacturers shown on this table are only a partial list of suppliers of these chips.

Disadvantages

The biggest disadvantage of the seven segment LED display is vastly reduced readability in high ambient light situations. This is shared by all displays that use LED junctions. They are hard to see when directly illuminated by sunlight or bright lights. Usage of the proper filter can increase readability many times in these brightly lit situations.

The seven segment LED can only display numbers. This is hardly a disadvantage, since numbers are all it is designed to display. However, other types of LED displays are capable of showing not only numbers, but alphabetical characters and even graphics. If there is anything but numbers to display, the dot-matrix or sixteen segment type of LED display is superior to the seven-segment type.

Table 5-2. BCD to Seven-Segment LED Decoder/Drivers.

IC number	Manufacturer	Output structure	Output current	Active state	Features
74LS47	T1, Fairchild, National	Open collector	24 mA	Low	Auto zero-blanking, lamp test
74LS48	T1, Fairchild, National	2 K pull-up	6 mA	High	Auto zero-blanking, lamp test
74LS49	T1, National	Open collector	8 mA	High	Auto zero-blanking, lamp test
8T04	Signetics	Open collector	40 mA	Low	Auto zero-blanking, lamp test
8T06	Signetics	Open collector	40 mA	High	Auto zero-blanking, lamp test
9368	Fairchild	Open emitter	– 19 mA	High	Constant current, latch
9370	Fairchild	Open collector	40 mA	Low	Latch, auto zero-blanking
9384	Fairchild	Current mirror	15 mA	Low	Constant current, latch
DS8669	National	Open collector	25 mA	Low	2 digits (14 outputs)
MC14511	Motorola	Npn bipolar emitter	– 25 mA	High	Latch, lamp test, blanking input
MC14547	Motorola	Npn bipolar emitter	– 65 mA	High	Latch, blanking input

Sample Applications

The following sample applications provide a set of building blocks that can be used in a variety of circuits. The idea is useful sub-assemblies, i.e., counters, voltmeters, etc. that can be used to construct other specific projects. The circuits shown here use off-the-shelf ICs to produce a number of basic devices using seven segment displays for readouts. The actual finished projects using these sub-assemblies are only limited by your imagination and ingenuity. For example, a voltmeter building block may readout voltage, or wind speed if measuring the output of an anemometer motor, or temperature if measuring the voltage drop across a silicon diode temperature circuit, and so on . . .

Universal Counter

This circuit is a universal counter sub-assembly using the ICM7226B counter/display driver made by Intersil. This IC contains a high frequency oscillator, a decade time base counter, an eight decade data counter with latches, a seven segment decoder, a digit multiplexer, and eight segment-digit drivers (seven for the number and one for the decimal point). This IC is capable of driving an eight digit, multiplexed, seven segment, LED display directly. No current limiting resistors are required. This IC is an LSI powerhouse and is very inexpensive at the retail price of about $40. An absolute minimum of external components are required to complete a working 10 MHz universal counter.

This universal counter can function as a frequency counter, period counter, frequency ratio counter (fA/fB), time interval counter, or a totalizing counter. It uses a 10 MHz crystal for its internal time base, or if desired an external timebase. Typical crystal parameters are C_L = 22 picofarads, and R_s = 35 Ω. An external time base can be used at pin 33 of the ICM7226B.

In this sample application, the display used has two 5082-7414 Hewlett Packard LED seven segment displays. Each 5082-7414 contains four digits. Both the display and the counter chip are designed for multiplex service. The 5082-7414 Hewlett Packard display requires very little power to operate, less than 5 mA per segment, making it perfect for portable, battery operated equipment. Figure 5-37 illustrates the schematic for the universal counter. Table 5-3 gives the truth table for the two switches used to set the universal counter's functions and ranges. This counter can be used with a 10× prescaler; this extends its input to 100 MHz.

Fig. 5-37. 10 MHz universal counter

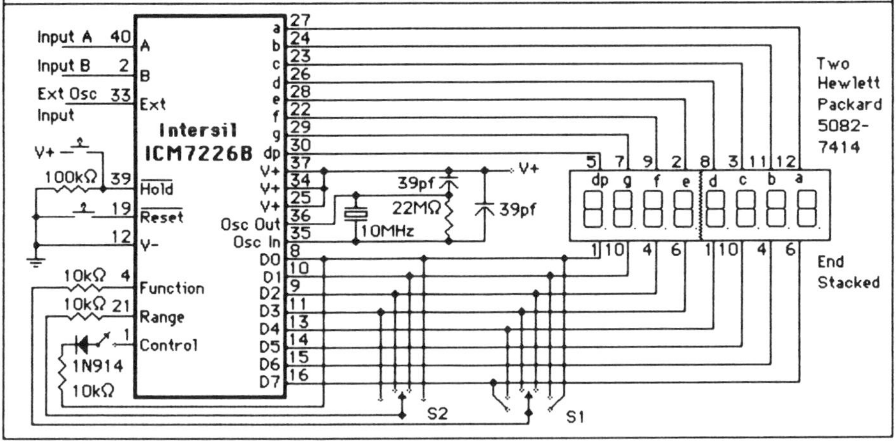

3-½ Digit Voltmeter

This digital voltmeter uses the ICL7107 integrated circuit made by Intersil. This CMOS IC contains the entire analog to digital converter, seven segment decoders, display drivers, a reference voltage, and a clock. Excluding the IC and the displays, only seven

Table 5-3. Switch Table for the Universal Counter.

Switch number	Function	Switch position
Function Input Switch 1 S1	Frequency	D0
	Period	D7
	Frequency ratio	D1
	Time interval	D4
	Oscillator freq.	D2
	Unit counter	D3
Range Input S2	.01 sec/1 cycle	D0
	.1 sec/10 cycles	D1
	1 sec/100 cycles	D2
	10 sec/1 K cycles	D3

Fig. 5-38. 3-1/2 digit voltmeter

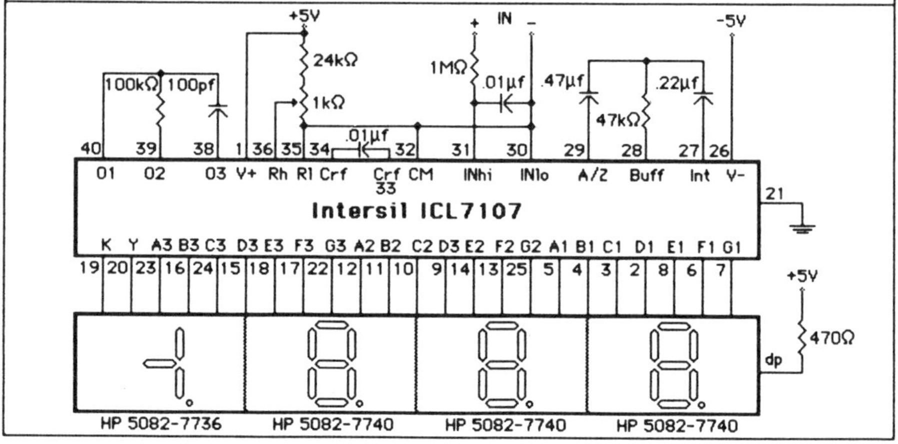

passive components are required to make a working digital voltmeter. The ICL7107 is designed to direct drive three seven segment displays and one overflow digit. The IC provides a constant current of 8 mA to the display segments. Retail price for this IC is around $13. In this sample application, three Hewlett Packard 5082-7740 and one 5082-7736, all common cathode, LED displays are used for readouts. The 0.3 inch tall, seven segment displays are end stacked to obtain a three digit display with overflow and polarity indication. Figure 5-38 shows the schematic for the digital voltmeter.

An Electronic Thermometer

An electronic digital thermometer can be constructed using the 3-½ digit voltmeter, and a diode-wheatstone bridge circuit. This circuit is based on the fact that a silicon diode's forward voltage loss is a linear function of temperature. A silicon diode's voltage drop is increased by 1.25 mV per degree F° or by 2.24 mV per degree C°. Figure 5-39 shows the diode thermometer "front end" used to measure temperature with any digital voltmeter functioning as the readout. R3 is used to zero the circuit to the freezing point of water. R5 adjusts the voltage so that there is a voltage change of 1 mV per degree. Note that two versions of the thermometer circuit are given, one for Fahrenheit and one for celsius degrees.

The circuit is simple to calibrate. Insert the diode probe into a slurry of ice and water. Adjust R3 until the digital voltmeter reads either 32° F or 0° C. Then insert the probe into boiling water and adjust R5 until the digital voltmeter reads either 212° F or 100° C. Repeat this adjustment procedure several times until the probe reads accurately. Since this circuit uses a bridge, it is essential that all resistors are within 1%, or use trimmer potentiometers.

This circuit has 6 to 24 Vdc as an input, which is then regulated to 1.5 volts by the LM317T for the bridge circuit. The voltage regulator can be eliminated by using a silver oxide battery as a power source. The absolute voltage to the bridge is not important, but a very stable voltage for the bridge is necessary if the thermometer is to be accurate. Several probes can be run into a single digital voltmeter, however, each diode must have its own bridge and be calibrated separately.

Seven Segment LED Display Cost

Seven segment displays are inexpensive. Single digits cost between $1.25 and $2.25 each depending on size. Two digit direct drive displays cost between $2.10 and $3.60 depending on size. Four digit multiplexed displays cost between $6.10 and $9.90 depending on size.

LED BAR GRAPH DISPLAYS

An LED bar graph is a collection of discrete LED lamps arranged in a straight line. This line of LEDs converts an analog signal into a visual display. The bar graph is quickly replacing analog meters

Fig. 5-39. Electronic thermometer

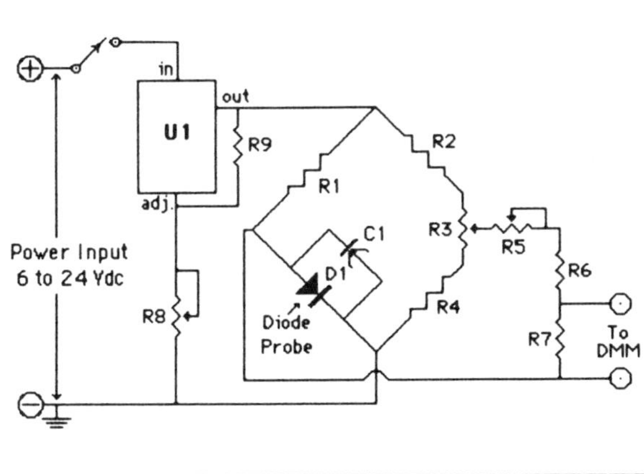

Part#	Fahrenheit	Celsius
R1	33 KΩ	33 KΩ
R2	82 KΩ	120 KΩ
R3	1 KΩ	1 KΩ
R4	56 KΩ	68KΩ
R5	10 KΩ	10 KΩ
R6	49 KΩ	120 KΩ
R7	220 KΩ	100 KΩ
R8	1 KΩ	1 KΩ
R9	240 Ω	240 Ω
D1	1N914	
C1	.01μf	
U1	LM317T	

in most consumer electronic devices. It is cheaper, more reliable, and far simpler for the manufacturer to implement. Most users prefer the bar graph aesthetically to the analog meter because it is easier to read, either up close or at a distance. The bar graph is so popular that it is now standardized into specialized display packages, with special ICs being manufactured to drive these bar graph packages.

LED bar graphs come in all the standard LED colors. Some manufacturers, such as Hewlett Packard, offer differently colored LED junctions within the same package. This makes the display easier to read and more communicative.

How It Works

The LED bar graph has a number (usually ten) of LEDs linearly assembled into a single rectangular package. Figure 5-40 illustrates a ten element bargraph's physical dimensions and internal construction. The device pictured is the Hewlett Packard HDSP-4830 display; it is typical and representative of the types made by other manufacturers.

The bar graph display uses the principles of "stretching," reflection, and diffusion to produce even illumination on the display's surface. The individual LED junctions are held in place within the package by a lead frame. Over each LED junction, there is a reflective cavity known as a scrambler. The scrambler reflects the LED junction's light out of the front of the package. The scrambler cavity is filled with a dyed epoxy diffusant which spreads the light output evenly over the display's emitting surfaces. The non-emitting surface of the bar graph package is dyed neutral grey to enhance its contrast with the individual LED elements. Filters can be used with the bar graph display in exactly the same manner as the seven segment LED displays.

The bar graph packages have their electrical leads spaced 0.100 inches apart on each side, with the two rows of leads being spaced 0.300 inches apart. This standard IC lead spacing makes the bar graph compatible with IC sockets. Figure 5-41 illustrates the internal electrical schematic of the bar graph package. Note that the anode and cathode of each LED junction within the package are available externally. This means that the bar graph array can be used in either common anode or common cathode service.

Advantages

There are several major advantages of using a bar graph package

Fig. 5-40. LED bargraph package

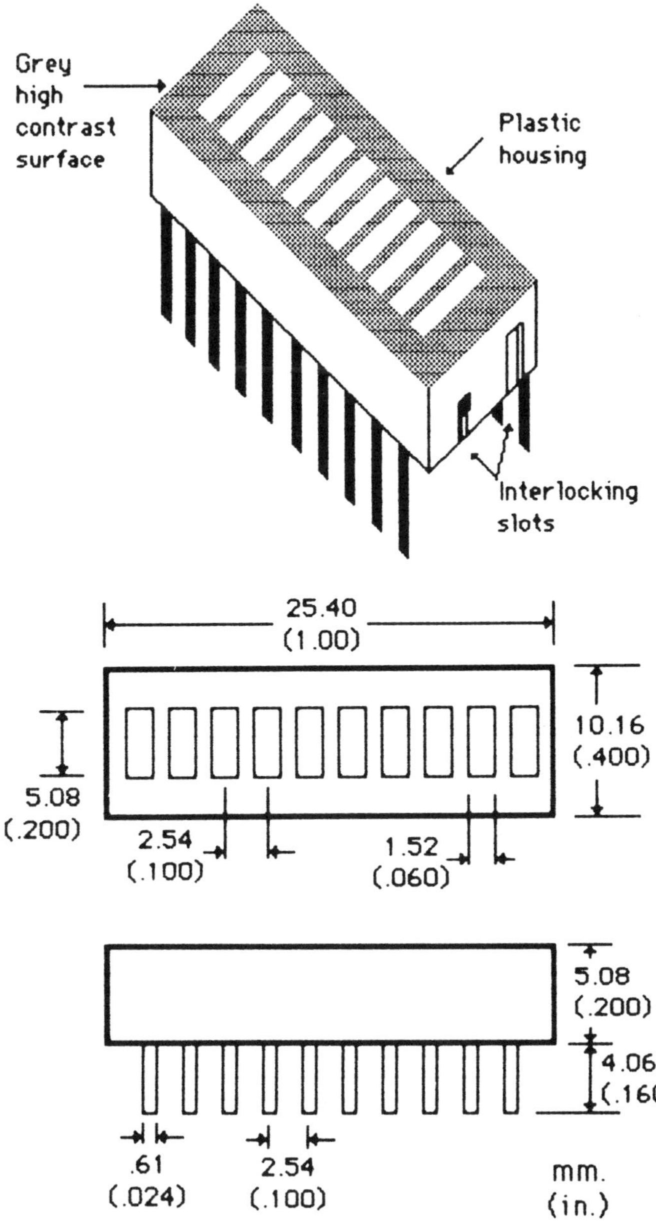

Fig. 5-41. Bargraph internal schematic

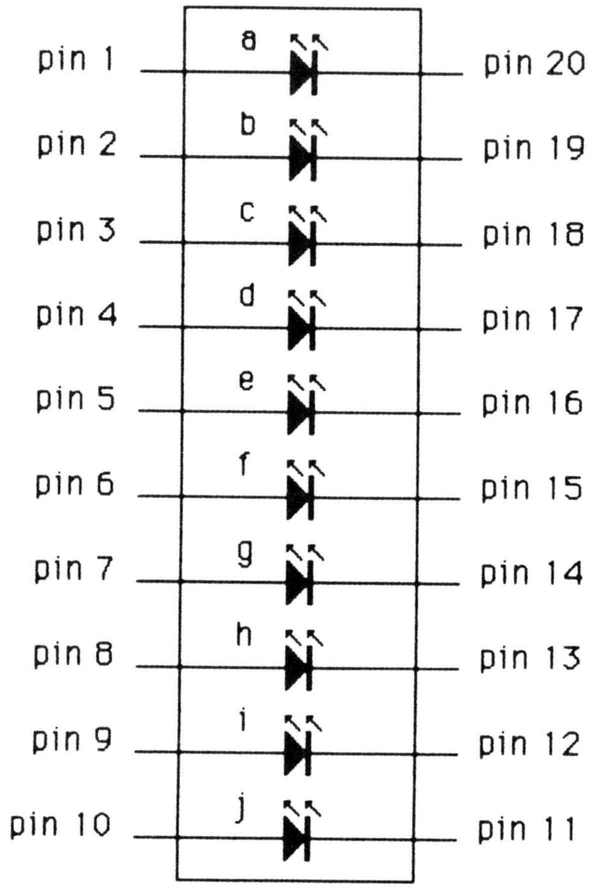

over a row of discrete LED lamps. The first is luminous intensity. All the LED junctions within the bar graph package are very carefully matched to provide the same luminous intensity for the same amount of junction current. This is difficult to achieve using discrete LED lamps. The wavelength (color) of each LED element in the bar graph package is also very closely controlled. The eye is very sensitive to even minute changes in the light's wavelength, especially in the regions of yellow and green. It is difficult to assemble a bar graph out of individual lamps that has complete color uniformity.

The bar graph package has two advantages over discrete lamps in the area of physical assembly. It is difficult to evenly space 10 LED lamps in a straight line, even using machine tools. It is far more difficult for the homebuilder using hand tools. The bar graph package solves this problem; all the elements are evenly spaced and absolutely straight to the eye. The bar graph packages are keyed on their ends so that several may be end stacked to produce displays with more elements. These "end keys" assure exact alignment between the individual bar graph packages. The physical electrical connections to the display are greatly simplified by using the bar graph packages. Simply plug the display into the appropriate IC socket; no soldering is required. If the bar graph is to be soldered use a good solder (>60% tin), and do the job quickly. Homebuilders are encouraged to heatsink the leads of the bar graph display while soldering. Treat them like any other semiconductor during assembly.

Disadvantages

The main disadvantage of the bar graph package is caused by its good points. There are at least ten LED junctions within the bar graph package. If only one of these fails, then the entire display has failed and it must be replaced. Fortunately, the LED junctions are very long lived. If the manufacturer's specifications are followed, there should be very few problems with LED failures. The bar graph package is an excellent place to derate the forward current through the individual junctions to about half. This insures long life.

Resolution of the information displayed by a bar graph is limited by the number of elements in the graph. For example, consider a bar graph of 10 elements which is designed to display analog voltage between 11 and 16 volts. Each LED element in the bar graph will indicate an increment of 0.5 volts [(16-11)/10)]. Measurements using this bar graph will have a resolution of less than 0.5 volts. It is possible to use more elements in the bar graph by stacking the displays and their ICs. This becomes cumbersome and hard to read when more than 20 elements are included in a single informational display.

Sample Applications Using Bar Graph Display Drivers

The bar graph package is so popular that entire families of integrated circuits are being made to drive them. Table 5-4 lists some analog input bar graph display drivers. This is a partial list, other suppliers do exist. Note that the table indicates that some of the drivers allow the user to program the forward current of the LED elements.

These drivers differ slightly from manufacturer to manufacturer but they are all based on the same principle. A block diagram of the internal circuitry of a typical analog bar graph driver is shown in Fig. 5-42. Each driver IC contains a voltage divider network of resistors. In some cases, this divider network can be fed from an internal, regulated, and adjustable voltage reference. The output of the voltage reference is divided by a chain of ten resistors. This yields ten equally spaced subreferences, one for each of the ten op amp comparators. Each of the ten comparators compares its individual subreference voltage to the input signal. If the input signal is higher than the subreference, the comparator enables its output driver and the LED is lit. If each of the resistors in the voltage divider chain has the same amount of resistance, then the bar graph will be linear (each LED indicates the same amount of input signal change). Some bar graph drivers contain a logarithmic voltage divider rather than a linear one. Logarithmic drivers have the value of their resistors arranged on a logarithmic scale rather than an equally spaced (linear) one. Such logarithmic drivers are intended for nonlinear uses such as audio level metering.

Table 5-4. Analog Input Bargraph Display drivers.

Number	Manufacturer	LED current	Scale	Elements	Comments
LM3914	National	2 to 30 mA	Linear	10	Bar/dot option
LM3915	National	2 to 30 mA	Log	10	Bar/dot option
LM3916	National	2 to 30 mA	Log	10	Bar/dot option
TL490	T1	≤ 40 mA	Linear	10	50-200 mV adjustable increments
TL480	T1	≤ 40 mA	Log	10	2 dB increments
TL491	T1	≤ −25 mA	Linear	10	50-200 mV adjustable increments
TL481	T1	≤ −25 mA	Log	10	2 dB increments
UAA170	Siemens	≤ 50 mA	External	16	Dot indicator only, user sets scale
UAA180	Siemens	10 mA	External	12	User sets scale
XR-2277	Exar	≤ 18 mA	Log	12	−30 dB to +6 dB, dot/bar option
XR-2278	Exar	≤ 18 mA	Log	12	−20 dB to +8 dB, dot/bar option
XR-2279	Exar	≤ 18 mA	Log	12	3 dB increments, dot/bar option
U237B	AEG-Telefunk	20 mA	Linear	5	200 mV increments (200 mV – 1000 mV)
U254B	AEG-Telefunk	20 mA	Linear	5	100 mV increments (100 mV – 900 mV)

Fig. 5-42. Analog bargraph driver

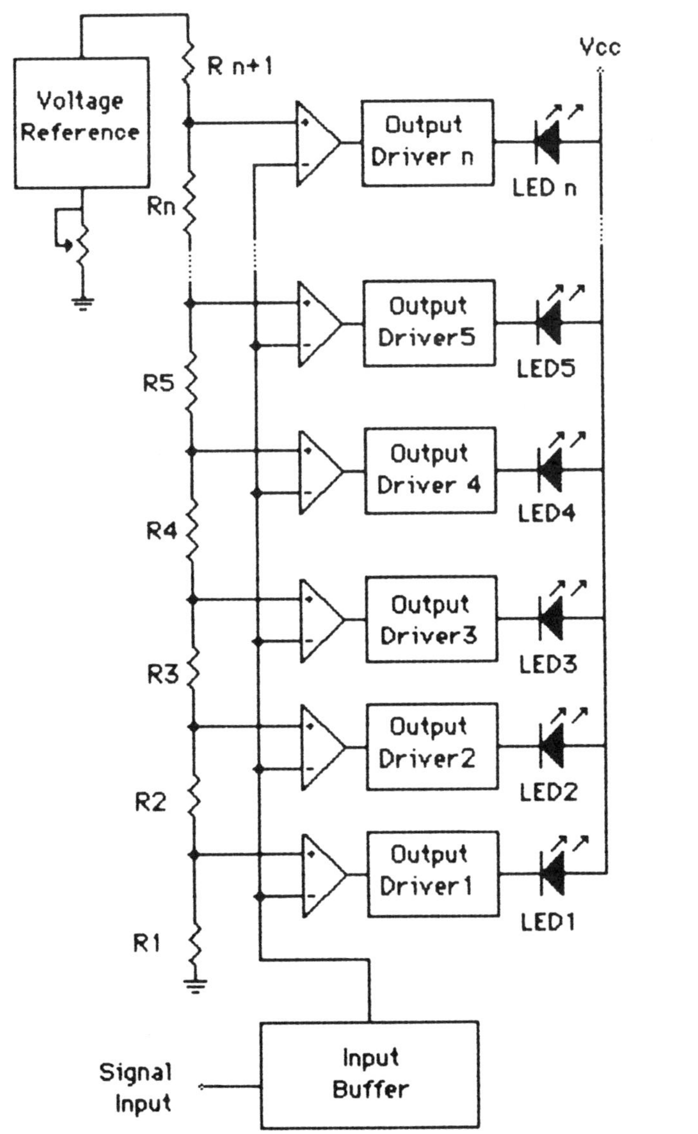

An Expanded Scale Voltmeter

This circuit uses the very popular LM3914 bar graph driver made by National Semiconductor to construct an expanded scale 11 to 16 Vdc bar graph voltmeter. Such a meter is very useful in 12-volt battery systems, and makes an inexpensive and very rugged automotive voltmeter. Figure 5-43 shows the schematic for this meter. When the input voltage under measurement reaches 11.5 volts the first LED is lit, and succeeding LEDs are lit for each increase of 0.5 volts. For example, two LEDs are lit for 12 volts, 4 for 13 volts, 6 for 14 volts and so on until all 10 LEDs in the display are lit at 16 volts.

Resistor 1 determines the amount of forward current flowing through each LED. Resistor 2 is used to set the internal voltage reference. The LM3914 uses the bar graph display in common anode mode. It does not require external current limiting of the LED elements. The voltage reference of the LM3914 supplies a regulated voltage across pins 7 and 8. This regulated reference is applied to R1 to obtain a constant current flow through this resistor. The current drawn by each LED element is about 10 times the current that flows from pin 7 (Reference Output). The actual amount of current flowing through any individual LED in the display can be calculated by:

Single LED current = (1.25V/R1)(10) **Equation 5-5**

Fig. 5-43. 11 to 16 Vdc bargraph voltmeter

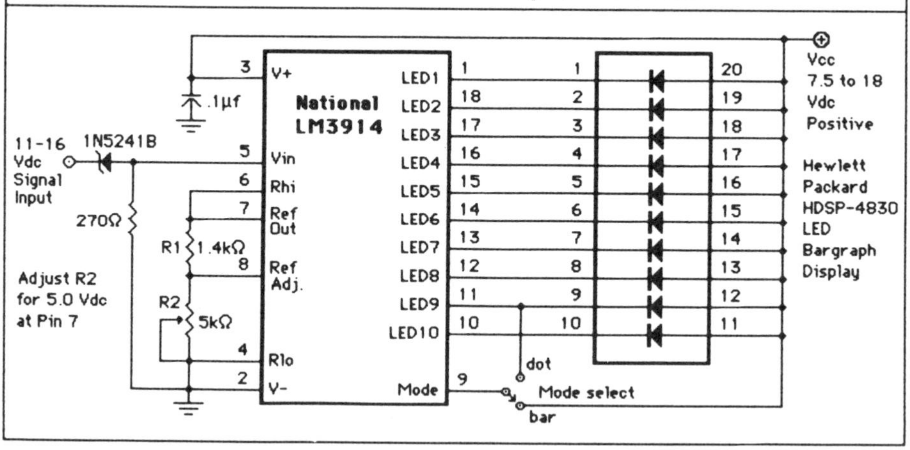

In the example, R1 is 1,480 Ω; this supplies 8.4 mA forward current for each LED element in the bar graph display. It is wise to determine R1 first and then determine R2. With each LED consuming 8.4 mA of current, then all 10 LEDs will consume 84 mA total and the LED portion of the display will dissipate about 1.3 watts. Note that the supply voltage of the circuit does not affect the amount of current flowing through the LEDs in the display. This makes the LM 3914 a very good chip to use in systems where the supply voltage fluctuates.

Power consumption can be minimized by switching the display from bar mode into dot mode. In dot mode, a single LED indicating the input signal's voltage is lit, rather than all the LEDs that are at or below the input signal's voltage. For example, consider an input signal of 13.5 volts. In bar mode, the lower five LEDs will be lit, while in dot mode, only the fifth LED will be lit. This mode change is accomplished by a bar/dot switch connected to pin 9. If pin 9 is connected to VCC, the display is a bar graph, or if pin 9 is connected to pin 11, the display is a single dot.

The amount of resistance of R1 and R2 determines the actual output voltage of the reference. This reference output is fed to the internal divider, and determines the scale of the bar graph. The high end of the divider is Pin 6, and the low end is Pin 4. The output voltage of the reference can be calculated by:

$$\text{Ref V Out} = 1.25\text{V}\,(1 + \text{R2}/\text{R1}) + 0.000075\,(\text{R2}) \qquad \textbf{Equation 5-6}$$

This equation allows the user to set the regulated voltage across the internal voltage dividers to the desired level. If pin 8 (Reference Adjust) is elevated from ground by a resistor (R2), the voltage of the regulated reference rises. 12 volts is the maximum available from the reference. If pin 8 is grounded, the reference's output voltage is at a minimum of 1.3 volts. The operation of the internal voltage reference is very similar to the operation of adjustable linear, series dissipative, voltage regulators such as the LM317T.

In this sample circuit, the potentiometer R2 is set to 4,540 Ω, while R1 is 1.47 kΩ (actually measured to be 1,480 Ω). Using the equation above, the reference output voltage is calculated to be 5.08 volts. In actual practice, the sample circuit was putting out exactly 5 volts at pin 7. Adjusting the reference output voltage gives us 5 volts to apply across the internal voltage divider, and results in a bar graph that will measure the 5 volts full scale. This same technique can be used to produce a bar graph meter of whatever range is desired. The input voltage of the entire circuit should be at least 2 volts higher than the reference's output voltage. This gives the internal reference 2 volts to dissipate during regulation. Once again, this is very similar to any linear voltage regulator.

The input signal of this circuit is ground referenced. This means that LED #1 will turn on at 0.5 volts on pin 5. Actually the circuit is a 0 to 5 Vdc meter. However, we wish to raise the meter's zero point and only measure the 5 volt interval between 11 and 16 volts. In order to elevate the zero point to 11 volts, we can process the input signal's voltage. This is accomplished by adding an 11 volt zener diode, reverse biased, in series with the input signal. In effect, this subtracts 11 volts from the input signal's voltage. Use a 1N5241B (5%) zener diode for accuracy, and leave its leads long for increased heat dissipation. Note the use of a 270 Ω resistor between the anode of the zener diode and ground. This linearizes the zener's voltage drop over the entire input signal range and greatly increases the accuracy of the finished meter. Worst case power dissipation by the zener is about 250 mW (at a signal input of 16 Vdc), far less than its 500 mW maximum rating.

An unusual characteristic of this circuit is its ability to measure the voltage of its own power source. This is not common in electronic metering. For example, consider this expanded scale voltmeter used in an automobile. The meter is measuring the battery's voltage. It is also being powered by the very same battery. Most electronic metering requires a separate, isolated power source. This isolated source must not be dc connected in any way to the voltage being measured. The problem is ground contention, and most manufacturers solve it by using a separate small battery to supply power for the electronic meter. The ability of this circuit to measure its own power source is a distinct advantage in automobiles, boats, alternative energy systems, and many other dc applications which use a common grounding scheme. This circuit does not require its own small battery. It can be run by the main battery in the system, and measure this main battery's voltage at the same time.

An Audio Level Display

LED bar graph displays are used in many types of commercially manufactured audio equipment. The LED bar graph is very fast acting and has no trouble displaying the rapidly varying audio peaks of music. It is far quicker than analog meters. The LED bar graph is a very pleasing visual display for music, especially in dot mode.

This circuit uses the LM3915 bar dot display driver manufactured by National Semiconductor. It is identical to the Lm3914 used in the previous example, except the LM3915's internal voltage divider is logarithmically scaled. It reads out in increments of −3dB. Figure 5-44 illustrates the schematic for this audio bar graph meter.

Note that R1, which controls each LED element's current, is 1 kΩ. According to Equation 5-5, this will result in an LED element current of 12.5 mA. This is brighter than the previous example, but still within allowable limits for both the chip and the display. Entertainment type displays are commonly driven much harder than informational types. Pin 8 (Reference Adjust) is grounded, producing a reference voltage of 1.3 volts at Pin 7 (Reference Voltage Out). This meter will read full scale when 1.3 volts appears on Pin 5 (signal input). Most audio signals are very much greater than 1.3 volts, so a voltage divider (R2) is used to process the incoming audio signal. It is easy to adjust. Just turn the audio source to maximum volume and adjust R2 until the highest LED just lights. Lowering the reference's output voltage to 1.3 volts allows this circuit to be powered by as little as 3 volts dc.

This audio metering circuit can share the same power supply and ground as the audio equipment under measurement. The LM3915 shares this characteristic with its close cousin, the LM3914. This meter makes an excellent audio level display for automotive audio equipment, or any other gear using a common ground.

Fig.5-44. LED bargraph audio meter

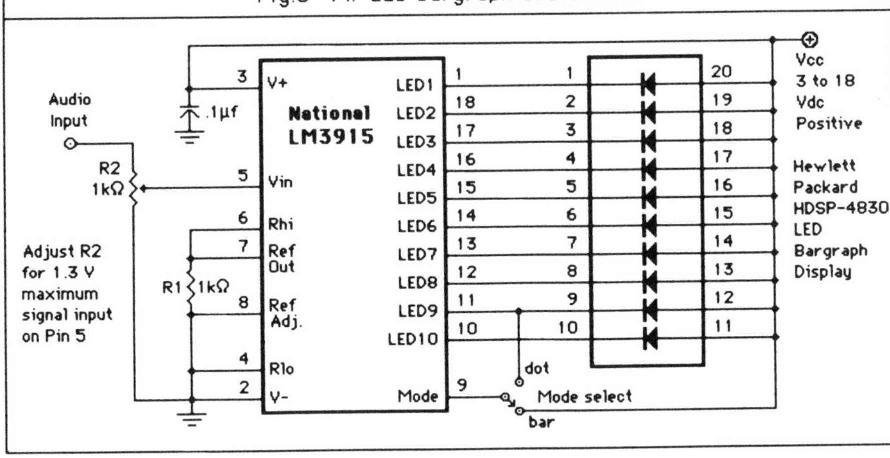

Cost

Ten element LED bar graph displays cost less then $4.00. Considering their ease of use and the perfect optical alignment of these displays, they are a bargain. Driver chips cost between $2.50 and $6.00. These components will produce a rugged, accurate, and visually exciting display for under $10.00.

Both the LM3914 and the LM3915 bar graph drivers are made by National Semiconductor with a built-in red LED bar graph display on a single PC board. This small (2 in. by 1 in. by 0.2 in. thick) circuit greatly simplifies assembly as all the LEDs are already connected to the driver. The linear version is numbered NSM 3914 and the logarithmic version is numbered NSM3915. They operate in the same fashion as the sample circuits given here. Each is under $10.00 and is an excellent value.

5 × 7 DOT MATRIX LED DISPLAYS

LED junctions are also arranged in dot matrix packages which can display alphabetical characters as well as numbers. These versatile dot matrix modules are commonly used in point of sale terminals (smart cash registers), electronic instrumentation, calculators, portable computers, computer peripheral, and industrial control equipment. The LED dot matrix display is in direct competition with CRTs and LCDs for some information displaying jobs.

How It Works

A dot matrix package contains 35 LED junctions constructed on a matrix that is 5 vertical columns by 7 horizontal rows. The individual elements of the matrix are selectively illuminated to form alphabetical and numerical characters. Figure 5-45 illustrates the physical package and electrical schematic of single character of a typical 5 × 7 dot matrix display. Such a matrix is said to be "X-Y addressable." These single characters, each composed of 35 elements, can be stacked horizontally to display a string of many characters. Most manufacturers making this type of display offer X-Y addressable packages that consist of 3 or more characters per package. This greatly simplifies the physical alignment of the individual characters within the display.

Figure 5-46 is a sample of the different characters formed by a 5 × 7 dot matrix. The LED elements that are illuminated are

Fig. 5-45. 5 X 7 Dot matrix display

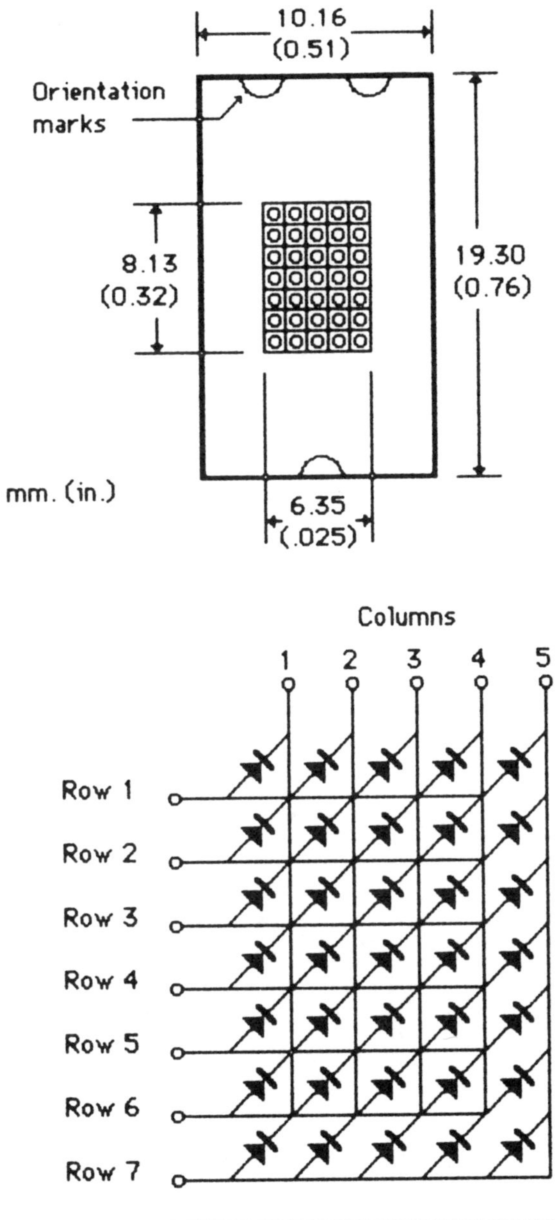

represented by solid black squares. Most of this character set is very readable, especially the upper case letters, and is even more readable in the "plastic" than it is on paper. Squinting at Fig. 5-46 will make the black elements stand out more clearly, and the characters will appear more as they do on an actual operating LED dot matrix display. The character set for the 5 × 7 matrix is extensive and capable of displaying upper and lower case text, numbers, punctuation, and some elementary mathematical symbols like equal, plus and minus.

In order to form characters, the dot matrix is scanned using a multiplex scheme, which is very similar to multiplexed seven segment displays. Information is sent to the display one row at a time, and the appropriate diodes in that row are illuminated. Information is then addressed to the next row, and so on until all seven rows in the display are addressed. The process then returns to the beginning and repeats itself. This scanning of the display occurs so rapidly that the display appears continuous to the eye. Each row in the display is scanned at least 100 times per second. Information is also sent to the display's columns at the same time it is directed to the rows. Hopefully, the two are synchronized and the desired characters are formed on the display.

This multiplex process is not very complex, but it is certainly a job for electronic encoding of the information for the display. Figure 5-47 illustrates a block diagram for a typical drive scheme used in row scanning a 5 × 7 dot matrix. The complexity here reflects the usage of "non-smart" matrix displays on computer encoded

Fig. 5-46. 5 X 7 Dot matrix character set

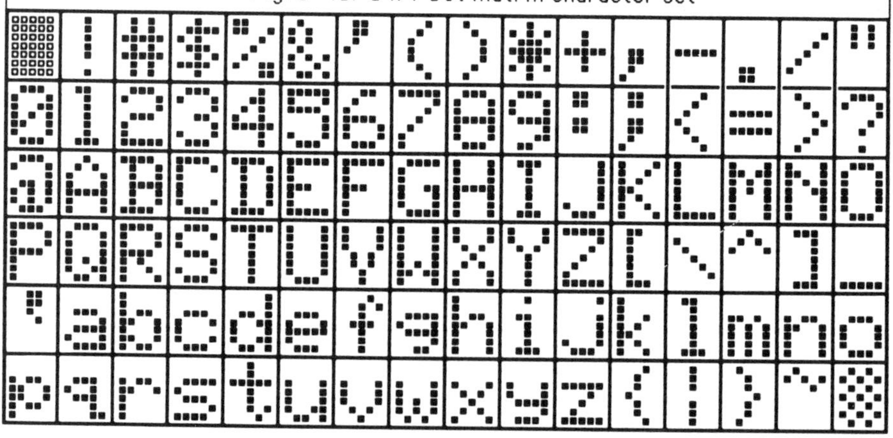

Fig. 5-47. 5 X 7 Dot matrix drive block diagram

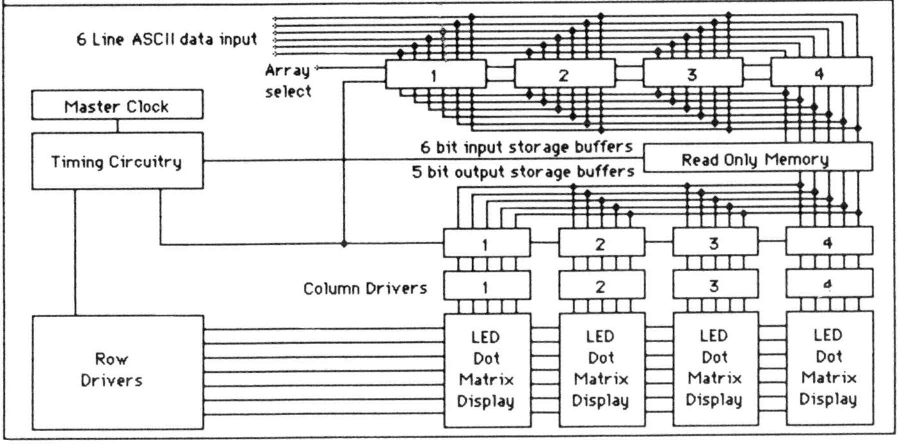

information. Other types of dot matrix displays containing as many as 36 characters are made. These large displays usually contain their own encoding and driving hardware, and are far simpler for the user to implement.

Power consumption is moderate in LED dot matrix displays. A single element (LED junction) within the display consumes around 10 mA. If all 35 LEDs that form a single character are lit then the power consumption of the entire character is less than 700 mW (0.7 W). this is not very much power. However, consider a dot matrix display with 36 characters, each of which is consuming 0.7 Watts. The entire display will consume around 25 watts. This is a considerable amount of power, comparable with small CRT displays and much greater than LCD displays used in the same type of applications.

Dot matrix characters are available in a variety of sizes from 3.8 mm tall to over 7 mm tall. The larger sizes are visible at much greater distances than alphanumerical displays of other types. This characteristic has led to their usage in industrial applications where data must be read from a distance.

Advantages

One of the main advantages that the 5 × 7 dot matrix display has over other LED displays is its ability to display alphabetical characters. Its other advantages are shared with all the members of the LED family. It is very rugged, and this has led to its use in military and aerospace applications. It is highly visible in low ambient light environments.

The dot matrix display is very compact. It can display the same information as a CRT in about a fifth the space. It is also very lightweight, less than a tenth the weight of a comparable CRT display. LED dot matrix displays can be directly powered by low voltage dc electricity, and are commonly powered by batteries. These factors have led to wide use in military, vehicular, and avionic applications.

Disadvantages

The main disadvantage of the X-Y addressable dot matrix is the complexity of the driving electronics. Each multiplexed character requires 12 electrical connections, plus the row and column drive electronics. If a display of only four characters is considered, the entire package will require 176 interconnections and 36 assorted electronic drive components. This factor has led to "smart" dot matrix displays which are assembled by the manufacturer into complete modules. These smart displays contain some of their own drive electronics, and all display interconnection is already made within the module. A four character "smart" display module will require as little as 11 active connections compared with the 176 of the "dumb" dot matrix display.

Sample Application—A Dot Matrix Computer Display

This sample application uses the HDSP-2000 dot matrix LED display module manufactured by Hewlett Packard. This module contains four, 5 × 7 dot matrix, characters in a single package. It also contains its own driving and encoding electronics. Figure 5-48 illustrates a block diagram of the internal circuitry of the HDSP-2000 series display modules. There are four LED dot matrices and two 14-bit, serial-in-parallel-out (SIPO), shift registers within each display module. Note that only 11 active connections are required external to the display. The SIPO shift registers have a constant current sinking output which drives the LED elements at a constant 12 to 14 mA of current.

The information to be displayed is loaded serially into the shift register at the high to low clock transition. While the data is being loaded, it is necessary to disable the column current to minimize current spiking between VCC, the columns, and ground. This is ac-

Fig. 5-48. HDSP-2000 Internal block diagram

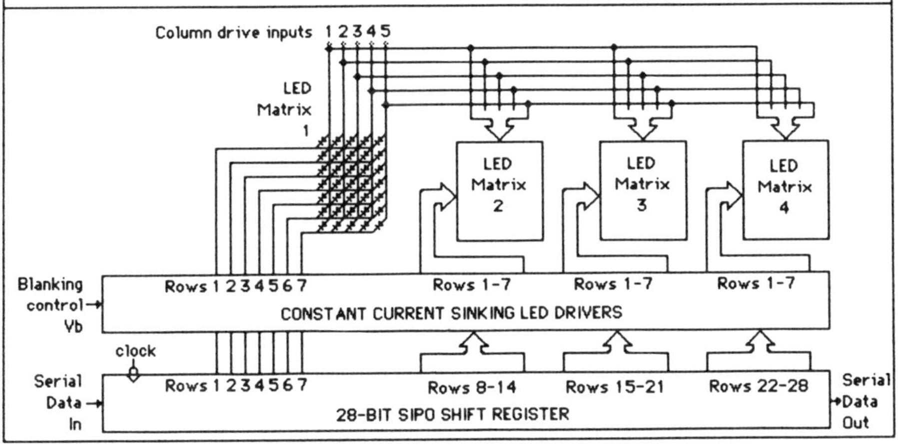

complished by supplying a logical "O" to the blanking input (pin 8).

In order to make a working computer display, some additional circuitry is required to interface the display with ASCII information. This additional circuitry supplies the timing pulses to properly strobe the display and to decode the ASCII data. Figure 5-49 shows a typical block diagram for interfacing the HDSP-2000 with a computer's central microprocessor (CPU). In this example the microprocessor treats the display as if it were RAM. Timing chores are handled by a counter driven by the main system clock. This example represents very efficient usage of the CPU. The microprocessor is only accessed when the display information is changed. The CPU requires very little time to load the display data as a dedicated ASCII decoder is used by the display. This example represents usage of an 8080A or 6800 series of CPU, interfacing with other types is similar.

Cost

The actual dot matrix LED displays are inexpensive, less than $3.00 each for a single character. The multiple character packages are cheaper per character. If a working, 128 character, computer display is considered, then the cost is about $200 including drive electronics. The additional cost and complexity of this type of display has limited their use to original equipment manufacturers. Its use is too complex and expensive for most homebuilders.

Fig. 5-49. CPU interface for HDSP-2000 alphanumeric display

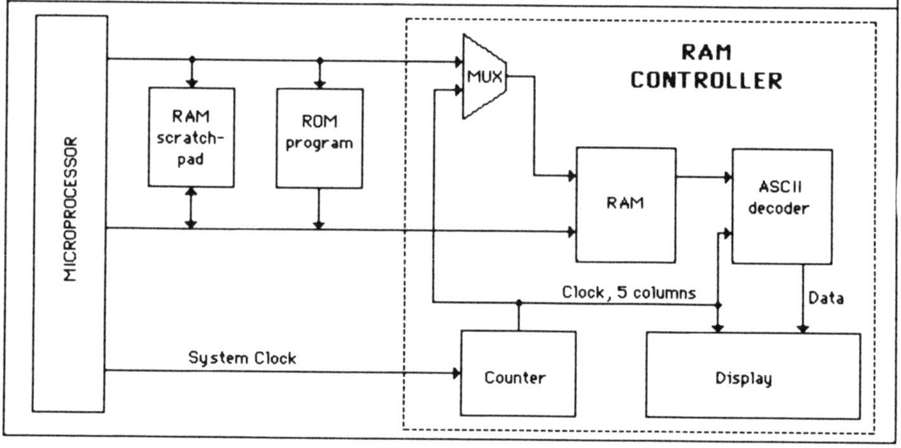

LISTING OF LED DISPLAY MANUFACTURERS

The following manufacturers contributed information to this chapter. Their complete addresses and telephone numbers can be found in Appendix A.

Hewlett Packard
Optoelectronics Division

General Instrument Corporation
Optoelectronics Division

AND

Leecraft Manufacturing Co., Inc.

Visual Communications Company

Data Display Products

Stanley Electric Co.

AC Interface, Inc.

6

Liquid Crystal Displays (LCD)

In the early 1970's, digital watches started showing up in the marketplace with a new and different type of display—the liquid crystal display or LCD. Chances are better than even that you are wearing one on your wrist at this moment. These tiny dark numerals have revolutionized battery operated electronic devices that require information displays. The LCD displays used in these early digital watches were very different from the LEDs they replaced. The LCD display is operating constantly, in contrast to the LED displays which required pushing a button to check the time. The reason for this is power consumption. While even a tiny LED display consumes a few milliwatts of power, the LCD consumes just microwatts of power. The LCDs are over 1000 times more efficient at their job than the LEDs they have replaced.

Since their commercialization in the '70s, LCDs are the most popular electronic display device made except one—the venerable CRT. They are now used in everything from multimeters to mixmasters. LCD flat panels are challenging the ubiquitous CRT as displays for television and computers. LCDs are now being produced in full color models. The time when we will hang a flat panel, color TV on our walls like a painting, is very close at hand. Since the LCDs have such low power consumption, this wall TV is likely to be cordless, i.e., powered by internal batteries. Small battery powered, lap-top computers are already using dot matrix LCDs as displays.

We can look forward to seeing LCD readouts in most of the consumer electronics we use.

The LCDs are not a single type of device, but an entire family of electronic display devices. The LCD exists now in many different forms, each building on the other and attempting to improve LCD technology. LCD technology is not static, but a rapidly developing display field.

HOW LCDs WORK

LCDs are light valves. The principle of the liquid crystal display's operation is radically different from all other display devices discussed in this book. LCDs are light modifiers, not light producers. All the other devices are self-illuminating; they produce their own light. The LCD does not make its own light, but operates by modifying light which is not produced by the LCD. This distinction is very important and is responsible for the low power consumption of the LCD. The external light modified by the LCD may be ambient light supplied from the sun, a table lamp, or other room light source. In some cases, there is a special light source installed within the device just to supply the LCD some light to modify. An example of this internal, dedicated light source is the tiny incandescent lightbulb contained in most digital watches. When the ambient light level is too low to supply the LCD with enough illumination to be readable, one simply pushes a button on the digital watch and a small bulb illuminates the LCD. Without some ambient light, the LCD has no illumination to modify, and it is not readable. In actual use, the LCD is exactly the same as the book you are now reading. The information on the page does not radiate its own light, but reflects the ambient light, just like the LCD. Both devices need ambient light to display information.

In order to understand the principle of the LCD's operation, we must first understand the idea of light's polarization. This concept of polarization is the principle that polarizers and some forms of sunglasses use to dim and modify light. LCDs are electrically controlled light polarizers. Light is considered by most physicists to be a traveling wavefront of photons. These photonic wavefronts are a transverse (perpendicular) combination of electric and magnetic fields. The electric and magnetic fields are perpendicular to each other and to the direction of the wavefront's propagation. The orientation of these fields gives each individual light wavefront a distinct polarization. By this we mean that the electric and magnetic fields are oriented in a certain angular direction. Figure 6-1 graphically illustrates a light wavefront with its electric and magnetic components. Note that the direction the light waves travel is perpendicular to both the electric and magnetic fields. If two light wavefronts have their electric and magnetic fields exactly parallel, then they have the same polarization. Such light is said to be coherent. Two individual sets of light waves can have the same exact polarization and be traveling in exactly opposite directions. Polarized or coherent light is not found in nature; it is man made. Lasers are one example of devices that produce coherent light of a single polarization. The sun, incandescent lights, and fluorescent lights are all examples of incoherent, nonpolarized light.

Ambient light is a combination of photon wavefronts of an infinite variety of polarizations. Natural lighting is a randomly oriented "soup" of photonic wavefronts, each with its own individual polarization. Ambient light is unpolarized and incoherent. The concept of light's polarization has resulted in the construction of devices known as polarizers. Polarizers are light filters which only allow light of a single polarization to pass through them. A polarizing filter is a network of infinitesimally small parallel lines. These lines are constructed on the molecular level by the transparent chemical compounds that make up the filter. The polarizing filter will only allow light waves parallel to the filter's lines to pass through it. The light transmitted by the filter is coherent, and light of all other polarizations is either reflected or absorbed by the filter; it will not be transmitted. Light which passes through a polarizing filter is said to be polarized,

Fig. 6-1. Light wavefronts

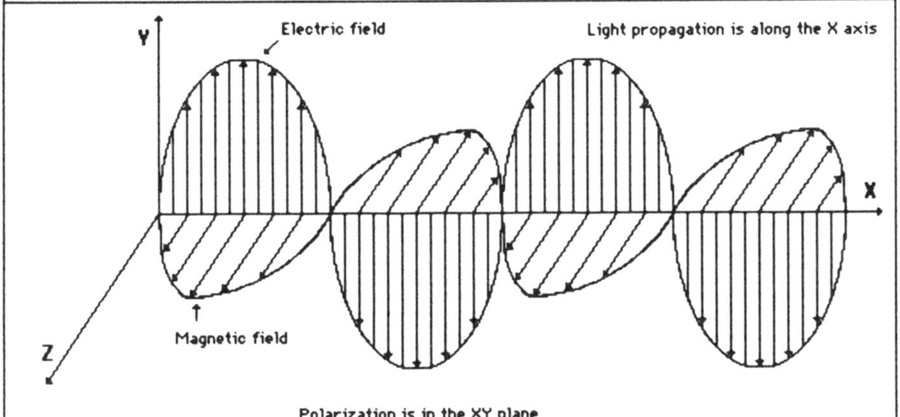

and is coherent. Figure 6-2 illustrates the operation of a polarizing filter. Randomly polarized natural light strikes the front of the filter. Only light of a vertical polarization is transmitted by the filter since the filter is vertically polarized. If the filter were rotated so that the plane of its lines were horizontal, then only horizontally polarized light would be transmitted. In each and every case, all light not polarized in the same direction as the filter will not be transmitted.

Two polarizing filters can be used together to actually stop the transmission of light through the combination of both filters. The first filter in the set is known as the polarizer, while the second is called the analyzer. The light passing through he first filter is polarized in a certain direction, and if the analyzer filter is oriented with its lines at right angles to the polarizer, no light will pass through the analyzer. If the analyzer is oriented with its lines parallel to the polarizer, almost all the light that passes through the polarizer will also pass through the analyzer. Figure 6-3 illustrates this effect. In this illustration the lines of the polarizer are perpendicular to those of the analyzer, and no light is transmitted through the filter set. The LCD uses a system of filters to display information that is similar to the operation of the polarizer and the analyzer.

Ambient light enters the LCD display through the front polarizing filter. The coherent light then passes through the liquid crystal medium. This liquid crystal medium is a collection of specific organic molecules which rotate the light passing through them. They change the polarization of the coherent light passed to them by the polarizer.

Fig. 6-2. Operation of a polarizing filter

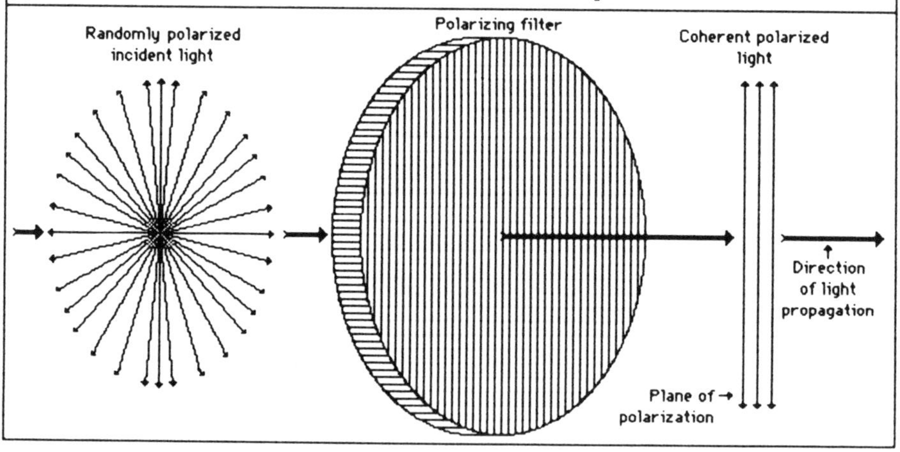

Fig. 6-3. Operation of two polarizing filters

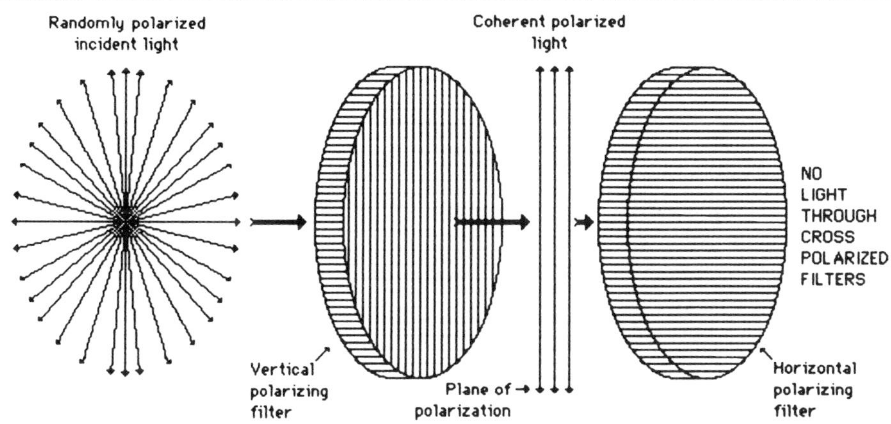

This rotation of the light's polarization may be from just a few degrees to over 270 degrees. In any case the light is still coherent, i.e., polarized. This effect of optical rotation is exhibited by a number of substances in addition to the liquid organic crystals used in the LCD, including quartz, sugar, tartaric acid, and turpentine. These compounds are said to be optically active because they will rotate the plane of polarization of coherent light that passes through them. These crystals can be thought of as twisted ribbons along which the light flows. In most liquid crystal compounds used in manufacturing LCDs, the amount of rotation of the light's polarization is 90 degrees.

The organic liquid crystals used in the LCD are dielectrically anisotropic, which is a scientific term meaning that they change their orientation in the presence of an electric field. When the liquid crystal changes its orientation, the polarizating rotation of light through the crystal is also changed. The liquid crystals used for LCDs are in what is called a "mesophase." This means that they exist as a form of matter that has some characteristics of a liquid and some of a solid. For example, the optical rotation demonstrated by the liquid crystal is a characteristic of solid matter, while its ability to change orientation under an electric field is a characteristic of a liquid. It is this effect that allows the polarization of the light passing through the liquid crystal to be rotated by the addition of a very small electric field. The effect is similar to rotating an analyzer in relation to a polarizer, the light passing through the system can be either turned on or off. Electrically, the operation of an LCD is very similar to another electric field device—the capacitor. Both are essentially ac operated devices that use the effects of the electric field.

Figure 6-4 schematically illustrates the operation of two polarizers with a liquid crystal sandwiched between them. In the first case, the coherent light is delivered to the liquid medium which rotates the direction of the light's polarization by 90°. Since the liquid crystal is not reoriented by an electric field, the crystal is at rest. The rotated light can then pass through the analyzer filter whose lines are oriented 90° to the polarizer filter. The display will appear bright due to the light passed through it. If an electric field is applied to the liquid crystal medium, it will reorient itself and no longer rotate the incoming coherent light. This means that the light will not pass through the second filter and the display will appear dark.

In actual operation, the LCD is somewhat more complex than the schematic in Fig. 6-4 shows. In most LCDs, the light actually makes two trips through the display. One trip is through the combination of filters and liquid crystal cells and another after it is reflected off the displays back surface. Since the liquid crystal display does not make its own light but modifies ambient light, a reflecting surface is added to the back of the display. This silvered surface reflects the ambient light passing through the display. The reflected light is sent back through the entire polarizer/crystal combination, out the display's front face, and into our eyes. Information is displayed by the LCD by stopping this processed, reflected light. LCDs are actually "light valves," they turn light on and off. If the

Fig.6-4. Operation of a liquid crystal cell

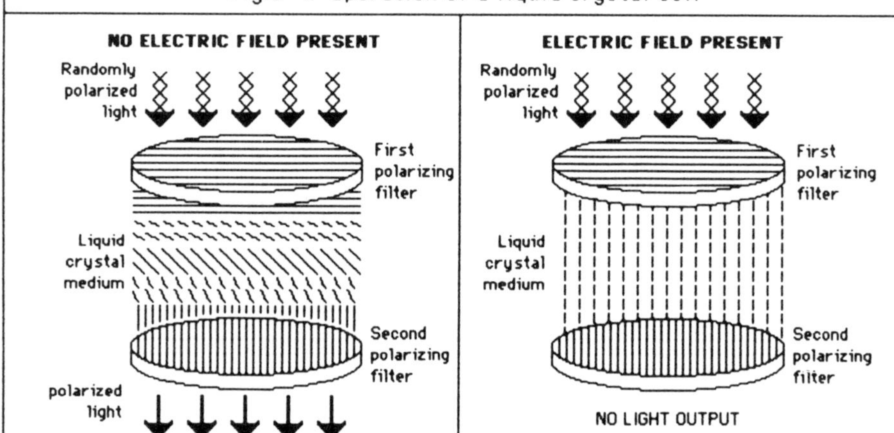

Fig. 6-5. Basic LCD construction

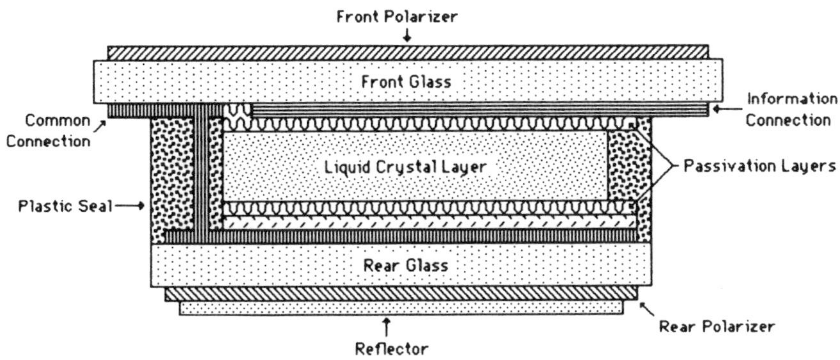

polarizers in an LCD are perpendicular, then the displayed information appears dark on a light background. If the polarizers are parallel, then the information appears light on a dark background. Most LCDs have perpendicular polarizers and display dark on light.

LCDs are among the most high tech of all the displays. Don't let their wide use, small size, and low power consumption fool you. These displays embrace some of the most abstract scientific concepts of light, organic chemistry, and crystalography. Since they use the ambient light around themselves to display information, they are the most efficient display type discussed in this book.

HOW LCDs ARE MADE

LCDs are commonly mass produced displays. As such, their physical construction is optimized for large scale machine production. Figure 6-5 illustrates the internal physical configuration of a typical liquid crystal cell. Many of these individual cells are assembled together to make a finished display. There are many different types of physical configurations used in LCDs, varying from manufacturer to manufacturer. The illustration shows one of the most common types of twisted nematic liquid crystal cells.

Ambient light enters the display through the front polarizer that is attached to the front glass. The light next passes through the pattern connection, which is a matrix of fine wires etched into the glass. These electrodes are patterned on the glass by photolithography. These pattern, or information, electrodes are made of indium tin oxide and are transparent. They lay like a grid over the display. They form half of the electrode set needed to electrically drive the display. Each cell has two electrodes, one which is distinctly its own and another shared in common with all the other cells. The common electrode is often called the ''backplane'' of the LCD.

The light then passes through the liquid crystal medium. Surrounding the liquid crystal medium is a transparent alignment coating that ensures that the liquid crystals are properly aligned to produce a 90 degree rotation of the incoming light. Use of this alignment coating increases the temperature operating range of the display. A transparent passivation layer is added before the back electrode to ensure display stability and long life. The passivation layer minimizes undesirable chemical changes in the liquid crystal medium due to electron transfer. Electrically, the LCD operates on the effect of the electric field surrounding the liquid crystal medium. Actual electronic flow (current) through the liquid crystal is undesirable and will destroy the cell.

The electrical connection for the backplane (common) electrode is brought to the same level as the electrical connections for the information electrodes by a signal crossover path. This path greatly simplifies the electrical connections outside the LCD package since they are all now in the same plane. The coherent light passes through the liquid crystal, the alignment coating, the common electrode, and through the back glass plate. Attached to the back glass plate is the rear polarizer, and then the last element of the display, the reflector.

LCDs are actually constructed on two sheets of glass. The front glass subassembly contains from top to bottom: the front polarizer, the front glass, the pattern (or information) electrodes, and the front alignment coating. The back glass contains from top to bottom: the back alignment coating, the passivation coating, the common electrode, the back glass, the second polarizer, and the reflector. These two glass subassemblies are sandwiched together with a thin film of liquid crystal contained between the two glass layers. A polymeric seal keeps the liquid crystal compound from leaking out of the display. Each cell or element within the display has its own distinct and separate reservoir of liquid crystal. The polymeric seal also compartmentalizes the liquid crystal medium into individual cells.

One of the most interesting characteristics of the LCD's construction is the behavior of its liquid crystal medium. Research into anisotropic compounds is very intense. None of the companies manufacturing or developing an LCD cared to be very specific as to the actual chemical composition of their liquid crystal mediums. In most cases, it was simply described as "an anisotropic liquid" of organic origin. The actual chemical composition of the liquid crystal varies from manufacturer to manufacturer, and this variety of LC compounds is primarily responsible for the difference in LCD operating specifications. Some manufacturers offer several LC (liquid crystal) compounds to meet a variety of display requirements. There is actually a wide family of organic compounds that will work in these displays. Some colesterol compounds, for example, are members of the dielectrically anisotropic family, and are used in some LC displays. The manufacturers and developers are all scrambling to have the best display, to find the ultimate LC medium. One cannot blame them for keeping secrets. Suffice it to say that all of these compounds are far too complex for the average amateur to construct.

LCD CHARACTERISTICS

As an electronic display device, the liquid crystal display has several very big advantages. Miniscule power consumption, high readability, ease of customization, and large size are but a few of its good points. On the minus side, narrow temperature operating range, narrow viewing angle, and slow speed are some of the problems associated with this display technology.

Liquid crystal displays have certain inherent limitations built into their structure. If we stay within these limitations, then the LCD can effectively display information at a fraction of the cost and power consumption of other types of displays. The information in this section is oriented toward the individual liquid crystal cell. These cells may be assembled in myriad ways to produce a variety of displays. One type is the numeric display which appears very similar to the seven-segment LED display, another is a dot-matrix display used in TV type service. Regardless of the displays final form, the essential operational characteristics of the LC cell remain the same.

The integrated circuits needed to drive LCDs are very common. Just about any standard measurement-display task can be solved by a specific large scale integrated circuit (LSI). These ICs contain all the logic and drive electronics necessary to effectively use the LC display. Application of LCDs are both simple and inexpensive. This is seen in their popularity with both large scale manufacturers and homebuilders.

Design

The liquid crystal display can display any form that can be drawn on a sheet of paper. It can display numbers, text, graphic symbols, and just about everything else. The construction of an LC cell is not bound to any shape. For example, the LED is essentially a point light source, and all displays made from LEDs are collections and modifications of points or dots. The LCD however is an area type display. It modifies light, it does not produce it. As such it can be virtually any shape and size. Displays built from liquid crystals can have smooth flowing curves, very fine definition, and a limitless array of pictographic symbols.

An LCD's final display form (or font) is totally flexible. This is one of the LCD's major good points. For instance, say you are a dairy farmer and have an application that requires a display to readout temperature in several locations. The temperature information can be displayed on a standard set of numbers, but you wish to identify the various temperature locations with little pictures. The house, the barn, the milk cooler, and the well, for example can be represented by small pictures instead of alphabetical names. These pictures can be drawn on paper and an LCD is made using these drawings as patterns. The finished LCD will display the pictures exactly as drawn. Words, pictures, or symbols used in this manner are called annunciators. The advantages of this approach are obvious; displays are pictographic and thereby multilingual, and much more communicative. This is especially true in pictographic languages such as Japanese and Chinese. It is very difficult to display pictographic characters on even a very fine dot matrix display. The LCD is the best type for displaying customized characters.

Power Requirements

The LCD has minimal power requirements. Currently, manufactured LCDs consume between 1 and 300 microwatts per square centimeter. This is the lowest power consumption of any display type now available. This very low power consumption allows most LCD products to be battery operated. From this fact, one might assume that the liquid crystal display is a direct current (dc) operated device. This is not true. The LCD is an alternating current (ac) operated device. If the actual LC cell is operated on dc, it will rapidly fail. The display's driving electronics produce a very symmetrical square wave to drive the LC cells.

Electrically, the LC cell can be modeled as a capacitor with both series and parallel resistive elements. Figure 6-6 illustrates the equivalent electrical schematic of a liquid crystal cell. R_s is the spreading resistance, while R_L is the leaking resistance of the LC cell. R_s is inherent resistance of the electrodes driving both poles of the LC cell, and is very low, less than 1 Ω. R_L represents the resistance to ac electron flow through the cell and is very high, usually over 10 MΩ. The capacitive element of the LC crystal is around 1000 picofarads.

The contrast of an LC cell is directly proportional to the peak voltage across the cell. Three to 10 peak-to-peak ac volts are used by most displays, with a very low dc voltage component. If the cell is subjected to dc voltages over 25 mV, the chemical composition of the cell is rapidly changed. These changes are catastrophic and lead to failure of the liquid crystal cell. In some cases, dc drive of the LC cell causes the indium tin oxide electrodes to be reduced to indium tin. While indium tin oxide is transparent, indium tin is not.

Fig. 6-6. Electrical model of an LC cell

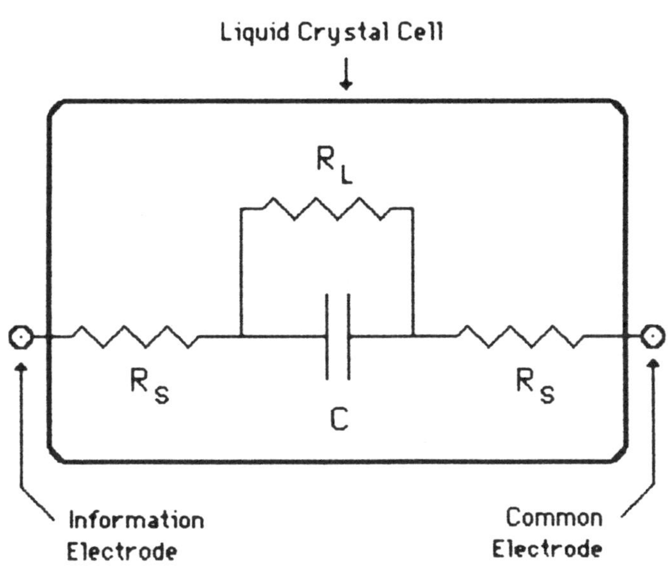

In other cases, the dc electron transfer across the LC cell can produce plating between the electrodes of the LC cell. In all cases, the LC cell is an ac operated device; the dc voltage component across the cell must be minimized.

There are many drive techniques used to convert the dc voltage contained within the battery to the ac voltage that is acceptable to the LCD. The most common scheme uses a 50% duty cycle square wave that is generated by an oscillator. This signal is applied to the LCD's common or backplane electrode. The same signal is applied to one input of an exclusive OR gate (EX-OR). The EX-OR's output is connected to the information electrode of the LC cell. When the other input to the EX-OR is at logic ground, then the output of the EX-OR gate is identical (in phase) with the common signal provided by the 50% duty cycle square wave oscillator. In this condition, there is no RMS voltage across the LC cell and no information is displayed. If the second input of the EX-OR is brought to logic level high, then the signal out of the EX-OR will be 180° out of phase to the square wave oscillator signal. This will cause a peak ac voltage of 2 times the supply dc voltage to appear across the LC cell. This ac voltage across the cell will untwist the internal LC material, the segment will go dark, and the cell will display information. Figure 6-7 shows this drive method in schematic form, along with the timing cycles involved. Note that the peak voltage across the LC elements are 2 times the supply voltage, while the rms voltage is equal to the supply voltage. It is very important to

Fig.6-7. LCD drive circuit and timing waveforms

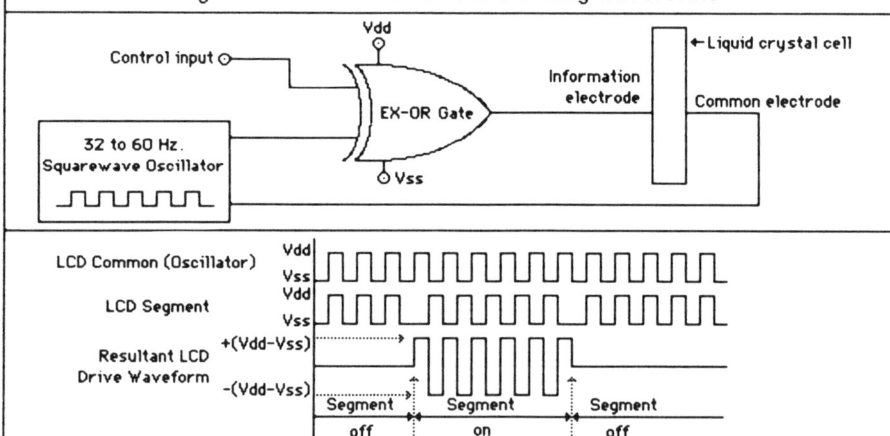

use CMOS electronics to drive LCDs. The ability of CMOS logic to switch very close to ground is necessary to reduce the dc voltage component across the LC cell.

The frequency of the square wave oscillator is critical. If the oscillator is running at less than 30 Hz, then the display will appear to flicker. The power consumption of the LC cell is directly proportional to the frequency of operation. Operation above 100 Hz increases the LC cell's power consumption. Most manufacturers recommend running their displays between 32 Hz and 60 Hz.

Operation at frequencies over 60 Hz also increases *ghosting* in the display. Ghosting is the partial activation of segments which should be deactivated. This is caused by capacitive coupling between the display's elements. Unused LC elements should be attached to the common terminal of the display. This reduces ghosting in the unused segments.

Contrast

The LCD is a light modifier, not a light producer. As such, its light output is measured in terms of contrast and not in terms of brightness. The contrast of an LC cell is measured as the ratio of how much light is being transmitted by inactive elements to the light being transmitted by active elements. Contrast ratios vary from 3 to 1 to over 20 to 1. This contrast ratio is relatively constant over the display's entire operating temperature and voltage range.

The contrast ratio of the LCD is also affected by the ac drive voltage. When this voltage falls below about 2 volts, the contrast ratio of the LCD comes very close to unity. In a typical LC cell, 10% contrast can be generated by 1.7 V_{RMS} at 25° C, while the same cell will take 2.0 V_{RMS} at 0° C. 90% contrast can be generated within the same cell by 2.8 V_{RMS} at 25° C, and 3.1 V_{RMS} at 0° C. Most LCDs are saturated at voltages between 3 and 5 ac rms volts, and contrast is not efficiently increased by further increasing the ac drive voltage. Excess drive voltage will increase ghosting problems and power consumption. You have probably noticed that your LCD watch's display becomes dim and hard to read when the watch's batteries are low. This is a practical example of the relationship between RMS drive voltage and contrast.

Resolution

LCD resolution is increasing at a very rapid rate. Early models LCDs were inherently low resolution devices. As dot matrix type displays, their pixel size was much too large. This was due in great part to the electrodes which conveyed information to the liquid crystal cells. The use of transparent electrode materials such as indium tin oxide have solved this problem. This allowed the LC displays to become more densely packed with pixels, thus increasing their resolution.

In the mid 1970's, high resolution in LCDs was 20 pixels per square centimeter. This is a pixel area of 5 square mm. By the early 1980's, the pixel density in LC displays was up to 528 pixels per square cm. This amounts to an individual pixel area of 0.19 square mm. The increase of the LCD's resolution increased over 25 times in 10 years. Modern researchers have experimental LC displays with 4039 pixels per square cm. This is a pixel area of 0.024 square mm. Such extremely high resolution LCDs are intended for television and computer monitor service. These prototype LCDs have resolutions four times greater than CRTs in television service today.

Resolution is no longer a problem for the LC display. The future holds the possibility of LCDs with over 230,000 pixels in an area of 57 square cm. This 4.25 inch diagonal LCD has just slightly less area than a five inch CRT commonly used on small TV sets, and about four times the resolution. Flat screen color television receivers should become commonplace and inexpensive before 1990.

Speed

Slow operating speed was one of the early problems with the twisted nematic (TN) LCDs. The display simply could not turn its elements on and off fast enough to display moving pictures. The reasons for this are built into the chemical nature of the liquid crystal medium and the physical cell construction. The speed of any particular LC cell's operation is greatly dependent on its temperature and drive method. An electric field must be maintained across an active liquid crystal or it will twist and the cell will become inactive. The time it takes the LC cell to respond to this electric field is called the turn-on time. Turn-on time is the sum of two factors. One factor is the turn-on delay before the electric field is established around the crystal, and the other is the rise time it takes the crystal to straighten out under the field's influence. The time it takes the crystal to retwist after the electric field is removed is called the turn-off time. Turn-off time is the sum of turn-off delay and the time it takes the crystal to respond after the field is gong (called decay time). Fig-

Fig. 6-8. LCD response time factors

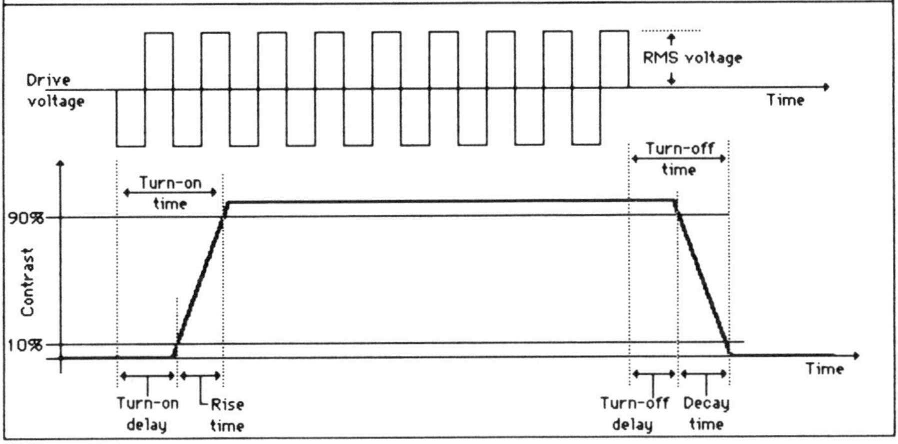

ure 6-8 shows the relationship between all these operating time factors for a typical TN liquid crystal cell.

In terms of real time, a typical LC cell will turn-on in 20 milliseconds (ms), and turn-off in 100 ms when the LC cell's temperature is at 20° C. If the temperature is lowered to 0° C, the turn-on time increases to 90 ms, and the turn-off time to 2000 ms. The longer turn-off time than turn-on time is a function of the liquid crystal medium. It simply takes the liquid crystal more time to retwist itself after the electric field is removed than it takes to straighten when the field is applied. Figure 6-9 illustrates graphically the relationship between response time and temperature for a typical LCD using standard LC material. This graph clearly shows the poor speed performance of LCDs at low temperatures. In some cases, the use of special LC materials has minimally extended the low temperature operation. A general rule of thumb is to only expect LCDs to operate quickly at temperatures above 0° C.

Color

Liquid crystal displays are available in two colored forms. The first has a single colored LC cell on another colored background. Such LC cells are called dichroic, meaning two colored. For example, the elements of the display may appear red on a silver background, or black on a green background. The LC technology used to make

Fig. 6-9.

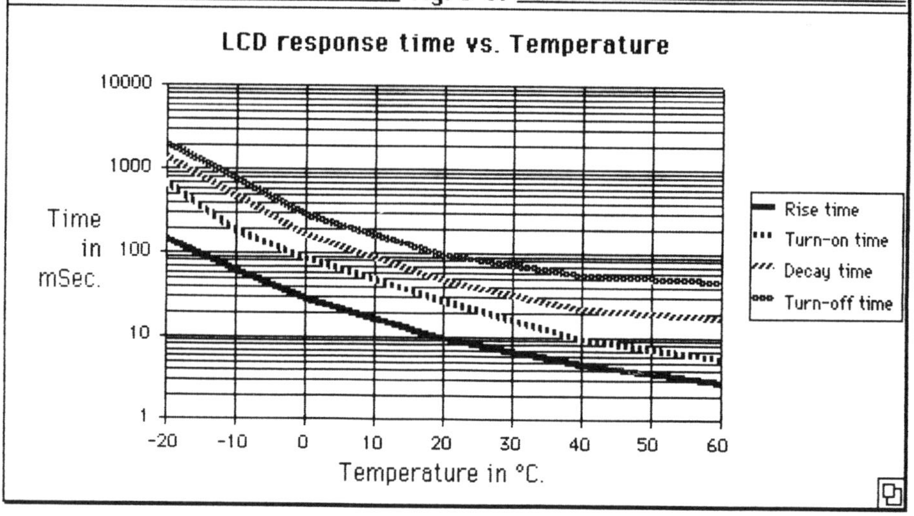

these dichroic displays is the Guest-Host technique and is described under that heading in this chapter. In some displays, two colors may be displayed by different cells against another colored background. Such displays are still called dichroic as individual elements, although colored differently, they have only one unchangeable color each.

The second type of LCD is designed for color television and color computer monitor service. In this type of display, each individual LC cell can appear as one or any combination of three colors, red, green, or blue. The full color LCDs display color images much in the same fashion as an RGB CRT monitor, or a three gun CRT used in standard color television service. The admixture of three primary colors (red, green, and blue) is used to produce a wide range of colors and tints. The technology used in most of these full color displays is the Thin-Film Transistor technique and is fully discussed under that heading in this chapter. These full color LCDs are usually backlit by a white light source, and do not rely on ambient light for illumination. Colored filters within each cell are shuttered by the LC media. This approach allows any, all, or none of the primary colors within the cell to be displayed.

LCD Size

The minimum element size of a liquid crystal cell is currently about 0.02 square millimeters. This remarkably small area appears to the eye as a dot at even close distances and is much smaller than the period at the end of this sentence. Individual LC elements can be constructed as large as required; there is no upper limit to the size of an individual LC cell.

Element Thickness

The thickness of an LC cell has a profound effect on the cell's viewing angle. The thicker the cell, the more narrow the viewing angle. The big push in LCD technology is toward thinner and thinner LC elements. LC cells are now commonly produced with thicknesses in the range of 1.5 to 5 millimeters. This dimension is the entire cell's thickness, including polarizers, electrodes, glass, and everything else necessary to implement the display. This size is decreasing rapidly as research is conducted on newer liquid crystal compounds and drive techniques.

Minimum and Maximum Display Size

The smallest numerical LCDs are used in watches. These small displays are assembled on an integrated circuit package of 32 pins. Figure 6-10 illustrates the physical dimensions of a typical small LCD display with 5.1 mm high digits. Larger numerical LCDs are used in digital multimeters, test equipment, calculators, and other commercial electronics. An example of a larger display with 25.4 mm high digits is shown in Fig. 6-11.

Fig. 6-10. A small numerical LCD

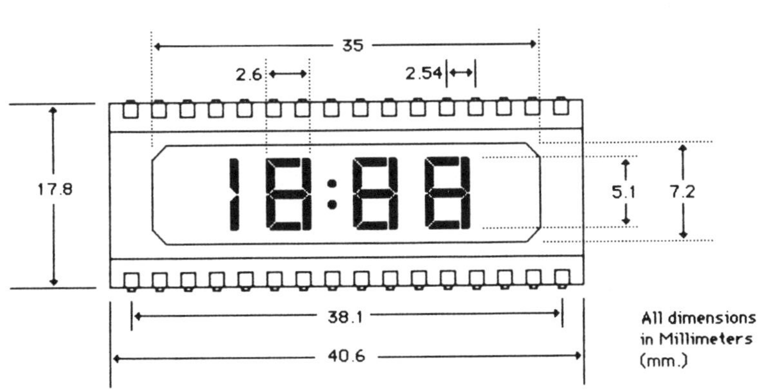

Fig.6-11. A large numerical LCD

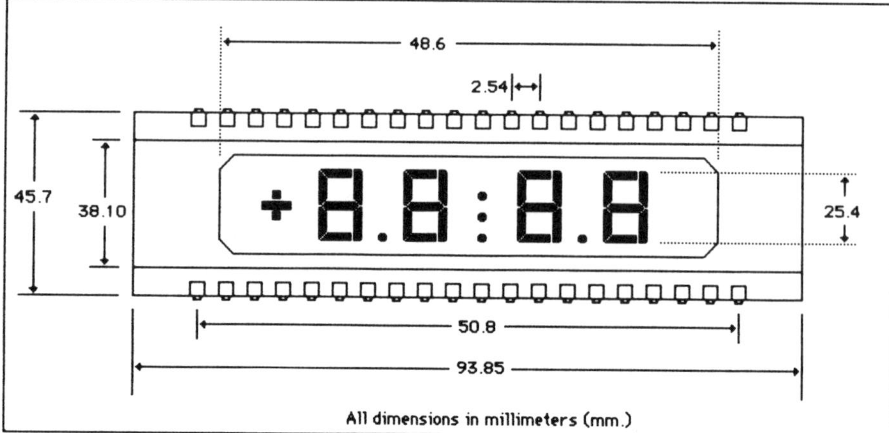

Liquid crystal displays intended for television service are growing very large. A monochrome display is available with a 9 in. diagonal measurement, while colored LCDs are available up to a 4.5 in. diagonal measurement. The problems with the large dot-matrix displays is manufacturing perfection. A large dot-matrix display can contain over 200,000 individual LC cells. Every one of these cells must function perfectly. Very tight manufacturing processes are necessary to produce a display of this size and density with no defects. When a display has this many pixels, the problem of addressing and driving these pixels becomes acute. Much of the current research on color LCDs is centered on this problem.

Operating Characteristics

In comparison to other display technologies, the operating characteristics of the LCD are somewhat limited. Factors such as temperature, viewing angle, and ambient lighting are critical to satisfactory LCD performance. A thorough understanding of the relationship between these factors and the LCD is essential. Within its limitations, the LCD offers effective image display with a minimum of power consumption. If these limitations are exceeded, the LCD offers poor performance and may even experience catastrophic failure.

Visual Angle

Early LCDs had very narrow viewing angles. This was due to their relatively large cell thickness, which was tied to the early manufacturing processes used to make the display. The actual operation of the LC cell depends on the passage of light through the cell. As such, the angle at which the cell is viewed is critical. The LCD exhibits its greatest contrast when viewed from 0°, i.e., perpendicular to its face. As the viewing angle is increased, the contrast of the display decreases. The rate of the decrease of contrast in relation to viewing angle is a function of the ratio of the smallest dimension of the LC cell to its thickness. The thinner the LC cell, the greater its viewing angle. It is simply a matter of geometry. Figure 6-12 illustrates the contrast to viewing angle curve for a typical wide angle numeric LCD display.

Narrow viewing angle LCDs lose all contrast (and thereby their image) when viewed from an angle as small as 10° on either side of a perpendicular to the displays face. Wide angle LCDs may be viewed at angles up to 35° on either side of the face's perpendicular. Narrow types are rapidly falling into disuse as the wider types become cheaper.

In order to get the maximum viewing angle and contrast on any LCD display, one should place the display so that ambient light is

Fig. 6-12.

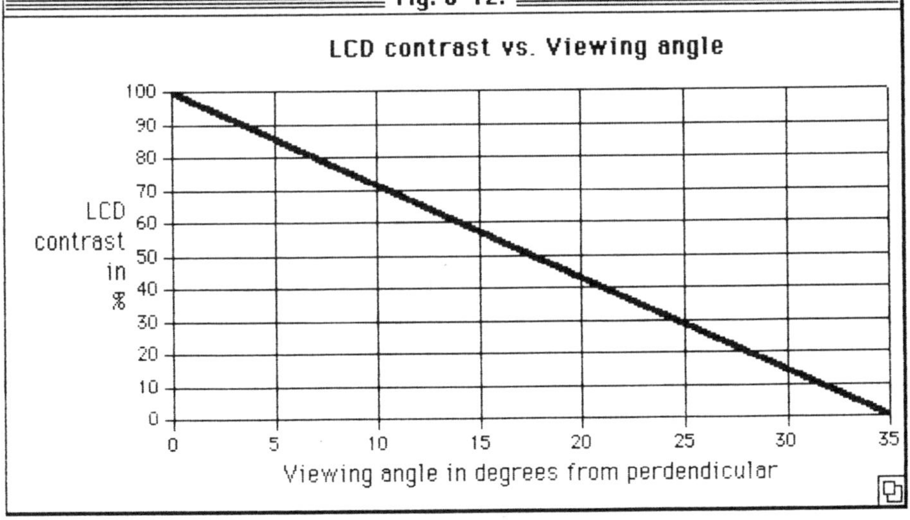

as near to perpendicular to the display's face as possible. This allows the maximum amount of light to make the round trip through the LC cell, and assures the widest angle of view possible. This technique is for LCDs that use ambient light sources, and backlit displays are excepted.

Memory

The LC cell does not exhibit any memory. It returns to its original twisted configuration when the electric field is removed. In fact, this is one of the problems encountered when driving LC displays with large numbers of pixels. Each and every pixel must be scanned over 30 times per second, or the display will appear to flicker. In order to give the cell memory or "persistence," thin-film transistors (TFT) are used to drive the cell. This TFT technique acts as virtual memory of the cell's on or off state, and the cell maintains its state without continual rescanning.

Operating Temperature Range

Temperature is a critical factor in LCD operation. The LCD has a relatively narrow range of operation temperatures when compared with any other display technology. Generally, LCDs are intended for use at temperatures above freezing. Below 0° C the speed of LCD operation is greatly decreased (see Fig. 6-9). The LC media is a liquid, and cooling it increases its viscosity, making it respond sluggishly to the electric field.

The LCD is not designed to operate at temperatures in excess of 50° C. At higher temperatures, the liquid crystals have sufficient thermal energy so that they will not hold their twist in the off state. This is due strictly to the heat caused molecular activity of the liquid crystal material. At temperatures above 60° C the entire display area goes dark, i.e., appears activated. This condition can be remedied by simply cooling the display. If LCDs are stored at temperatures above 85° C they may be permanently damaged. Excessive heat can rupture the polymeric seals between the individual LC elements and ruin the display. Never leave LCD devices on the seat of a closed car in the hot sun. This is a quick way to permanently destroy the display.

LCD Longevity

One of the major advantages of all LCDs is their incredibly long lifetime. Most types of LCDs last over 50,000 hours of operation before catastrophic failure. This amounts to over 5 years of 24 hour per day display operation. In normal 8 hour per day use, the LCD will last over 15 years. Parametric failure, or display dimming, is not a problem with the LCD.

Longevity in LCDs is assured by not exceeding their operating limits. Temperature is the first factor to consider. Keep the display within the 0° C to 50° C range. Storage above 85° C for even short periods can produce immediate catastrophic failure. Drive voltage is another factor. Keep drive voltages to less than 5 Vac RMS for maximum display life.

LCD Viewing Modes

Liquid crystal displays operate by modifying ambient light. In order to deal with a wider variety of ambient lighting situations, the LCD is manufactured in three viewing modes—reflective mode, transmissive mode, and transflective mode. In the reflective mode, the display uses the ambient light which enters the display's front panel. Reflective mode LCDs are readable only in the presence of ambient light, they do not contain a dedicated light source on board for night time use. Reflective mode LCDs can accept ambient lighting only from the display's front panel. Transmissive mode LCDs use a dedicated on-board backlight all the time, and do not use ambient light for modification. Transmissive LCDs will only accept light for modification from behind the display. Transflective mode LCDs use both viewing methods, reflective and transmissive. Transflective LCDs can operate from either ambient lighting or from an on board light source contained near the LC display. Transflective LCDs can accept light from either side of the display, front or back. Figure 6-13 illustrates these viewing modes, how they operate, and their characteristics.

One major disadvantage of the transmissive mode is that it requires continuous operation of a light source. This consumes thousands of times more power than the actual LCD, and nullifies the LCD's best feature—low power consumption. The transflective mode offers the best of both worlds, ambient light is used by the display unless it is necessary to turn on its internal light source. This keeps power consumption down. LCD watches with tiny incandescent lightbulbs inside them for night viewing have the transflective type of LCD. It is best to use this built-in lightbulb sparingly as it draws over 2000 times the power of the basic watch electronics and the LCD.

Fig. 6-13. LCD viewing modes				
Viewing Mode	Transmissive	Reflective Bead	Reflective Foil	Transflective
Description of Mode	Doesn't use reflector. Illuminated from behind by a bulb.	Uses a reflective surface to reflect ambient light back through the liquid crystal cell.		Uses both reflector and/or backlighting.
Advantage	Backlighting assures readability in all ambient lighting situations.	Minimal shadow effect. Low power consumption	Highest contrast Brightest background Low power consumption	Display readable in all lighting situations. Controlable power consumption
Disadvantage	Reduced viewing angle. High power consumption.	Low contrast ratio when viewed from straight ahead		Lowest contrast ratio of all types.

The illumination source for transflective and transmissive mode LCDs does not necessarily have to be an incandescent lamp, although this is the most common illuminator used. Both LEDs and electroluminescent panels can also be used for backlighting. The LED is very much more efficient at this job than either the incandescent lamp or the electroluminescent panel. However, the LED is not capable of high levels of illumination, and transmissive displays illuminated by LEDs are hard to read in high ambient light situations. The electroluminescent panel (ELP) has the distinct disadvantage of requiring a fair amount of power at ac voltages in excess of 100 Vac for operation. This puts the ELP out of this illumination job for portable battery powered equipment. One novel approach to LCD backlighting is the use of slightly radioactive (but safe to humans) tritium gas to excite a phosphor panel to glow behind the LCD. This tritium backlight consumes no electricity, but its faint green glow is hard to read at twilight. Figure 6-14 shows how several different types of backlights can be applied to LCDs.

TWISTED NEMATIC LCD (TN)

The twisted nematic (TN) LCD is the oldest and most common type. The TN LCD is commonly found in watches, digital meters, calculators, and most consumer electronics that use LCDs. The TN LCDs are monochromatic, information appears as dark areas against a light background.

How It Works

The operation of the TN LCD is thoroughly described in the beginning of this chapter. See Figs. 6-4, and 6-5 for pictorial presentations of the TN cell's operation. One technical characteristic of all TN LCDs is that they are directly switched by the driving electronics which are external to the display. This is radically different in performance from other types such as the TFT LCD which carry some of their driving electronics on board.

One might think that the TN LCD technology is static and being surpassed by other types of LCDs. This is not true. There is still much research being conducted on the TN LCD. One promising technology applies a special LC compound that undergoes 270° rotation from its on to its off state. This new LC material offers higher contrast ratios and wider viewing angles than conventional TN LC materials.

Advantages

The major advantage of the TN LCD over other types is cost. All LCD share the definite feature of low power consumption. At this time, there is no display technology that uses less power than the LCD. The TN LCD is the simplest type of liquid crystal display to manufacture, and its price reflects this. The TN LCD shares the easy to customize characteristics of all LCDs. Virtually anything that can be drawn on paper can be displayed on the TN LCD in monochrome.

Fig. 6-14. LCD backlighting techniques

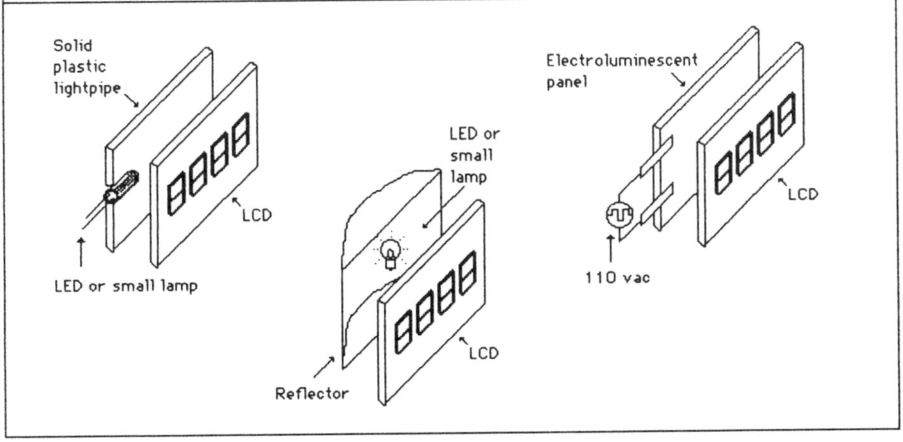

Disadvantages

The TN LCD suffers from several disadvantages, among which are, restricted viewing angle, slow speed, and narrow temperature operating range. In spite of these drawbacks, the TN LCD is now the most commonly used electronic display device except the CRT. Operating temperatures within the human environment are well within the displays range. In most applications, such as watches and calculators, the TN LCD is more than fast enough to do the job. It is only when displaying moving graphics (like TV) that the TN LCD is too slow. Viewing angle is also not a problem with small items like calculators and watches, we simply orient the entire device so that the display's contrast is peaked.

In both the reflective and transflective modes of operation, the TN LCD requires two polarizers and a reflector. As no optical media is 100% efficient, there are losses of the light with each and every element placed in the light's path. The use of two polarizers and a reflector reduce the TN LCD's contrast in comparison to other types of LCD.

In comparison with other display technologies, the LCD seems to have many disadvantages. In fact, these disadvantages are real, but are miniscule in comparison to the display's positive points. The LCD really fits in with modern trends in electronics. All electronic devices are shrinking in size and power consumption. The LCD is the perfect display medium for these new electronic devices.

Sample Applications

The sample applications described below are of a simple nature. They are suited for homebuilders. These applications are based on an entire family of ICs which are designed to encode and drive the LCD. The ICs and circuits listed for the TN LCD are direct drive, not multiplexed. Table 6-1 lists the IC's purpose, the number of digits it handles, the IC's manufacturer, and number.

TN LCDs are usually employed in direct drive service. Multiplexing the LCD requires greater speed and contrast than the TN LCD can deliver. Multiplexed service is reserved for LCDs such as the TFT LCD. Some of the circuits below, such as the seven segment decoder/driver, require the user to supply a separate oscillator to drive the display. Figure 6-15 shows a circuit using the TLC 555 timer to provide a 32 Hz, 50% duty cycle, square waveform. This timer is available from Radio Shack for under $2. This timer circuit is easy to build and inexpensive. Use a low leakage

Table 6-1. Driver ICs for Direct Drive LCDs.

Function	# of digits	Manufacturer	Manufacturer's part number
BCD to 7 segment decoder/driver	1	RCA/SGS	CD4054
BCD to 7 segment decoder/driver	1	RCA/Mitel	CD4055A,CD4056A
BCD to 7 segment decoder/driver	4	Hughes	HLCD0437
BCD to 7 segment decoder/driver	4	Intersil	ICM7211
BCD to 7 segment decoder/driver	4	Siliconix	DF411,DF412
BCD to 7 segment decoder/driver	4	National	DM7211
Digital volt meter/LCD driver	3½	Intersil	ICL7106,ICL7116
Digital counter/LCD driver	4½	Intersil	ICM7224
Up/down counter	4	National	MM74C945,MM74C947

capacitor, such as a tantalum type, for the timing chain. The resistors should be within 1% of the specified value if the circuit is to be accurate in frequency and duty cycle.

A Seven Segment Decoder/Driver

This circuit is all that is necessary to display a decimal number on a seven segment LC display. The circuit uses the timer building block shown in Fig. 6-15. The timer is combined with a CD4055A seven segment decoder/driver to produce a working LCD of one digit. The CD4055A is manufactured by RCA, and accepts BCD data as its input. It does not require an external EX-OR gate to drive the LCD. The CD4055A is a CMOS IC and will operate on voltages as high as 20 Vdc. In this example the circuit uses 5 Vdc as a supply

Fig. 6-15. TLC 555 circuit to drive LCDs

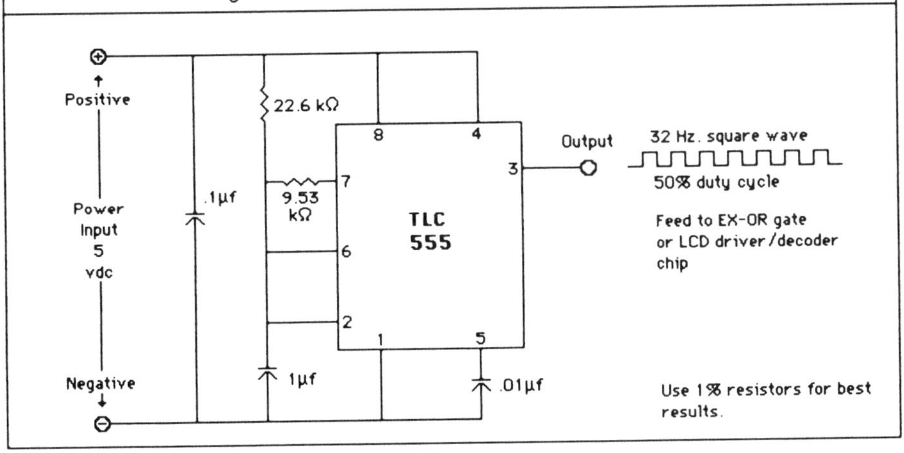

voltage. Keeping the supply voltage at 5 volts is desirable since anything more will not produce a display of more contrast, but it will increase power consumption. The input current of the CD4055A is less than 10 mA, and the package is capable of dissipating 300 mW.

Figure 6-16 shows the schematic for a single digit of seven segments. The circuit is very similar to those used to drive seven segment LEDs. The major difference is that the LCD is not a dc operated device like the LED. It is necessary to provide a symmetrical square wave to drive the LCD. If additional digits are required, then the same circuit may be applied to each. Each digit requires its own CD4055A decoder/driver. The timing circuitry may be shared by all the digits in the display. The encoding of the segments of the digit is exactly the same as the seven segment LED displays. See Figure 5-27 for the segment identification information.

A Digital Voltmeter

This circuit uses the 7106 integrated circuit made by Intersil. This chip contains a 3½ digit analog to digital converter, an on-board oscillator, and all the active circuitry necessary to complete a working digital voltmeter with an LCD. The signal input accepts an analog voltage of up to 200 mv, and can be fed with a resistive voltage divider for voltages over 200 mv. The decimal point on the display is set manually by a series of switched EX-OR gates. The decimal point switch and the signal input voltage divider selection switch can be

Fig. 6-16. Single digit LCD driver

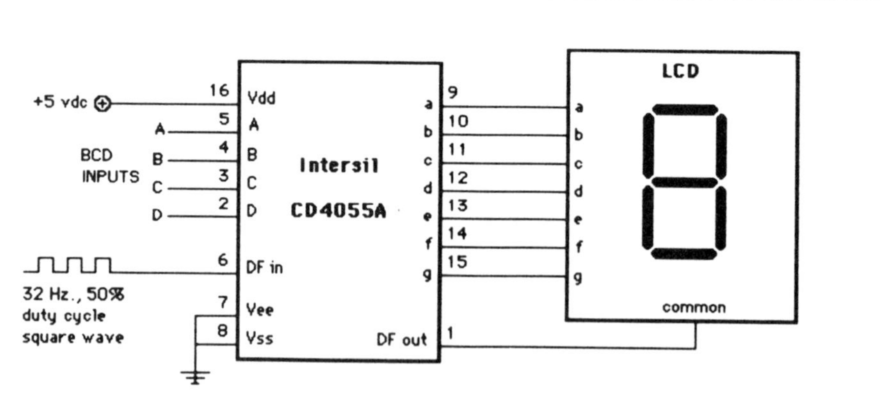

Fig. 6-17. 3 1/2 digit LCD voltmeter

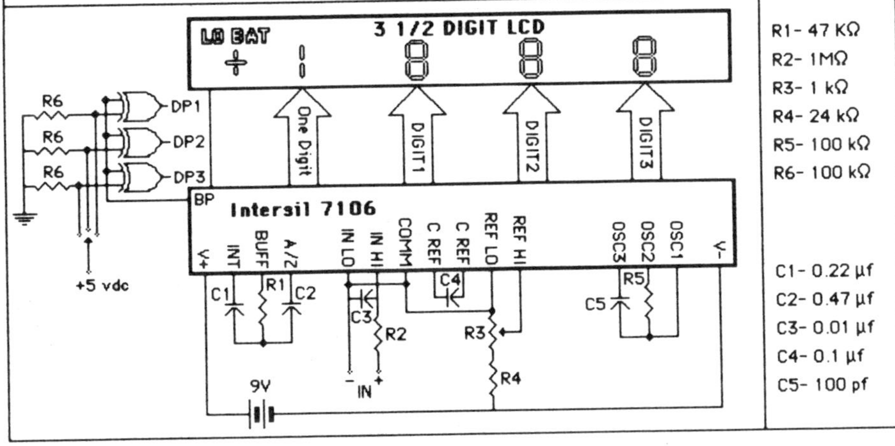

the same multi-decked switch. This simplifies the DVM's use to measure a wide range of voltages. Use 1% resistors for the input signal's voltage divider. This will assure accuracy on readings above 200 mv.

Figure 6-17 shows the schematic for the 3½ digit voltmeter. The 7106 is a 40 pin DIP and requires a very small number of external components to complete the circuit. The 7106 is available for under $15.00. The entire digital voltmeter is powered by a standard 9V transistor radio battery. Power consumption on this project is very low, the 9V battery will last for months of continuous service. It is a very good idea to use a socket for the 7106 when constructing this project. Even though this meter measures voltage, it can display a wide variety of other information. For examples, if the meter is connected across a wire shunt it will measure current, if the meter is wired to the thermometer probe in Fig. 5-39 it will measure temperature. The possibilities are only limited by your imagination.

The LCD chosen for this project has four digits, 0.5 inch tall. The most significant digit is a 1, while the other digits are seven segment types. There is a "LO BAT" annunciator included in the display, along with a plus or minus sign preceeding the 1. Figure 6-18 shows the physical layout of a typical LCD that may be used in the digital voltmeter.

Seven segment LCDs come in many sizes and packages. The method of mounting these various packages differ. Some of the LCDs come equipped with pins like a standard IC. The spacing on these

Fig. 6-18. 3 1/2 digit liquid crystal display

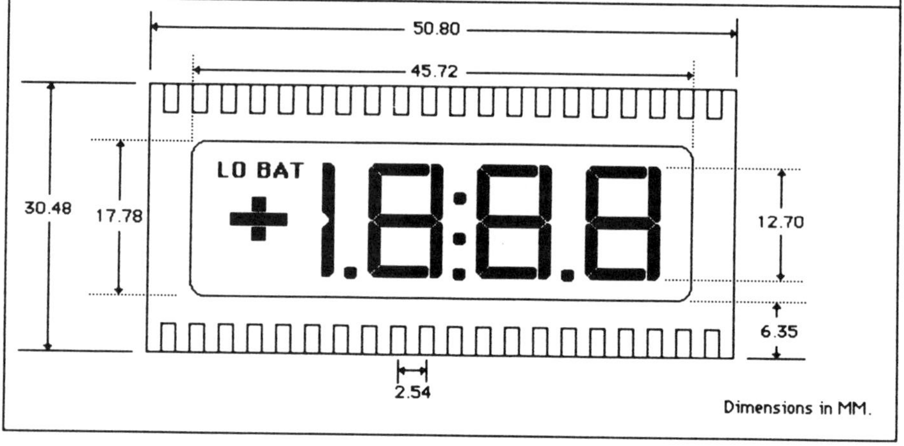

pins, however, is not standard IC pin spacing. The LCD is too wide to fit in standard IC sockets and special sockets must be used for "pinned" LCDs. Other LCDs are pinless and mount in several fashions. Some LCDs have their connections on a single edge, while others use both edges of the display for interconnection. Single edged LCDs are often mounted perpendicular to the printed circuit board in a special in-line socket. This method requires no soldering to the LCD, and allows for rapid installation and replacement. Figure 6-19 shows some of these LCD packages and their mounting methods. Note the use of conductive rubber spacers to both support the LCD and to conduct electricity to its contacts.

Cost

TN LCDs are the most inexpensive type of LCD. Most of the TN types available are either seven segment types or bar graphs. They cost between $5 and $20 depending on the size and complexity of the display. Including the extra electronics necessary to implement these displays, they are initially more expensive than the LED type. This additional expense is justified when one considers the savings in power, and thereby batteries. The LCD is the most efficient type of display to use in battery operated equipment.

METAL-INSULATOR-METAL LCD (MIM)

One of the major problems with some TN LCD designs are that

they require electrodes etched in the glass, both above and below the actual liquid crystal cell. We view the display through one of these etched layers of electrodes. The electrodes are made of transparent, conductive material deposited into the etched channels. Even though the material itself is transparent, it does not have the same index of refraction that glass does. The net result is that the etched electrode paths distort the light passing through the display. As TN LCDs grew in pixel density, the electrodes became a significant portion of the display's area and began obscuring the display. The metal-insulator-metal (MIM) type of LCD is an early attempt to reduce this problem of the LC cell's electrodes by limiting the lines etched into the glass to the backplane of the cell.

The MIM LCD is an "active" LCD type as it uses semiconductor junctions with the display itself. This distinction is important. The direct drive TN LC cells are passive devices; they do not contain switching or amplifying transistors. The MIM LCDs are the forerunners of the modern TFT LCDs as they are the first to use active devices within the actual display. The MIM LCD also differs from the TN type in that it is designed for matrix service and uses three electrodes per cell, one more than the two electrodes used in a direct drive TN cell. Two electrodes, called data and scanning gelectrodes, form the x-y addressable matrix, and the remaining electrode is held in common by all the display's pixels.

Fig. 6-19. LCD mounting techniques

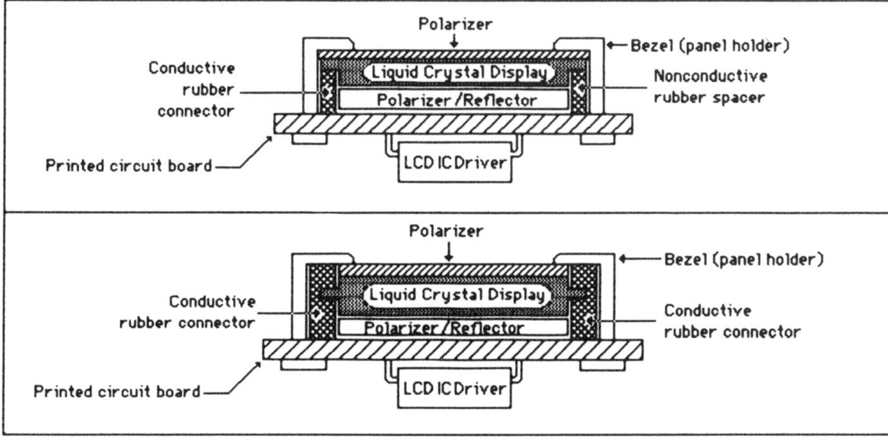

How It Works

The LC cells data (x) and scanning (y) electrodes are engraved on the same piece of glass located below the LC cell. These two lines form the x-y addressable matrix used to drive one of the cell's electrodes. The other electrode is the common electrode located above the LC cell. This common electrode is a continuous plane of transparent, conductive material which is deposited on glass. There are no lines etched on the glass which holds the common electrode. As such, there are no differences in the index of refraction through the common electrode/glass layer which serves as the display's faceplate.

The lower piece of glass forms the backplane of the display, and its etched lines do not appear on the display's face. There is a thin insulative layer deposited between the x and y lines to prevent short circuits between these lines. If electrodes were placed this closely on a standard TN type LCD, there would be extensive ghosting in the display due to capacitive coupling between the x and y lines. The very small distances that separate the x and y lines makes capacitive coupling between both these lines inevitable. TN LCDs which had all their electrodes in the same plane suffered greatly from partially activated LC cells (ghosting) and thereby greatly reduced contrast. In order to overcome this coupling effect, the data lines are isolated from their electrodes by a MIM junction.

The MIM junction is electrically equivalent to a bi-directional zener diode. This MIM junction is constructed by sandwiching a thin film of tantalum-pentoxide between two conductive metal layers. This MIM junction has a bi-directional voltage threshold below which electrons will not traverse the junction. If the voltage of the data signal is below this threshold, the LC cell is not activated. The use of this MIM junction allows the LC cells to ignore the low level capacitive coupling between the x and y lines.

Figure 6-20 shows an equivalent electrical schematic of a single MIM LC cell. Note that the MIM junction is represented as if it were two zener diodes wired anode to anode. This points out the bi-directional nature of the MIM junction. This bi-directional current flow is necessary as the LCD is driven by symmetrical square waves with virtually no dc component. Figure 6-21 shows the physical configuration of a single MIM LC cell. Note that the x-y electrodes and their lines are on the same piece of glass and in the same plane. This diagram shows only the lower backplane of glass. The upper

Fig. 6-20. MIM LC cell schematic

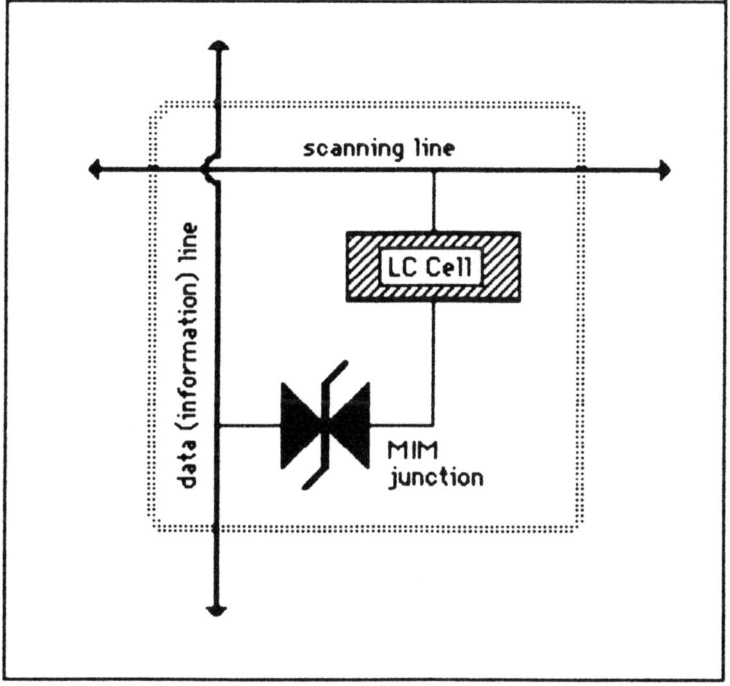

piece of glass, with its continuous common electrode, is placed above the LC cell.

Advantages

The elimination of the top, etched, electrodes from the LC cells produced two great advantages. Since there is no top layer of electrodes and their associated lines, the LC cells are thinner and thereby have greater viewing angles. The viewing angle of an LCD is geometrically related to the ratio of the cell's thickness to its horizontal size. Figure 6-22 illustrates the geometric relationship graphically. From this diagram, it is obvious why manufacturers are striving for ever thinner LCDs. As the thickness of the cells decreases, the display area of each pixel can also be decreased without reducing the display's viewing angle. Thinner LC cells are necessary if the LCDs are to have greater pixel densities.

Fig. 6-21. MIM LC physical construction

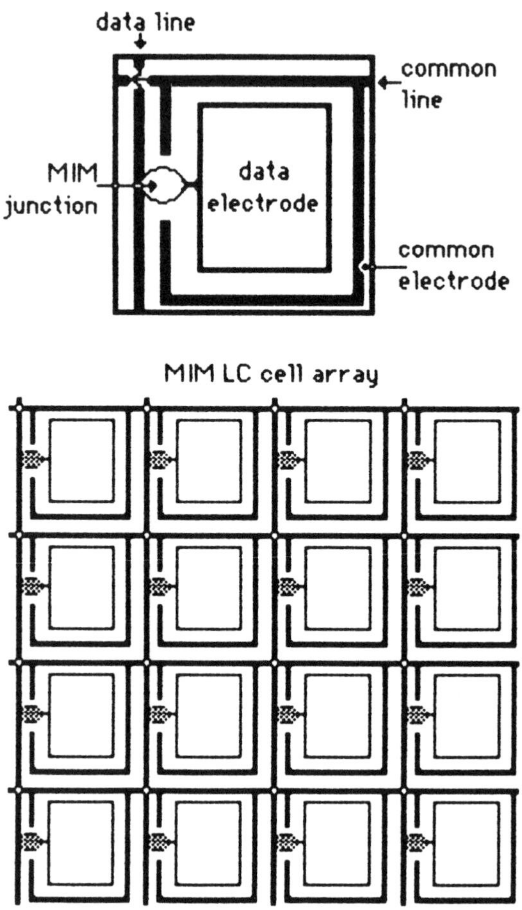

The lack of an etched upper electrode layer presents the light moving through the display with one less non-homogeneous layer to pass through. There are no problems with uneven refraction from the display's face. This increases the display's contrast by allowing the unactive cells to pass more light. The use of the MIM junction techniques gives this type of LCD greater contrast than the TN LCDs.

The MIM junction's line isolation characteristics also make the display better suited for multiplex service. In multiplex service, the driving waveforms are very fast square waves, many times faster than the square waves used to drive the TN LCDs. The higher speed of multiplex service increases capacitive coupling and ghosting. The MIM junction alleviates this problem, and allows this LCD to perform when multiplexed.

Disadvantages

Along with the MIM LCDs good points come several distinct disadvantages. The use of the MIM junction allows only two states for the LC cell, either on or off. There are no grey levels available from the MIM LCD as there are from other LCD technologies. The MIM junction avalanches once its voltage threshold is exceeded; it is not possible to partially activate the MIM junction. This fact has limited the MIM LCDs to a narrow range of devices that do not require any grey levels to be displayed.

An MIM LCD is more difficult to make than a direct drive TN LCD. Using the same plane to carry both the data (x) and the scanning (y) electrodes for the display increases the density of the traces on this plane. This increased electrode density complicates the manufacturing process. Manufacturing of the MIM LCD is also made more complex by the existence of semiconductor junctions within the display. Each and every pixel within the display has its own individual MIM junction. The manufacturing difficulties of

Fig. 6-22. LCD visual geometry

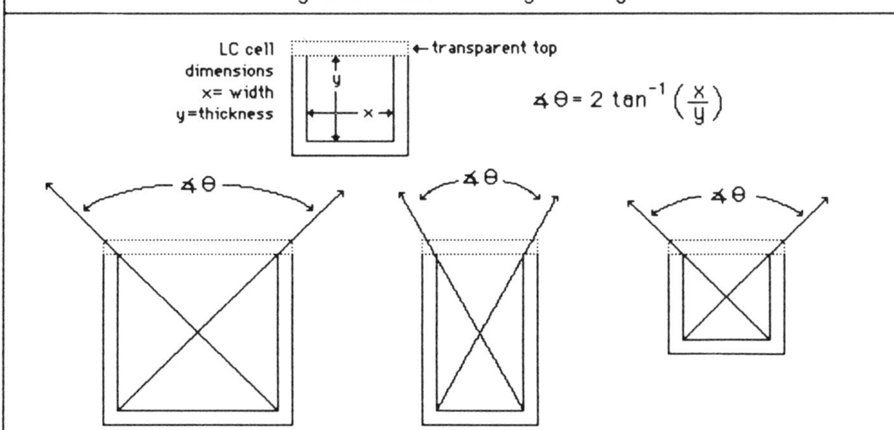

producing a display with thousands of perfect, densely packed MIM junctions, all of which work, are considerable. This factor drives up the cost of MIM LCDs, and all LCDs that use active, i.e., semiconductor, elements.

MIM LCD Applications

MIM LCDs are best suited for application in devices such as computers and test instrumentation. In these types of devices, high contrast displays are required. The MIM LCDs' lack of grey scale rendering makes them less suitable for entertainment uses such as television displays. Black and white LCD TV sets, with MIM LC cells, were produced as early as 1984, but were quickly replaced by more advanced TFT technologies.

Cost

MIM LCDs are no longer commercially available as they have been surpassed by the TFT varieties. They are mentioned here to show the progression of LCD technology as MIM types are the technical forerunner of the TFT devices.

THIN-FILM TRANSISTOR LCD (TFT)

The thin-film transistor (TFT) LCD is an extension of the ideas first applied in the MIM approach. The major differences is that the MIM junction is replaced with a transistor junction. The transistor junction gives more control over the LC cell's state and increases operating speed. The TFT uses the same matrix approach to multiplexing as does the MIM.

The TFT technology holds the greatest promise for color flat screens able to display moving graphics. They have high resolution, acceptable speed, and low power consumption. The active matrix addressing approach to LCD technology is the only now available type to meet these requirements.

How It Works

The physical construction of the TFT LC cell is very similar to that of the MIM LC cell. The x-y matrix lines are once again contained on the same glass backing plate of the display. The front glass plate is uniformly coated with the common electrode. The MIM junction is, however, replaced with a transistor junction. This junction serves the same purpose as the MIM junction but offers several advantages in addition to line isolation. The TFT junction can be constructed as a flip-flop. As a flip-flop, it will hold the LC cell in either an on or an off state until changed by the control circuitry. This gives the display a defacto memory and solves many problems with addressing and refreshing large, hi-res, displays.

The TFT junction can also respond to changes of state much more quickly than the MIM junction. The TFT operates as a current amplifier to more rapidly change the state of the electric field surrounding the LC cell. This increase in speed allows this type of LCD to display acceptable moving graphics. This additional speed is also required to meet the rigors of multiplex service. For example, take a 4 pixel by 4 pixel display. It contains 16 elements addressed on an x-y matrix. Each row or column must be addressed in turn. This means that each row or column is only individually addressed 25% of the time. If the LC cell is not quick to respond, then moving graphics would "smear" as they moved across the display. The flip-flop type of memory also saves the central video processor the chore of continually updating unchanged pixels.

Each and every pixel within the display has its own discrete thin-film transistor junction. For example, in a display with 200,000 pixels there will also be 200,000 TFTs. These transistor junctions can be made with a variety of semiconductor technologies. Poly-crystaline silicon, amorphous silicon, and cadmium selenide are some of the types now in use. The process of fabricating these TFTs in the LCD is a very involved hi-tech process. Semiconductor construction techniques like laser recrystalization, film deposition, and ion implantation are employed. In some cases, the TFTs are fabricated right on the glass backplane of the display, in others, the TFTs are made separately and transferred to the backplane. The electrical schematic of a typical TFT LC cell is shown in Fig. 6-23.

The TFT junctions that drive the LC cell are very small and consume very little power. A typical unit will have a current drain of less than 0.1 μA at 5 Vdc. Even in LCDs with very small pixels, the TFT is still miniscule and occupies less than 2% of the LC cell's surface area. Figure 6-24 illustrates the physical construction of a typical TFT LC cell's backplane. This illustration is very magnified, actually the entire LC pixel is smaller than this period.

The TFT transistors that control this type of LC display can be driven in linear mode. This means that the transistor junctions can be turned partially on and not necessarily saturated. This allows the TFT LCD to be partially activated and to display a wide range of grey tones. Monochrome TFT LCDs are currently manufactured

Fig. 6-23. Electrical schematic for a TFT LC cell

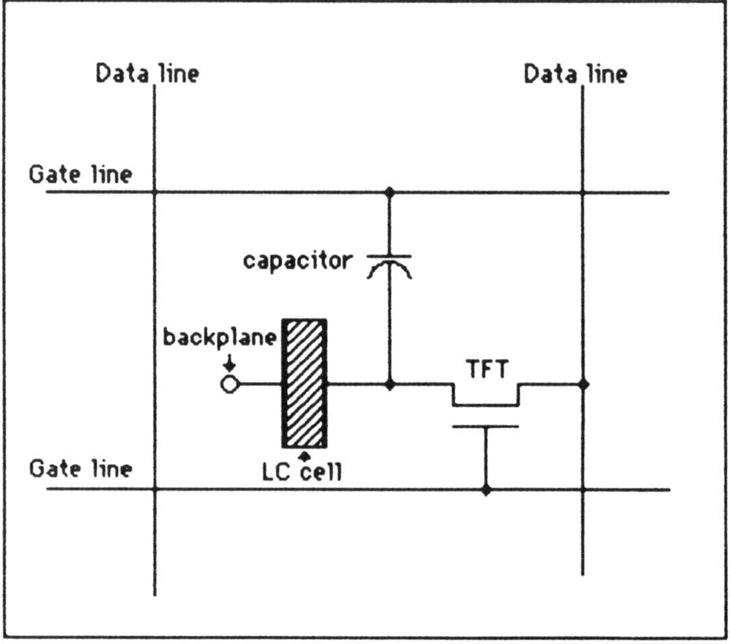

Fig. 6-24. A TFT LC array

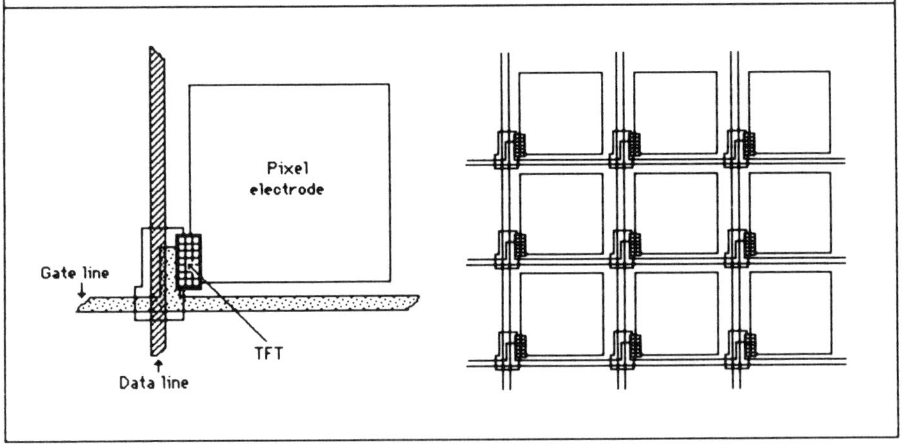

that can display 16 shades of grey. The use of grey scales complicates the encoding of the multiplexed signals driving the display's pixels. In the linear mode, TFTs cannot be used as flip-flops, but must be driven and refreshed with an analog voltage level. This places additional speed demands on the driving electronics used in LCD's displaying grey tones.

Advantages

The TFT LCD offers many advantages over the earlier MIM types. The TFT is over three times faster. The increase in speed makes larger flicker-free displays possible. The TFT LCD is thinner, allowing for increased pixel density and thereby resolution. Pixel sizes in commercial displays are down to less than 0.04 square mm per pixel. This is fine grained enough to display moving graphics even when viewed at close range. Along with smaller and thinner pixels comes a greatly increased viewing angle. Some modern TFT LCDs have acceptable viewing angles of up to 160°. Wide viewing angles are essential with large LC displays where it is impossible to view all pixels perpendicularly at the same time.

The TFTs are able to drive the LC cells harder than the MIM type due to the truly active nature of the TFT. The TFT is capable of establishing a more intense electric field, more rapidly, around the LC material. This combined with newer LC fluids give the TFT displays greatly increased contrast. TFT LC displays with contrast ratios of over 15 are now common; this is 5 times greater than the contrast of past TN LCDs.

The TFT is the technology that will produce a workable color LCD television at a marketable price. The TFT is currently the only LCD technology that possesses both the resolution and speed necessary for colored moving graphics. See the sample application below for a thorough description and discussion of the operation of a color TFT LCD.

Disadvantages

In a word, expense. The TFT is the most difficult of all LCD types to manufacture. It is, thus, the most expensive type. The TFT types are being made in larger sizes, up to 15 inches diagonal measurement, with over 300,000 individual LC pixels. Each of these pixels is fed by two electrical lines, and switched via its own thin-film transistor. This amounts to over 300,000 TFTs fed by over 600,000 matrix points. The complexity of such a display is staggering.

The density of the individual components on the backplane alone necessitates the very tightest manufacturing tolerances. Inevitably, many of the displays finish the manufacturing process in less than perfect operating condition. These losses, plus the overall complexity of the display give rise to its greatest disadvantage—it's expensive.

Sample Application—A Flat Screen Color Television

Several types of color LCD televisions are currently being manufactured. This type of service is where almost all TFT LC arrays are used, whether colored or monochrome. The most common method of displaying color on an LCD is to insert a single layer of colored filters between the upper glass and the common electrode layer of a transmissive TFT LCD. These filters are alternating colors of red, green, and blue and are thicker than the actual LC cells. They are positioned in a single layered checkerboard pattern over the LCD, with each colored filter having its own individual LC cell. A full color display is obtained by mixing these three primary colors, much in the same fashion as a conventional color CRT or RGB monitor. Figure 6-25 illustrates the color matrix filter arrangement. The layer of filter material is placed on the upper glass portion of the LCD by either electrodeposition or photolithography. Electrodeposition offers smaller pixels and higher resolution than the photolithography process. One of the major problems with both processes of attaching the colored filters to the upper glass is overlap. The individual filters are very small and even a

Fig. 6-25. Structure of a full color TFT LCD

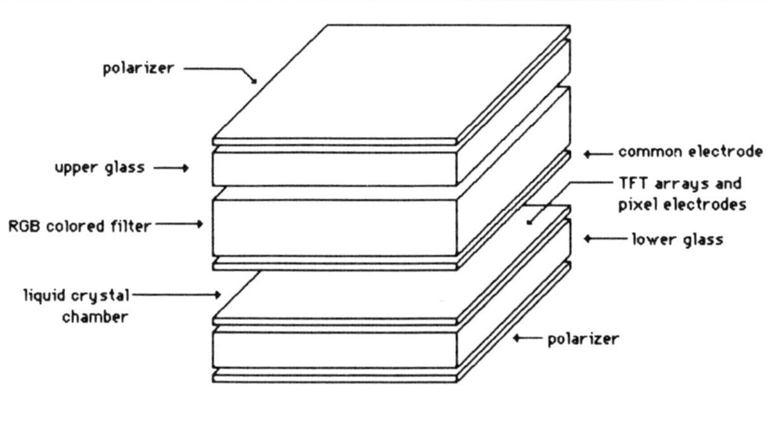

Fig. 6-26. Color LCD filter matrix

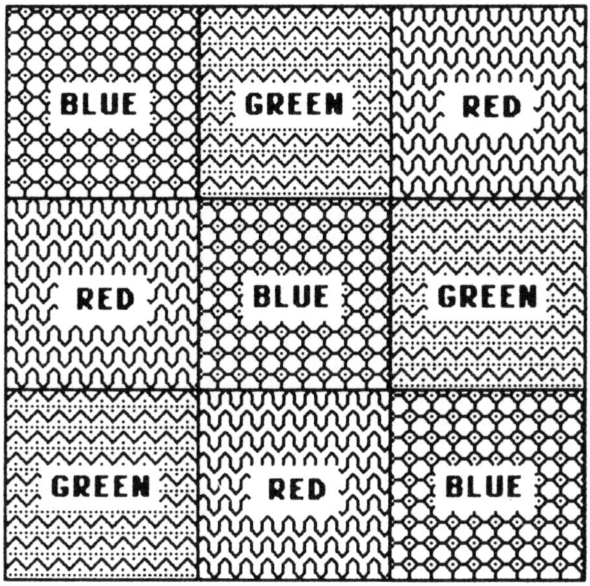

miniscule amount of overlap between the colored filters produces very noticeable dark lines in the finished display.

The colored filter approach demands a very pure and highly concentrated white light source for color correct operation of the LCD. As such, this type of device is transmissive and backlit by a dedicated on board light source. This source is usually fluorescent which emits a very balanced, intense white light. This backlight is responsible for most of the power consumed by the color TFT LCD. Figure 6-26 illustrates the configuration of a representative small section of a color TFT LCD. This illustration shows a block of nine pixels, three red, three blue, and three green. This is only a very small section of a display which actually contains hundreds of thousands of these individual elements.

Some of the problems associated with the colored filter technique are lost light within the filter and reduced resolution in comparison with monochrome TFT LCDs. In order to obtain acceptable color, the filters are very thick in relation to the LC cells.

These filters are not perfectly transmissive, some light is lost within the filter. The thicker the filter, the greater the loss. Losses within the filters are compensated for by increasing the brightness of the display's backlight. This results in increased power consumption. The filter technique also reduces the effective resolution of the LC display. Since each colored filter has its own individual LC cell, it takes a minimum of three cells, one red, one green, and one blue, to display a single white element. LCD manufacturers are already producing the individual LC cells as small as possible. The filter approach effectively reduces the displays resolution to one-third of a monochrome display constructed of the same sized LC cells. This reduction in resolution is inherent in assigning each colored filter its own individual LC cell. In most colored LCDs, the pixel density is so high that the loss of resolution is apparent only at very close (under 2 cm) distances.

Colored TFT LCDs now used in commercially available TVs range in size from 54 mm to 110 mm in diagonal measurement. Pixel density varies from 240 × 240 to 480 × 480 pixels. All commercially available color LCDs use the filtration technique to develop their color. All types also use some form of TFT matrix drive technique.

Cost

Color LCD TVs are currently listing for around $150 to $250. As consumer items, they are often heavily discounted. Monochrome TFT LCDs designed for video use vary in price from $80 to $150 depending on size and operating characteristics. While this may sound expensive, it amounts to less than a tenth of a cent per pixel. Considering power consumption, size, and longevity, the TFT LCDs are an excellent bargain in video display devices.

DYNAMIC SCATTERING LCD

The dynamic scattering mode LCDs are very similar to the TN LCDs but they do not require the use of polarizers. The liquid crystal medium differs chemically and effectively from those of the TN family of LCDs. In theory and practice, the dynamic scattering mode LCDs operate more directly as light valves. The dynamic scattering mode not only simplifies the display but also offers better operating characteristics and lower power consumption.

How It Works

The LC molecules used in dynamic scattering LCDs allow light to pass through the cell when the cell is not surrounded by an electric field. In their normal relaxed orientation, these liquid crystals tend to align themselves with the walls of their container. In this organized molecular orientation, the LC compounds used in the dynamic scattering mode are transparent. In the "off" state, the cell passes light. If the cell is "on" or energized, then the electric field causes the LC molecules to become disorganized and adopt a random orientation. With the random molecular orientation, the LC compound becomes opaque and blocks the passage of light through the cell. Figure 6-27 illustrates the operation of the dynamic scattering LC cell.

Operation of the dynamic scattering mode LCD does not require the use of polarizers as the light can be controlled within the cell without them. In the TN mode, the LC medium changes the polarity of the light passing through the cell. Polarizers are necessary so that the change in polarization can affect a change in the cell's light output. In the dynamic scattering mode, however, the LC media does not rotate or change the light's polarization,but merely transmits or absorbs the light. This eliminates the need for polarization. The dynamic scattering mode is more direct and simplier than the TN approach.

Drive voltages used in dynamic scattering LCDs are higher than those of the TN types. Drive voltages as high as 15 Vac are used in contrast with 5 Vac for TN mode LCDs. Response time is about the same as TN types—100 ms.

Fig. 6-27. Operation of a dynamic scattering LC cell

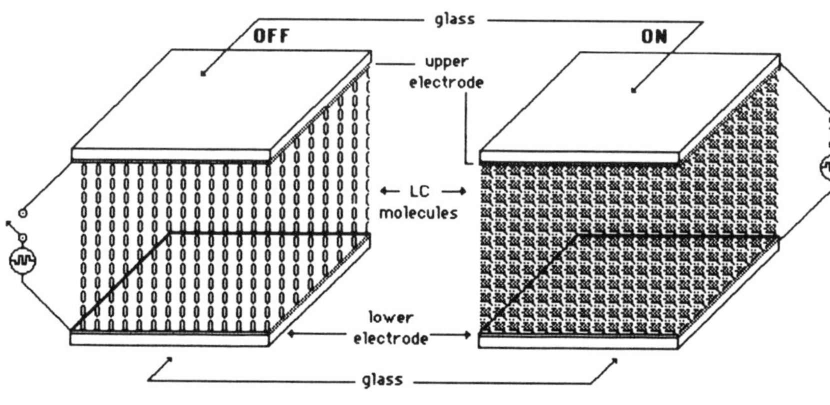

Advantages

The major advantage of the dynamic scattering mode is the elimination of the polarizers. The polarizers limit the viewing angle of the LCD by their very nature. Polarizers are superfine lines and as such they have a restricted viewing angle. They also are far from perfect transmitters of light, absorbing some 10% to 60% of the light passing through them. Elimination of the lossy polarizers allow backlighting intensity to be reduced which greatly lowers the display's power consumption. Both these factors give the dynamic scattering mode LCDs larger viewing angles and higher contrast ratios than the TN types. Viewing angles are more than doubled and contrast is increased by more than three times, all by merely eliminating the two polarizers. The elimination of the polarizers also minutely reduces the display's manufacturing cost. One example of a prototype dynamic scattering LCD has a pixel density of 420 × 780 pixels and a viewing angle of over 170°. This experimental display will update the entire screen in less than 0.84 seconds and consumes less than 5 watts of power.

Disadvantages

The dynamic scattering mode LCDs have much the same operating limits as TN LCDs with respect to temperature, power, and speed. These limits are inherent with the use of LC medias now available. The elimination of the polarizers has no negative effects on the display operating characteristics. The increased ac drive voltages on the cells reduces their operating lifetime to about 30,000 hours, some 60% of that of TN type LCDs.

SMECTIC LCD

Smectic LCDs use a specific class of liquid crystal compounds that respond to heat in addition to electric fields. Their main advantage is that they produce a relatively nonvolatile LCD display. The information written on the display will stay there until the central processor changes it.

How It Works

Smectic liquid crystals undergo changes in crystal orientation when they are heated. Their operation is very similar to that of the dynamic scattering mode, with the LC medium acting directly as a light valve within the LC cell. When the crystals are relaxed they act as light conductors. When the crystals are stressed by either heat or an electric field they become opaque. Smectic LC cells use a combination of both electric fields and heat to produce changes between the LC molecules.

A prototype smectic LCD contains 256 × 640 pixels within a 125 mm × 165 mm area. Pixel size is 0.25 mm × .48 mm. This prototype smectic LCD is capable of displaying 25 rows of 80 characters at the same time. It is constructed of two glass sheets with smectic liquid crystal sandwiched between them. The upper glass layer is etched with a grid of transparent indium tin oxide electrodes. The rear glass contains a network of heating electrodes. This display is capable of writing approximately 2000 characters per second, with a full screen update taking about 1 second. The ac electric current that establishes an electric field around the cell also heats the cell. Other than the heating effect, the smectic LCD works in much the same fashion as the dynamic scattering types.

Advantages

The major advantage of this type of LCD is that it is nonvolatile. Cells which are activated by the display's processor stay activated until the processor deactivates them. This frees the display's main processor of the time consuming chore of constantly updating unchanged cells. This results in greater effective operating speed for the display's electronic processing. Viewing angles and contrast are the same as the dynamic scattering mode LCDs, and are better than the TN types.

Disadvantages

The major disadvantage of smectic LCDs is their relatively higher power consumption. Power consumption is some 10 to 70 times greater than the other LC types. Drive voltages are up to 10 to 50 Vac for the smectic LC cells. This is due directly to using electricity to provide the resistance heating for driving the display. The usage of smectic liquid crystals also narrows the temperature operating range of a display type already plagued by temperature restrictions. The operating temperature range of smectic LCDs is now within 10° C to 30° C, making them unsuitable for outdoor use.

MULTIPLEXED LCDS

All types of LCDs are found in multiplex service. Structure of the LCD's electrical connections is radically different from the direct drive type of LCD. The direct drive LCD has a discrete set of electrodes for each and every LC element within the display. This works fine for small and relatively uncomplicated displays, but becomes cumbersome in larger, denser displays. When the display begins to have hundreds of elements or more, then a multiplexing technique is required. Multiplexing is basically a hardware time sharing technique.

The necessity of providing an ac drive waveform greatly complicates the multiplexing of liquid crystal displays. The advantages of multiplexing, however, do outweigh its disadvantages. If an LCD contains a large number of elements, then the simplification of its external electrical connections alone justifies the additional complexity of multiplexing the display. Multiplexing an LCD means that the individual LC cells' electrical terminals are arranged on an X-Y matrix. In the case of LCDs, the X axis is called the "common plane", while the Y axis is called the "segment plane."

Matrix Formats

While all multiplexed LCDs use an X-Y matrix, not all types arrange the matrix in the same format. Three basic formats are in common usage—the 2×4 format, the 3×3 format, and the 5×7 format. In all these cases, the first number refers to the common plane (X axis), while the second number refers to the segment plane (Y axis). One dimension of the matrix in all currently manufactured multiplexed LCDs is limited to no more than 16. This is due to the contrast to voltage response, and speed limitations, inherent in liquid crystal use. Any greater multiplexing results in poor contrast and reduced readability.

The 2×4 format is used in seven segment LCD packages. Figure 6-28a and b illustrate the common and segment planes of a two digit, seven segment display arranged in a 2×4 matrix format. In this arrangement, like elements of each digit are connected horizontally to form the common plane. Each digit also has two discrete Y lines forming its vertical segment plane. These two planes are illustrated separately in Fig. 6-28a and b. Note that while the matrix form is based on an X-Y matrix, this matrix is not rectilinear. Figure 6-28c illustrates the combination of both planes into a single 2×4 matrix and illustrates the internal electrical schematic of the digit.

The 3×3 matrix format is also used to drive seven segment displays and is similar in application to the 2×4 format. Figure 6-29a

Fig. 6-28. 2X4 matrix format

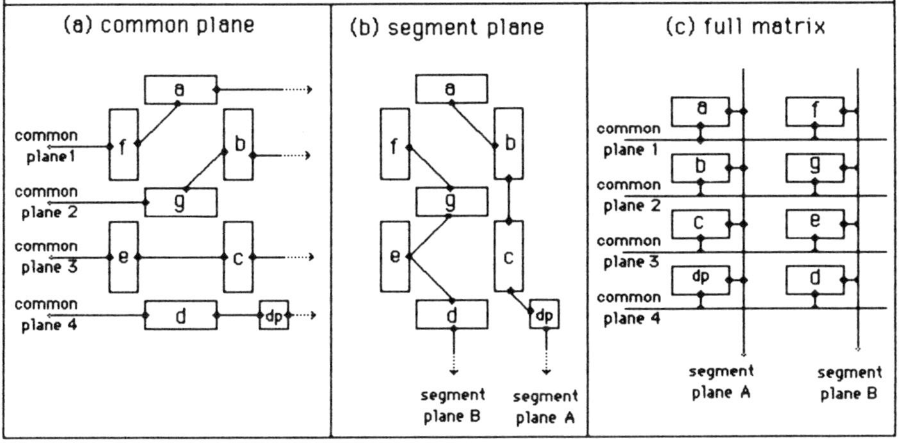

and b illustrates the common and segment planes of a 3×3 matrix format. This format has one additional address available. In the illustration, a colon is added to the display. Figure 6-29c illustrates both planes of the matrix joined and gives the electrical schematic of the digit's inards.

The 5×7 matrix format is the most versatile and is used in numeric, alphabetical, and graphics displays. Here there are seven horizontal planes and five vertical planes. This produces a 35 dot matrix capable of displaying text and graphics in addition to numbers.

Fig. 6-29. 3X3 matrix format

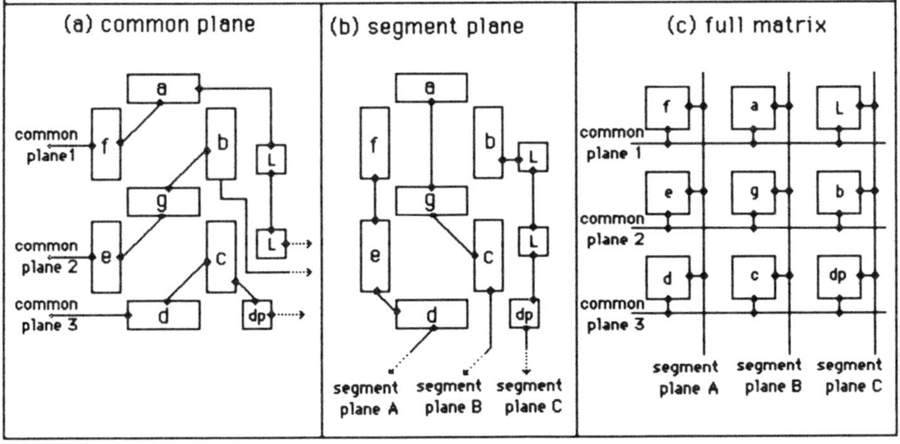

Figure 5-46 illustrates a complete character set based on a 5×7 matrix. Figure 6-30 illustrates a single 5×7 matrix. The 5×7 matrix is rectangular and capable of being stacked both vertically and horizontally to produce a multiplexed display of many characters.

Many more multiplexing formats exist and are limited only by the physical performance characteristics of the LC material being used. In most cases, limiting the maximum number of planes in one dimension of the format to less than 16 is essential for satisfactory display operation. This is necessary because the LCD requires a

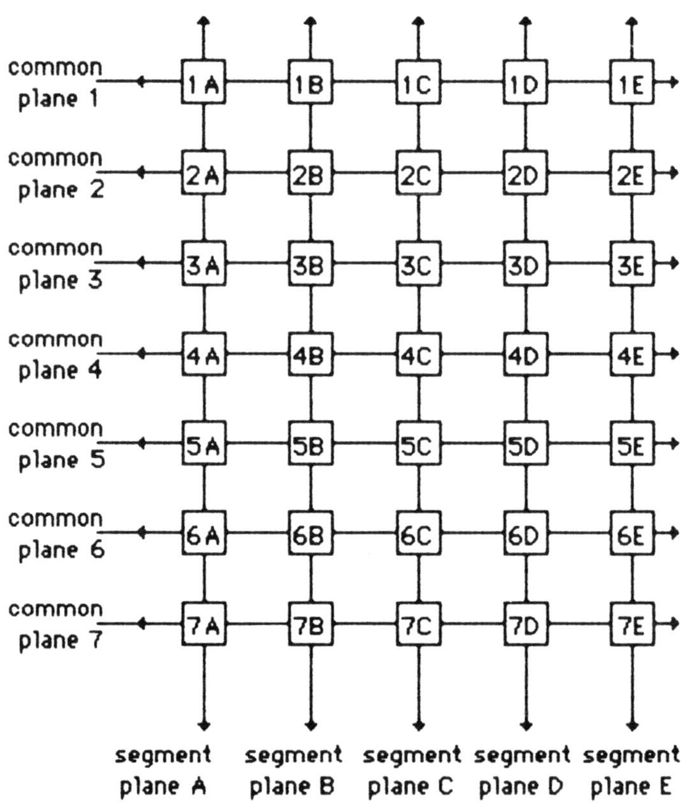

Fig.6-30. 5X7 matrix format

symmetrical ac waveform for drive power. Multiplexing is essentially a time division and sharing of this ac drive energy by all the elements within the display. This time division is equal to the number of common planes in the format times two. Multiplication by two is necessary as the LC cells require a symmetrical ac wavefront to prevent irreversible electrolysis. The necessity of maintaining this waveform with no net dc component is the main factor that limits and complicates the multiplexing of LCDs.

Matrix Format Drive Waveform

The driving waveform of a multiplexed LCD depends on the matrix format in use. Let's consider a simple format, the 2×4 matrix format. Figure 6-31 illustrates the drive waveform necessary to display the number "4" on a seven segment display using a 2×4 format. Waveforms (a), (b), (c), and (d) are the common plane drive waveforms. These are constant and do not change; they are the bipolar strobe pulses which select the individual common planes. Waveforms (e) and (f) are the segment plane waveforms that cause the number "4" to be displayed. The actual waveform occurring at each LC cell is the algebraic sum of the segment and common plane waveforms for that cell. For example, segment "a" of the seven segment display is not activated and its waveform is illustrated by (g), while segments "b" and "c" are activated and the resultant waveforms on segments "b" and "c" are illustrated by waveforms (h) and (i).

In order to provide the analog voltage levels necessary for switching and driving the display's segments, a series network of resistors is used as a voltage divider. A typical network, providing four voltage levels, is illustrated in Fig. 6-32. This network is used as a stepped voltage supply for the switching circuits that actually drive the display. Note that four voltages are provided by the divider network—V_a, V_b, V_c, and V_d, these plus V_{dd} give five voltage levels; this is enough to drive a display with five common planes. Since the display's elements must be provided with a symmetrical ac waveform, the following criterion must be met between these four voltages:

$$(V_a - V_b) = -(0 - V_b),\ V_b = V_a/2,\ \text{and}\ (V_c - V_b) = -(V_a - V_b)$$

These mathematical equations express the symmetry necessary to provide a satisfactory driving waveform to the LC segments. Any

Fig. 6-31. 2X4 format drive waveforms

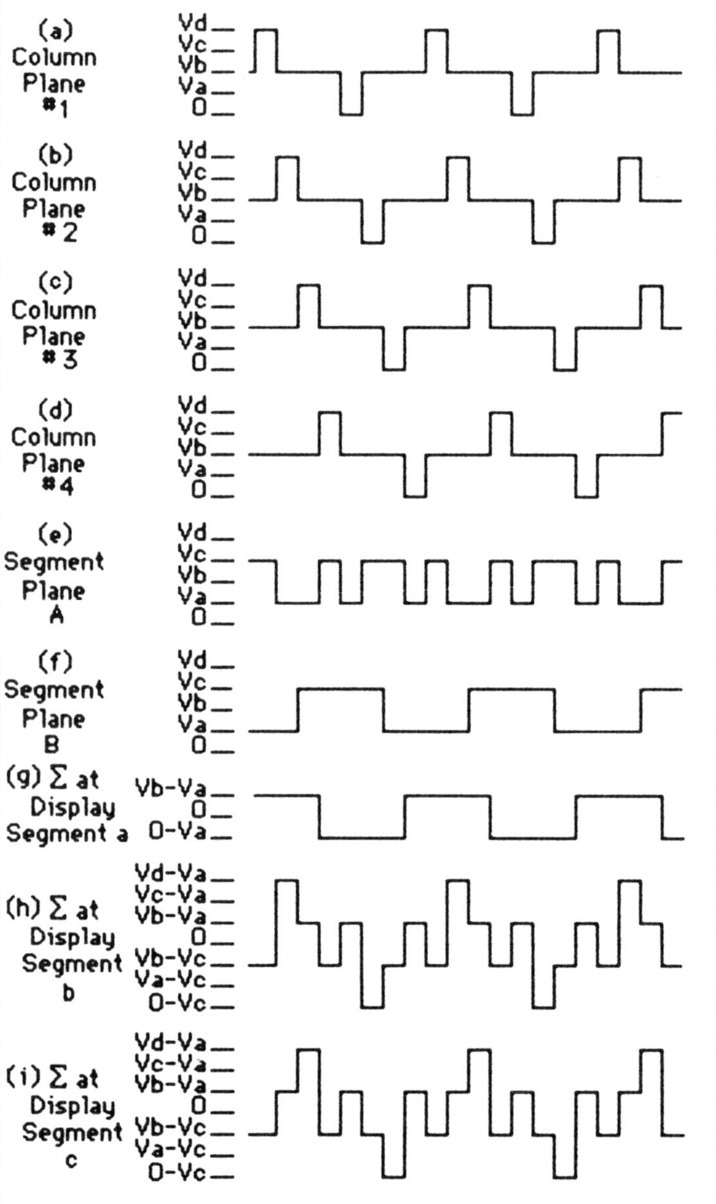

Fig. 6-32. LCD MUX voltage divider network

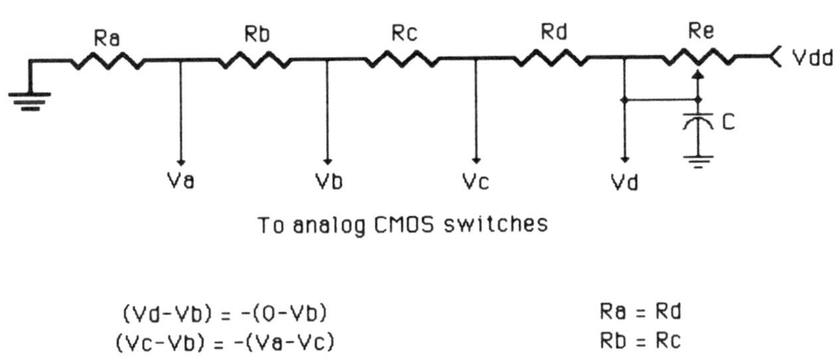

waveform based on these relationships will have a resultant zero net dc component and will drive the display without ruining it.

The actual voltage levels of all the driving ac waveforms are critical. It is essential that the waveforms occurring at the LCDs segments have zero net dc voltage in both the on and off states. The net RMS voltage occurring across the display's segments is optimized on the basis of the number of common planes within the matrix. Since the display is multiplexed, the individual RMS voltages determine the supply voltage of the display. The absolute minimum dc voltage input for powering the entire display can be expressed mathematically by:

$$V_d = V_{off_{RMS}} \left(\frac{2N}{1 - \frac{1}{\sqrt{N}}} \right)^{1/2} \qquad \textbf{Equation 6-1}$$

V_d = minimum supply voltage for display driving in volts dc
$V_{off_{RMS}}$ = cutoff voltage- LC cell inactivated
N = number of common planes

This equation clearly shows the relationship between the voltage necessary to power the display and the number of common planes in the display. The more planes, the more dc input voltage is necessary. This however, is not the entire situation. This dc input voltage must be divided and switched into N different symmetrical ac waveforms, one for each common plane. The equations which express the relationship between N and both the drive voltage on

RMS and drive voltage off RMS are:

$$V_{off_{RMS}} = V_d \left(\frac{1 - \frac{1}{\sqrt{N}}}{2N} \right)^{1/2}$$ **Equation 6-2**

$$V_{on_{RMS}} = V_d \left(\frac{1 + \frac{1}{\sqrt{N}}}{2N} \right)^{1/2}$$ **Equation 6-3**

$V_{off_{RMS}}$ = optimized off ac drive voltage RMS
$V_{on_{RMS}}$ = optimized on ac drive voltage RMS
V_d = minimum supply voltage for display driving in volts dc
N = number of common planes

Most LC cells require at least 2 Vac RMS to be activated, this translates to a minimum power supply voltage of 1 Vdc for $N=1$. As N is increased, the supply voltage is divided between N common planes. If N is greater than 16, then the RMS ac drive voltage is too low to activate the LC cell. Figure 6-33 graphically illustrates the relationship between the number of common planes, and the normalized display drive voltage V_d. The normalization point for drive is $N=1$. Note that the on voltage and the off voltage converge as the number of common planes (N) increases. When the voltage difference between Von and Voff becomes less than 2 Vac RMS, then the display has become too large for a single multiplex format. The decrease in RMS drive voltage for each common plane requires that the LCDs used in multiplexed displays have a very high contrast to drive voltage ratio.

LCD Multiplexing Electronics

The complexity of multiplexing a large LCD has given rise to specialized integrated circuits just to drive multiplexed LC displays. In many cases, the LCD manufacturers are constructing encoding and drive electronics for their displays, and including these electronics with the display module. Displays with on board processing are termed "smart," while those without are called "dumb." A smart module greatly simplifies a very complex job for the eventual end user of the display module.

Table 6-2 is a list of integrated circuits designed specifically for

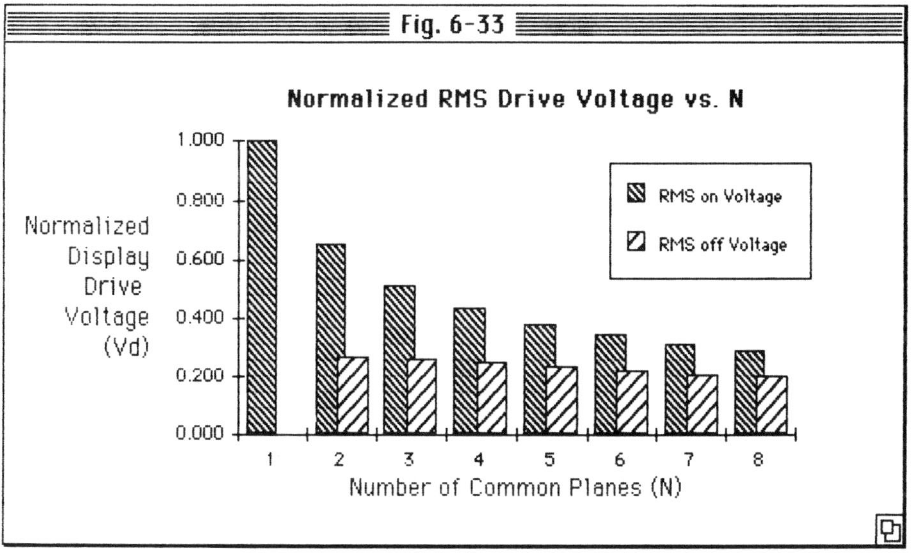

multiplexed LCD service. In most cases, LCD multiplexing chips and smart LCD modules are designed to accept input from a computer. This computer input may be either serial or parallel. The use of the word "μproc" in the column entitled "Input" on the table indicates that IC possesses a microprocessor or central processing unit (CPU) on board. The IC voltage refers to the dc input voltage required to operate the IC.

Disadvantages of Multiplexing

Multiplex service for LCDs requires complex electronic drive schemes as discussed above. These electronics significantly increase the power consumption of a display type which is mainly selected for its low power consumption and portability. Multiplex service requires that the LCD be of very high quality in order to work with lower ac drive voltages. The lowering of the ac drive voltage also lowers the display's performance in the areas of contrast, temperature operating range, and speed.

Listing of LCD Manufacturers

The following manufacturers of LCDs and LCD drivers have contributed information to this chapter. Their complete addresses

Table 6-2. Multiplex LCD Driver Integrated Circuits.

Maker	IC #	IC Type	IC V.	Input	Package	Features
Hitachi	HD 44790	Matrix Driver (smart)	5	µproc	80 pin flat	4X32, 2KROM, 128RAM
Hitachi	HD 44795	Matrix Driver (smart)	3	µproc	80 pin flat	4X32, 2K Expandable
Hughes	HLCD 0488	Matrix Driver (dumb)	3.-8.	parallel	40 pin DIP	16X16 Matrix
Hughes	HLCD 0510	Matrix Driver (dumb)	3.-10.	serial	40 pin DIP	25 columns X 8 rows
Hughes	HLCD 0550	Matrix Driver (smart)	3.-10.	ASCII	40 pin DIP	12 columns X 8 rows
Hughes	HLCD 0607	Matrix Driver (dumb)	3.-12.	serial	40 pin DIP	30 columns X 4 rows
Intersil	ICM 7231	8 Digit, 7 segment	4.-5.5	parallel	40 pin DIP	3X3 MUX format
Intersil	ICM 7232	10 Digit, 7 segment	4.-5.5	serial	40 pin DIP	3X3 MUX format
Intersil	ICM 7233	4 Digit, 16 segment	4.-5.5	parallel	40 pin DIP	6X3 MUX format
Intersil	ICM 7234	5 Digit, 16 segment	4.-5.5	serial	40 pin DIP	6X3 MUX format
Intersil	ICM 7280	10 row MUX Driver	5.-15.	parallel	40 pin DIP	TBA
Motorola	MC 145000	Matrix Driver (half)	3.-6.5	serial	24 pin DIP	12 columns X 4 rows
Motorola	MC 145001	Matrix Driver (slave)	3.-6.5	serial	18 pin DIP	11 columns
National	COP 472	Matrix Driver (half)	2.4-5.5	serial	20 pin DIP	12 columns X 3 rows
National	MM 58201	Matrix Driver (half)	3-18	serial	40 pin DIP	24 columns X 2-8 rows
NEC	µPD 7225	Matrix Driver (smart)	2.7-5.	serial	52 pin flat	32 columns X 1-4 rows
NEC	µPD 7227	Matrix Driver (smart)	2.7-5.	serial	64 pin flat	40 columns X 7-8 rows
NEC	µPD 7228	Matrix Driver (smart)	2.7-5.	serial	80 pin flat	50 columns X 7-8 rows
NEC	µPD 7502	Matrix Driver (smart)	2.7-5.5	µproc	64 pin flat	2K ROM, 128 RAM
NEC	µPD 7503	Matrix Driver (smart)	2.7-5.5	µproc	64 pin flat	4K ROM, 224 RAM
Philips	MH 100	Matrix Driver (dumb)	2.3-6.5	serial	40 pin DIP	20 columns X 2 rows
Philips	MH 110	Matrix Driver (dumb)	2.3-6.5	serial	40 pin DIP	30 columns X 2 rows
Philips	MH 111	Matrix Driver (dumb)	2.3-6.5	serial	40 pin DIP	32 columns X 2 rows

and telephone numbers are listed in the Electronic Display Devices Manufacturers Data Base in Appendix A.

AND, Inc.

Hamlin, Inc.

LXD, Inc.

Mitsubishi Electric Corp.

RCA Laboratories

Stanley Electric Co., Ltd.

Texas Instruments Inc.

UCE, Inc.

7

Vacuum Fluorescent Displays (VFD)

Vacuum fluorescent tubes have been in wide usage for over ten years. The most common applications are in seven segment numerical displays used in automobiles, TVs, cassette machines, cash registers, and professional desktop calculators. The VFD is chosen for these applications because it is bright and readable. The VFD is more difficult to implement than an LED and is more commonly used in the more expensive types of equipment. The job is almost invariably displaying decimal numbers using a series of seven segment VFDs.

You can best recognize most VFDs in service by their intense blue-green color and high light output. This color is currently not commercially available in LEDs and is very distinctive. The blue-green color lies within a spectrum where the eye is very sensitive. This, plus high levels of luminosity, make the VFD very readable. The color output of the VFD may be varied into many shades with filters, so you may encounter colors ranging from blue to yellow to green.

Within the last two years, much interest has been focused on the VFD as a fast, dot matrix display for computers. This area of "flat-screen" displays for computers is very competitive. The VFD must compete with electroluminescent and plasma technologies. Currently, the latter two have the edge. Let's examine the inner workings and principles applied in the VFD, and we'll see why.

HOW VFDs WORK

The VFD is a highly specialized and miniaturized fluorescent light; it has many points in common with the fluorescent tubes used for area lighting and with CRTs. The principle used to produce light is basically the same as that used in the CRT. High energy electrons are forced to collide with a fluorescent material. The fluorescent material converts some of the kinetic energy of the colliding electron into light. The intensity of the light output depends on the amount of energy the electrons possess and the conversion efficiency of the phosphors used. The color of the VFD is dependent on the type of phosphor and filter employed.

The type of fluorescent tube used in the VFD has been specifically engineered to this service. The tube is highly miniaturized. Since the VFD is used to display data, it must be capable of being rapidly updated. The design used in fluorescent tubes for area lighting is very slow to respond to changes, far too slow to display flicker free data or images. To overcome the problem of speed, the VF tube used a grid to control the electronic flow. This allows the tube to be partially biased in the ON state, and the flow of electrons controlled by the grid. The principle is the same used in many vacuum tubes. This speeds up the VF tubes operation into the millisecond ranges necessary for flicker-free operation.

Like all vacuum tubes, the VF tube is a voltage operated device. This differs radically from the current operated LED. The anode and control grid of the VF tube can require voltages in the hundreds of volts, fortunately at very low currents. The use of high anode voltage is essential for the operation of the phosphors. The high voltage provides the essential kinetic energy for the electrons. Without this energy, there would be no fluorescence.

HOW VFDs ARE CONSTRUCTED

VFDs are constructed in a wide variety of shapes and sizes. Regardless of physical configuration, the operating elements of the tube are the same. All these elements are enclosed within an evacuated glass envelope. Figure 7-1 illustrates schematically the elements present within all VFDs. The VF tube has three active elements, similar to any triode type vacuum tube.

The cathode of the VF tube is the source of the electrons being accelerated through the tube. This cathode is constructed of thoriated tungsten, and is directly heated by low voltage dc energy. The control grid is a very thin metal mesh located near the cathode, and is located

Fig. 7-1. VF tube elements

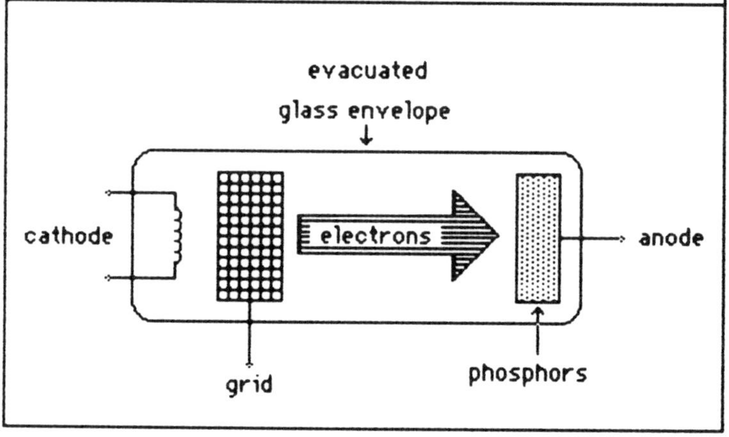

at the opposite end of the tube from the cathode. The anode is formed on an insulative base. The anode is coated with the fluorescent phosphors, and its shape determines the shape of the light radiating area. In the case of seven segment displays, the anodes within the package are linear, while in dot matrix displays, the anodes are small points. Each anode within the display is held electrically separate allowing each to be selected only when needed.

The unfiltered blue-green color of most VF tubes is due to the use of zinc-oxide as a phosphor. Actually, this is but one of many colors available by using different phosphors and filters. Zinc-oxide is easily available and inexpensive. Most observers find the blue-green color pleasing and highly readable; this has led to the majority of VFDs using the zinc-oxide compounds as phosphors.

VFD CHARACTERISTICS

The VF tube is arranged in many fashions to display a variety of types of information. Regardless of its configuration, all VFD use the same basic VF tube as elements. It is the basic characteristics of the elemental VF tube that interest us here. All VFDs are merely collections of this one basic element.

Design

The VFD is available in a number of designs. The most common is the standard seven segment package used to display decimal numbers. This configuration accounts for over 95% of the VF tubes implemented into displays. The next most common configuration is the fourteen segment display. This configuration can display both numbers and upper case alphabetical characters. The dot matrix designs are the least common configuration. Dot matrix VFD with 5×7 and 5×12 character dot matrixes are available. The 5×7 and 5×12 character matrixes are capable of displaying lower case alphabetical characters as well as upper case and numerals. Lastly, the least common type of VFD is the large dot matrix configurations. These large units are used to display graphics and may have tens of thousands of individual dot elements. No matter how many elements or how they are arranged, each element is a single VF tube. Figure 7-2 illustrates the variety of designs commercially available using the basic VF tube element.

Power Requirements

The VFD can be electrically considered a vacuum tube. The anode voltages can range from 100 volts to over 400 volts dc. The anode currents are very low, in the microamperes. The control grid requires voltages in the range of 60 to 120 Vdc. Every effort is made to keep the control grid voltages as low as possible to facilitate their switching by semiconductor junctions. In fact, the development of flat screen displays using high voltage switching has given rise to a whole family of semiconductor driver ICs designed to switch 60 to 120 volts quickly and reliably. These ICs will drive not only the

Fig. 7-2. VFD configurations

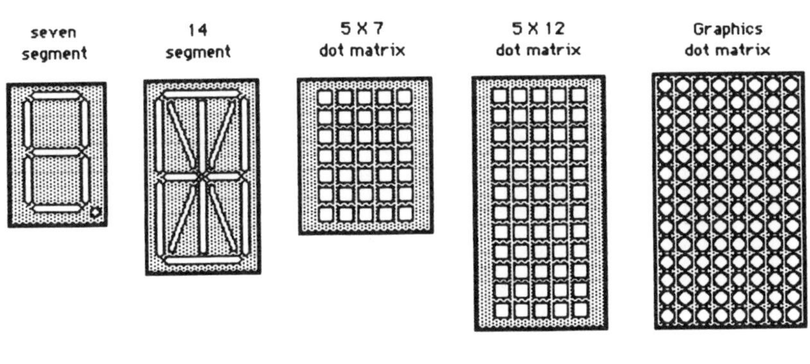

VFDs, but also the electrolumineiscent and plasma flat screen displays.

If the display is powered by a standard 120 Vac, 60 cycle input, there is no problem obtaining the required voltages. A transformer or voltage doubler/tripler can supply the required voltages. If, however, the power input to the display is low voltage dc, like the 12 Vdc available in an automobile, then a micro inverter must be used. This very small inverter steps up the low voltage dc source to the higher voltages required by the VFD. In most cases, the manufacturer of the display module has taken care of the power supply requirements, and provides the micro inverter on board with the display. Voltage input to the micro inverter is 5 Vdc to 18 Vdc.

Figure 7-3 illustrates a schematic for a micro inverter that will supply 60 Vdc and 180 Vdc from a 11 to 16 Vdc source. The NE 555 timer is used to generate a 2 kHz, 50% duty cycle, square wave which is stepped up by the transformer to the voltages required by the control grids and anodes of the VFD. Note that the power requirements by the VFD are so low that the NE 555 timer can directly drive the transformer without current amplification. After inversion and transformation, the power is rectified and filtered. The anode voltage is fed directly to all the individual anodes in the display. The grid voltage is fed to the IC drivers that control the information flow through the display. A voltage divider obtains both the anode and grid voltages from the same supply.

The power consumption of the VFD is very small, often less

Fig. 7-3. NE 555 micro-inverter for VFDs

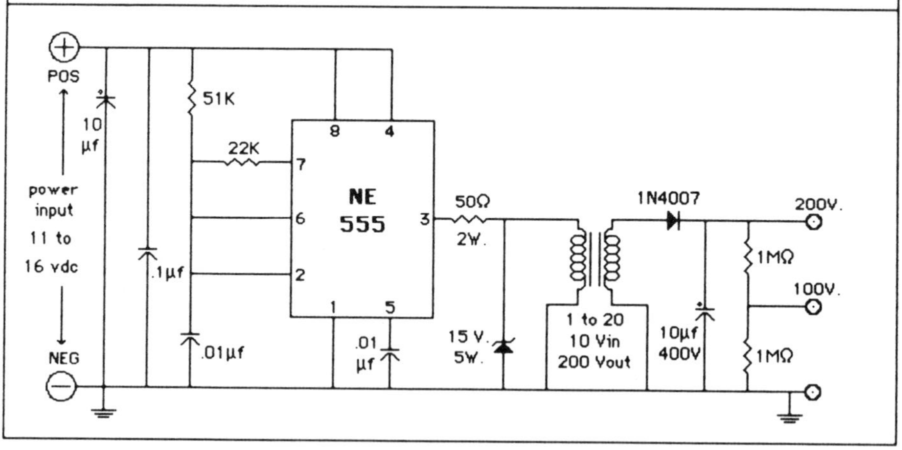

Fig. 7-4.

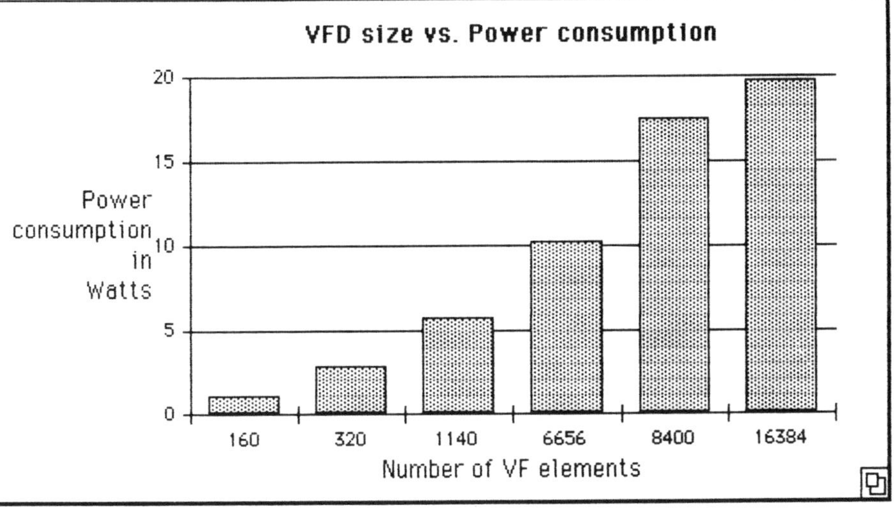

than 65 milliwatts per character. The actual power consumption of a particular VFD is proportional to the size and number of elements within the display. Basically, the larger the display the more power it consumes. Figure 7-4 is a bar graph showing power consumption of various sizes and types of VFDs. In general the VFD is a very small consumer of power, less than either LEDs and plasma panels. A small ten character 14-segment VFD will consume less than 3 watts of power. The larger dot matrix graphics VFD with an active area of 25 square cm may consume as much as 35 watts of power.

Brightness

The brightness of VFDs are dependent on several factors. Among these are size of the VF tube, anode voltage, and the type of phosphors selected for the VF tube. Absolute brightness of VF elements range from 150 to over 1000 foot-Lamberts. An average VF element in a seven segment display will have a brightness in the neighborhood of 200 ft-L. VFDs designed for outdoor operation in the sunlight have brightnesses around 600 ft-L.

There is no doubt that the fluorescent principles applied in the VFD are very efficient at converting electricity into light. The VFD is not only among the brightest of displays, it is also among the most efficient. Many VFD manufacturers supply their display modules with adjustable anode voltages. By raising or lowering the anode voltage, the display's brightness and power consumption can be controlled. Adjustable brightness, high brightness, and overall efficiency have made the VFD a favorite for use in areas with high ambient light.

Resolution

The effective resolution of a VFD is directly tied to the size of an individual VF element. Remember we are dealing with a miniaturized fluorescent light. The resolution of a VFD is totally dependent on how small a VF element can be made. Currently manufactured VF elements have minimum areas in the neighborhood of 0.5 square mm. A large graphics display will have some 16,384 individual elements within an area of 68.8 square cm.

The resolution of the VFD currently challenges those of both the LED and the LCD type displays. This, coupled with their high brightness, has led to VFD use in many environments having changing light levels, such as automotive service. VFD resolution is currently lagging well behind what is possible with the CRT. For this reason, VFDs are not expected to replace CRTs in high resolution computer display service.

Speed

The VFDs are very quick. An individual element can be written or unwritten in less than 1 microsecond. This type of high speed performance is to be expected from a device that is, after all, essentially a vacuum tube. Only solid state devices like an LED can switch faster (around 10 nanoseconds). The VFD is almost as fast as the electroluminescent and plasma technologies. The VF element is many thousands of times faster than the LC cell. A VFD graphics module displaying over 16,000 pixels can be updated in less than 20 milliseconds. This is more than fast enough to display moving graphics without flicker.

The overall speed at which a VFD will display information is also related to the information handling capabilities of the display module. Most manufacturers offer the choice of either serial or parallel TTL or RS-232 type information inputs on VFDs used in computer service. The advantage of parallel TTL data input is that the computer treats the display like RAM. Data input times are commonly very fast, less than 10 microseconds per byte. VFDs operate over a wide range of serial baud rates, from 1200 to 9600 baud. In any case, the essential VF tube is faster than the processing and information processes required to prepare the image for display. VFDs have the potential of increased speed if newer and faster information processing ICs, employing high voltage switching, are developed. Since the VFD's processing and power levels are similar to those of the electroluminescent and plasma displays, specialized ICs for driving these displays are sure to be made soon. In this case, the VFDs are receiving benefit from their more popular luminescent and plasma competitors.

Color

The VFDs are available in the following colors, blue, blue-green, green, yellow, orange, amber, and red. These colors are produced by the combination of differing phosphors in conjunction with a wide range of filters. The current trend is to use phosphors with a wide range of frequency output. In this fashion, the displays output color can be easily modified after manufacture by changing the filter covering the screen. The use of filters is similar to that of the LED technologies, and the reader is referred to the information on filters in Chapter 5. The general information on phosphors in Chapter 4 on CRTs also relates to the phosphors used in VFD manufacture. The majority of VFDs now made are constructed with zinc oxide as their phosphor. This gives a blue-green color characteristically associated with VFDs. The zinc oxide's fluorescent light also can be easily filtered into blue, green, amber, orange, red, or even grey light.

There have been attempts to produce VF tubes which have three anodes, each coated with a different phosphor. The anodes are coated with red, green, and blue phosphors. The individual anodes are addressed to make the VF tube light up in any one or a mixture of three primary colors. This would produce a VFD that could display full colored images. Unfortunately the difficulties and expenses involved in producing such a full color display in large sizes has eliminated commercial production.

Size

The VFDs are available in many sizes from a single seven segment digit to a large array-type graphs display. Large sizes are not a problem for what is essentially a high-tech fluorescent light. Small sizes, or densely packed high resolution matrixes do, however, prevent some very real problems. Once again, as with most display technologies, the display's strong points define its weaknesses.

Element Thickness

The elemental thickness of the VF tube is limited by its voltage operating characteristics. Since the anode voltage of the VF tube is at least 100 volts, a certain amount of distance must be placed between the cathode and the anode. Without this gap, the tube would internally arc over and be uncontrollable. The current minimum limit for this elemental thickness is about 5 mm. This minimum is not likely to be reduced unless new materials become available that fluoresce at very low energy levels. This would allow reduction of the anode voltage and thereby reduction of the VF tube's thickness.

Minimum and Maximum Display Size

The largest VFD yet made measures over 1000 square meters, contains some 150,000 individual elements, and is designed for viewing by large audiences. Such very large scale implementation is no problem for what is essentially a fluorescent light. VFD seven segment displays are available in the same sizes as their LED competitors, and these represent the smallest package in which a VFD is commercially manufactured. VFDs are not made in single lamp packages like LEDs and incandescent lamps.

When the VF tubes are assembled into displays, the high anode and grid potentials once again cause problems. With operating voltages in the hundreds of volts, great care must be taken to provide adequate separation and insulation for all lines, conductors, and connectors. This places minimum spacing requirements on the display's connections. Arcover between differing VF tubes can easily result if the interconnections are too densely packed.

Let's examine a VFD designed for computer use. Such a display is formatted for 5×7 dot matrix characters, with 6 lines of 40 characters displayed. Overall size of the display is 270 mm × 126 mm, with the active area being 188 mm × 46 mm. The characters displayed by this VFD are 3.5 mm × 5 mm. Figure 7-5 illustrates such a computer display. This display represents the larger types commercially available for computer use.

Operating Characteristics

The VFD possesses a number of fine operating characteristics that have led to its wide usage in its seven segment form. Some of the VFDs strong points are a wide range of operating temperatures, wide viewing angle, very long lifetime, and extreme

Fig. 7-5. VF alphanumeric computer display

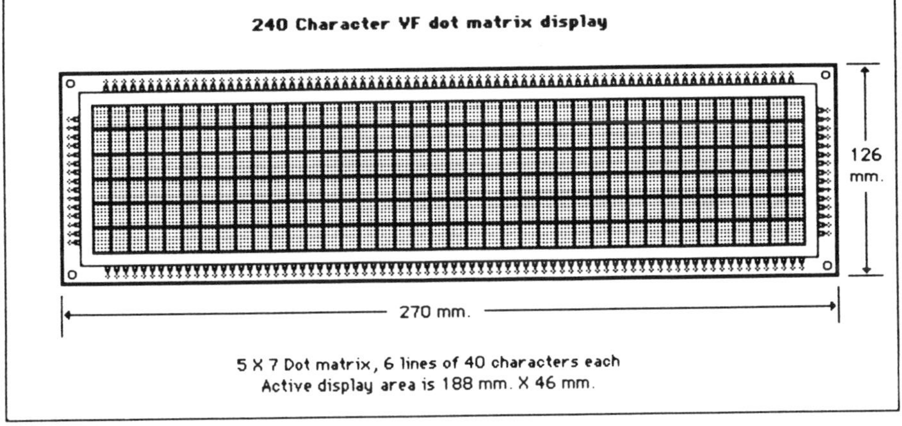

mechanical ruggedness. These factors coupled with high brightness have led to the use of VFD in military and commercial applications such as aircraft cockpits and automobile instruments.

Visual Angle

The VFDs have wide viewing angles. They are comparable with the CRTs, plasma panels, and other flat screen technologies. Viewing angles for VFDs are in the region of 120°. The fluorescent tube is encased in glass and can radiate its light over very wide angles in three dimensions. The physical orientation and matrix geometry of the individual elements of the VFD play a great part in the overall viewing angle of the finished display. The 120° viewing angle of currently made VFDs represents their usage as flat screen displays. There are no engineering limitations preventing construction of a spherical display using VF elements. Such a display would have an unlimited viewing angle. The VFDs constructed today are designed as readouts for electronic equipment or computers. In this type of service, the 120° viewing angle of the VFD is overkill.

Longevity

The VF element has a very long operating lifetime. Single VF elements are projected to last between 100,000 to 300,000 hours before catastrophic failure. Parametric element failure, such as some loss of brightness, begins at around 10,000 hours of operation. The

VF tube gradually decreases in brightness until it reaches about 50% output at 50,000 hours. This decrease in light output is caused by electronic impact which erodes the phosphors on the VF element's anode. These performance characteristics make the VF element the most reliable light producing display element now manufactured. Basically, a VF element is capable of 40 hours per week operation over a period of five years with less than a 15% loss in brightness.

The longevity of a VF element is closely related to the anode voltage across the VF tube. The higher the anode voltage, the quicker the VF element loses its brightness. The higher energy attained by the electrons at higher voltages erodes the phosphors faster. Higher anode voltage increases the light output of the VF element, but it also wears the tube more quickly. Figure 7-6 illustrates the aging process of VF elements run at full light output versus those run at half output. Note the direct relationship between display light output and longevity. What this tells us as display users is to turn the display's brightness to a minimum acceptable level and our VFD will keep its brightness longer.

The VF element uses high voltages in its operation. When a large number of VF elements are assembled into a densely packed display package, problems of arcover arise. This reduces the longevity of the overall display. Most densely packed VFDs are rated to run over 40,000 hours before catastrophic failure. This figure means that the VFD is more long lasting than the CRT, the LED,

Fig. 7-6.

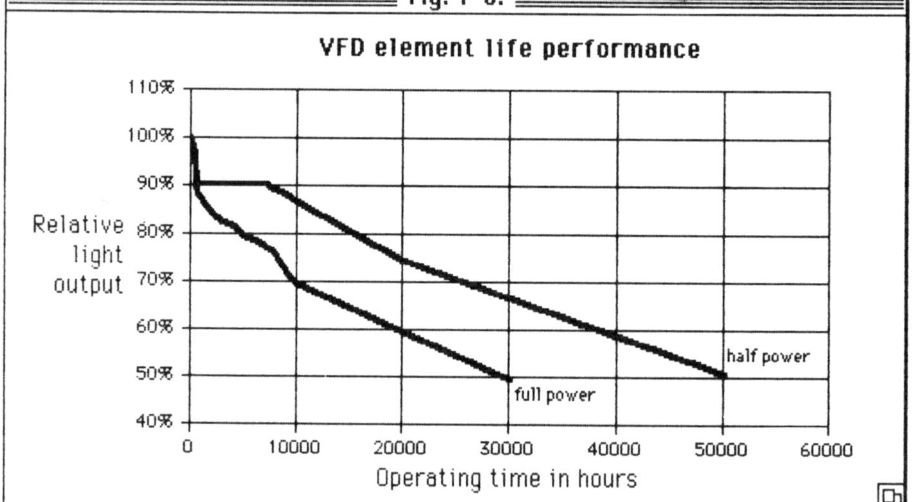

plasma displays, and most LCDs. Longevity is really the VFDs long suit.

Operating Temperature Range

The VFD is capable of operating just about anywhere a person can exist to watch it. On the low side, the VFD can operate at temperatures as low as −40° C. VFD operation is possible at temperatures as high as 85° C. This represents a range that is as wide as the CRT, wider than most LEDs, and far surpasses any current LCD technology. This wide temperature range is a significant factor in VFD use in all types of vehicles. The VFD will produce an acceptable display in an automobile, even if the car is buried in the snow, or parked in a blazing hot parking lot all day. These conditions will at least cause an LCD to not operate, and may possibly cause permanent failure. In terms of temperature, the VFD is about as rugged as electronic display devices get.

Mechanical Characteristics

The VFD is the most physically rugged display type now manufactured. The VFD is capable of withstanding mechanical shock up to 100 Gs. This strength is due to the material construction of the VF elements, and has led to the use of VFDs in aircraft cockpits. The factor limiting the VFD's shock performance is the interconnection between the VFD elements and the electronics that drive them. The actual VF tubes are capable of resisting even higher accelerations.

VFD ADVANTAGES

The list of VFD advantages is large. Start with high brightness for example. The VFD is as bright as any type and exceeds most. The VFD will operate in temperature environments that would destroy other types. The VFD is the most mechanically rugged display type now produced. The VFD is available in a variety of colors. The VFD offers low power consumption, and is the lowest among the light producing display technologies. Power consumption is less only in light modifying displays like LCDs. And finally, the VFD has the greatest longevity of any commercially produced display technology.

So why with all these good points does the VFD remain implemented in small applications like the frequency numerical readout in radios? The answer lies in the VFD's prime disadvantage, which alone has limited its spread into computer and video displays.

VFD DISADVANTAGES

The prime factor limiting the VFD is its use of high voltage. Both the anode and the control grid use voltages that can be in excess of 100 volts. This voltage level is difficult to implement in the densely packed arrays necessary to attain high resolution information output. The problem is arcover. Since the voltage levels are necessary for the operation of the VF tube, the VFD technology has reached an impasse.

The VFD uses voltages that are higher than those of the electroluminescent and plasma technologies. This higher voltage level has rendered the VFD incapable of competing with these technologies in terms of resolution. The lower voltages used in other display technologies make it easier to pack the individual elements into dense matrixes.

SAMPLE VFD APPLICATION—A COMPUTER DISPLAY

This sample application describes the state of the art in VFDs. Here a dot matrix of VF tubes is assembled into an array of 200 elements horizontally and 42 elements vertically, 8400 VF tubes in all. This VFD can display alphanumerics as 6 lines of 40 characters. Each character is based on a 5 × 7 dot matrix. See Fig. 5-46 for an example of an alphabet display on a 5 × 7 dot matrix. This same VFD can also display graphics, and pictographic characters. This degree of versatility makes this VFD suitable for ideographic languages such as Japanese.

This example VFD is used as a display for a computer. In physical appearance it is similar to the one illustrated in Fig. 7-5. This VFD is a complete module that contains the encoding and switching logic necessary to run the display. Data can be sent to the VFD in either high speed serial or RS-232 forms. In its RS-232 form, the display can show 192 different characters, more than contained in the standard 96 ASCII character set. The display takes 10 microseconds to accept a single character, or about 3 milliseconds to accept the data for an entire new screenful of information. This is very quick.

One advantage of the TTL serial input is that the computer can treat the display as random access memory (RAM). This simplifies display to computer interface and speeds up the data transmission process. The VFD module takes care of matters such as character generator, screen refresh, control logic, and power supply. The module only requires 5-volts dc for operation. An on board inverter converts the low voltage dc into the higher voltage required by the VF tubes. Power consumption is around 3 amperes at 5 Vdc.

VFD COST

Seven segment VFDs are more expensive than their LED competitors, about $3.00 per digit. This cost does not include the power supply and switching logic necessary to implement the display. Alphanumeric VFD modules cost in relation to their size. A small module capable of 10 characters costs about $125. A 40 character module costs around $260. The larger displays with 240 characters are the most expensive at around $1000. VFDs with graphics capabilities are slightly more expensive for the same number of pixels as their alphanumeric cousins. This is due to the additional complexity and speed necessary in the driving electronics.

At these prices, it is easy to see why the VFD is not considered a serious competitor for the CRT in computer use. Currently the CRT offers greater resolution, comparable brightness, and larger size at a fraction the VFD's cost. Since the individual, miniaturized VF tubes are complex to manufacture and assemble into dense arrays, it is not likely that the VFD will replace the CRT as the most popular computer display. The additional problems of high voltage switching and transmission to the display are inherent in the VF technology and are not likely to be solved.

VFD MANUFACTURERS

The following manufacturers of VFDs and their driving electronics have contributed information for this chapter. Complete addresses and telephone numbers are available in the Electronic Display Devices Manufacturer's Data Base in Appendix A.

Digital Electronics Corp.

Enterprise Systems Corp.

Texas Instruments Inc.

8

Electroluminescent Displays (ELD)

The electroluminescent display is a serious contender to replace the CRT in many applications. Computer displays, especially in portable and military applications, will be the first to use ELDs. The ELD is reliable, very bright, and has moderate power consumption. Modern models have resolution slightly less than a high resolution CRT. Electroluminescent effects were first discovered in 1936 by Georges Destriau. He noticed that zinc sulfide doped with copper gave off light when stimulated by an electric field. Destriau called the effect "photoluminescence." The ELD was first commercially produced by the Sharp Electronics Corp. in the mid 1970s. Early prototypes were plagued by arcing problems, lack of adequate semiconductor drivers, and short lifetimes.

Currently, electroluminescent displays are not commercially produced in full color. This is under development and is practical, although difficult. All the problems associated with a monochromatic ELD are present in the full color attempts, only times three. If full color can be realized in this display type, then it will be able to replace CRTs in television use, and many other video applications. EL technology promises to be the first, full color flat panel display that can effectively compete with the CRT.

The ELD is a matrix addressed array, much the same as dot matrix LCDs, VFDs, or Plasma displays. The rigors of addressing any mega-pixel array are considerable. Many of the problems confronted when employing matrix addressable displays are in the driving electronics. In no case is this more true than with ELDs. The necessity of feeding the display a high voltage, high frequency, ac waveform places considerable demands on the driving electronics. In fact, in the case of ELDs, the display technology has exceeded the technology of the required electronic drivers. The panels are now waiting for the processing and switching technologies to catch up with them.

The ELD's good points are many. Its light weight, very thin profile, moderate power consumption, and very high level of brightness make it attractive to designers of portable and ruggedized equipment. The ELD is very rugged as it is a completely solid-state device. It is the only completely solid-state challenger for the CRT's job. LCDs are liquid state devices, while both VFDs and plasma displays are gas state. Being a solid-state device gives the ELD the edge in mechanical ruggedness and allows it to operate over wider temperature ranges than its competitors. All of these are desirable characteristics for a display used in portable, vehicular, or military service.

There are several types of electroluminescent technologies. The ac driven thin film ELD (AC TFEL) is emerging as the most popular and likely to succeed. Other types such as the ac and dc dispersion types are not being developed as quickly as the AC TFEL. Currently the AC TFEL is the only type commercially available, and the material in this chapter relates specifically to this type.

HOW ELDs WORK

The ELD is an electrostatically operated solid-state device. It bears a strong similarity to a capacitor. A single EL pixel can be visualized as a capacitor with a light emitting dielectric. The presence of a relatively intense electric field around and through the dielectric causes the EL compound to emit light. The material used for the dielectric is very special. Only a few compounds are capable of converting electric fields into visible light. Figure 8-1 illustrates an electrical schematic representation of a single EL cell. The resistor shunting the capacitor represents the light output of the cell, while the back-to-back zener diodes reflect the minimum electric potential necessary before the dielectric material will emit light. The capacitor itself simulates the capacitive electrical nature of the entire EL cell assembly. Overall capacitance for a single EL cell is

Fig. 8-1. Schematic for an EL cell

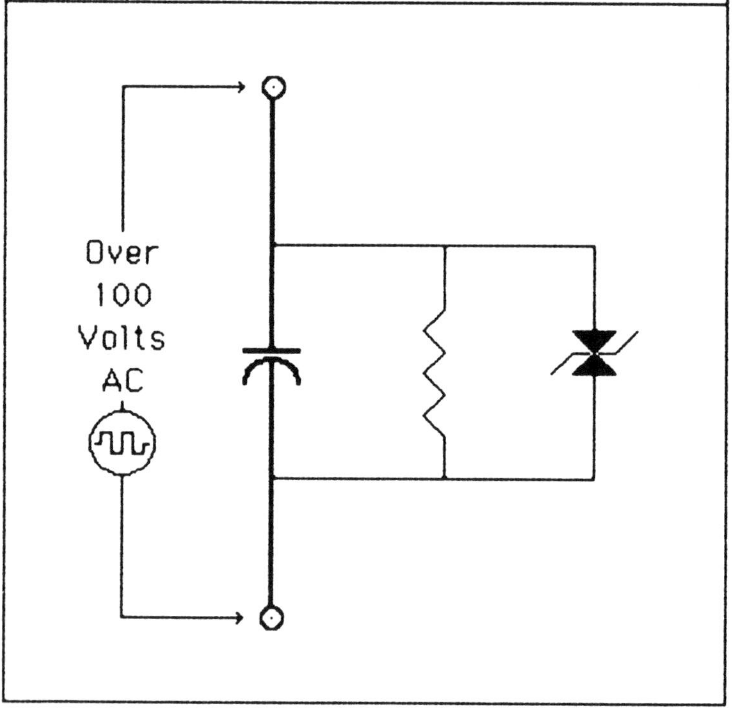

approximately 4 picofarads in currently produced models. It should be stressed that this schematic is only a symbolic electrical representation of the operation of the EL.

The actual physical mechanisms involved in the EL cell are still theoretical. It is simply a case of "we know it works, but we aren't too sure why." The most current and popular theory holds that the electric field surrounding the electroluminescent material generates "hot" electrons. These hot electrons are kicked loose from the interface of the dielectric and the EL material. The electric field within the EL cell is intense—over 1 million volts per cm. The hot electrons are accelerated by the electric field. These hot electrons collide with the manganese dopant atoms. This collision has a radiated photon as one of its results. This quantum energy exchange accounts for the very discrete frequency output of the EL cell. This quantum energy transfer is very similar to the theoretical operation of the LED junction, where energy lost within a semiconductor junction is converted into light. In the case of the ELD, an intense ac electric field is converted into light. An ac electric field is necessary to operate the EL cell. Without an ac field, the EL cell would become depleted of electrons for collision with the dopant—the cell would become polarized. The use of an ac field insures that the boundary layer between the insulating layers and the EL material always has electrons available for acceleration.

The practical engineering problems associated with the EL technology are many. First of all, there is the discovery and manufacture of EL compounds that will perform well in the role of dielectric in the EL cell. The criteria for these EL compounds are basically threefold. One, the compound's hot electrons must radiate their lost energy as photons within the visible spectrum. Two, the compound must radiate visible photons with the lowest possible electric potential applied across the working EL cell. And three, the compound must be as easy and inexpensive as possible to implement in the finished display.

The electrical connections that supply the energy to the display's matrix are a critical area that has caused problems. The number of connections is very large and all these connections must be made in a very small area. The problem is complicated by the necessity of using transparent indium tin oxide (ITO) as electrodes. ITO has relatively high resistance as a conductor. With rapidly switched high voltage ac waveforms, arcover is constantly a problem in densely packed areas. Special flexible, low loss, connectors are employed to solve this problem. As the number of pixels within the array increases, the frequency of the high voltage driving waveform also increases. The connector problem is made more critical by the higher frequency drive energy.

One more problem with AC TFEL implementation is maintaining a net zero dc potential across the EL cell. The driving waveform of up to 200 volts is strictly ac. There should be a minimum net dc potential allowed across the EL cell. The situation is not as critical as with the ac driven LCD. An LCD can be quickly and forever ruined by applying dc voltage across the cell. The EL cell is not damaged by the dc component, but the dc component reduces the net electric field surrounding the cell, reducing luminosity and efficiency.

The practical luminous efficiency of the ELD is very high. These displays are very efficient at converting electricity into light. They are more efficient than the plasma panel, although the ELD lags behind the CRT in terms of efficiency.

HOW ELDs ARE MADE

The ELD is constructed like a sandwich. the conductors that form the plates of the capacitors are built as an X-Y matrix of columns and rows. The row conductors lie on the top of the sandwich, while the column conductors are located on the sandwich's bottom. The EL dielectric is located in the middle, between the rectangular matrix formed by the row conductors on top and the column conductors below. Actually, the dielectric material is separated from the conductors by two layers of insulative material, one above and the other below the EL layer. Figure 8-2 gives a graphic representation of a single EL cell. Note that the sandwich actually consists of six distinct solid-state layers. There are no liquids or gasses employed in the ELD. All these layers are transparent, except for the very bottom layer.

Fig. 8-2. EL cell cross section

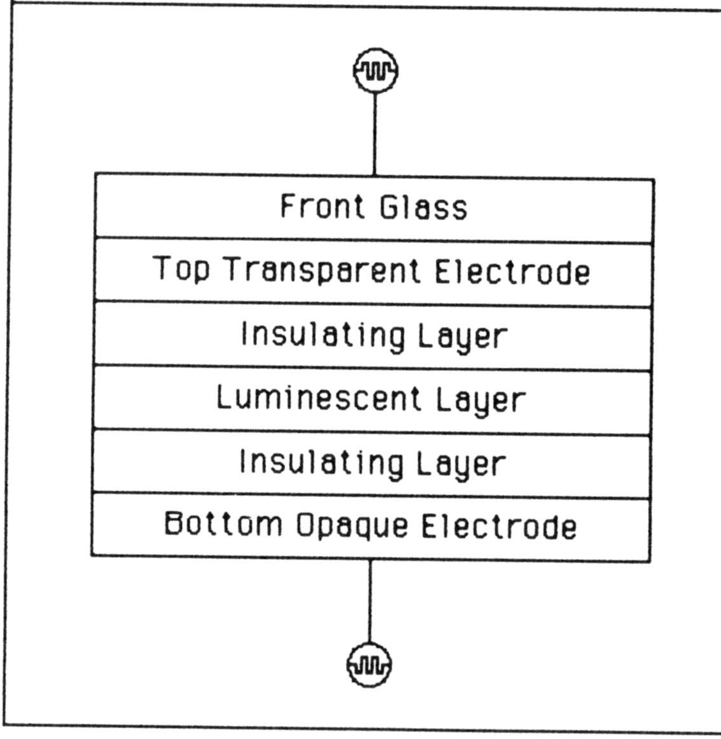

The material most commonly used as an EL dielectric is manganese doped zinc sulfide. This material is very efficient in converting electric field energy into free photons. The light output of this compound is very discrete, centered about 585 nanometers. This translates into a bright yellow-orange light. Other EL compounds do exist and will be discussed below under the section on color. The use of zinc sulfide doped with manganese is by far the most common and is used in most currently made, monochrome, commercial ELDs. This compound's high brightness, readable color, and good longevity have led it to become a standard.

The top layer of electrodes resides on the front glass of the display. These top electrodes are made from indium tin oxide and are transparent. They must be transparent in order not to block the light produced by the dielectric. This layer of electrodes is separated from the dielectric by a very thin layer of insulating material, usually yttrium trioxide or silicon dioxide. The thin film techniques of chemical vapor deposition, vacuum deposition, and layer epitaxy are used to place both the insulating layers and the very thin film of manganese doped zinc sulfide onto the sandwich. The bottom layer of the EL display is the back electrodes, which are opaque and usually made of aluminum. Figure 8-3 illustrates a physical cross section of a single EL cell. A complete display consists of thousands of these individual EL cells assembled into a rectangular matrix.

The thickness of the dielectric EL layer and the two insulating layers that surround it are critical areas of manufacture. Currently, layer thicknesses are less than 1 micrometer. The voltage at which

Fig. 8-3. Physical cross section of an EL cell

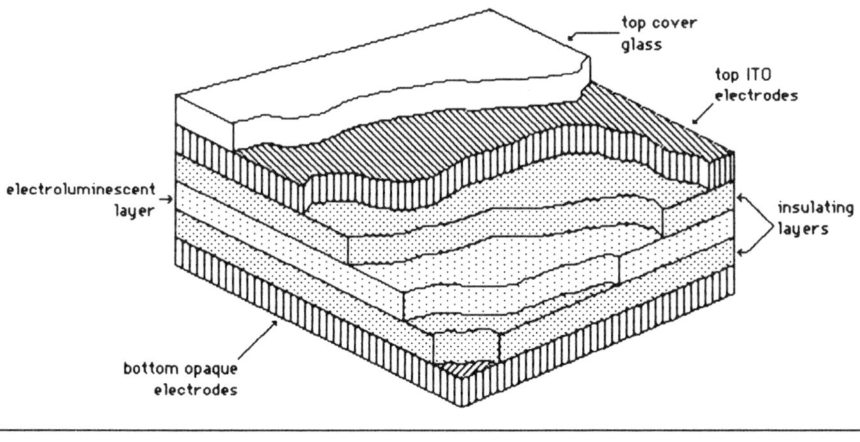

the cell emits light (or "fires") is directly related to the thickness of these layers. Remember, the EL cell is electrically a capacitor. The EL layer and its insulators are essentially the capacitor's dielectric. As such, the thickness of these layers is a major factor in determining the voltage at which the cell fires. The thicker these layers are, the higher the ac drive voltage must be in order to fire the EL cell. Thin layers in the EL cell mean that the driving electronics have to handle less voltage, making the drivers cheaper and easier to construct and implement. Total display performance is not all due to thinness however. If the layers are too thin, the display suffers very short longevity. The development of thin film deposition technologies have made manufacture of the ELD possible.

ELDs are now just becoming mass produced. Currently, they are made to quality control standards that are very high. Less than one pixel in 10,000 is allowed to have less than half light output. On a display with over 130,000 pixels, this means that only 13 are allowed to be weak or inactive. This is a tremendous triumph of manufacturing technology, but to meet such standards, 3 out of every 10 displays manufactured are discarded as defective. Current ELD manufacture is less than 200,000 units worldwide yearly. This will increase rapidly as the ELD technologies mature.

ELD CHARACTERISTICS

The electroluminescent display offers many desirable characteristics for the electronics designer. At the current state of ELD technology, their implementation is still complex and best suited for the professional. ELDs still have some growing up to do before they are as simple for the home experimenter to use as LEDs and LCDs. These characteristics presented here specifically refer to the AC TFEL. Other EL technologies offer similar characteristics, but are just not up to the high levels shown by the AC TFEL.

Design

The ELDs currently manufactured are without exception configured as dot matrix displays. These dot matrix units may be optimized to display either text or graphics by their electronic processing. The complexity of manufacturing and implementing the EL technologies has restricted their use as seven segment displays. This market is already adequately served by several less expensive display technologies.

Power Requirements

The ELD requires only a moderate amount of power considering the high level of light output produced by the display. Power consumption varies from about 150 milliwatts to 750 milliwatts per square centimeter of actual display area. This variation in consumption is due to differing brightness levels. Overall power consumption for an ELD displaying 24 lines of 80 characters in an area of 195 mm by 97 mm is about 30 watts. This figure includes all the driving electronics as well as the actual ELD panel.

The EL cell is inherently a high voltage ac operated device. The actual voltages required to fire the cell are dependent on layer thickness and phosphor/dopant material. Some cells require up to 210 Vac to fire, while the current minimum voltage required on experimental EL cells is around 120 Vac. Since the switching waveforms have frequencies in excess of 4 MHz, this high voltage requirement places considerable stress on the switching junctions. Every effort is being made to reduce the amount of voltage required to fire the EL cell. Even with thinner films making up the EL cell, there are physical limitations. The technique of producing light by electric field stimulation of EL compounds places a lower limit on drive voltage at around 100 Vac. The ELD will remain basically a high voltage ac operated device.

The overall power consumption of the ELD is likely to decrease as the technology is perfected. For example, Hewlett Packard is working on a scheme that promises to reduce the overall consumption of the ELDs by up to 50%. The basic idea is to treat the capacitive load of the EL panel as a portion of a resonant LC circuit. This may lower the overall power requirements by recovering some of the energy previously wasted while driving the display.

ELD panels require two types of voltage, high voltage ac to excite the panel and low voltage dc to supply the driver logic. If an ELD panel alone is being implemented by a designer, then he must take care that power supplies meet the required voltages without exceeding the acceptable voltage switching levels of the driving semiconductors. Many ELD manufacturers are offering their displays with all the driving electronics and power supplies in place. This greatly simplifies the user's work in implementing the display. Manufacturers now offer complete ELD modules that require only low voltage dc as input power. The high voltages required are generated by the on-board driving electronics through inversion.

Usually both 5 Vdc and 15 Vdc are required as power to these modules. The 5 Vdc is used by the display's logic, while the higher 15 Vdc is inverted into the 160 Vac or more required to excite the EL panel.

Brightness

The ELD is the brightest competitor for the CRT's job. Currently manufactured models have screen brightnesses in the neighborhood of 20 to 30 foot-Lamberts. For a similar screen size, the ELD is almost as bright as the CRT, and does the job with less power consumption.

The luminous efficiency of EL cells is in the neighborhood of 0.5 to 1 lumens per Watt. This is high in comparison with plasma panel efficiencies of about 0.3 lumens per watt. For those accustomed to the high light output levels of the CRT, the ELD makes the brightest substitute. This reason alone is a major factor spurring on ELD research.

The ELD usually does not display grey levels. The cell is either firing or not, i.e. when it's on, it's full on and when it's off, it's full off. Less than full luminosity is obtained from the EL cells by "dithering." Dithering means that the on pixel is not refreshed on every cycle, but only on some cycles. In some cases adjacent pixels are alternately fired. If this process is carried on quickly enough, the eye does not notice the very short drop out times of the pixels. The light output appears continuous, but at a lower luminosity level. This technique is very successful and, for all intents and purposes, the ELD appears to be displaying grey levels even though it is not. Dithering is commonly implemented in the system via software. Another attempt to bring grey scales to the ELD is the use of analog drivers which amplitude and pulse width modulate the ELD's driving waveforms.

Resolution

The ELD is approaching the area now commonly defined as "high resolution," but it still lags somewhat behind the hi-res CRT. When it is considered that a color ELD has all its colored elements in the z plane, while the CRT's colored elements are in the X-Y planes, then it is apparent that the ELD theoretically offers greater resolution than the CRT. The geometry of the ELDs gives them zero misconvergence between the colored elements that comprise a single pixel. It is simply a matter of shrinking the dimensions of the individual EL pixels for the ELD to surpass the CRT in resolution.

Currently, manufactured ELD models offer adequate resolution for computer display service. For example, a display with a 512 by 256 dot matrix (131,072 pixels) occupies an area of 19,032 square millimeters (195 mm by 97.6 mm). This amounts to an individual pixel area of 0.145 square mm, or almost 7 pixels within an area of 1 square mm. While such densities are not quite as great as those of the hi-res CRT, this is much greater resolution than the average garden variety CRT used in television service. If full color can be achieved by the ELD, then it is ready for a full scale "blitzkrieg" on the CRT's hold on the high resolution electronic display market.

Speed

The ELD is a fast operating display. Single Pixels can be written on the screen in less than 2.9 microseconds. An entire row of pixels can be written in about 25 microseconds. This is more than fast enough to display high resolution data at screen update times in excess of 60 Hz. Each row is scanned in a 60 Hz system for about 16 milliseconds. The ELD is definitely capable of 60 Hz flicker-free operation with up to 640 rows. In fact, the ELD is some ten times faster in its operation than its plasma competitors, but also some ten times slower than the fastest CRTs, and 1000 times slower than the superfast LED.

Color

The subject of full color operation is critical to the future of the ELD. If the ELD can be commercially manufactured for full color operation, then the last large barrier to its widespread use will be removed. The lack of full color operation is all that is keeping the ELD from replacing the CRT in many applications.

Color can be achieved in the ELD by stacking three EL cells one atop the other. Figure 8-4 illustrates the physical structure of a prototype full color EL cell employing three primary colored sub-cells. Each of the sub-cells contains a differing phosphor/dopant material. All these phosphor materials are rare earth doped alkaline earth sulfides. The red cell contains calcium sulfide (CaS). The blue cell contains strontium sulfide (SrS). The yellow-green cell contains barium sulfide (BaS). These compounds are capable of producing a full color display by the addition of primary colors. It should be emphasized that this approach is only one of several methods being

Fig. 8-4. Full color EL cell

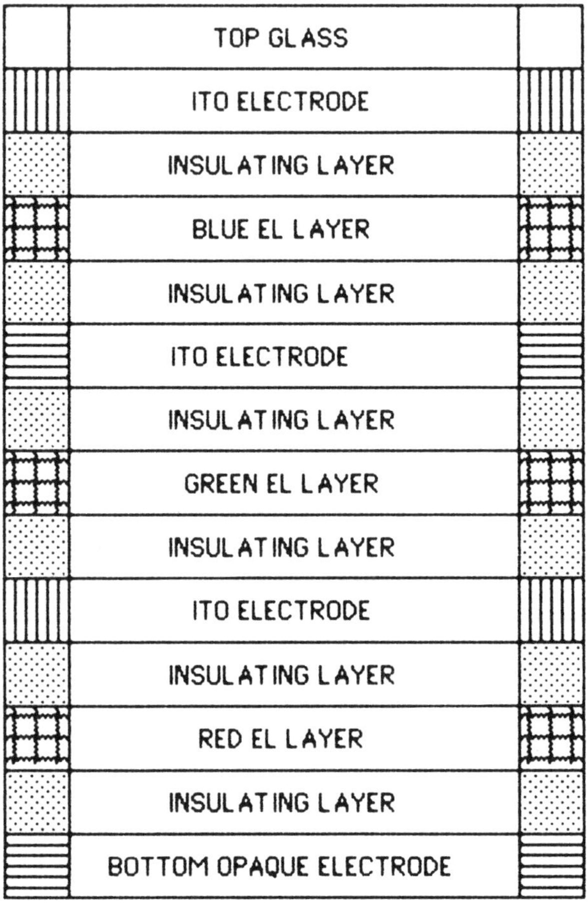

researched in order to bring full color to the ELD. Some full colored ELD prototypes use side-by-side placement of the colored elements that make up a single pixel. While this approach simplifies construction of the EL panel, it also results in a display with inherently less resolution.

One problem plaguing the full color ELD is that the colored layers making up a single pixel do not have the same relative brightnesses. This is true whether the colored layers are arranged one atop the other or side by side. For example, the CaS red compound emits about 100 Cd. per square meter, while the blue SrS compound emits 650 Cd per square meter, and the yellow-green BaS phospor emits 350 Cd per square meter. The luminous intensity of these compounds appears to be closely linked with their temperature during the process of thin film deposition. Much research is centered around this process, and every attempt is being made to equalize the light output of these differing phosphors.

The ELD technologies appear to be closing on the problem of color faster than the plasma technologies, but not as quickly as LCDs. The completely solid-state nature of ELDs gives them the edge in development over plasma types. This fact alone gives the ELD a significant advantage in the race to replace the aging and bulky CRT. Many differing phosphor/dopant combinations are being tried, in addition to several differing physical configurations of the colored cells within the matrix. Time will tell, but several sources expect a full color ELD before 1990. Other than phosphors and their configuration, several problems still remain. Among these are the difficulty of addressing a matrix with three times the number of points within the same area. The high density of interconnection is a real problem associated with the increased physical density of the electrical conductors. Another problem is the very rapid high voltage switching of the increased number of pixels required for full color display. This places additional demands on the semiconductor processing necessary to drive the full color display. These additional demands are placed on a semiconductor technology that is already hard pressed to keep up with monochrome ELDs.

Element Size

Element size is the prime factor determining the ultimate resolution of any display. There are limitations placed on the minimum size possible in an EL cell. The first factor is the voltage of the driving waveform. With voltages over 100 Vac being rapidly switched, arcover between the electrodes is possible if the lines of the matrix are located too closely. Very small dimensions between the electrodes also result in capacitive coupling between the electrodes, thus degrading the driving waveform. These factors place a lower limit to the density of EL cells assembled into dot matrix displays. Current ELD prototypes are displaying pixels with areas of less than 0.10 square millimeters. The real problem is not shrinking the EL element's size, but in assembling these small elements into densely packed arrays.

There are definite limits on the size of an EL matrix, and this is detailed below under a section called display size. There are, however, few limitations on the maximum size of a single EL cell. ELDs are being considered for very large scale displays for this reason as well as for their high brightness.

Element Thickness

The ELD is a sandwich of thin films. In no display technology is the thickness of the elements more critical. Too thin and the EL cells will self-destruct. Too thick and the driving voltages will be prohibitive. Currently, the EL active layers vary from 200 to over 500 nanometers in thickness. This is an incredibly thin layer, and makes apparent the ELD's dependence on thin film deposition technology.

In terms of overall display thickness, the completed EL panel is very thin, less than 4 mm. Once the driving electronics and connectors are added, the overall package will be between 0.37 inch to 2 inches thick. This is as thin as an overall display module now gets. Consider that the plasma panels are over twice as thick, while the CRTs are about 15 times thicker. ELDs are the most compact displays capable of replacing the CRT.

Minimum and Maximum Display Size

The ELDs now manufactured are relatively small in size. One sample ELD measures 7.68 inches by 3.84 inches of active display area. This represents a medium sized commercial display. This area is divided into 512 pixels by 256 pixels. The pixels are configured as 25 lines of 80 characters each. Characters are displayed in a 5 by 7 character matrix. What this reduces to in practical terms is about half a page of text displayed on the screen. An active area of 5.14 inches by 11.14 inches represents the maximum size now commercially available. This sample unit is also set up as a 512 by 256 pixel matrix.

ELDs have size limitations caused by the use of ITO for the transparent electrodes. The high electrical resistance of ITO attenuates the driving signal at the extreme ends of the matrix. Lower voltages at the extremes of the matrix result in intermittent "drop-outs" of these remote pixels. The high resistance of the ITO electrodes is increased as the display resolution increases. Increased pixel density means thinner cross sections for the ITO electrodes and greater electrical resistance. Since the EL cells are essentially capacitive loads, the driving signal is also degraded by capacitive coupling to all the cells along the electrode. The longer the electrodes, the more cells are coupled to the electrode, and this increases the problem of capacitive degeneration of the drive signal. Some manufacturers have attempted to solve these problems by breaking the drive matrix into a series of subassemblies, each with its own electrodes and drivers. As with other display technologies, like LCDs and plasma displays, the ELD's operation can be greatly improved by the development of transparent conductor materials of low resistance.

Operating Characteristics

The ELD is a very readable display; it has many of the desirable operational characteristics required of a display. It is primarily the ELD's exceptional operating characteristics that have led to its use by the military. It is rare among electronic display devices to find one that offers the combination of high brightness, overall display module thinness, moderate power consumption, and extreme ruggedness.

Visual Angle

The visual angle of the ELD is limited by the geometry of its individual cells and the use of ITO as an electrode material. The situation is similar to that of the LCD, and is illustrated in Fig. 6-22. The main limiting factor is the thickness of the EL cell. The thinner the cell can be constructed, the wider the possible viewing angle. At the current state of ELD technology, visual angles vary from 80° to 150°. The use of a transparent ITO grid over the light emitting portion of the display introduces refraction. This refraction distorts the display's light output. This amount of refracted light in relation to nonrefracted display output is also related to the viewing angle. The more obtuse the viewing angle, the higher the proportion of refracted light. As with most display technologies that use transparent ITO electrodes, the ELD is best viewed straight on.

Memory

The AC TFEL is generally considered not to have any inherent memory within its display elements. An EL pixel will glow only for about 1 to 3 milliseconds after electrical activation has stopped. The EL's memory characteristics are very similar to those of the CRT. Light persistence after electrical stimulation has ceased is a function of the phosphor's composition and excitation voltage. In general, the ELD remains a display on which the information must be continually refreshed.

Experimentation is directed at developing an EL cell with high persistence characteristics, i.e. a memory. The big advantage of a memory in this case is the elimination of refreshing unchanged pixels. The disadvantage is that pixels must be electrically erased rather than losing their light output naturally. High persistance phosphors under development for use in ELDs are still based around zinc sulfide compounds with the addition of fluorine and terbium oxides. The development of high persistance EL phosphors is being attempted to make driving the display easier. If the ELD's electronic drivers are improved, and they certainly will be, then the advantage of an ELD with a memory disappears. The ELD will be commercially implemented in its non-memory form.

Operating Temperature Range

Wide temperature operating range is one of the ELD's strongest operating points. The temperature operating limits of the ELD are determined more by the driving electronics than by the actual EL panel itself. With military specification drivers, the ELD will operate between −40° C and 55° C. The use of commercial drivers reduces the temperature operating range to 0° C to 55° C.

The ELD can survive storage over a wider temperature range than other types of non-solid state flat panel displays. With military driving electronics, the ELD can be stored from −55° C to 105° C. Commercial grade electronics allow ELD storage at between −40° C to 85° C. These storage characteristics are essential for displays used in aircraft and other military vehicles. An aircraft parked in the sun can experience cockpit temperatures that will permanently destroy some display devices such as LCDs.

This wide temperature operating range is strictly a function of the completely solid state construction of the ELD. Plasma and LCD panels use gas and liquid states, and these are greatly affected by temperature. Theoretically, the electron tunneling technology used in the ELD is only slightly affected by temperature.

Longevity

The ELD's solid state ruggedness really pays off in terms of longevity. The ELD is very long lived, over 20,000 hours. The luminance of the panel in relation to drive voltage gradually decreases by 20% over the first 10,000 hours of operation. Aging of the panel continues until about 50% of the light output remains at 20,000 hours.

The longevity of the ELD is a function of several factors. The ELDs suffer greatly shortened lifetimes if continually operated at over 80° C. Another factor affecting longevity is the symmetry and voltage of the driving waveforms. Asymmetrical driving waveforms can cause permanent electron migration in the EL cell. Overvoltage can cause arc over within the EL cell, resulting in instantaneous cell destruction.

AC TFEL Driving Waveforms

The actual EL panel itself is really a simple device. This simplicity is had at the price of complex driving requirements. These driving requirements are threefold. One, the EL panel requires a symmetrical high voltage ac waveform to produce the constant di/dt necessary to stimulate the EL compounds into light emission. Two, this HV ac voltage must be applied to a rectangular row/column matrix to activate the appropriate pixels. And three, the information to be displayed must be encoded onto the HV ac waveform applied to the matrix. And all this must happen very quickly; driving waveforms are commonly over 4 MHz in EL panels.

Most of the information encoding schemes used in ELDs are designed to be compatible with CRT encoding techniques. The use of a raster scanning and refresh encoding system allows the ELD to more directly compete with the CRT. It also allows the ELD to use commonly available video processing ICs, character generators, and graphics chips. The biggest advantage of using raster scanning is that it allows the ELD to directly display information already encoded for CRT display. It makes the ELD and the CRT interchangeable as display devices. All the information presented here is based on a CRT raster scan compatible system. This is by no means the only way to encode information for the ELD, it is simply the most common.

First, let's take a look at an electrode matrix that allows us to fire individual locations on the ELD's screen. An AC TFEL panel has a matrix of columns and rows to address the individual pixels within the EL array. The vertical electrodes (columns) have their electrical connections at the top and bottom of the display. The odd numbered column's connections are at the top, while even numbered columns are connected at the bottom. The configuration is similar for the horizontal electrodes (rows). Odd numbered rows are electrically connected at the left side of the EL panel, while even numbered rows connect at the right side of the panel. Figure 8-5 illustrates this matrix arrangement. Remember that the EL panel is an electric field operated device. This means that each electrode need have only one connection to function. Electric field operation also means no direct dc connection between the row and the column electrodes.

The vertical electrodes are the transparent ITO conductors that form the top of the sandwich. In the middle, the EL layers and its insulators act as a dielectric. The EL/insulator layers prevents dc contact between the electrode pair that fires any particular location. The bottom of the sandwich is the aluminum electrode network that forms the rows. A pixel is addressed by applying the electric field to its location. For example, if row #3 and column #4 are simultaneously electrically charged to the proper voltage, then that pixel location will fire. The situation here is entirely similar to the usage of matrixes in both LED and LCD displays.

Fig. 8-5. ELD matrix

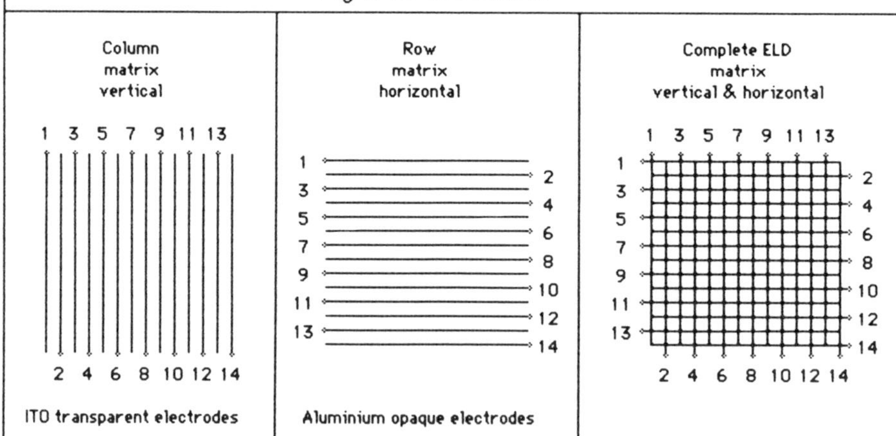

The ELD's screen is scanned one pixel at a time in a standard raster scan pattern borrowed from the CRT. The upper left hand pixel (column #1, row #1) is scanned first, and may be fired or not fired as desired. The second pixel scanned is column #2, row #1, and the third pixel scanned is column #3, row #1, and so forth . . . When all of row #1 is completely scanned, the entire process is repeated on row #2, beginning with column #1, row #2. This scanning technique is a direct copy of CRT operation. Its use assures that data encoded for CRT raster display can also be displayed on this particular ELD. In this system, the row signals function in the same manner as vertical deflection signal in a CRT display system.

The EL pixel in this sample application requires in the neighborhood of 210 V to fire. This voltage potential is split between the columns and the rows. The columns are ground referenced and charged to around +50 V. The rows are not ground referenced, but float, and are charged to −160 V. The resulting electrostatic potential between a row and column intersection is the absolute difference between +50 V and −160 V, or the 210 V necessary to fire the pixel.

Let's take a look at a complete scan of the ELD's screen. The ELD has all of its columns simultaneously rounded before beginning a scan. While the columns are grounded, all the rows receive a positive refresh pulse around +160 volts. This initial refresh pulse is applied to the entire panel and is required to achieve maximum brightness for the EL panel. This special positive refresh pulse assures discharge of the panel (it's a capacitor, remember?) and sets it up for the negative illuminating pulses to follow.

Now that housekeeping matters are done, the display scans its first pixel. If the pixel at row #1, column #1 is required to fire, then row #1 receives a negative pulse of −160 V and column #1 receives a positive pulse of +50 V. This procedure is repeated until a complete raster scan of all the display's pixels is completed. Figure 8-6 illustrates the operational waveforms employed in this ELD. This illustration shows only the first 3 columns and rows, but the situation is identical for the remaining rows and columns. In this scheme, the data is carried by the column waveforms, while the row waveforms carry the enabling pulses. Note that this illustration also includes the input waveforms used to control the row and column driving electronics.

This waveform may not seem exceedingly complex, and it really is not. The major wrinkle in making this scheme work in an actual ELD is the semiconductors that are used to accomplish this very

Fig. 8-6. ELD waveforms

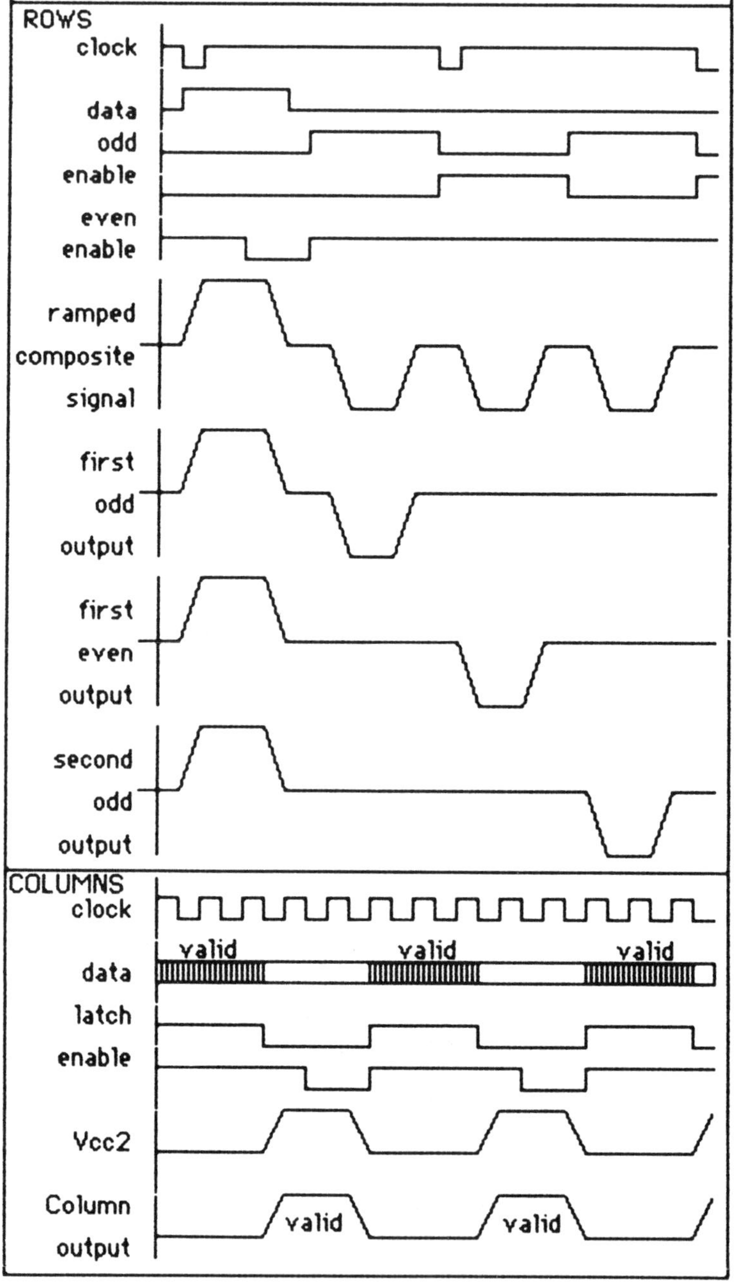

rapid switching of hundreds of volts, some negative and some positive. Until recently we lacked the semiconductors to accomplish this job.

AC THIN-FILM ELD DRIVERS

The semiconductors that drive the ELD are a very specialized type. They are divided into two classifications—row drivers and column drivers. These devices are so specialized that the odd and even driver chips have their pin-outs reversed to facilitate their installation around the edges of the display. These drivers are available in 16, 32, and 64 electrode models. Regardless of size or manufacturer, these chips have one basic function—to properly switch the high voltage required by the ELD. The magic of the ELD resides not in the display, but in these very advanced semiconductors. The price of the ELD also resides in the driving electronics which account for over half of the completed ELD's cost.

The problem faced by ELD drivers is to switch the high voltage ac required by the display. This problem is more complicated for the row drivers which do not have their output junctions referenced to ground, but are floating. The row drivers must handle both positive and negative voltages. Operation of semiconductors at voltages as high as those found in ELDs is a fairly recent development (within the last four years).

Texas Instruments has developed a high voltage switching technology for use in electroluminescent and also plasma displays. This patented process is called BIDFET which stands for bipolar, double diffused, N-channel and P-channel MOS transistors on the same chip. This process succeeds in placing NPN, PNP, CMOS, DMOS and JFET semiconductor technologies all on the same monolithic substrate. This unique process allows these driver ICs to process high voltage energy while still retaining their LSI logic capabilities.

The Texas Instruments SN75551/2 row driver and SN75555/ column driver ICs are capable of switching 32 display lines. A display with 512 columns and 256 rows would use 16 column driver ICs and 8 row driver ICs. The two numbers for each chip refer to the odd and even packages. These packages are electrically identical, but have their pin-outs reversed to simplify their electrical connections around the panel's edges.

The SN75551/2 row driver uses high voltage open drain N-channel DMOS outputs. These outputs are rated at 225 volts maximum, with a breakdown voltage of over 450 volts. Figure 8-7

Fig. 8-7. SN75551/2 ELD row driver

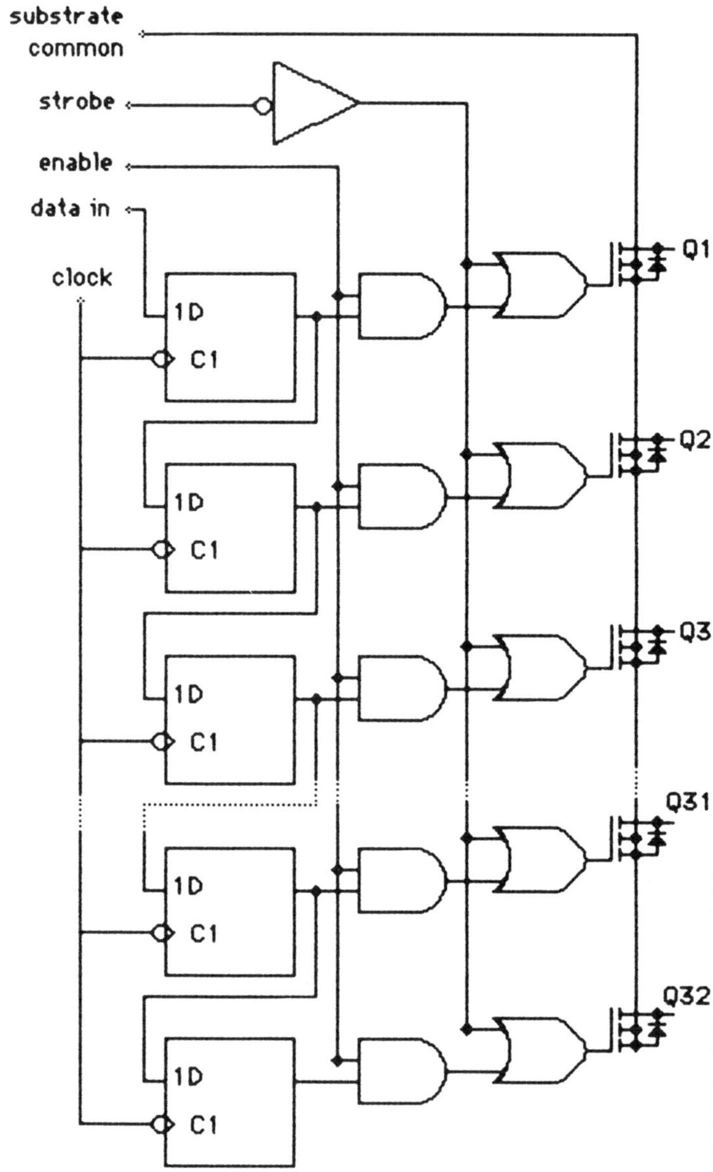

illustrates a functional block diagram of the SN75551/2. All inputs of this chip are compatible with CMOS logic. Serial data is sequentially loaded into the shift registers on transition of the clock from high to low. A high pulse at the enable input sends all DMOS outputs into conduction if their respective register also contains a logical high state. If their strobe input is low, then all DMOS outputs conduct regardless of the condition of their respective shift registers. The refresh pulse is accomplished by a low pulse on the strobe input of the row driver. In this manner the row data is translated into the actual high voltage signal needed to active the ELD's rows.

The TI SN75555/6 column driver ICs contain bipolar over DMOS totem pole outputs. These outputs are capable of switching 90 volts and are ground referenced. Figure 8-8 shows a functional block diagram of the SN75555/6 column driver IC. All inputs of this IC are CMOS compatible and diode protected. The 32-bit shift register is capable of operation at 6.25 MHz, and registers accept data on the positive edge of the clock. Clamp diodes from ground to the outputs protect the outputs from the high negative and positive voltages needed to drive the ELD's columns. Figure 8-9 illustrates the output semiconductor configurations of both the row and column driver activating a single EL pixel. Note the use of diodes to protect the output devices from the high voltages involved.

These row and column EL drivers are mentioned as examples. Companies other than Texas Instruments are also involved in ELD driver manufacture. It is on the continuing development of these driver ICs that the future of the ELD depends. If the ELD is to become less expensive and larger in area, then the price and complexity of these driver ICs must decrease. As it stands now the driving electronics form the bulk of the completed ELD's cost.

SAMPLE APPLICATION: A FLAT SCREEN COMPUTER DISPLAY

The ELDs are now being implemented as flat panel computer displays. Using the matrix addressing techniques and driver ICs mentioned here, the use of the ELD in computer service is possible and gaining rapidly in popularity. Several computer manufacturers offer portable models with ELDS.

Figure 8-10 illustrates a block diagram of an ELD used in computer service. The 512 × 256 EL panel is surrounded by its row and column drivers. In actuality, this circuit requires 16 row drivers and 8 column drivers of the 32 bit variety. The block diagram

Fig. 8-8. SN75555/6 column driver

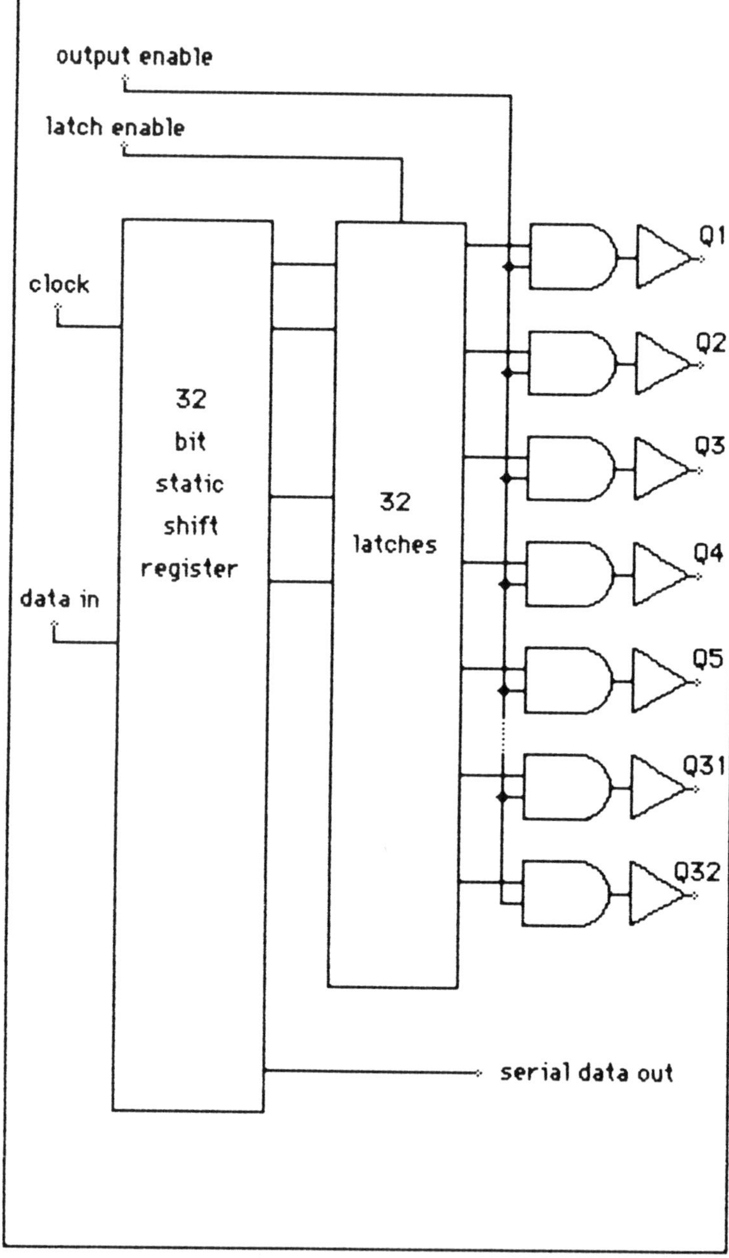

Fig. 8-9. ELD driver outputs

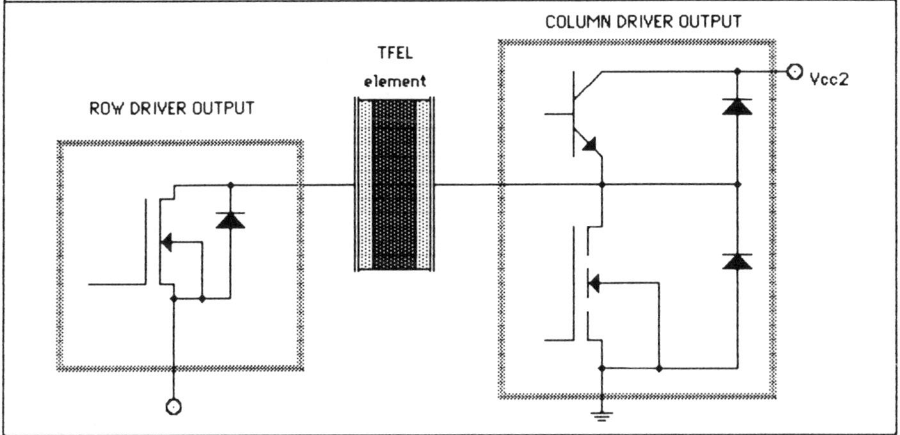

only illustrates the first and last of the required drivers. These drivers are buffered to the data by a coupling circuit. The ramped composite generator synthesizes the bipolar high voltage waveform required by the rows. This ramped composite generator is controlled by a signal provided by the computer's display controller.

Figure 8-11 illustrates a block diagram for the entire display system including the remainder of the circuitry not shown in Fig. 8-10. Note that this block diagram differs very little from a standard raster-scanned CRT display. In this system, the ELDs logic functions

Fig. 8-10. ELD block diagram

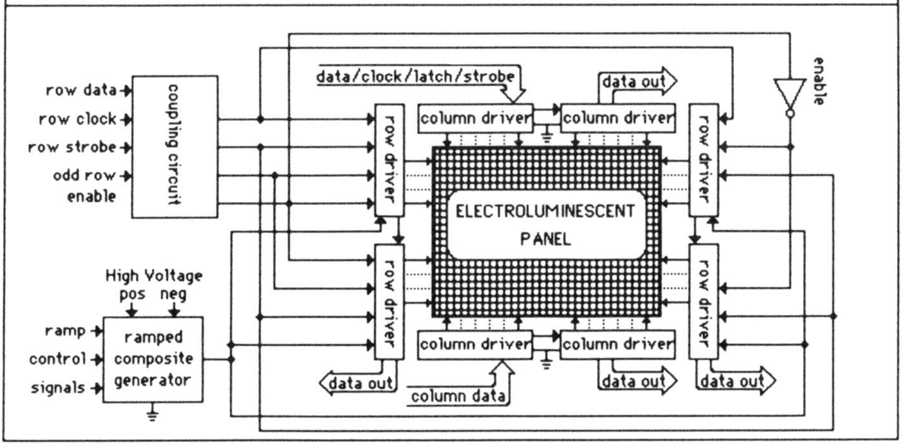

Fig. 8-11. ELD/Computer block diagram

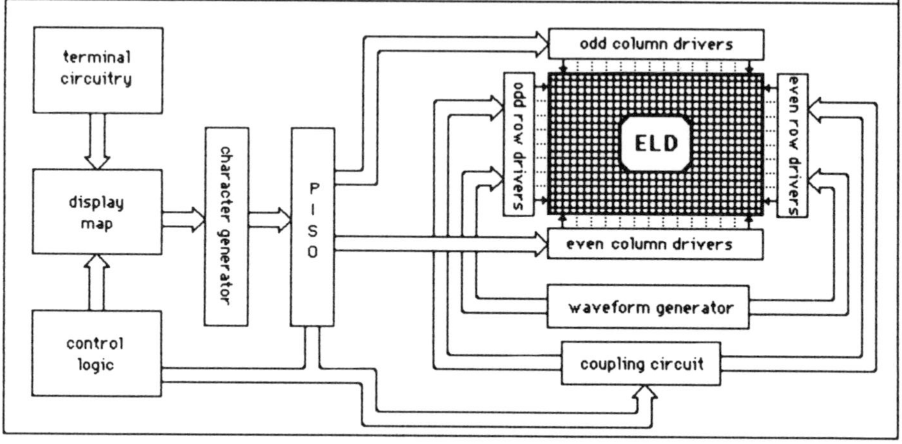

in the same manner as the CRT's raster system. The parallel-in-serial-out (PISO) register stores the character information. The PISO accepts this data in a parallel form and passes this data to the column drivers in a serial stream. After a complete line of information is transferred to the column drivers, the PISO accepts the next line of data.

ELD COST

The ELD still remains one of the more expensive display devices. The prices mentioned here represent complete display modules. These modules include the EL panel, driving electronics, and inverter power supplies. Only the addition of the appropriate data and low voltage power is necessary for the modules operation. Currently ELD modules start at about $1,900 and go up to over $3,000 depending on size and number purchased. The cost of the actual El panel, sans electronics, varies from about $60 to over $700, once again depending on size. If the ELD is already implemented in a computer, it adds about $1,000 to the cost of the system over using a medium resolution CRT or LCD flat panel.

ELD MANUFACTURERS

The following companies contributed information on ELDs and their drivers to this chapter. A complete list of their addresses and telephone numbers can be found in Appendix A Electronic Display Devices Manufacturers Data Base.

Texas Instruments Inc.

Digital Electronics Corporation

Infodex, Inc.

Siliconix Inc.

Sprague Electric Co.

9

Plasma Displays

The plasma display is a flat panel, light producing, gas discharge display. The plasma panels are attempting to do the same basic job as the CRT—visual electronic display of text and graphics information. Modern plasma panels are now making inroads into the computer display market. The future for these high brightness and compact displays looks very promising. The plasma panels are now the most commonly used light producing replacement for CRTs.

Plasma display technology is fairly recent, and was first developed in the early 1960's. The theoretical basis of plasma displays is some 20 years older than the electroluminescent displays. Early attempts produced very small (3 cm × 3 cm) plasma panels with 16 × 16 pixels and very short lifetimes. Currently manufactured plasma panels now measure in the meters on a side, with pixel counts over one million. Plasma displays are matrix addressed in much the same manner as LED, LCD, and ELD matrix types. The physics behind the operation of the plasma panel is very basic. The principle is the same as the common, everyday, neon sign—neon gas emits light when electrical current is passed through it. As in the case of most display technologies, the actual physical principles underlying the display's operation are simple. It is the actual implementation into a hi-res, mass produced, operating display that is very complex. The plasma panel requires very sophisticated manufacturing and operating techniques for mass implementation.

Plasma displays are currently competing with electroluminescent (ELD) types for the lucrative military and industrial display market. The flat profile of the plasma panel fits into tight spaces such as military vehicles. This market is able to bear the additional cost of plasma panels in relation to CRTs. As in the case of the ELDs, the cost of the electronics driving the plasma panel represent most of the overall display's cost. If plasma display technology can be refined and made less expensive, then a large consumer market is sure to follow.

HOW PLASMA DISPLAYS WORK

The plasma panel is a super complex collection of neon lights. Plasma is an ionized and electrically conductive gas. The principle of its operation was first discovered by physicists (such as J.J. Thomson, discoverer of the electron) late in the nineteenth century. They experimented by passing an electrical current through gases at low pressures. These physicists were not trying to invent a lighting or display device; they were probing into the nature of matter in general and the electron in particular. They noticed that some gases glowed under electronic flow. The intensity and color of the light depended on the gas being used, its pressure, and the amount of electrical flow through it. Credit for the development of neon lighting goes to the French chemist, Georges Claude. In 1910, he introduced a working neon light that glowed red under electrical flow.

Figure 9-1 illustrates an early apparatus used in investigation of the electron's nature and the subsequent, accidental, discovery of the neon lighting effect. This early apparatus demonstrates the essential features of modern plasma cells based on neon gas mixtures. These early gas discharge tubes used air as the gas. The physicists noticed that if the gas was partially evacuated from the tube, then a purplish-pink light was emitted by the gas when the electrodes were charged with high voltage. The air would not glow at higher or lower gas pressures. The gas pressure within the tube is an indication of the density of the gas within the tube. If there are too many gas molecules per unit volume within the tube, the electric field within the tube will not cause the gas to glow. The situation is similar if there are too few gas molecules per unit volume in the tube. The reason for this is found in the physics of the energy transfer between the electrons moving through the tube and the electronic structure of the gas molecules.

Fig. 9-1. An early gas discharge tube

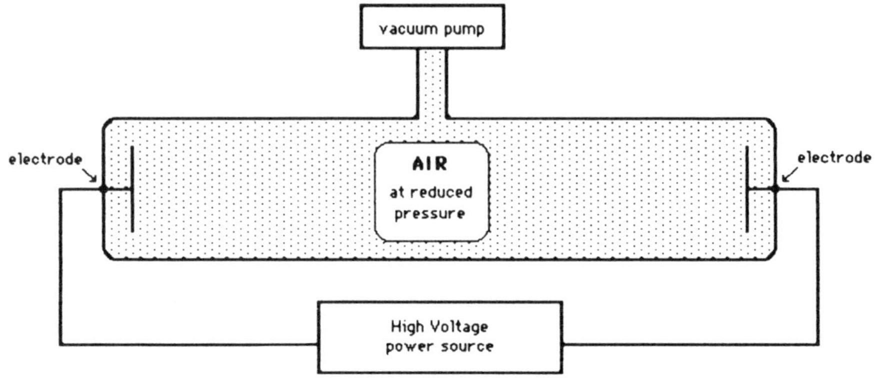

As the electrons move through the gas, they ionize the individual gas molecules. The gas molecule, while ionized, rearranges its electronic configuration and dissociates into a positive gas ion and an electron(s). This rearrangement is not an electrically stable electron configuration and rapidly decays to a more stable form. Decay, in this case, means that a gas ion absorbs one (or more) of the free electrons. During this decay process, some of the energy gained from ionization is radiated as a visible photon(s).

The voltage potential at which the gas becomes a plasma and conducts electricity is called its ''breakdown'' voltage. This breakdown voltage varies with the chemical composition of the gas, and with the pressure of the gas. Plasma displays commonly use gases in the inert gas (noble) family, usually neon, argon, and xenon. The actual gas in the plasma display is often a mixture of these noble gases. Small amounts of other ''dopant'' gases are sometimes added to the noble gas mixture to obtain variations in color.

Plasma displays are currently made in two forms—dc plasma and ac plasma displays. Figure 9-2 illustrates schematically the difference in construction of these two forms of plasma displays. The dc plasma display is operated, as its name implies, by dc electricity and electronic flow through the gas. The ac plasma panel operates on ac electricity, and also by actual electronic flow through the gas plasma. Both types are gas (plasma) discharge tubes. The only physical difference between the two types is the absence of the dielectric, insulative layers separating the electrode from the gas mixture in the ac plasma cell. In the dc plasma cell, the gas is in direct electrical contact with the electrodes of the cell. The dc plasma display has no inherent pixel memory and is refreshed much in the same manner as ELDs and CRTs.

While the physical principles used in both ac and dc plasma panels are the same, their operation and implementation are very different. The ac plasma panels require an ac drive voltage because of the insulating layers separating their electrodes from the gas plasma. The ac plasma panel is capacitively coupled to its driving waveform, while the dc model is dc coupled. This makes the driving waveform and electronics of ac types much more complex. The ac plasma panel contains a limited cell "memory" that the dc model does not. This limited pixel memory is inherent with the use of the insulating dielectric layers. This pixel memory is the prime advantage of the ac plasma cell over the dc type, but necessitates more complex driving techniques.

Figure 9-3 illustrates the electrical models of both the dc and ac plasma cells. Note that the dc plasma cell is represented by a parallel circuit of a single capacitor and a spark gap. The capacitor is made up of the cell's electrodes with the gas plasma playing the role of dielectric. The spark gap signifies the cell's operation when the voltage is high enough to fire the cell, i.e., operation at breakdown voltage. Note that the ac plasma cell is electrically represented by a series string of three capacitors, with a spark gap paralleling the center capacitor. The two layers that insulate the electrodes from

Fig. 9-2. DC and AC plasma cell schematics

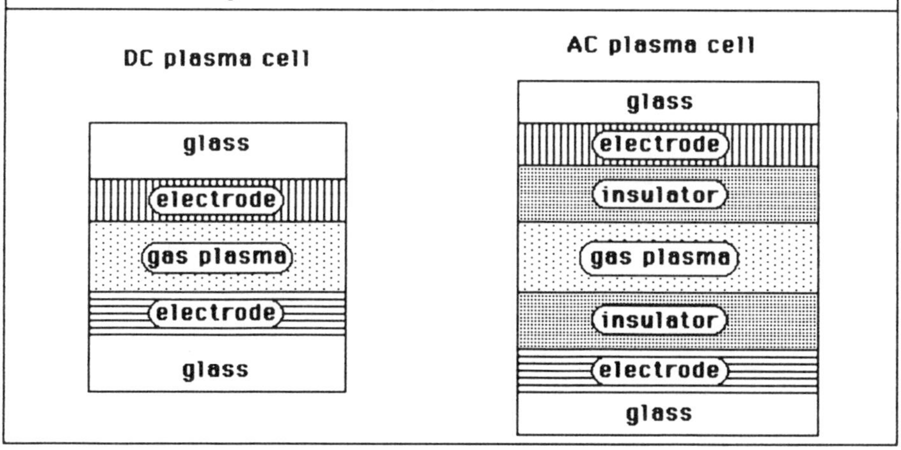

Fig. 9-3. Electrical models of ac and dc plasma cells

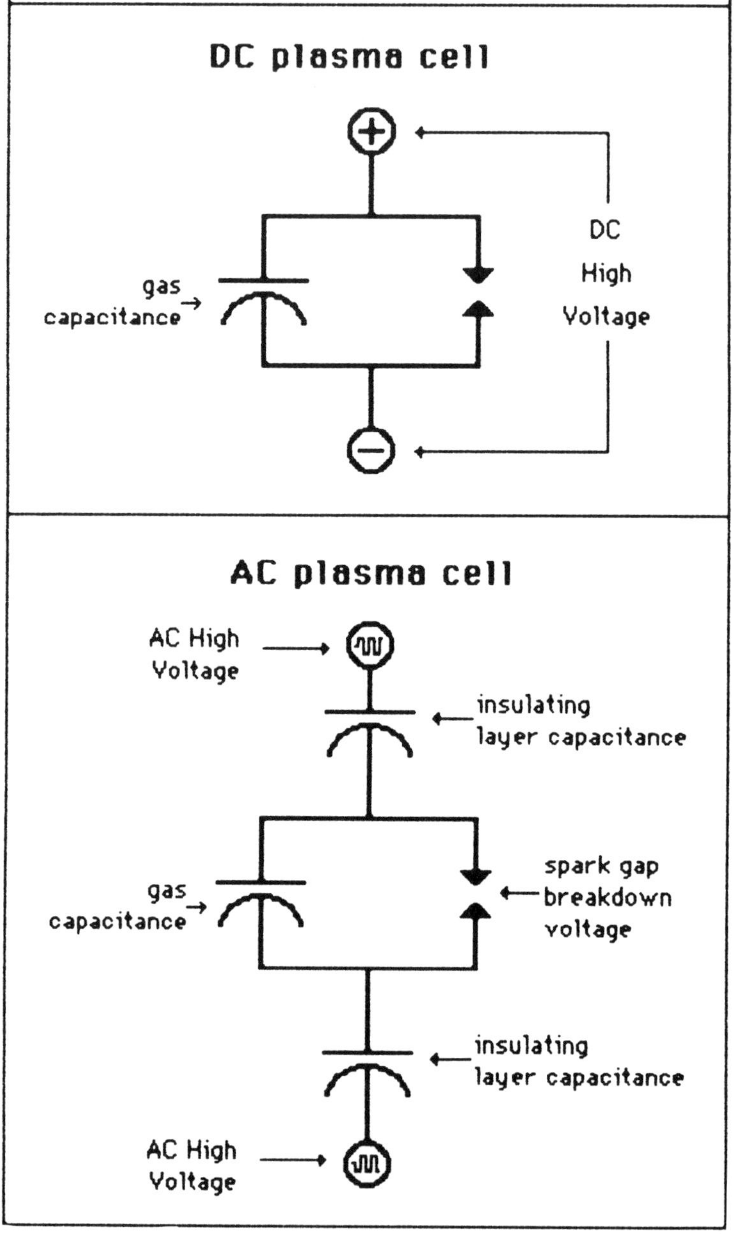

the gas plasma contribute to the overall capacitance of the ac cell. The dielectric constant of the insulating material is much higher than that of the gas plasma. The insulating layers are also much thinner than the gas plasma layer. The overall effect is that the gas plasma capacitance is much lower than that of the insulating layers. This is a very important fact that gives the ac type its limited cell (pixel) memory, and is thoroughly discussed under the section titled Memory.

HOW PLASMA DISPLAYS ARE MADE

Both ac and dc plasma displays start out with the same construction. Two sheets of glass, each about 6 mm (about 0.25 inches) thick, are vapor deposited with very thin gold lines that form the display's addressing matrix. The gold lines forming the electrode matrices vary from 0.07 mm (3 mils) to 0.20 mm (8 mils) in width, depending on display size and type. The plasma display's matrix is rectilinear and identical to that of the ELD illustrated in Fig. 8-5. The only difference between the ELD's matrix and the plasma display's matrix is that the plasma type uses gold as a conductor rather than the transparent indium tin oxide (ITO). The plasma display is a gas discharge type, and as such, it does not require the large conductor surface areas of the ELD which is field operated.

One piece of glass forms the back of the display and the other forms the front. In the case of the dc plasma display, the two pieces of glass, with their vapor deposited electrode lines, are assembled with an edge seal and spacers. This forms a gap of some 0.1 mm (about 4 mils) between the two glass sheet subassemblies. This gap volume is evacuated and filled with the inert gas mixture at reduced pressures. The basic dc plasma panel itself is then ready for operation. The dc plasma display's matrix is addressed in the same fashion as ELD types, with the odd and even rows and columns being arranged around the edges of the display. Figure 9-4 illustrates the physical construction of a dc plasma panel. Note that there is no insulating barrier between the electrodes and the gas filled cavity within the center of the display.

The ac plasma panel has a thin film of magnesium oxide vapor deposited over the glass plates and their attached gold electrode lines. This film of magnesium oxide acts as an insulator and dc isolates the electrodes from the gas mixture. After these insulative layers are deposited on the glass sub-assemblies, they are then assembled in the same fashion as the dc plasma panels. Figure 9-5 illustrates

Fig. 9-4. DC plasma panel physical construction

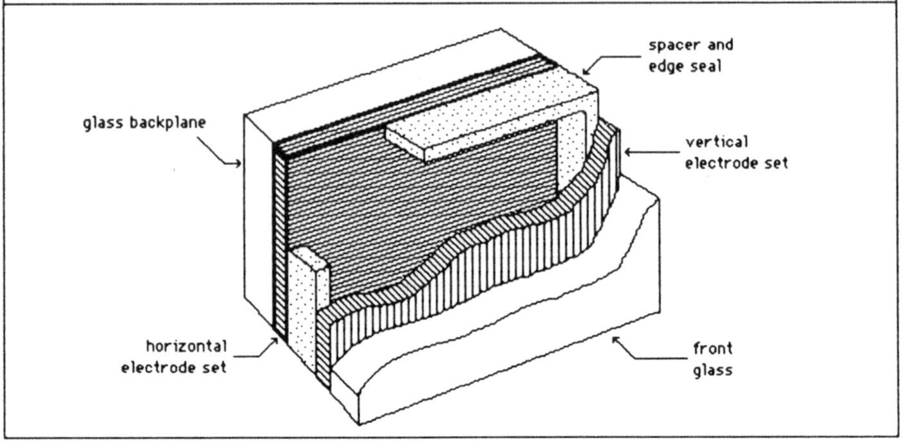

the physical construction of an ac plasma panel. The use of these insulating layers is the only physical difference between the ac and dc plasma displays.

The manufacture of plasma panels, especially large area ones, is a difficult affair. The large pieces of glass must be handled carefully to prevent contamination, scratching, or chipping. The glass may be contaminated by dust, solvents, and/or moisture. In addition to these problems, a large area plasma panel may contain as much as four miles of ultra-thin gold electrodes. Breakage of any one of these

Fig. 9-5. AC plasma panel physical construction

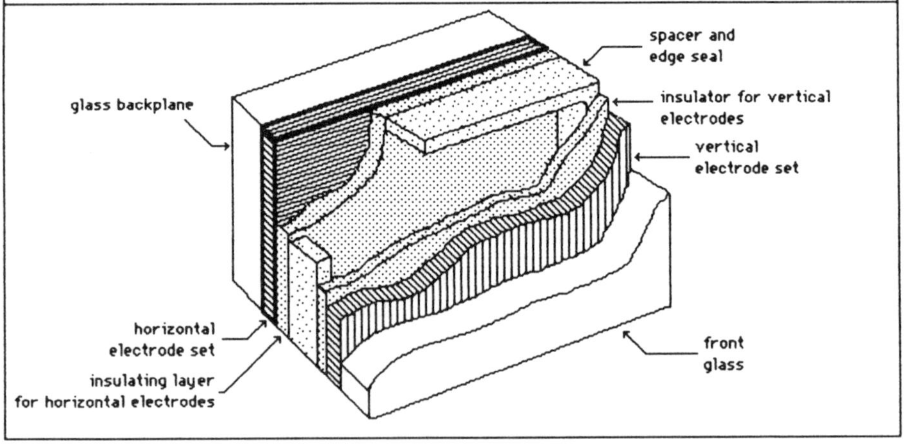

electrodes can cause an entire row or column to be inoperative. A large plasma panel may have as many as 300 hours of expensive, quality control before being considered complete.

PLASMA DISPLAY CHARACTERISTICS

Both the ac and the dc plasma displays offer about the same operating characteristics. They are both relatively bright, compact, and power efficient. They do, however, differ greatly in both the waveforms and the electronics that drive them. Due to the inherent memory of the ac types, they appear to have the edge in the marketplace and are much more commonly used. As such, most of this information is specifically directed at the ac type of plasma display. The advantages of the ac type's memory is likely to be erased in the future by faster and less expensive driving electronics.

Design

Plasma panels are available in just about every display configuration we have discussed to this point. Plasma display come in seven segment, fourteen segment, sixteen segment, and many bar graph forms. By far the most popular form of the plasma display is the dot matrix type. The versatility of the dot matrix type makes it the logical type to consider for computer use. The dot matrix types will display both text and graphics, something not possible on the segmented displays. Figure 9-6 illustrates the physical dimensions

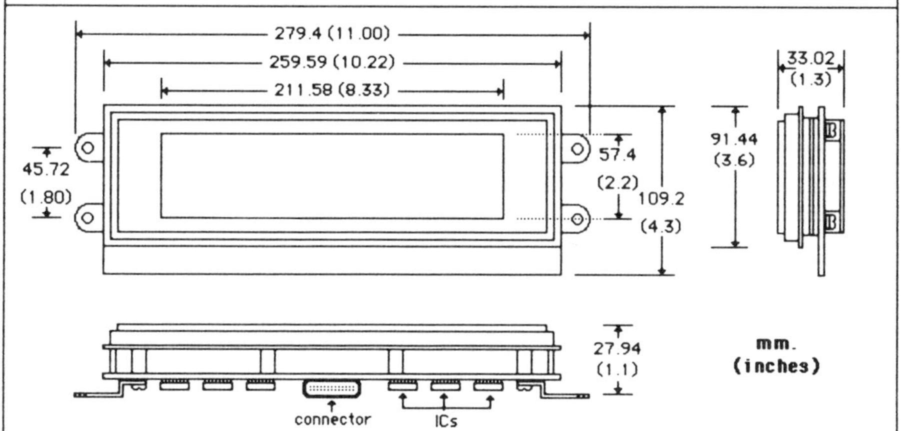

Fig. 9-6. Physical dimensions of a plasma display module

of a typical dot matrix type plasma panel. Note that the overall display module is very thin. This panel is capable of displaying 240 characters on 6 lines of 40 characters each. Each character is made up of a standard 5 × 7 dot matrix.

Power Requirements

The basic plasma pixel needs to have a potential of at least 200 volts before it will fire. The exact amount of voltage required depends on the panel's geometry, the type of gas used, and the gas's pressure. The prime factor in the panel's geometry is the thickness of the gap between the two electrode matrices. Wider gas gaps require higher voltages before they will fire. The high voltage requirements are inherent with the use of gas discharge technology. The amount of current flowing through the plasma cell when it fires is very low, between 1 and 10 microamperes.

Most plasma displays are offered as modules by the manufacturer. These modules contain power supplies that provide the necessary high voltage for the driving electronics. These on-board inverters that provide the driving power accept a wide variety of input voltages, everything from 5 Vdc to 24 Vdc. Some models have power supplies that accept 120 Vac as input, and are designed to operate on the power mains.

The ac plasma panel dissipates between 1 mW and 2 mW per pixel. The dc coupling and absence of the insulating layers of the dc plasma panel allow its pixels to be fully illuminated at about 0.6 to 1.5 mW per pixel. These figures include operation of the display's logic and on-board inverter power supplies. This level of power consumption is moderate, and is slightly more than the ELDs, but much less than a CRT of the same size.

In terms of a sample unit, let's consider the plasma panel illustrated in Fig. 9-6. The logic driving the display requires 5 Vdc at 210 mA, while the inverter uses 12 Vdc at 1 ampere to make the high voltage necessary to fire the panel. Total panel power consumption is less than 14 watts. At this power level, small dc plasma displays are compatible with portable battery operated equipment. Larger ac plasma panels require more energy to operate. For example, a large panel with a diagonal measurement of 1 meter will require about 200 watts of power to operate. Considering the area and brightness of such a display, over 5.3 square feet, this is very moderate power consumption.

Brightness

The plasma displays are among the brightest of the flat panel displays. Only the electroluminescent panel is brighter and more efficient at converting electricity to light. Plasma technologies are now producing between 0.2 and 2.0 foot-Lamberts of light per watt of input power. The actual amount of light output by a plasma display depends on its size. For example the display illustrated in Fig. 9-6 has a cell brightness of 30 foot-Lamberts. Larger panels are equipped with larger cells, and have cell brightnesses in excess of 100 foot-Lamberts.

Many plasma displays are now designed for military operation. As such, they use a filter in front of the screen. This filter is designed to enhance the display's contrast, and to provide shielding from electromagnetic and radio frequency interference. The use of this filter reduces the display's effective brightness by about 50%. Displays not used in military environments do not employ this filter and as a result are brighter and more efficient.

Resolution

The limit of resolution for the plasma panel rests on how small an individual plasma pixel can be constructed. The plasma pixel uses gold thin-film electrodes that are opaque. The width of this electrode limits the cell to areas greater than 0.008 square mm. At a pixel area less than this, the opaque electrode blocks the light output of the cell. High resolution plasma panels now constructed do, in fact, have about half their light output absorbed by the gold matrix lines.

At current technological levels, plasma panels with pixel densities between 100 and 900 pixels per square cm are being commonly produced. Prototype and experimental displays have exhibited pixel densities of 4000 pixels per square cm, which amounts to an area of 0.025 square mm per pixel. This is very dense, and modern plasma panels are already among the highest resolution displays. The use of opaque material for electrodes places a definite limit on how small a pixel can be made. This deficiency is not shared by the electroluminescent displays which use transparent material as electrodes. In any case, modern high resolution, plasma panels can display virtually seamless data and graphics when viewed at distances as close as one meter.

Speed

An individual cell within a plasma panel can be activated or deactivated in less than 20 μs. This is somewhat slower than the CRT and the LED, but on a par with the ELDs. When the individual plasma pixel is arranged with thousands of others on a matrix, then things slow down considerably. The individual pixels must each wait their turn for information from the matrix. In general, the more pixels a plasma panel has, the slower it performs. This is a function of the time it takes to effectively matrix address the large number of pixels, and has very little to do with the actual operating speed of the individual plasma cells.

Small plasma panels that display less than 250 characters of 5 $\times$ 7 text are screen updated very rapidly, in less than 125 milliseconds. Data is transferred to the plasma panel's logic in parallel at rates up to 1 MHz. Baud rates of up to 19,200 are available in some small plasma panels designed for computer service.

Plasma panels that contain more than 1 million pixels are slower. The main factors affecting speed in larger panels are the configuration of the matrix and the method used to apply the information to the matrix. In large plasma displays the matrices are often subdivided into a number of smaller and more quickly managed sub-matrices. Figure 9-7 illustrates the division of a plasma panel's matrix into sub-matrices. The more the entire matrix is subdivided, the smaller each sub-matrix becomes, and the faster the overall display can be operated. Each sub-matrix is smaller and has its own driving electronics, drive electrodes, and information supply. As such, it operates much faster than a larger matrix. The use of sub-matrices increases the number of address lines in the display, and this is the techniques major disadvantage. The microprocessor used in the display module has the task of keeping all the sub-matrices in synchronization, and of computing their individual packets of information. The largest and most sophisticated plasma panels now employ 16 or 32 bit microprocessors, driving many sub-matrices, to produce updates at speeds over 3.2 million pixels per second.

Dc plasma panels are commonly raster scanned much in the same manner as the CRT or the ELD. As such, their speed is limited by the raster scanning system used. Most plasma panels use a standard 60 Hz raster frequency. Video bandwidths vary from 16 MHz to over 40 MHz. This keeps them compatible with information and video processing electronics used in CRTs. Remember, the plasma panel is the new kid on the block, and needs acceptance by the display-using public. The closer plasma panels can imitate the commonly used CRT, then the faster will be their acceptance.

The ac plasma type has some degree of pixel memory. Ac plasma

Fig. 9-7. Matrix subdivision

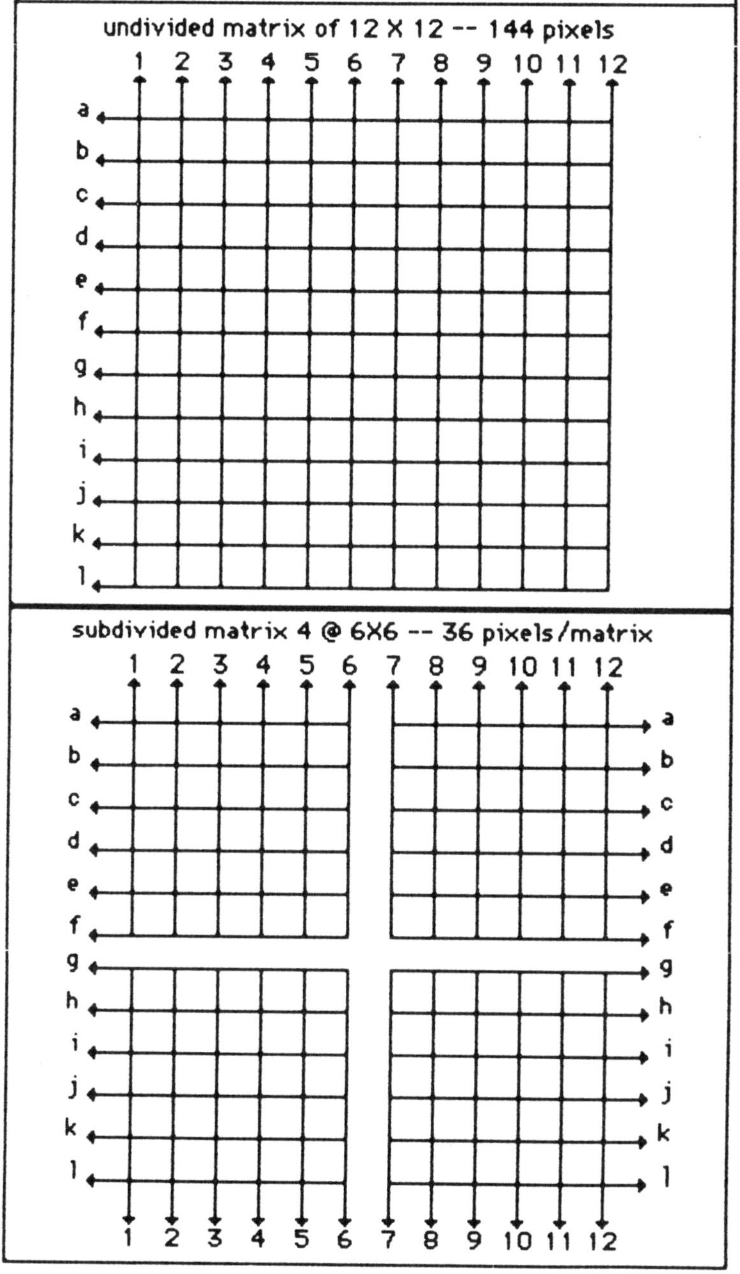

types require specialized and complex encoding techniques to take advantage of this pixel memory. If this pixel memory is managed properly, then pixels which do not require a change of state can be mass updated. This saves the microprocessor and the driving electronics much time. The net result is that the ac plasma types can make more efficient use of their processing and driving electronics. This leads to a faster operating display. This increase in speed is had at the expense of the display's complexity and cost. Plasma panels with over 750,000 pixels are being screen updated in as little as 20 milliseconds.

The bottom line is that all plasma displays, regardless of type, are much faster than they currently need to be. Using encoding techniques developed for CRTs limits the plasma panels to operation at speeds far slower than their potential. This is simply a case of the sacrifice of performance to gain compatibility. If video encoding techniques can be updated from 1940's raster technology, then the plasma panels may realize their potential speed. Speed in a display basically means that high resolution data can be displayed without flicker. Many manufacturers are now offering their display modules with information encoding designed specifically for plasma panels. These displays operate many times faster than raster models, and require complex on-board video processing. As with most displays, speed means additional cost and complexity.

Color

Plasma displays are based on light emitted when electrical current passes through a gas. The chemical composition of the gas determines the color of the light output. Many gases do not emit photons within the visible spectrum, and many others emit so weakly as to be worthless in displays. Most plasma panels produced now use neon as the basis of their gas mixture. Some add xenon, argon, or other inert gases to improve the display performance and to alter the wavelength of the emitted photons. Neon based plasma panels emit photons with wavelengths in the neighborhood of 5852 Angstroms. This is a yellowish orange light.

Inert gas compounds, other than neon, give the plasma panel the possibility of colors other than orange. It might seem strange to discuss compounds made with inert gases, but in fact, the inert or noble gases do enter into some chemical combinations with other elements. Several of these man-made compounds are used in plasma panels. Xenon chloride (Xe_2Cl) produces a blue-green color when used in plasma displays. Xenon oxide (XeO) produces a green color under reduced pressure and electrical discharge. These compounds are expensive and difficult to make. In all cases, they are dim, and do not offer the luminous efficiency of neon mixtures. Research is centered around these compounds because they offer the chance of full color plasma displays. The situation here is similar to that of the illusive blue LED. There are simply no readily available gas compounds that are bright and produce blue light. The complexities of incorporating three (red, green, and blue) colors in the same plasma panel has yet to be solved. The plasma technology is farther from the development of a full colored display than are the LED, LCD, and ELD technologies. If full colored plasma panels are manufactured, many technical problems must be solved. This is not likely to take place within the next ten years. Plasma panels are now best considered as monochrome displays.

One novel approach to the production of a full colored plasma panel is interesting. The gas mixture used in this approach does not emit its light within the visible range. Instead of viewing the plasma panels light directly, the nonvisible light is used to stimulate photoluminescent phosphors which in turn emit the visible photons. This approach allows the usage of a wide variety of photoluminescent phosphors which can be stimulated by the non-visual photons to produce a full range of colors. Research on this type of plasma display was funded by the U.S. government in the early 1970s. This approach was later dropped as the prototype panels had very short lifetimes, low brightnesses, and were subject to extensive crosstalk between adjacent pixels. This full color technique required several stepped, high voltage, waveforms to produce selective activation of the three colors within the panels. At that time, the electronics necessary to accomplish this did not exist.

Size

One of the plasma display's strong points is its size potential. Most display technologies have inherent problems that limit their size. In the case of the ELD, the problem is the resistance of the ITO material used in their electrodes. In the case of the CRT, larger cathode ray tubes have real problems with misconvergence and edge distortion in larger sizes. The plasma display technology is one of the few that has no inherent upper size limits. Plasma displays have been custom made to cover entire walls, with areas of over 4 square meters. In fact, the plasma display is the only type commonly used in large wall sized displays.

In many cases, very large plasma displays are constructed from individual sub-modules. While these displays are complex, there is no upper limit to the size of the overall display. Plasma displays are now produced with pixel counts of 2048 by 2048, and 4096 by 4096 is possible in the near future. With displays of this density, an entire wall can be covered with several of these panels to produce an enormous, high resolution, display panel with a diagonal measurement well over 3 meters. Displays of this type are used in stock & commodity markets, corporate boardrooms, and, extensively, by the military in their control centers.

In terms of thickness, the plasma panels are among the thinnest made. Only the electroluminescent panel is thinner. The actual thickness of the plasma panel is about 12 mm, about twice the thickness of the ELD, but many times thinner than the bulky CRT.By the time that the driving electronics, power supplies, and matrix connections are added, the overall thickness of the plasma display module becomes between 50 mm and 100 mm. This is definitely thin enough to give the CRT a run for its money.

The only size limitation placed on the plasma panels is that they may not be made in very small and high resolution displays. This is inherent in their construction and is discussed in the section titled Resolution. Since the plasma panel has already surpassed the average TV type CRT in resolution, it is possible to consider the plasma panel as a replacement for the CRT in monochrome applications.

Operating Characteristics

Plasma panels have a very desirable set of operating characteristics. They offer wide angles of view, inherent memory (in the ac type), and a very wide temperature operating range. It is these characteristics, coupled with the thinness and brightness of the plasma display, that have led to its acceptance by industrial and military users. In terms of the operating characteristics of modern flat panel displays, the plasma type is slight ahead of the ELD and lightyears ahead of the LCD types.

Visual Angle

The visual angle of plasma panels varies from 120° to 160°. This viewing angle is slightly greater than ELDs, but much greater than the LCDs. The main factors affecting the plasma panel's viewing angle is the thickness of the gas gap between the electrodes, the width of the gold electrode lines, and the density of the electrode lines. In general, the thinner the gas gap within the panel, the wider the viewing angle. The wider the electrode lines, the more narrow the viewing angle becomes. And finally, the denser the pixels are in the panel, the more of the panel's surface is occupied by the electrodes, and this results in narrower viewing angles.

If a plasma panel is intended for wide angle viewing, then the panel should not be of the higher resolution type. Since most plasma panels are viewed from a distance, the issue of resolution is not as important as if the panels were intended for close viewing. Large panels viewed from many locations in a room require large viewing angles rather than high resolution.

Some types of plasma panels are equipped with a touch sensitive face. This touch sensitive face allows the user to enter data by simply touching the appropriate position of the panel's face. This touch sensitive face requires another transparent layer to be added over the display's front glass. This touch sensitive layer reduces the viewing angle of the plasma panel to about 60°. Since this type of plasma panel is usually viewed at close ranges, and from directly in front, the reduced viewing angle does not represent a real problem for the operator.

Memory

The ac type of plasma panel offers a limited form of cell memory. In the case of the plasma panel, this does not mean that once a pixel is fired that it will stay lit. It means that the ac pixel can be immediately reactivated by supplying less energy than it initially required to fire. This effect is due to the ac panel's additional insulative layers within the cell, and is generated by the ac plasma cell's capacitive nature.

Let's look at the firing process of an ac plasma cell. The ac plasma cell can be represented electrically by a series string of three capacitors and a spark gap, see Fig. 9-3. The capacitance of the gas layer is low in comparison with the capacitance of the insulative layers. This means that, when the cell is firing, the voltage drop across the gas layer is much greater than the voltage drop across the insulative layers. This inequality between the potentials within the cell causes ions to collect on the inner surfaces of the dielectric layers. This "wall charge" allows the cell to be immediately refired with about half the voltage required to initially fire the cell. Figure 9-8 illustrates this process schematically. Section (a) of this illustration shows the initial firing of the cell. Section (b) shows the

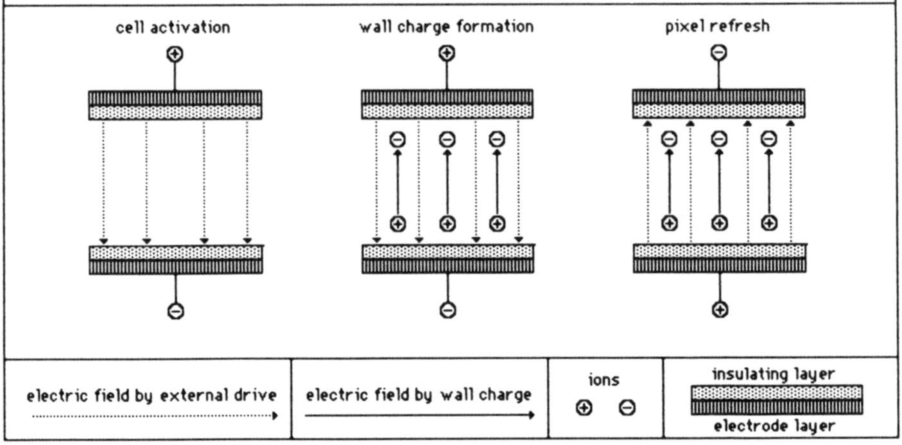

Fig. 9-8. AC plasma cell memory effect

charges collecting on the walls of the ac cell. Section (c) illustrates the usage of this wall charge to refire the cell with a lower voltage. A special waveform is used to provide the lower energy sustaining pulses to the ac cells. More on this later in the section called Driving Waveforms.

This "memory" of the ac plasma cell is not without its problems and limitations. For example, the wall charge of the cell rapidly dissipates if the cell is not refired. In order to take advantage of the wall charge, the ac cell must be refired by the sustaining signal within approximately 50 μs. The actual time involved is a function of several factors—gas pressure, gas gap thickness, and insulative layer thickness. Sustaining waveforms are commonly used with frequencies around 40 kHz. The use of the sustaining waveform complicates both the information processing and the display's electronic drivers. This technique is only employed in displays with large numbers of pixels because of the additional complexity and expense. Smaller plasma displays are usually of the dc type because it is easier and cheaper to update the entire screen rather than to implement the ac type's memory.

Operating Temperature Range

The plasma panel operates over a wide range of temperatures. Plasma panels will operate from −30° C to 55° C. These flat panels can be stored at temperatures from −60° C to 75° C. These temperature ranges are very broad, much greater than the LCDs.

The only flat panel display that has a wider temperature range is the ELD, and this is due to its solid state construction. The plasma displays use gas state technology. This gas is sealed within the display at reduced temperatures. It is the failure of the gas seals at low and high temperatures that restrict the operation and storage of the plasma panel at extreme temperatures. Temperature extremes can cause the plasma panel to lose its gas and become inoperative. Plasma panels in this situation require refilling with gas before they will become reoperative.

Ac & Dc Plasma Display Driving Waveforms

The driving waveforms of the dc and the ac plasma panels differ radically. The dc type's waveforms bear strong similarities to those of the ELD. Dc types use a constant refresh technique that updates the entire screen at every scan, much the same as the CRT. The ac types, however, require three different waveforms to control the display—one for writing, one for erasing, and one for sustaining the image. Let's look at the dc types first as they are far simpler.

The matrix that makes up the dc plasma panels electrode network is divided into two sections—the row electrodes, which are horizontal lines and the column electrodes, which are vertical lines. The columns are on the front of the display while the row lines are on the bottom. The gas occupies the space between them. A pixel is formed anywhere that the two matrices intersect. The high voltage waveform driving the dc plasma panel is divided into two components, one is ground referenced and one is floating. It is the sum of these two voltage components that adds to the 200+ volts necessary to fire the pixel. One component is applied to the column matrix while the other is connected to the row matrix. The row signal is a constant floating square wave of about 100 volts. This row signal selects the appropriate row electrode by its timing. The row waveform performs the same function as the horizontal retrace signal in a CRT signal. The actual luminosity information is carried by the ground referenced column waveform. This column waveform of 100+ volts carries the pixel information. A pixel is illuminated when these two waveforms coincide. Does this sound familiar? That's right, the situation is virtually identical to the waveforms that drive the electroluminescent displays. Further details on this type of encoding and waveforms are available in Chapter 8—Electroluminescent displays. The dc plasma panel is driven in exactly the same manner as the ELD. In fact, many of the ICs used to drive to drive these displays will work on either the ELD and the plasma panel. The only major difference is that the plasma panel's waveforms are of higher voltages than those of the ELD.

The situation is more complex with the ac type of plasma panel. In order to use its inherent cell memory, the mode of information encoding and driving waveforms must be different. The physical setup of the ac plasma display's matrix is exactly the same as the dc type. The matrix is composed of rows and columns. Once again, the rows float while the columns are ground referenced. The driving waveforms are applied to this horizontal/vertical line matrix.

The first of the three waveforms used in the ac plasma display is the write waveform. This waveform initiates the firing of a previously unactive pixel. This write waveform is split between the rows and columns. Half the voltage is applied to the ground referenced column while the other half is floating and applied to the row. Their sum at the pixel creates the 200+ volt potential difference necessary to fire or ''write'' the cell. This write waveform is similar to the waveforms employed in activating the pixels of dc plasma panels and ELDs.

The second waveform employed in the ac plasma panel is the sustaining waveform. This waveform keeps all cells that are currently firing in the firing (on) state. The sustaining waveform makes use of the wall charges which are present in activated plasma cells. It will not cause inactive pixels to fire as its peak voltage is only about 100 volts. The sustaining waveform is ground referenced and applied only to the column matrix. In this waveform, the row drivers output no voltage. *The sustaining mode is the basic operating mode of the ac plasma panel.* Data is sustained on the screen by this waveform at speeds of 30 to 60 kHz. Data may be either added to the screen by the write waveform, or deleted by the third type of ac plasma display waveform, the erase waveform.

The erase waveform simply discharges the wall charge within the ac plasma cell. It accomplishes this by applying around 100 volts of the opposite polarity to the cell. This discharges the cell and makes it unresponsive to the sustaining waveform; the cell stops firing. The cell will not refire without another application of the write waveform at its location. Actually, the erase waveform is applied to an entire line of the display at a time. The entire line is erased, and then any pixels that should be activated in the newly updated line are refired by the write waveform. If a line contains no changed pixels, then the erase waveform is deleted and the line's state is maintained by the sustaining waveform.

All three of the ac plasma driving waveforms are illustrated in Fig. 9-9. Note the base waveform of a 100 volt square wave shown in the illustration. This base waveform is used to generate the three distinct waveforms, and for timing purposes. Note also that the sustaining waveform is totally carried by the columns, while the rows are held at zero potential. All of these waveforms may seem complex and more than a little confusing. Actually, it really is. Why go to all this trouble simply to take advantage of a short-term pixel memory? The answer is speed.

The sustaining waveform takes the burden of refreshing unchanged pixels away from the microprocessor and the driving electronics. For a few microseconds, the screen itself is actually capable of remembering its own data. While the sustaining waveform keeps the panel's information constant by operating 40,000 times per second, the screen data itself need only be changed about 10 to 60 times per second. This frees the microprocessor from the continual, repetitive, and time consuming operation of keeping the display illuminated. Instead, the microprocessor is free to perform image calculation and other image generation chores. In high resolution plasma panels, this means speed increases by as much as 20 times over dc plasma panels. This is the prime advantage of the ac types and the reason why dc types are not made in large or high resolution models. The additional cost and complexity of the ac type is thought worthwhile because of its increase in speed and, thereby, resolution. It should be remembered that the pixel memo-

Fig. 9-9. AC plasma display waveforms

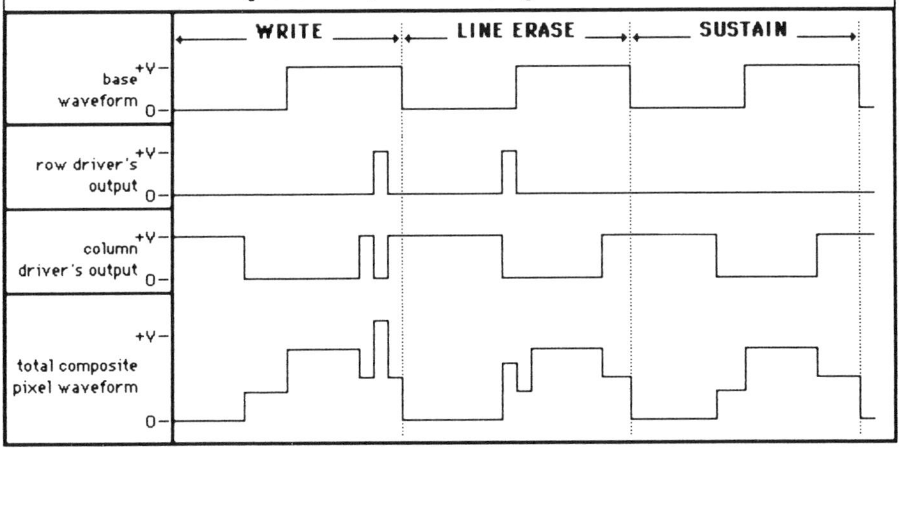

ry here is inherent in the panel. Its use is roughly equivalent to adding an entire screen's worth of RAM to the display. Large high resolution displays may require over 4 megabytes of RAM to form a screen memory. All this is already contained within the ac plasma panel. When thought of in terms of this, the usage of the ac plasma cell's memory, however complex, seems like a good deal indeed.

DC PLASMA DISPLAY DRIVING ELECTRONICS

Dc plasma displays are most commonly used in seven segment packages. Their electronic drivers reflect this use and are fabricated on a smaller scale than are the ac drivers. These drivers are very similar to those used for electroluminescent seven segment displays, and those requiring additional information of these drivers are directed to Chapter 8. Multiplexing may be used to decrease the interconnection complexity between drivers and display. The dc plasma drivers are capable of switching the high voltages necessary to fire the dc panel. In most dc plasma applications, the refresh of the display is accomplished by electronics other than the actual display drivers.

Most dc drivers accept standard TTL, MOS, or CMOS inputs. They all require an external source of high voltage for switching through their final transistors. Segment current driver levels are set for the entire display by using a resistor to program the driver. This sets the brightness of the segments that make up the display.

Dc plasma panels are also available in small to mid-sized dot matrix packages. In these cases, the electronic drivers are not more complex, but simply more numerous. The standard drivers are ganged and arranged in exactly the same fashion as those of the ELD. Some specialized types of dc drivers carry on board RAM, data processing, and accept very rapid (19,200 baud) transfer of serial or parallel computer data.

Figure 9-10 illustrates the block diagram of a dc dot matrix panel functioning as a computer display. This dc plasma display module is designed to be compatible with signals encoded for a CRT. As such, this example represents the bulk of the techniques used in dc plasma implementation. The dc plasma panel in this example displays 256 characters in a 5 × 7 dot matrix format. There are 8 lines of 32 characters each for a total of 8960 pixels. The driving electronics of this panel accept serially encoded column data and generate the required high voltage waveforms necessary to display this data on the plasma panel.

Fig. 9-10. DC plasma display module block diagram

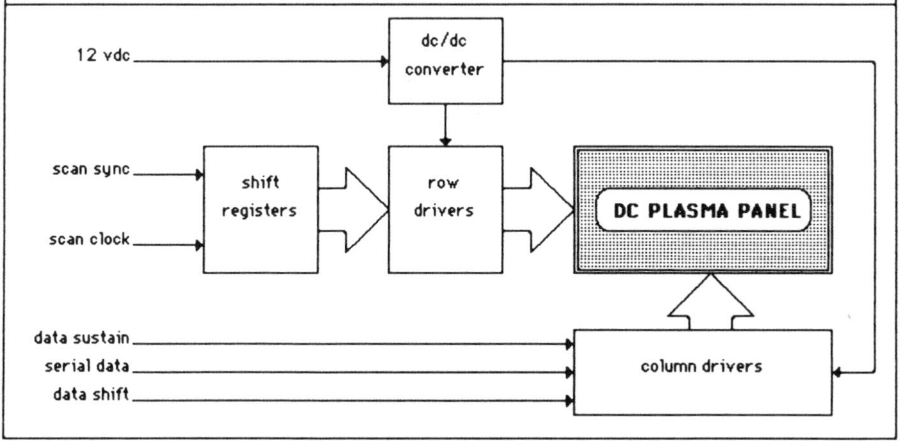

This particular module is designed to scan the panel row by row, beginning with the top row. Each character is 5 dots wide and there are 32 characters per row. This means that each row of pixels within this display can be represented by 160 bits of data (5 × 32). The display's column drivers accept 160 bits of serial data, and this represents a single row. This information is then transmitted to the column driver's output transistors which fire the appropriate pixels. The column driver then accepts the data for the next row and so on until the screen is completely scanned. This process is continually repeated, about 80 times per second; the panel appears continuous and flicker-free.

The scan clock input of the display module works just like the horizontal sync signal used in a CRT. The scan clock is used to advance the row pointer vertically down the display as the scan proceeds. The scan sync input functions in the same manner as the vertical sync signal in the CRT display. It instructs the plasma drivers that a complete screen full of data has been displayed and that it is time to return to the top of the panel to begin again. This panel is typical of most as it includes a dc to dc converter in order to make its own high voltage.

In many cases, the manufacturer of the dc plasma panel can also supply an optional controller board. This board eliminates using the host computer to generate characters, remember the screen in RAM, and other image processing chores. This makes the dc plasma display easier to implement within the computer. The optional controller board makes the host computer operate faster as it need not bother with the mundane details of the image's display. Figure 9-11 illustrates the block diagram of such a controller board which is compatible with the display module shown in Fig. 9-10. Note that this controller employs a microprocessor with its own clock. It also contains its own character data generator, character clock, RAM, and video controller. This circuit encodes incoming 8 bit parallel data from the host computer into a serial, controlled format that is suitable for the plasma module. The function of this dc plasma control board is similar to the CRT controller circuits used in CRT displays.

AC PLASMA DISPLAY DRIVING ELECTRONICS

The ac plasma panels are usually much larger and more densely packed with pixels than are their dc relatives. This additional density, and the additional signal needed to sustain the panel's inherent memory require additional processing that is not used in the dc types.

The electronic scheme used to drive the ac plasma display is similar to the dc types and ELDs in some areas. The matrix is once again broken into rows and columns. The columns are operated at true ground (0 volts) and the rows are floating, and operated with a composite waveform that is negative in relation to the columns. Using a floating ground for the row drivers eliminates dc signal coupling with the microprocessor, and necessitates the use of optical

Fig. 9-11. DC plasma display controller block diagram

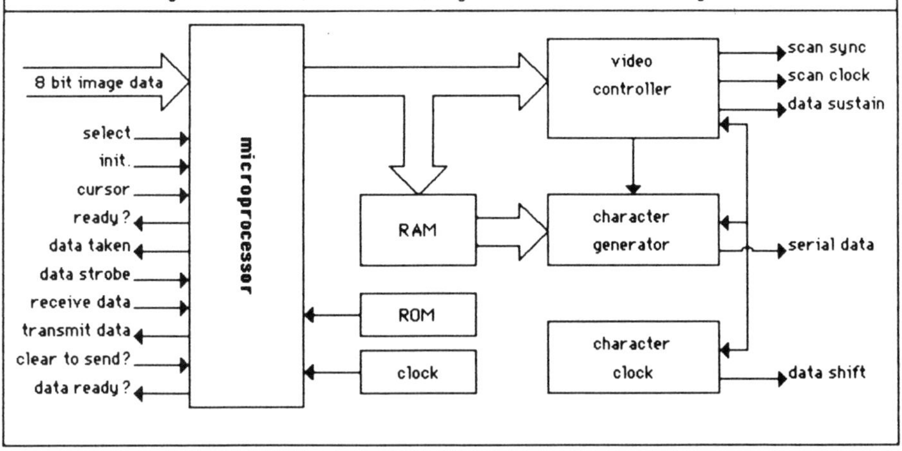

signal coupling. These operating parameters require that the electronic row drivers differ electrically from the ground based column drivers. Both drivers have one similarity, however, they both accept serial data input which they translate to parallel output. This input process can be carried on at speeds over 4 MHz.

Let's look at a typical row driver. This example contains an 8 bit optically coupled input section, and a two to four line decoder. The computer inputs the row sequence to the shift register in four chunks of 8 bits each. Each 8 bit slice of the image row information is sequentially loaded by the shift register contained within the row driver. This assures that the rows are enabled at the proper time to mesh with the actual image data encoded on the column drivers. The row information is then relayed to the 32 output sections of the row driver, which sequentially switch the high voltage waveform to the actual rows of the plasma panel. Figure 9-12 illustrates a block diagram of a row driver. Each 32 row segment of the panel requires its own row driver.

The column drivers operate differently than the row drivers. For one thing, the column drivers carry the actual image information. For another, the sustaining waveform necessary to use the ac plasma panel's memory is directly coupled to the column driver ICs. Think of the row drivers being the canvas and the column drivers are the paint. Image data is serially loaded into the 32-bit shift register of the column driver. This data is coupled to the 32 output sections of the driver and applied as parallel high voltage signals to the panel. All outputs of the column driver can be switched low at any time, if the sustaining input of the driver is switched low. This is the sustain pulse that activates the panel's memory. The sustaining pulse does not affect the contents of the shift register memory, which holds its data during the mass refresh of the panel. Figure 9-13 illustrates the internal block diagram of a typical column driver used with ac plasma panels.

The output gates of the row and column driver IC are identical. Figure 9-14 shows the output configuration of both plasma drivers. Both outputs contain pairs of DMOS transistors in a "totem-pole" configuration that can either source or sink up to 20 mA of up to 100 volts of high voltage current. All the outputs employ both sink and source clamping diodes to protect the junctions from the high voltage transients generated when switching high voltage into capacitive loads. This type of output configuration is very similar to that used in the ELD drivers.

Fig. 9-12. AC plasma row driver

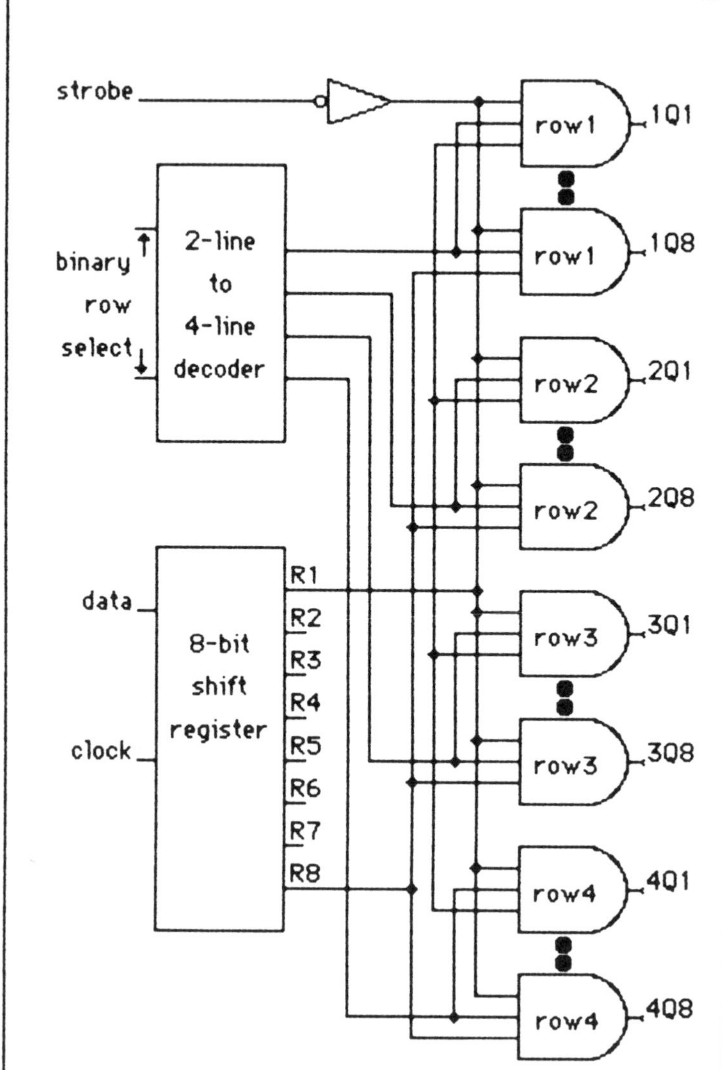

Each row contains 8 outputs. Only the first and last are illustrated.

Fig. 9-13. AC plasma column driver

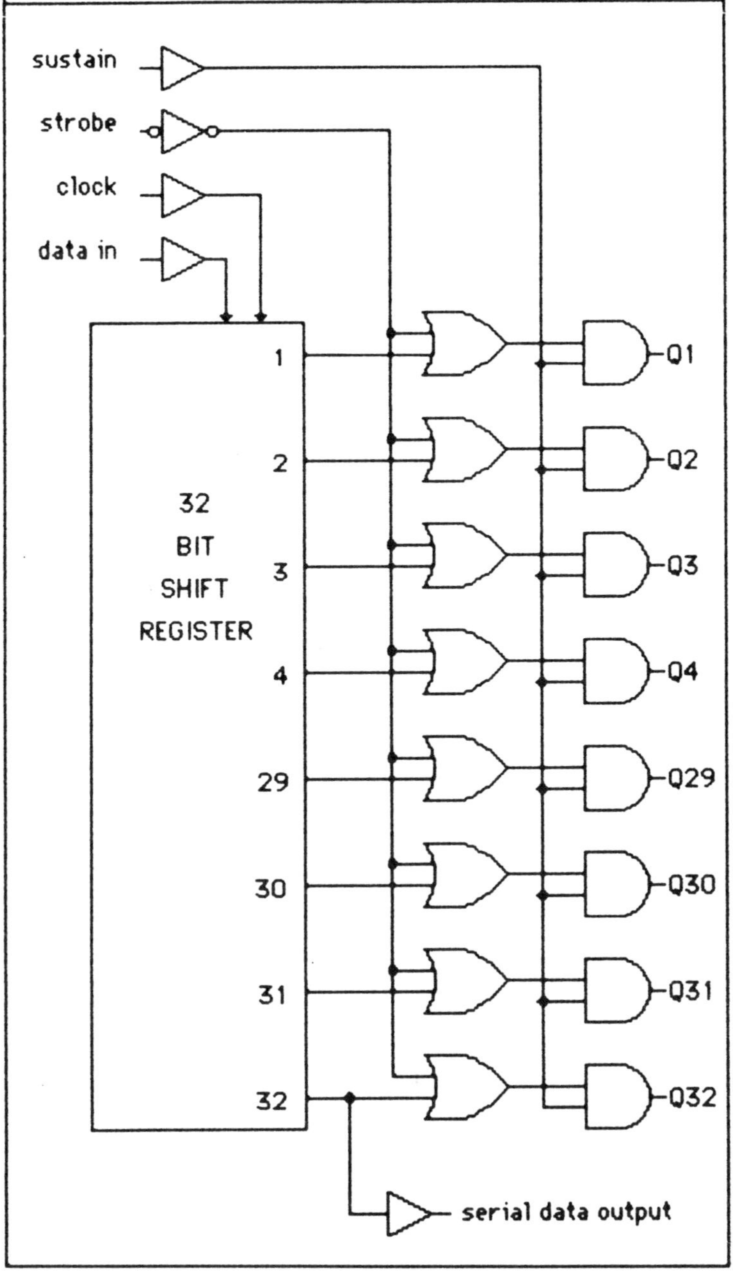

Fig. 9-14. Plasma driver output gates

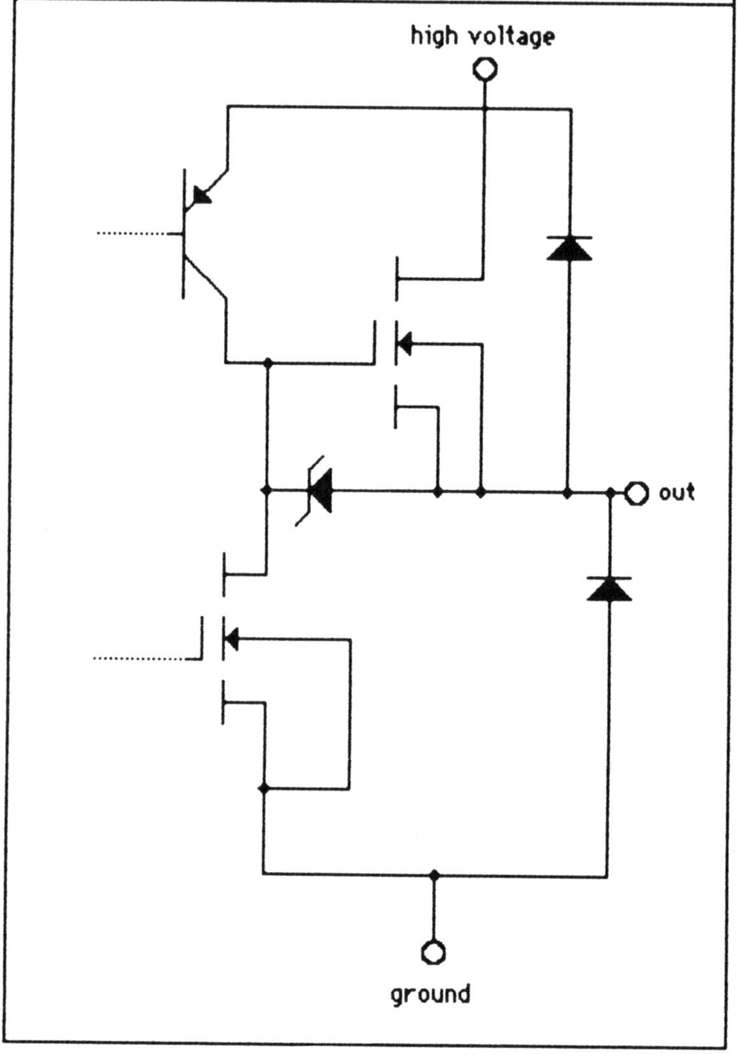

SAMPLE AC PLASMA DISPLAY APPLICATION— COMPUTER DISPLAY

Plasma panels are now becoming an option for a variety of computers. It is the thinness and portability of these displays which makes them so attractive in computer service. These displays use the encoding techniques and electronic drivers that we have discussed to this point. Now we are going to assemble the whole lot into a working display for computer use. This example represents only the most common method of plasma display application. There are indeed, many ways to skin this cat, and we are looking only at the most commonly used method.

Ac plasma displays used in computer service are densely packed with pixels. For example, IBM offers an optional plasma panel for its personal computers. This panel is capable of displaying 1000 characters. It is arranged in a matrix of 960 vertical columns by 768 horizontal rows. This panel has 74,000 pixels within an area of about one square foot.

The driver chips are arranged radially around the display's edges, in exactly the same manner as in the ELDs. These drivers, one each for each group of 32 horizontal rows and one each for every group of 32 vertical columns, are activated by information encoded specially for the display by the CPU of the computer. In many cases, a separate IC is used to process the image data for display on the panel. Figure 9-15 illustrates a block diagram of an ac plasma panel used as a computer display. This illustration is simplified. The row and column drivers are shown only on one edge of the display each.

In order to process and efficiently transfer the large mass of data that makes up a high resolution image, the image data is broken into chunks. In this case, the panel accepts data for 16 rows at a time. When these 16 rows are encoded and displayed, then the

Fig. 9-15. AC plasma computer display

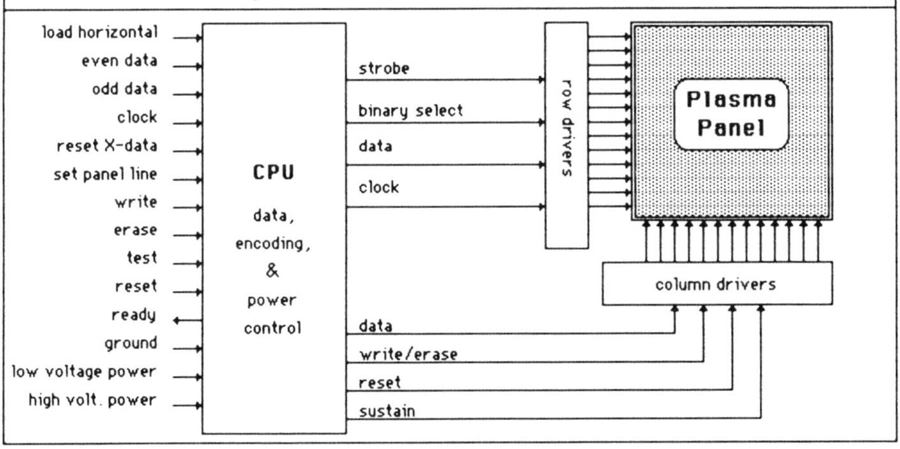

display moves on to the next 16 rows of the image. This technique yields complete screen updates in as little as 200 ms. Frame rates for these displays are usually held to 50 to 60 Hz in order to ensure compatibility with image and processing electronics used with CRTs.

PLASMA DISPLAY COST

The plasma displays are among the most expensive types now produced. Plasma displays large enough to function as a computer display cost between $890 and $4300. The use of a plasma panel can add a minimum of $1000 to a computer system. Very large wall sized plasma panels can cost well over $30,000. Smaller dc plasma panels in bar graph or seven segment configurations vary in cost from $185 to over $700, depending on size and complexity.

Most of the cost associated with plasma panels is due to their driving electronics. For example, one manufacturer is asking $3570 for a complete display module including all encoding and driving electronics. The ac plasma panel used in this module can be purchased by itself from the same source for $1064. The complexity of driving large matrices with high voltage power just about triples the overall cost of the plasma display. For this reason, we are not likely to see plasma displays used in small scale, low end, applications. Figure 9-16 is a column graph showing where your money goes when

Fig. 9-16.

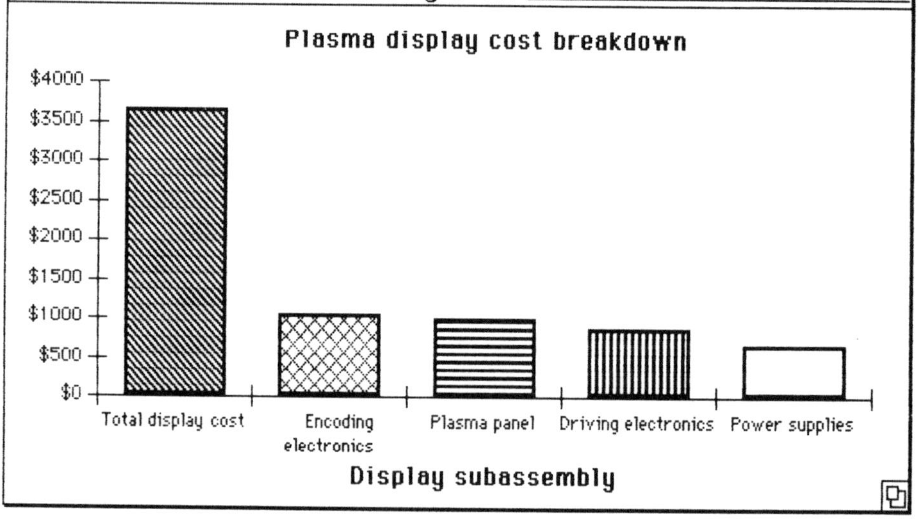

you purchase a plasma display with enough capacity to be useful in computer service. Note that the actual plasma panel's cost is small in relation to the overall display's cost.

PLASMA DISPLAY MANUFACTURERS

The following manufacturers of plasma displays and their related electronics have contributed information to this chapter. Complete addresses and telephone numbers are available in Appendix A The Electronic Display Devices Manufacturers Data Base.

Dale Electronics Inc.

Displays, Inc.

General Digital Corporation

Interstate Electronics Corporation

Photonics Technology, Inc.

SAI Technology Corporation

Texas Instruments Corporation

10

Using Electronic Displays

The aim of this chapter is to enable the reader to properly select and implement the right display for any particular job. All the displays discussed to this point have varying characteristics. This chapter compares these characteristics, their strong points, and their weak points. Some displays are much more suited and effective for certain types of applications. In some cases, a particular user requirement may indicate a specific display technology. For example, if a computer is to have a display capable of showing over a thousand pixels, and this display must be powered by batteries and be compact, then there is only one choice—an LCD.

For the purposes of discussion, these electronic displays are divided into two broad and non-exclusive categories—segmented displays and dot matrix displays. In general, the segmented displays show only small amounts of information at a time, usually in the form of numbers. Examples of segmented displays are the seven segment LCDs or LEDs so commonly used to display numbers in watches and calculators. The dot-matrix type of displays are used for the display of more massive amounts of information. This information may be numerical, alphabetical, or graphics images. The images may be static or moving. Examples of the dot matrix type displays are the ELD and plasma display. CRTs are also included in the dot matrix types even though they are not actually matrix addressed devices.

Segmented Displays

If you want to display small quantities of numerical information, then the segmented display is the one to use. Segmented displays are now used almost exclusively for the display of numbers. The characters that make up a complete set of arabic numbers can be displayed with a minimum of seven segments. In some cases, the number of segments used to display a character is fourteen or sixteen. These types of segmented displays are said to also have the ability to display alphabetical characters in addition to numbers. The alphabetical characters formed by the 14 and 16 segment displays are, quite frankly, crude and difficult to read. In general, unless there is a very small amount of text to be displayed, dot matrix displays are far better suited to the display of alphabetical information.

Segmented displays can be used to display one number or many numbers. Display packages contain a single, two, four, or eight digits. Segmented displays are usually multiplexed if they contain four or more digits. Segmented displays are manufactured in a variety of technologies—LED, LCD, VFD, and plasma types are the most common. Each of these technologies has radically different characteristics.

If you are going to display less than 24 digits of information, then the segmented displays offer ease of use, low power consumption, and most of all low cost. It simply is not efficient to use a large dot matrix display to show a few numbers.

Dot Matrix Displays

The dot matrix displays are the most versatile type available. These units will display virtually any type of visual information. They are also manufactured in a very wide variety of sizes and resolutions to meet any requirement. These displays are manufactured using just about every available display technology. Computer displays offer the widest variety of different display types. Computer displays use CRT, LCD, ELD, and plasma panels in very large sizes and high resolutions. In fact, it is the market for computer displays that has been responsible for the development of many of the new display technologies. The demand for specialized computer displays is now considerable and increasing yearly with the demand for computer equipment. For an example of the worldwide demand for flat panel, dot matrix displays see Fig. 10-1. This column graph shows the worldwide demand for LCD, ELD, plasma, and flat CRT displays in 1982, and demand projections for 1987 and 1992. With a projected

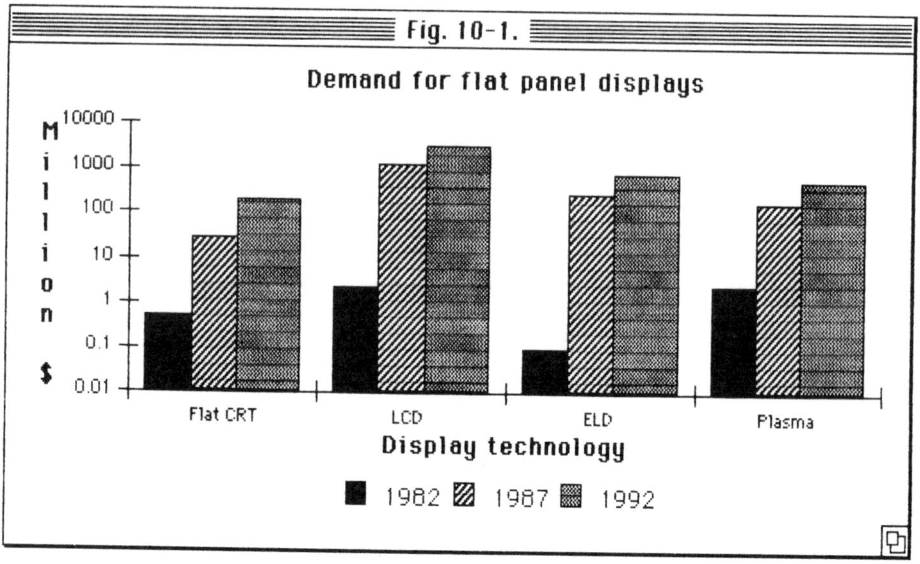

demand for 4.5 billion dollars worth of flat panel displays by 1992, this industry represents a very big business indeed. Please note that the y-axis, representing the dollar demand for the various displays, is charted on a logarithmic scale.

CHOOSING THE RIGHT DISPLAY FOR THE JOB

The choice of the right display is determined by three factors—type & amount of information to be displayed, operating environment, and power availability. Basically it boils down to—what do you want to display, where do you want to display it, and how much power do you have to give the display. All three of these requirements must be met for successful use of any particular display technology.

The power requirements should be considered first. Any display is worthless if you don't have the power to run it. If the display is to be battery powered and portable, power consumption is the prime factor. Operating environment is the next consideration. If the display is used in high ambient light environments (like outside in the sun) then it must be of the brightest type. If the display is used outside or in a vehicle, then it must be able to withstand the temperature fluctuations encountered in this service. If a display is not suited to its operating environment, then it will certainly fail to do its job. Lastly, after the power and environmental requirements are met, we have a list of possible display technologies to consider for the third criteria—information type and size. It is in this third category that the display's size, resolution, and speed become factors in the display's choice.

Let's now compare the different display technologies based on the three criteria we have discussed—power, environment, and information. For the purposes of these comparisons, we will consider these display technologies—CRT, LED, LCD, ELD, plasma, and VFD. In some categories, the display characteristic data is normalized in order that the information be meaningful. For example, a CRT displaying a full page of text is not compared to a small LCD seven segment display, but to an LCD with the same informational capacity and resolution. In some cases, the displays are compared on the level of their individual smallest element (pixel). In all the displays charted, we are looking at the commonly available commercial versions. What is represented is the mainstream of display technology rather than its cutting edge. Prototype and experimental displays may exceed these specifications. Let's consider power consumption first.

Display Power Consumption

Figure 10-2 is a bar graph comparing the power consumption of different display technologies. The y-axis of this graph shows the relative power consumption per unit of display area of each display

Fig. 10-2.

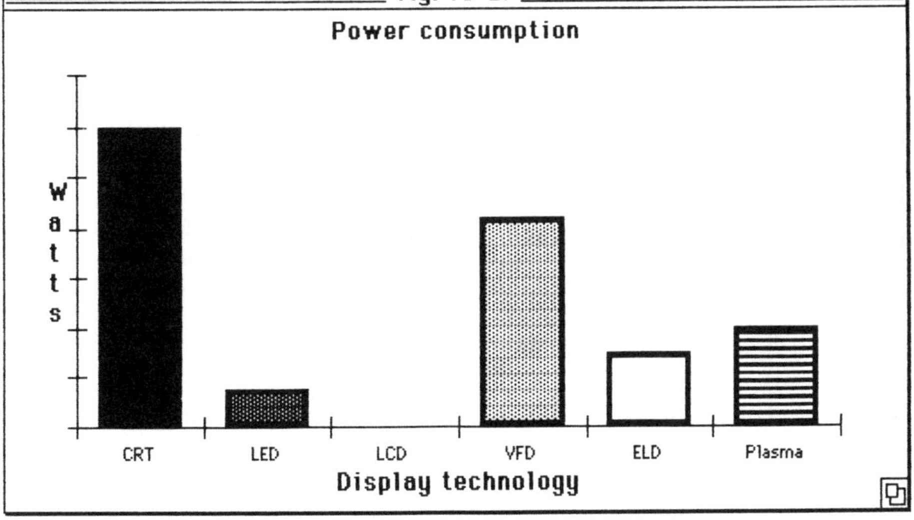

technology in a normalized and linear fashion. The y-axis of this graph is not logarithmic. While it may appear that the information on the LCD's power consumption has been omitted from this graph; this is not true. It is just that the LCD's power consumption is so low that it doesn't even register on the graph. When it comes to power consumption, the LCD is the all time champ. These displays consume so little power that they are commonly left operating all of the time in applications such as digital watches and clocks. This is even more amazing when one considers that these devices are powered by miniature button cell batteries with very small energy capacities. If you are thinking battery powered, portable display, then there is really only one choice offered today—the super-efficient LCD. This is due to the fact that the LCD is a light modifier, using ambient light as its source, rather than a light producer as are the rest of the displays charted. In terms of the remainder of the displays, the CRT consumes the most power, while the ELDs and plasma types can display the same area at about half the power consumption. The LED remains the most efficient self-illuminating electronic display device. For small scale or intermittent use, the LEDs can be used with batteries as power sources. Even so, the LED consumes many times the power of the LCD. The LCD remains the most practical display to consider for battery operation.

Display Operating Voltage

Figure 10-3 shows the voltages required to operate a specific display technology. The voltages illustrated here are those necessary to operate a display element, and not the input power voltages to the entire module. In all cases, where the cell operating voltage differs from the normal commercial lines, the display's manufacturer includes a power supply to make the required voltage from either the 120 Vac mains, or from some source of low voltage dc. Note that the y-axis, representing cell voltage, has a logarithmic scale. This shows the very wide range of operating voltages within the sample of displays. Operating voltages vary from over 20,000 volts in the CRT to less than 2 volts for the LED. In some cases, the high voltages used in the CRT produce unacceptable hazards. Consider a display used in a plant manufacturing potentially explosive chemicals. The failure or damage of the CRT, with some 20 kV used in its interior, may produce sparks that could set off an explosion. For this reason, many industrial and military uses are now requiring other display technologies to replace the high voltage CRT.

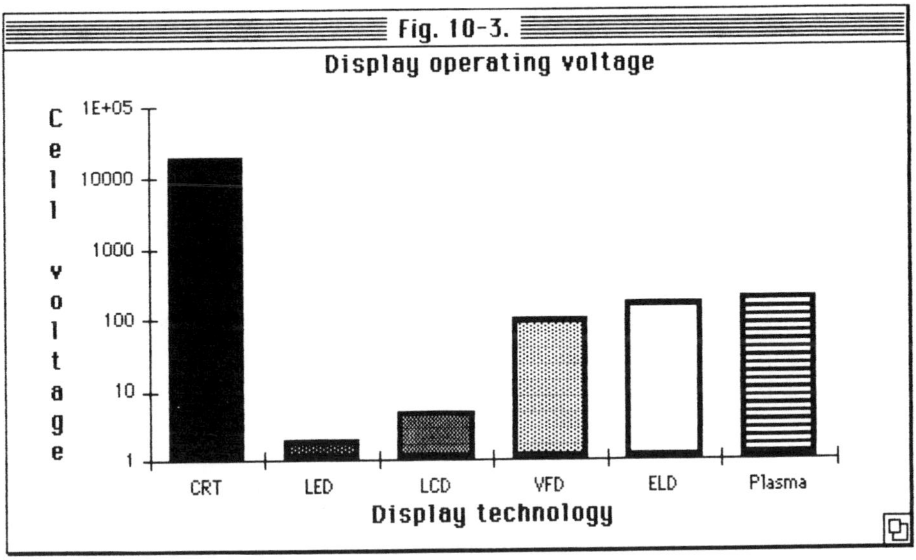

Low voltage operation makes a display technology applicable to portable and battery operation. The only two display types which meet these requirements are the LCD and the LED. While the LEDs use very low dc voltages directly, the LCDs are ac operated and require that their low dc voltage be inverted into a symmetrical ac square wave. Fortunately, this is very easily and efficiently accomplished, and LCDs emerge once again as the battery operated champion. While the ELDs, VFDs, and plasma type do require higher voltages for their operation, their operating voltage levels are some 100 times less than those of the CRT.

Operating Temperature Range

The question of operating temperature range is not critical for displays operated in a controlled environment, such as inside a building. If a display is to be operated in a vehicle, or outside as a portable, then temperature range is a critical factor. Figure 10-4 illustrates the operating range of the six different types of displays under discussion. The y-axis of this column graph is linear and calibrated in degrees centigrade (°C).

The CRT offers the widest temperature operating range, followed by the VFD and the LED. ELDs have a slightly wider operating range than plasma panels, especially in the colder

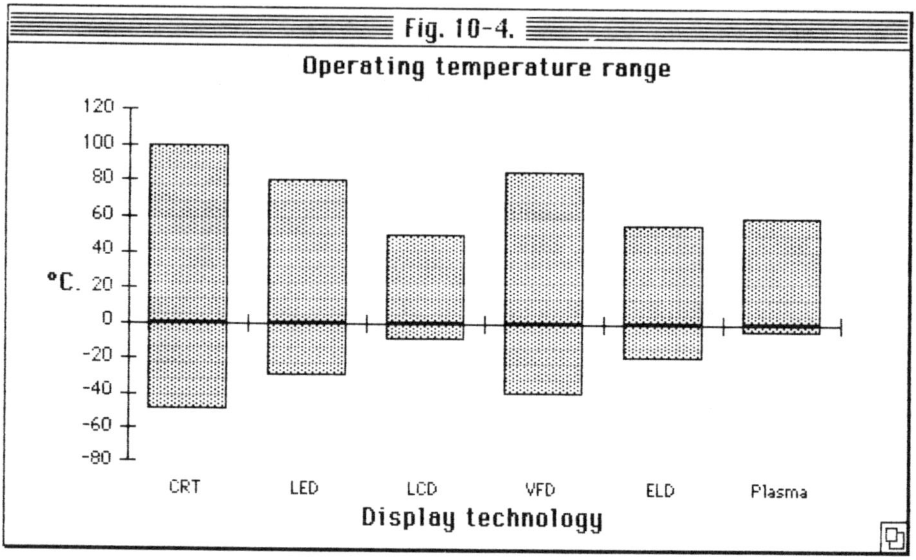

temperatures. The LCD comes in last. In general, all these display devices will operate within the ranges of human comfort. They perform their tasks in environments that will leave a human dripping with sweat, or cold enough to require a heavy coat.

This graph shows us some sad news. The LCD has the narrowest temperature operating range of all the displays. While the LCD is eminently suited for battery powered, portable service, care must be taken not to let its temperature exceed its limits. This is sometimes difficult in an outside environment. For example, an LCD left in a vehicle could be subjected to temperatures above 50° C or below 10° C. In general, LCDs can be reliably stored within these limits. If these limits are exceeded, the display can be permanently ruined. If a display is used outside, don't leave it to get hot in the sun. Don't leave electronic displays (especially LCDs) in cars parked in the sun with the windows up.

Display Brightness

Brightness is an important factor to consider in the choice of a display. Figure 10-5 rates the displays based on their brightness. The y-axis of this graph is linear and normalized. The CRT wins out as the brightness champ, being much brighter than ELDs and plasma panels. The VFD displays are also very bright, but usually don't compete with the CRT because of their relatively small size.

Note that the LCD is not listed on this graph. This is because the LCD is not a light producing display, but a light modifying display. LCDs are not rated in terms of brightness, but in terms of contrast ratio. Contrast ratio is the amount of light difference the display can produce across its surface. Modern LCDs have contrast ratios between 5 to 1 and 20 to 1.

Electronic displays that are operated outside should be of the brightest types. The outside environment is flooded with high levels of ambient light at times, and the display must overcome this light to be effective. If any light producing display is used outside, position it so that the sun does not directly shine on its screen. Use the display in the shade, or position the screen facing away from the sun. LCDs are the one exception to this rule. Since they use ambient light for modification, they function best in high levels of ambient light. They work best of all when illuminated by direct sunlight.

The light output of any display used inside can be enhanced by proper positioning of the display within the room, and by proper positioning of any artificial lighting. In general, position the display so that sunlight shining through the windows does not fall directly on the display's screen. The same is true of artificial lighting, don't position it so that it falls directly on the screen's face. This simple technique reduces glare, reflections, and gives the maximum visual effect to the light produced by the display.

Fig. 10-5.

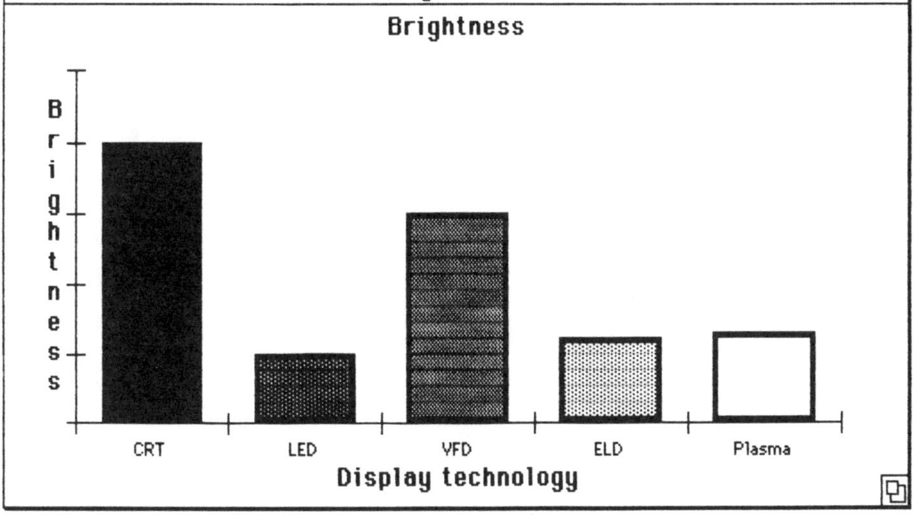

Visual Angle

Wide visual angles are really only necessary for displays that are viewed by many people at the same time. In general, if you are sitting in front of the display you will receive its maximum effect. Figure 10-6 illustrates the viewing angles of several display technologies. Here the y-axis is linear and calibrated in degrees. The plasma panel has the widest viewing angle, almost 160°, wider even than the CRT. The LED comes in second, but it should be remembered that the viewing angle of an LED is a function of its lens. The LED charted has the widest angle lens available. The ELD offers a narrower angle of view than the plasma panel. This is exclusively due to the use of the ITO electrode lines in the ELD (see Chapter 8). The narrowest viewing angle is exhibited by the LCD. Once again, ITO is used in LCD electrodes.

The narrow viewing angle of the LCD is primarily a function of the LD cell's thickness. Restricted viewing angle has long been one of the LCD's major problems. Modern LC cells are being made thinner all the time, and modern types have viewing angles up to 75°. If you are using an LCD, it is worth the trouble to position the display so that you are viewing it directly head on. This position assures the maximum contrast on the LCD's screen, regardless of the type of LCD used. Since most LCDs are used in portable equipment, it is usually easy to properly position the display.

Fig. 10-6.

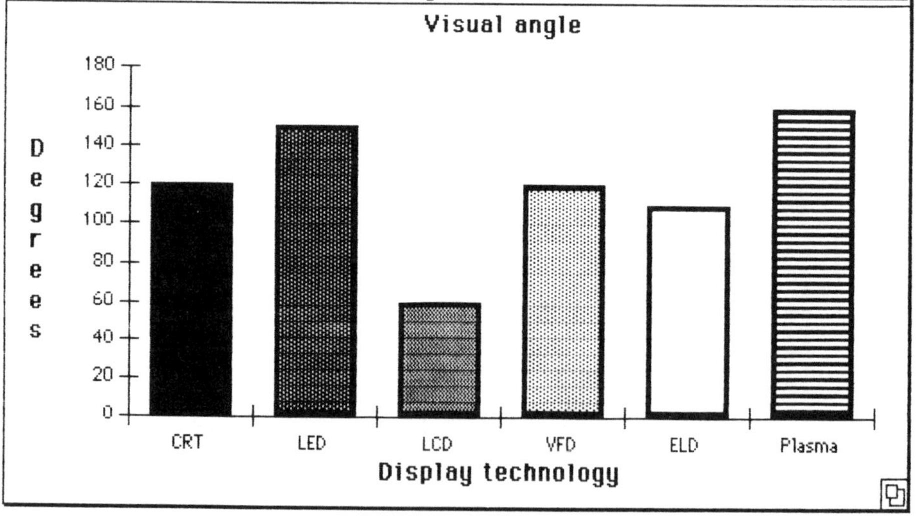

Fig. 10-7.

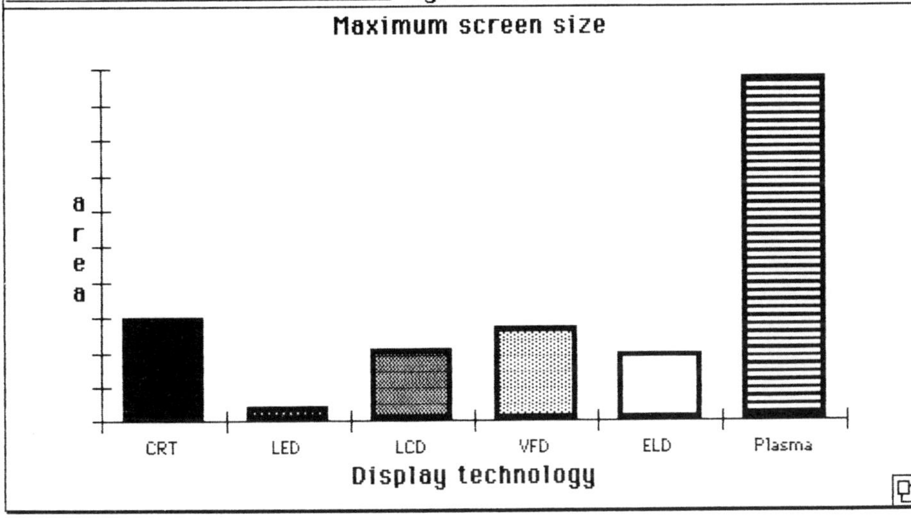

Maximum Screen Size

Figure 10-7 shows the maximum screen area that can be produced by the sample display technologies. The y-axis here is normalized and linear. The plasma panels are currently capable of producing gigantic displays with many times the area of other types. These large area plasma panels are actually composed of smaller sub-panels. The CRT, VFD, LCD, and ELD are all also available in large sizes capable of displaying a full page of data visible from up to 3 meters. The CRT charted here, for example, is a 35 inch diagonal, direct view type, not a projection type.

The LED comes in last in the category of screen size. LED displays are generally only manufactured in smaller sizes. Their poor showing on Figure 10-7 is a function of what is being made now and does not reflect any inherent limitation in LED technology. For example, assume that the elusive blue LED junction can be economically produced. If sets of three LED junctions, one red, one blue, and one green, can be assembled in a very small space, then LED full color flat panel displays can be made. This could be accomplished by using a matrix drive scheme with switching transistors built into the same semiconductor substrate as the LED junctions. The situation is very similar to the TFT LCD panels now used as the full colored TV displays. The hypothetical LED, full color, flat panel display mentioned here would offer incredible advantages. It would be bright, very efficient in power consumption, very thin, make its own light, and have great longevity. In terms of screen size, the LED could possibly compete with the rest of the flat panel displays used in computers.

The user makes a decision as to the screen size required for any particular application. The first criteria in this decision is the distance from the display to the viewer's eye. The closer the viewer is to the display, the smaller the display should be. Let's consider a display used in computer service. In most physical computer configurations, the viewer is very close to the display, usually within 1 meter. At close distances such as this, the larger screen actually exhibits less resolution than a smaller one. For example, a 12 in CRT offers greater apparent resolution at 1 meter than does a 25 in CRT. Both CRTs display the same number of lines, but the linear nature of the display is more evident in the larger CRT. The lines tend to merge on the smaller display, and the apparent resolution is greater. This effect is a function of the resolving power of the human eye, and varies from person to person.

Most computer applications feature screens that are in fact oversized. A 19-in CRT should be viewed from at least 1.5 meters or its apparent resolution is decreased. If you are saddled with an oversize CRT at work or at home, then position it farther away from your eyes, By doing this, you will notice an apparent increase in resolution and thereby a reduction in eyestrain. If you are buying a display for your computer, then give careful consideration to the viewing distance. If this is within 1 meter, then the screen size to consider is between 9 to 15 inches in diagonal measurement. Displays used in entertainment service are usually viewed from greater distances, averaging around 3 to 5 meters. As such, entertainment displays are usually required to be larger in screen area.

Resolution

Figure 10-8 illustrates the resolution of various display technologies. The y-axis of this graph is normalized and linear. Note that the resolution champ is the CRT. In commonly produced electronic displays, the CRT is capable of producing an image with up to twice the resolution of any other technology. The CRT charted here represents a high resolution computer monitor with over 4 times the resolution of the CRTs used in TV service. Plasma displays come in second, with resolutions that also surpass the CRTs used in TV service. Of the lower resolution display technologies, only the LED

Fig. 10-8.

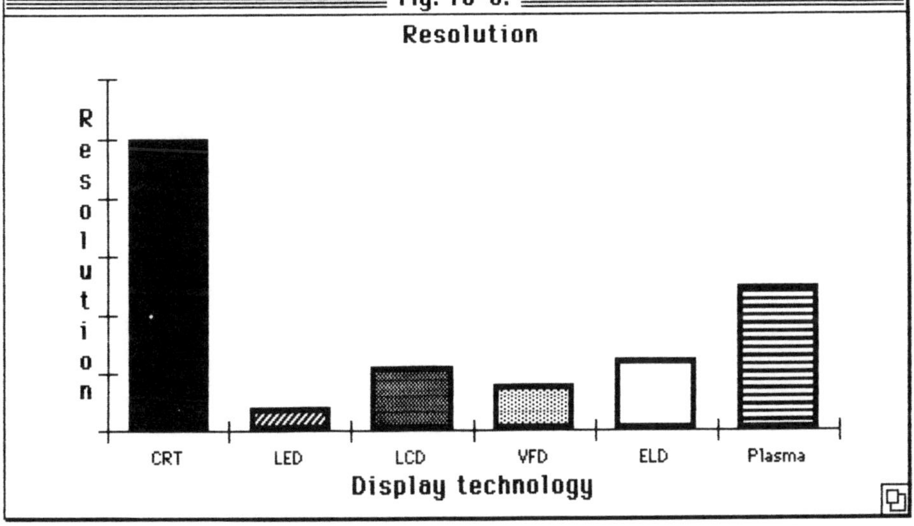

is not inherently limited by its design and technology. Both the ELD and the LCD use ITO electrodes which place limits on the resolution that the technology can produce. This point may be considered moot if one considers that currently made LCDs offer enough resolution to display TV pictures (in full color no less).

The computer display market is currently in the grips of "resolution mania." This means that many CRT users are purchasing more resolution than they actually need. For the display of text and simple images, resolutions of 512 by 512 are more than adequate. Consider that many displays with twice to four times this resolution are needlessly purchased for these applications. How much resolution is needed in a computer display? Unless you are designing ICs with a CAD program or other intensely graphic activity, what is termed "medium" resolution (1024 × 1024) is overkill.

The cost of a CRT display for computer service goes up geometrically with the resolution of the CRT. CRT monitors with twice the resolution will cost about four times as much. The additional density of the pixels within a high resolution display means more memory and drivers (in the case of flat panels) to handle the image. It also means more processing time to generate the image. Unless your computer system is up to the additional processing requirements, the addition of a high-res monitor will dramatically slow down the entire system. These are the trade-offs involved in higher resolution display systems. The higher the resolution is, the higher the cost will be and the more hardware will be required for satisfactory display operation. If you are currently dissatisfied with the resolution of your computer's display, then place it further away. By increasing the distance between the viewer and the display, the display's apparent resolution is increased. In other words, the resolution of your display may be OK for your usage, but you are simply sitting too close to the screen. This technique costs nothing and is certainly worth trying if you think your system needs more resolution.

If a high resolution display is called for in your application, then there are several avenues open that can cut cost and information processing time. The first is color. Does your application really require a full color display? If not, a monochrome high resolution monitor becomes a less expensive, and about three times faster, solution to the problem. The reason is simple, the monochrome display is only concerned with one set of luminosity information per pixel, while the color system must display and process three sets of luminosity information for each pixel. Resolution is the same in both systems, but only one displays in full color. Applications involving word processing and data entry have little use for color, but higher resolution can reduce both eyestrain and operator fatigue. However, some applications can benefit from both increased resolution and color. Applications such as computer aided design (CAD) use color for the simulation of three dimensional space on a two dimensional surface (the display's screen). In applications like machine design, both high resolution and color are necessary.

A second technique for reducing high resolution display cost and complexity is the choice of screen size. Resolution is being compared on the basis of pixels per unit of area. As such, the actual pixel count on the screen's surface rises geometrically with the screen's area. For example, assume a 10-in (edge measure) square display with 1000 pixels per square inch. The total pixel count of the entire screen is 100,000. If the same pixel density is produced in a 20-in square display the total pixel count rises to 400,000. That's four times as many pixels for a doubling of the screen's linear size. Each and every pixel has to be computed and displayed, making the larger display four times slower than the smaller one. If high resolution is required, then keep the monitor's screen as small as possible. This will help reduce both cost and information processing time. The trade-off involved here is that the screen actually displays less data.

Speed

The question of speed in a display technology only becomes critical in higher resolution systems. Figure 10-9 illustrates the speed of various display technologies. Note that the speeds here are those of the actual display device, and do not consider the time spent in image computation. The y-axis is logarithmic and calibrated in operations per second. The undisputed speed demon is the LED. It can display information over 10 times faster than its nearest competitor, the CRT. The VFD, ELD, and plasma panels are capable of displaying entire pages of data in medium resolution without flicker.

To display information without flicker is the problem that defines the lower limit of a display's speed. All display technologies are capable of this, but the LCD comes the closest to not "making the cut" for flicker. The speed at which a pixel may be changed from light to dark and back again has long been a weak feature of the LCD. They are by far the slowest device, operating just faster than the flicker rate (between 30 to 60 Hz) of the human eye. Considering the liquid phase construction and physics of the LC cell, it is highly unlikely that LCD speeds will increase more than a factor of 10.

Only the high resolution displays require high speeds. High resolution, in this case, means a pixel count of 1024 × 1024 or more. Here the situation involves displaying massive amounts of image data

Fig. 10-9.

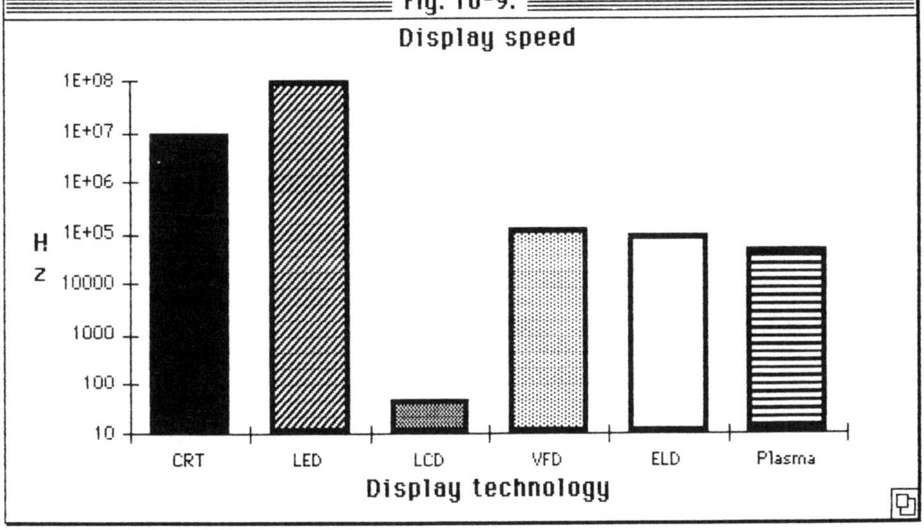

in a time period of less than the eye's flicker rate. The only technology that is currently capable of doing this is the CRT. In a very definite sense, the speed of a display's operation places very real limits on the resolution of the image it may display. The speed of a display must increase geometrically with the increase of resolution. Modern high resolution CRTs must maintain video bandwidths of up to 200 MHz in order to display this massive amount of data within the flicker period.

Longevity

Longevity is a factor in the economics of electronic display use. The longer it lasts, the less often it has to be replaced. Figure 10-10 illustrates the longevity of various display types. The y-axis of this display is linear and calibrated in thousands of hours. The longest lived display technology is definitely the LED. Projected lifetimes of LEDs are in excess of 20 years of continuous operation. With intermittent operation, it is likely that an LED display will survive longer than either you or I. The LCDs come next. With their low voltage, liquid phase operation, they will run for many years without losing their contrast. This is in keeping with the LCD continuous operation in watches and clocks. ELDs and plasma panels will last for several years of continuous operation. Since the ELD is a

Fig. 10-10.

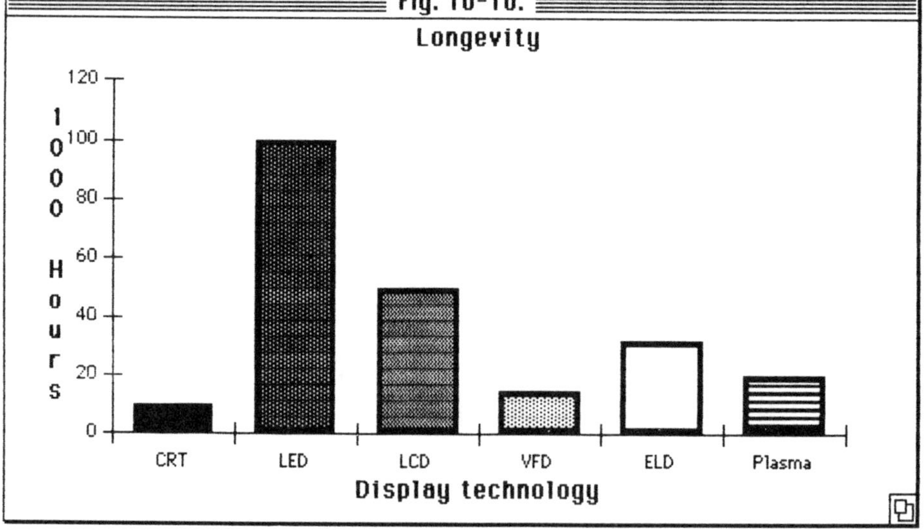

relatively new, solid state device it is very likely that this longevity figure will greatly increase in the future. The CRT remains the shortest lived electronic display device, with lifetimes of about 10,000 hours of continuous, full brightness, operation. In common & intermittent operation, a CRT will last some ten years before becoming dim enough to require replacement.

Longevity is one factor that the user can control. Most displays that are self-illuminating contain a brightness control. If this control is adjusted to the minimum illumination necessary for satisfactory service, then the display's life can be greatly extended. In terms of CRT operation, if you turn the brightness down to the minimum acceptable level, then you can extend the effective life of your CRT by as much as four times. It is high luminosity levels that wear out the display the fastest. This is also true, but to a lesser extent, with LEDs, ELDs, and plasma panels.

PROPER DISPLAY POSITION AND DISPLAY READABILITY

Assuming that the previous information has enabled you to select a display, then this display still must be installed and arranged. The position of a display plays a great part in the display's operation. Simply imagine yourself watching the display and operating the device. Arrange the display for ease of viewing. Straight on viewing from about a meter is usually best for displays used in computer service. Computer displays should not require turning the head for viewing. You should be able to look from the key board to the display easily and without any exaggerated motions. The same is true of the documentation area. The computer work area should provide simultaneous and easy visual access to these three areas—the display, the keyboard, and the paper documentation area.

If you are designing a project that incorporates an electronic display, then pay special attention to the panel layout. If the device contains any controls, then they should be placed so the hand operating them does not obscure the display. For example, consider building a digital clock using four digits, each composed of a seven segment LCD. This device will contain switches to set the time, alarm and whatnot. If the switches are located below the display, then they can be operated without covering up the display. Since most folks are right handed, the best general place for the display is in the upper, left-hand corner of the device. This leaves the bottom and right hand section for controls.

The position of the display in relation to ambient lighting is critical. In all displays, except LCDs, position the display so that a minimum of ambient light will fall on its screen. The situation is just the opposite with the LCD. Position the LCD so that a maximum of ambient light falls on the screen. While this may sound both familiar and trivial, it is in fact of the utmost importance. If you require experimental proof, simply place a self illuminating display (like a CRT) where direct sunlight falls on its screen. You will notice that the brightness of your display cannot compete with the sun's luminance. The same is true of artificial light sources. They are usually much brighter than the display. Position your display so that it doesn't have to compete with other light sources.

DISPLAY INTERCONNECTION-RELIABILITY AND EMI

If the display is remote from its processing, as many computer displays are, then special attention is required for its electrical connections. The image data can be delivered to the display in several fashions—as rf, or composite video, or in a variety of RGB encoding systems. All these transmission systems have one thing in common. They move data at very rapid rates. In physical terms, this data is carried on electronic signals that are high enough in frequency to be considered radio frequency (RF) energy. As such, they will radiate if given the opportunity. Anyone who has ever operated radio equipment near a computer is familiar with this type of electromagnetic interference (EMI).

EMI is more than just a nuisance to other equipment and to our neighbors. It is a sign that the computer (or whatever image source) to display path is faulty. This path is leaking energy. If this leak is severe enough, it can interfere with the data being supplied to the display, and result in poor display contrast and/or resolution. Each system of data source-to-display transmission requires a slightly different technique, but all are related to good RF feedline design. The basic characteristic of a good signal path from source-to-display is the same as a good after-dinner speech. Keep it as short as possible. This applies to RF, composite video, or RGB systems of signal transfer.

First, let's consider a video signal that is being transmitted as vhf rf. This is the situation for TV receivers and computers that use rf modulators to send their data to TV receivers. This information also applies to computers, video gear or whatever, using composite video signal encoding. In this case of VHF RF signal, we are usually working on TV Channels 2 or 3, about 50 to 60 MHz. A composite video signal has a bandwidth of about 6 MHz. Treat all these entire circuits as rf, just like an antenna and feedline combination. Don't do anything to the signal path that you wouldn't do in a proper antenna installation. Shortcuts, like twisted mechanical connections instead of soldering, are to be avoided.

First of all, keep the cable as short as possible. Secondly, use high quality connectors that are properly installed. Most TV sets and composite video displays use 75 Ω coaxial cable. Use a good grade of coax, with good coverage on its shield braid. If you have your choice of connectors use the BNC type, rather than the F type or RCA types. The BNC connector, while more expensive and difficult to install, produces less impedance changes in the signal path. This results in greater signal transfer, and vastly reduces EMI. Do not bundle the coax with other cables. No coaxial cable is completely shielded, and bundling rf cables with other lines is just asking for interference and cross-talk. If your video system exhibits ghosts in the image, the problem may be in the video feedlines. If the coaxial cable is of some length, it may produce standing waves which are perceived by the display as ghosts. The situation is identical with high standing voltage waves (VSWR) in an antenna system. If coaxial cable runs exceed several meters, then the coax may be tuned to reduce ghosting. Tuning may be accomplished by using a cable length of odd multiples of ¼ wavelength (i.e. ¼, ¾, 5/4 . . .) at the operating frequency. Be sure to include the specific velocity factor of the coaxial cable in use in this computation.

RGB image transmission systems differ widely from system to system. The more expensive varieties use coaxial cable for signal transmission. As such, treat them just as rf, as mentioned above. Some systems do use, however, cables that are not coaxial, but sets of conductors, or twisted pairs of wires. The situation for non-coaxial cable carrying RF signals, is much more sensitive. First of all, keep the wire lengths to an absolute minimum. Don't route these wires near other wiring or the metal cases of other equipment. If other wiring must be crossed by the signal wires, then let it be at right angles. Fortunately, most manufacturers using non coaxial feedline supply a cable harness for the display. This harness is usually tuned and equipped with DB series, shielded, connectors. If you must lengthen this cable, triple its length and you will maintain its tuning. Multiplication of the cable's length by odd numbers assures that it will remain tuned.

DEVELOPING DISPLAY TECHNOLOGIES

To this point, we have discussed a variety of display technologies. These technologies were examined in terms of what is now happening. The vast majority of the devices we have discussed can be purchased just about anywhere in mass produced versions. But what does the immediate future hold in the field of electronic information display? Let's look a few years into the future.

The following discussion omits several display devices—VFDs, analog meters, and incandescent lamps. These displays are displays of the past and are rapidly being replaced by other technologies. The reasons for this are detailed in the chapters on these three types. There will always remain some specific applications for analog meters and incandescents. But these applications are not plentiful enough to spur additional research into technologies that are basically dead end. Analog meters are more expensive, mechanically more complex (less reliable), and less accurate than digital types. In the case of incandescent lights, they consume too much power, have poor longevity, and cost more than the LEDs that are replacing them. These displays are simply obsolete, and no further development is expected of them.

DEVELOPING CRT TECHNOLOGIES

Since the CRT is the most popular electronic display, many manufacturers are spending fortunes on CRT research. We can expect definite image display improvements from CRTs within the next five years. More resolution and larger screens are in the future. Much research is also directed at the one of the CRT's major defects—large size. The development of flat CRTs is proceeding at a frantic pace. Color is becoming more common in all CRT applications. Considering the age of the basic concepts involved in the CRT, this amount of continuing research is amazing. There's life in the venerable CRT yet.

Resolution in CRTs will increase. Within five years, resolutions of 1024 × 1024 will be common in CRTs used in average computer service. High end computer systems will be equipped with resolutions up to 4096 × 4096. Full RGB systems of color will be implemented in these systems. These newer CRTs will cost a fraction of what current, very high resolution, types do. Expect these new high-res CRTs to have multiple electron guns. Instead of three guns, as in current color types, we will see up to 18 guns commonly used within the next five years. There is no real upper limit to the number of guns that may be used. Eight electron guns within a CRT are under development and successful testing now. Increasing the number of guns allows the signal encoding to be broken in smaller segments. This allows the display of higher resolution images without flicker. Multiple guns, in effect, lower the frequency of the video waveforms used. This simplifies and speeds image encoding. Multiple guns also allows lower frequency operation of all the analog image drivers. This frees the CRT from the problem of too slow driving electronics.

With the use of multiple guns, we will see the screen area of the CRT increasing. The problems of high deflection angles, high deflection voltages, and poor resolution involved in the larger screens is also solved by multiple guns. Instead of three guns (one for each primary color), the multi-gun CRT will use, say 18 guns. This means that various guns need only be focused on portions of the screen, rather than cover the entire screen. The use of 18 guns in effect divides the screen into 6 smaller screens. Each of these sub screens has reduced deflection requirements from its electron guns. Screen area will increase in multi-gun CRTs to over 3 square meters.

Research began in 1952, and is continuing, on flat panel CRTs. This is an attempt to extend the CRT into display applications that require compactness and portability. The most common approach to a flat screen CRT also involves the use of multiple electron seams. Matsushita Electric of Japan, for example, is experimenting with a flat screen CRT using 3000 separate electron beams. This system uses 15 cathode guns and 200 electron-beam-control electrodes to produce 3000 distinct electron beams. The total pixel count of this screen is 192,000 pixels. This prototype has screen dimensions of 20.32 cm (8-in) by 27.94 cm (11-in), and is only 9.9 cm (less than 4-in) thick. An added advantage of this technology is the reduction of the CRT's anode voltage. This prototype requires only 10 kV of anode voltage, while producing brightnesses over 70 foot-Lamberts. This is a better than 50% reduction in anode voltage over conventional CRTs of the same size, and without loss in brightness. Matsushita uses a proprietary Matrix Drive and Deflection System (MDDS) in this flat CRT. The screen is divided into 200 horizontal and 15 vertical "picture cells." This MDDS is configured to reproduce the 270 line conventional broadcast TV system.

Other attempts are also being made to produce a flat CRT. Philips Research Laboratories (Redhill, England) is working on a system. This system uses electron multipliers to amplify low energy electron beams which, in turn, excite the phosphor screen. This prototype is noteworthy as the low energy beams are actually folded back onto themselves to achieve a flat display profile. This prototype has a 12-in diagonal screen, and is configured for the display of conventional TV images. On other fronts, Sony of Japan is actually marketing a 4-in diagonal flat screen CRT in some of its shirt pocket TV receivers. Flat screen CRTs may be practical reality in small sizes during the next five years.

The market for computer displays fuels CRT research. It is only computer technology that has progressed rapidly enough to require more performance from the CRT. As such, most CRT research is directed at the computer display market. If there were consumer demand for say, a better television display, then things will be different. It is highly probable that manufacturers will attempt to introduce high definition TV (HDTV) into the marketplace. The necessity of maintaining compatibility with all existing TV equipment has long delayed this project. Several companies are developing systems that are compatible with the NTSC video system. If this can be accomplished and sold to the public, then high-res CRTs will become more common and cheaper.

Developing LED Technologies

The big news in LEDs during the next five years will be the development of a viable blue LED junction. Currently it is possible to actually purchase blue LEDs. They are very expensive—over $50.00 apiece in quantities of 100. These junctions are difficult to make, and are not very bright. The reason all this work is being done on the blue junction is not just to add another color to the LEDs repertoire. This is the last of the primary colors that the LED cannot effectively display. If a blue LED can be inexpensively made, it will complete the LED's primary color triad (red, green, and blue). This means that the LEDs can be used to display full color images.

Along with the development of the blue junction, comes a reduction of size of all LED junctions. The currently made junctions occupy small enough areas so that they may be assembled into dot matrix displays. If these dot matrix displays can be compressed even more, it will be possible to display full color moving images on a screen of LEDs. Junction brightnesses will also rise in all forms of LEDs. The increase in junction brightness is necessary if flat panel LED displays are to compete with the bright CRTs and plasma panels. If these research goals can be met, then the LED could emerge as the most versatile, and most common, display technology.

Developing LCD Technologies

LCDs are going to be used in many types of truly portable computer equipment, and in flat screen TVs. The flexibility and small power consumption involved in LCDs makes them ideal for this purpose. Look for LCDs to become larger and to offer more resolution. The screen areas of LCDs will become large enough to display an entire 8-in × 11-in page of text within the next four years. Resolution will increase to that exhibited by the conventional (512 × 512) CRTs within the same period. Full color LCD technology is on the edge of mass production. Full color LCDs will become commonly available and much cheaper within the next three years.

One major factor slowing down the development of all LCDs is the use of indium tin oxide as their electrode material. The transparent ITO electrodes have relatively high electrical resistance when compared with other electrode materials. If a transparent, electrically conductive, material can be developed with less resistance, then the LCDs could become larger in size and offer greater resolution. This is of critical importance, not only to LCDs, but also to the ELDs which also use ITO electrodes.

Developing ELD Technologies

Currently, the ELD has the same size problem as the LCDs, ITO electrodes. The ELDs are limited in screen size by the resistance of their ITO electrodes. Techniques of sub-dividing the screen re being used to overcome this problem. Look for ELDs to become larger, up to 5 in by 7 in within the next five years. Resolution will also increase to the point where glitch-free moving video can be displayed.

The ELD is an excellent candidate for the development of a full color flat panel display in the very near future. The use of solid-state electroluminescent technology makes the full color ELD a matter of lots of money and a little time. Research is centered on finding electroluminescent compounds that emit the three primary colors with consistent luminosities and good longevity.

One of the problems facing the ELD technology is the cost and complexity of the driving electronics. This problem is gradually being solved by the manufacture of high voltage driver ICs specifically designed for ELD service. Now, over 60% of the cost involved in a working ELD is tied up in the driving electronics. Look for this to drop to less than 25% within the next five years. Companies such as Texas Instruments, Sharp, Siliconix, Supertex, and Telmos are all now manufacturing drivers specifically for the ELDs. This points out that many people within the actual display industry regard the ELD as having a bright and prosperous future.

DEVELOPING PLASMA DISPLAY TECHNOLOGIES

The coming thing in plasma displays is size. They are going to be made with enormous screen areas. Plasma panels will measure in the meters in the very near future. Plasma panels with 3-meter diagonals are now being prototyped, and units over twice this large are not far away. Large screen size is really the plasma panel's strongest point, and this is sure to be exploited in the future. Wall sized displays for business, sports, and entertainment are all going to be made with plasma technologies. With this increase in size will also come an increase in resolution. Currently about four million pixels is the upper limit for plasma panels. This resolution figure will more than double in the next three years.

Industrial and military markets have been swift to accept the plasma panels as replacements for CRTs. As such, much of the current plasma display research has been directed at these specific applications. Look for the plasma panels to be used in many more diverse consumer applications in the near future. Computers and vehicles are some of the first applications that will begin using these large, bright flat panel displays. Already, the use of plasma panels on some IBM personal computers has led to greater public acceptance of this display technology.

The problem of full color image display has yet to be solved by plasma technology. From the looks of this knotty problem, it is highly unlikely that full color plasma panels will be developed within the next five years. The problems involved in using gas discharge technology are formidable. The use of thin gold electrodes creates problems with the stacking of differing gas cells in the z dimension. The resulting layers have a very narrow viewing angle; and this angle is inherent with the use of opaque electrode material. So any attempt at a full color plasma panel will require that the differing colors be stacked side by side, rather than vertically. This greatly limits the resolution of the finished plasma panel.

The driving electronics of the ac plasma panels are even more complex than the ELD. The switching voltages are very high for conventional semiconductors. While most early production models of the plasma panel actually used driver ICs developed for the ELD, this is no longer true. Several IC manufacturers are spending R&D time working on drivers specifically designed for plasma displays. If these efforts are successful, then the price of the plasma panel (mostly due to its driving electronics) is sure to fall.

Appendices

Appendix A

Electronic Display Device Manufacturers

Aborn Electronics 3675 Enochs St. Santa Clara, CA 95051 Tele: 408-746-0505	*LED display devices.*
AC Interface Inc. 17911 Sampson Lane Huntington Beach, CA 92647 Tele: 714-841-6090	*LCD LED display devices.*
ADAC 70 Tower Office Park Woburn, MA 01801 Tele: 617-935-6668 Attn: Russ Ver Nooy	*CRT display devices.*
Advanced Dimensional Displays 16742 Stagg St. #102 Van Nuys, CA 91406 Tele: 818-785-6563	*Laser display devices.*

AEG-Telefunken Corp. PO Box 3800, Rt. 22, Orr Dr. Somerville, NJ 08876 Tele: 201-772-9800	*CRT LED LCD display devices.*
AFP Imaging Corp. 50 Executive Blvd. Elmsford, NY 10523 Tele: 914-592-6100	*CRT display devices.*
AG Electro Optics Tarporley, Cheshire CW6 0TW England Tele: (08293) 3305	*Laser display devices.*
Amperex Electronic Corp. Providence Pike Slatersville, RI 02876 Tele: 401-762-3800	*LCD display devices.*
Ampex Corp. 401 Broadway Redwood City, CA 94063 Tele: 415-367-4423 Attn: Dave Detmers	*CRT display devices.*
AND 770 Airport Blvd. Burlingame, CA 94010 Tele: 415-347-9916 Attn: Stephen A. Way	*LED LCD display devices.*
Ann Arbor Terminal Inc. 6175 Jackson Road Ann Arbor, MI 48103 Tele: 313-663-8000 Attn: Beth Turner	*CRT display devices.*
Applied Data Systems Suite 213, 9811 Mallard Dr. Laurel, MD 20708 Tele: 301-953-9326	*CRT display devices.*
Applied Micros Sugarland, TX 77478	*Plasma display devices.*

Arcolectric Corp. Canoga Park, CA 91304 Tele: 818-700-1933	*LED display devices.*
ARS Electronics PO Box 7323 Van Nuys, CA 91409 Tele: 818-997-6200	*Storage Tubes display devices.*
Audiotronics 7428 Bellaire Ave. North Hollywood, CA 91605 Tele: 213-781-6700	*CRT display devices.*
Auto-Trol Technology Group 12500 N. Washington St. Denver, CO 80233 Tele: 303-457-3424	*CRT Storage Tubes display devices.*
Aydin Computer Systems 401 Commerce Dr. Fort Washington, PA 19034 Tele: 215-542-7800	*CRT Projection display devices.*
Ball Electronic Systems Div. 4501 Ball Rd. Circle Pines, MN 55014 Tele: 612-786-8900	*CRT display devices.*
Beckman Industrial Inc. 2500 Harbor Blvd. Fullerton, CA 92634 Tele: 714-773-6753	*DCGas Electrofluorescent Plasma display devices.*
Brian B. O'Brien, P.E. 15 Country Dr. Weston, MA 02193 Tele: 617-891-7014	*Laser display devices.*
Calcomp 2411 West La Palma Avenue Anaheim, CA 92803 Tele: 714-821-2000 Attn: Renee Randall	*CRT display devices.*

Calcomp/Sanders 14151 North 76th St., Suite 100 Scottsdale, AZ 85260 Tele: 602-988-4800 Attn: David P. Peters	*CRT display devices.*
California Computer Products Inc. 2411 W. La Palma Ave. Anaheim, CA 92801 Tele: 714-821-2011	*CRT display devices.*
Calrad-Hanovia 100 Chestnut St. Newark, NJ 07105 Tele: 201-589-4300	*DCGas Plasma Projection display devices.*
Camax Systems Inc. 7225 Ohms Lane Minneapolis, MN 55435 Tele: 612-831-0604	*CRT display devices.*
Cambridge Digital Systems POB 568, 65 Bent St. Cambridge, MA 02139 Tele: 617-491-2700	*CRT display devices.*
Cambridge Instruments Inc. 40 Robert Pitt Dr. Monsey, NY 10952 Tele: 914-356-3331	*CRT Sequential Scan display devices.*
Centronic Inc. 1101 Bristol Rd. Mountainside, NJ 07092 Tele: 201-233-7200	*CRT display devices.*
Centronic Ltd. King Henry's Drive, New Addington Croydon, CR9 0BG England Tele: (0689) 42121/8 Attn: J.O. Miller	*CRT LED display devices.*

CGX Corp. 42 Nagog Park Acton, MA 01720 Tele: 617-263-3222	*CRT display devices.*
Cherry Electrical Products Corp. 3600 Sunset Ave. Wawkegan, IL 60087 Tele: 312-662-9200	*Plasma DCGas Electroluminescent Electrofluorescent LED display devices.*
Chugai International Corp. 1 Ames Court Plainview, NY 11803 Tele: 516-349-9080	*CRT display devices.*
Clinton Electronics Corp. 6701 Clinton Road Rockford, IL 61131 Tele: 815-633-1444 Attn: Joe Beck/Applications Engineering Mgr.	*CRT display devices.*
Codar Technology Inc. 1428 Florida Ave. Longmont, CO 80501 Tele: 303-776-0472	*CRT Vector Scan display devices.*
Colorgraphic Communications Corp. 2379 John Glenn Drive Atlanta, GA 30341 Tele: 404-455-3921 Attn: Elyse Mintz	*CRT display devices.*
Communications & Display Systems Inc. 24 Fitch St. Norwalk, CT 06855 Tele: 203-852-9814	*LCD display devices.*
Computer Systems Co. 26401 Harper Ave. St. Clair Shores, MI 48081 Tele: 313-779-8700	*CRT display devices.*

Computer Talk Inc. PO Box 148, 2800 S. Rooney Rd. Morrison, CO 80465 Tele: 303-697-5485	*CRT display devices.*
Comrex International Inc. Suite 120, 3701 Skypark Dr. Torrance, CA 90505 Tele: 213-373-0280	*CRT display devices.*
Conrac Div. 600 N. Rimsdale Ave. Covina, CA 91722 Tele: 818-966-3511	*CRT display devices.*
Controlyne Inc. 16 Church St. Montclair, NJ 07042 Tele: 201-746-8900	*Electrofluorescent display devices.*
Crystaloid Electronics PO Box 628 Hudson, OH 44236 Tele: 216-655-2429	*LCD display devices.*
Dage MTI Inc. 208 Wabash Street Michigan City, IN 46360 Tele: 219-872-5514 Attn: Hank Bogardus	*CRT display devices.*
Dale Electronics Inc. 2064 12th Avenue Columbus, NE 68601 Tele: 402-564-3131	*Plasma DCGas Colored Plasma display devices.*
Data Display Products PO Box 91072 Los Angeles, CA 90009 Tele: 213-640-0442	*LED Incandescent display devices.*
Data General 4400 Computer Dr. Westboro, MA 01580 Tele: 617-366-8911	*CRT display devices.*

Data Type Inc. 2615 Miller Ave. Mountain View, CA 94040 Tele: 415-949-1053	*CRT display devices.*
Datacopy Corp. 191 Post Roa West Westport, CT 06880 Tele: 203-222-9195 Attn: Watson S. Coverdale	*CRT display devices.*
Densitron Corp. 20775 Western Ave. Torrance, CA 90501 Tele: 213-618-9647	*DCGas Electroluminescent Incandescent LED LCD Plasma display devices.*
Dialight Corp. 203 Harrison Pl. Brooklyn, NY 11237 Tele: 212-497-7600	*Incandescent LED display devices.*
Digital Electronics Corp. 26142 Eden Landing Rd. Hayward, CA 94545 Tele: 415-786-0520	*Electrofluorescent LCD Electroluminescent display devices.*
Digital Graphics Systems 2629 Terminal Bl. Mountain View, CA 94043 Tele: 415-962-0200	*CRT display devices.*
Digivision 4980 Carroll Canyon Rd. San Diego, CA 92121 Tele: 619-458-1111	*Projection display devices.*
Dionics Inc. 65 Rushmore St. Westbury, NY 11590 Tele: 516-997-7474	*Plasma DCGas Electrofluorescent display devices.*
Dipix Inc. 10220 Old Columbia Rd. Columbia, MD 21046 Tele: 301-596-0505	*CRT display devices.*

Dixy Corp. Yokohama, Japan	*Plasma display devices.*
Dotronix, Inc. 160 First Street S.E. New Brighton, MN 55112 Tele: 612-633-1742	*CRT display devices.*
Dwight Cavendish Co. Ltd. 2117 Chestnut Ave. Wilmette, IL 60091 Tele: 312-256-0937	*Laser Projection display devices.*
Dwight Cavendish Displays Ltd. Unit 5, Bydand Lane, Little Paxton, St. Neots Huntington, Cambridgeshire PE19 4ES England Tele: 0480 217567 Attn: W.G. Stewart	*Laser Projection display devices.*
Dyma Engineering Inc. Box 1535 Los Lunas, NM 87031 Tele: 505-865-6700	*CRT Vector Scan LED LCD display devices.*
EEV Canada Ltd. 67 Westmore Dr. Rexdale, Ontario M9V 3Y6 Canada	*CRT LCD Projection Storage Tubes display devices.*
EEV Inc. 7 Westchester Plaza Elmsford, NY 10523 Tele: 914-592-6050	*Plasma CRT Electroluminescent Laser LCD FlatPanel display devices.*
Elec-Tek Inc. 10280 Alliance Road Cincinnati, OH 45242 Tele: 513-793-7937 Attn: Rick Groth	*LED display devices.*

Elector USA Inc. 5128 Calle del Sol Santa Clara, CA 95050 Tele: 408-727-1506	*CRT Projection display devices.*
Electronic Image Systems 4146 Woodedge Dr. Bellbrook, OH 45305 Tele: 513-327-7579	*Beam Tubes CRT Vector Scan Projection display devices.*
EMCEE Broadcast Products Box 68 White Haven, PA 18661 Tele: 717-443-9575	*LEDDrives display devices.*
Engineering Automation Systems Inc. 936 Silas Deane Hwy. Wethersfield, CT 06109 Tele: 203-529-3200	*CRT display devices.*
Enmark Associates Inc. 610 Franklin Ave. Nutley, NJ 07110 Tele: 201-667-8114	*Laser display devices.*
Enterprise Systems Corp. Box 698 Dover, NH 03820 Tele: 603-742-7363 Attn: Valerie Sawyer	*CRT Vacuum Fluorescent display devices.*
Essco Industries Box 515 Sierra Madre, CA 91024 Tele: 213-355-8825	*DCGas Electroluminescent Electrofluorescent Incandescent LED LCD Projection display devices.*
Evans & Sutherland PO Box 8700 Salt Lake City, UT 84108 Tele: 801-582-5847	*CRT Vector Scan display devices.*
Fibervision 2200 Shames Drive Westbury, NY 11590 Tele: 516-334-6800	*FiberOptics display devices.*

Finlux Inc. PO Box 2535, 12623 Cambridge Dr. Saratoga, CA 95070 Tele: 408-725-1972	*Electroluminescent display devices.*
Florida Computer Graphics 1000 Sandpond Rd. Lake Mary, FL 32746 Tele: 305-321-3000	*CRT display devices.*
Folsom Research Inc. 526 E. Bidwell St. Folsom, CA 95630 Tele: 916-985-2481	*LCD display devices.*
Futaba Corp. Tokyo, Japan	*Vacuum Fluorescent display devices.*
General Digital Corp. 700 Burnside Avenue East Hartford, CT 06108 Tele: 203-528-9041 Attn: Gary Budzak	*Plasma display devices.*
General Electric Co., Lamp Components & Technical Prod. 21800 Tungsten Road Cleveland, OH 44117 Tele: 216-266-2451	*Incandescent Analog Meter display devices.*
General Instrument Corp. Optoelectronics Div. 3400 Hill View Ave. Palo Alto, CA 94304 Tele: 415-493-0400 Attn: Michael L. Bottini	*LED display devices.*
Gigatek Limited Box 498 Scarborough, Ontario M1S 3C5 Canada Tele: 416-439-4104	*CRT display devices.*

Gilway Technical Lamp 165 N. New Boston St. Woburn, MA 01801 Tele: 617-935-4442	*LED display devices.*
GIXI Inc. 7808 Glenroy Rd. Minneapolis, MN 55435 Tele: 612-893-1350	*CRT display devices.*
Gould Inc. Deanza Imaging Division 1870 Lundy Ave. San Jose, CA 95031 Tele: 408-263-7155	*LCD CRT LEDDrive display devices.*
Graphics Technology Corp. 1777 Conestoga St. Boulder, CO 80301 Tele: 303-449-1138	*CRT display devices.*
Great American Market 826 N. Cole Ave. Hollywood, CA 90038 Tele: 213-461-0200	*Incandescent Projection display devices.*
Grid Systems Mountain View, CA 94042	*Electroluminescent FlatPanel display devices.*
Grimes Div. Midland Ross Corp. 550 Route 55 POB 247 Urbana, OH 43078 Tele: 513-652-1431	*Electroluminescent Electrofluorescent Incandescent LED LCD display devices.*
Grinnel Systems Corp. 6410 Via del Oro Dr. San Jose, CA 95119 Tele: 408-629-9191	*CRT display devices.*
Hamlin Inc. 612 East Lake Street Lake Mills, WI 53551 Tele: 414-648-2361 Attn: Walter A. Bruenger	*LCD display devices.*

Hartman Systems 360 Wolf Hill Rd. Huntington Station, NY 11746 Tele: 516-427-7500	*CRT LED LCD display devices.*
Hitachi Yokohama, Japan	*CRT Hi-Res display devices.*
Hitachi America Ltd. 50 Prospect Ave. Terrytown, NY 10591 Tele: 914-332-5800	*CRT display devices.*
HMW Enterprises Inc. 604 Salem Rd. Etters, PA 17319 Tele: 717-938-4691	*CRT display devices.*
Holotek Ltd. 300 East River Road Rochester, NY 14623 Tele: 716-424-4996 Attn: Peter A. Pizzutelli	*Laser display devices.*
Honeywell Optoelectronics Inc. 830 E. Arapaho Rd. Richardson, TX 75081 Tele: 214-234-4271	*LED display devices.*
Hoppmann Corp. 14560 Lee Rd. Chantilly, VA 22021 Tele: 703-631-2700	*Projection display devices.*
Hughes Aircraft Co., Corp. Marketing PO Box 1053 El Segundo, CA 90245 Tele: 213-414-6838	*LCD Plasma Storage Tubes display devices.*
Hughes Aircraft, Industrial Products Div. 6155 El Camino Real Carlsbad, CA 92008 Tele: 619-438-9191	*Projection display devices.*

Hycom Inc.
16841 Armstrong Ave.
Irvine, CA 92705
Tele: 714-557-5252

Electroluminescent display devices.

I. Robotics Inc.
11 Melcher St.
Boston, MA 02210
Tele: 617-482-9138

CRT display devices.

ID Systems Corp.
6175 W. Shamrock Ct.
Dublin, OH 43017
Tele: 614-876-1595

CRT display devices.

IEE Industrial Elec. Engin. Inc.
7740 Lemona Ave.
Van Nuys, CA 91405
Tele: 818-787-0311

Plasma DCGas FlatPanel Electrofluorescent Incandescent LED LCD display devices.

Ikegami Electronics USA Inc.
37 Brook Avenue
Maywood, NJ 07607
Tele: 201-368-9171
Attn: Richard Spallone

CRT display devices.

Image Magnification Inc.
739 Airway Circle
New Smyrna Beach, FL 32069
Tele: 904-427-5294

Projection CRT display devices.

Industrial Devices Inc.
Edgewater, NJ 07020
Tele: 201-224-4700

Incandescent LED display devices.

Info-Lite Corp.
422 Cliff Street
Fairview, NJ 07022
Tele: 201-941-4455
Attn: Joseph M. Cartelli

Incandescent LED display devices.

Infodex Inc.
395 W. Main St.
Waterbury, CT 06702
Tele: 203-757-9291
Attn: Robert R. Bartoletti

CRT Electroluminescent display devices.

Intecolor Corp.
225 Technology Park
Norcross, GA 30092
Tele: 404-449-5961

CRT display devices.

Intermedia Systems
10601 S. DeAnza Blvd.
Cupertino, CA 95014
Tele: 408-996-0900

CRT Sequential Scan display devices.

International Imaging Systems
1500 Buckeye Dr.
Milpitas, CA 95035
Tele: 408-262-4444

CRT display devices.

International Instrumentation Inc.
31131 Via Colinas Bldg., 602
Westlake Village, CA 91362
Tele: 213-991-9614

Analog Meter display devices.

Intraaction Corp.
3719 Warren Ave.
Bellwood, IL 60104
Tele: 312-547-6644

Laser display devices.

Ise Electronics Corp.
Ise, Japan

Vacuum Fluorescent display devices.

ITT Courier
Tempe, AZ 85282

LCD FlatPanel display devices.

ITT Information Systems
2350 Qume Drive
San Jose, CA 95131
Tele: 408-945-8950
Attn: Teena Genetti

CRT Printer display devices.

Jewell Electrical Instruments Grenier Field Manchester, NH 03108 Tele: 603-669-6400 Attn: Jean C. Kelleher	*Analog Meter display devices.*
JKL Components Corp. 13343 Paxton St. Pacoima, CA 91331 Tele: 818-896-0019	*Incandescent LED Electrofluorescent display devices.*
Joely Industries Inc. PO Box 38489 Los Angeles, CA 90038 Tele: 213-569-8155	*Electrofluorescent display devices.*
Jupiter Systems 1100 Marina Village Pkwy. Alameda, CA 94501 Tele: 415-523-9000	*CRT display devices.*
Kel Inc., Kanematsu Electronics Ltd. 400 West Cummings Park Woburn, MA 01801 Tele: 617-933-7852 Attn: Barbara J. Vandulek	*CRT display devices.*
Kel Inc./K.G. USA Inc. Suite 4811, 1 World Trade Center New York, NY 10048 Tele: 212-524-8319	*CRT display devices.*
Koyo Corp. Hibiya Park Bldg. 908, 1-8-1 Yurakucho, Chiyoda-Ku Tokyo, 100 Japan Tele: (03) 213-1571	*Laser display devices.*
Krystal Image Engineering Inc. 6837 Canoga Ave. Canoga Park, CA 91303 Tele: 418-992-7670	*LED LEDDrive display devices.*

Lamp Technology Inc. 141-A Central Ave. Farmingdale, NY 11735 Tele: 516-454-6464	*LED display devices.*
Laser Beam International Bld De Smet De Naeyer, 182 Brussels, 1090 Belgium Tele: (02) 428 10 30	*Laser display devices.*
Laser Engineering Inc. 1396 Main St. Waltham, MA 02154 Tele: 617-647-1920	*Laser display devices.*
Laserworks PO Box 2408 Orange, CA 92669 Tele: 714-832-2686	*Laser display devices.*
Leader Instruments Corp. 380 Oser Ave. Hauppauge, NY 11788 Tele: 800-645-5104 Attn: Marc Reiner	*CRT Vector Scan display devices.*
Lectron Industries Inc. Box 317, 117 Chestnut St. Roscelle, NJ 07203 Tele: 201-245-5858	*LCD LED display devices.*
Ledco Div. 240 Plato Blvd. St. Paul, MN 55107 Tele: 612-222-2291	*LED display devices.*
Leecraft Mfg, Co. Inc. 21-02 44th Rd. Long Island City, NY 11101 Tele: 718-392-8800 Attn: Mario Staltari	*LED Incandescent display devices.*

Leo Beiser Inc. 151-77 28th Ave. Flushing, NY 11354 Tele: 212-353-7298	*Laser display devices.*
Levison Sales Co. Inc. PO Box 345, 351 Larkfield Rd. E. Northport, NY 11731 Tele: 516-266-5020	*CRT display devices.*
Lexidata Corp. 755 Middlesex Tpk. Billerica, MA 01865 Tele: 617-663-8550	*CRT display devices.*
Librascope Div./Singer Co. 833 Sonora Ave. Glendale, CA 91201 Tele: 213-502-7301	*Electroluminescent Laser LCD Plasma display devices.*
Light Impressions Inc. PO Box 832 Ben Lomand, CA 95005 Tele: 408-458-1991 Attn: Ellen Nugent	*Holographs display devices.*
Link Electronics Ltd. North Way Andover, Hants SP105AJ England Tele: (0264) 61345	*Projection CRT display devices.*
Lite-On 4951 Airport Parkway Dallas, TX 44122 Tele: 214-239-3565	*LED display devices.*
Litton Industries, Electron Devices Division 1215 South 52nd Street Tempe, Arizona 85281 Tele: 602-968-4471 Attn: Jim E. Wurtz	*DirectViewCRT display devices.*

LXD Corp.
24500 Highpoint Road
Beachwood, OH 44122
Tele: 216-292-3300

Matsushita Electric Industrial Company Ltd.
1006 Kadoma, Kadoma City
Osaka, 571
Japan

Electroluminescent FlatPanel LCD display devices.

McMahan Assoc. Inc./Electro-Optical Div.
2160 Park Ave. N.
Winter Park, FL 32789
Tele: 305-645-0463

Laser display devices.

Megatek Corp.
3985 Sorrento Valley Blvd.
San Diego, CA 92121
Tele: 619-455-5590

CRT Vector Scan CRT display devices.

Metheus Corp./Graphics
PO Box 1049
Hillsboro, OR 97123
Tele: 503-640-8000
Attn: John L. M. Huges

CRT display devices.

Microtex
80 Trowbridge St.
Cambridge, MA 02138
Tele: 617-491-2874

CRT display devices.

Miltope Corp.
Melville, NY 11747
Tele: 516-420-0200

Plasma display devices.

Mitsubishi Electronics America, Inc.
991 Knox Street
Torrance, CA 90502
Tele: 213-515-3993

CRT display devices.

Motorola Display Systems 1299 E. Algonquin Rd. Schaumburg, IL 60196 Tele: 312-576-5403	*CRT display devices.*
Motorola Inc. 4800 Alameda Blvd. NE. Albuquerque, NM 87113 Tele: 505-822-8801 Attn: Al Lowenstein	*LCD display devices.*
Mouser Electronics 11433 Woodside Santee, CA 92071 Tele: 619-449-2222	*LED display devices.*
MPB 1725 N. Service Rd., Trans Canada Hwy. Dorval, Quebec H9P 1J1 Canada Tele: 514-683-1490	*CRT display devices.*
NEC Kanagawa, Japan	*Vacuum Fluorescent display devices.*
New Media Graphics Corp. 279 Cambridge St. 5 Burlington, MA 01803 Tele: 617-272-8844	*CRT display devices.*
Ocean Technology Inc. 2835 North Naomi Street Burbank, CA 91504 Tele: 213-849-7111 Attn: E. Grant Corcoran	*CRT display devices.*
OCLI-Optical Coating Lab. Inc. 2789 Northpoint Parkway Santa Rosa, CA 95407 Tele: 707-525-7037	*LCD display devices.*

Omega Organization Int. PO Box 687 Mercer Island, WA 98040 Tele: 206-232-6256 Attn: Sheila Chatelaine	*Incandescent Laser Projection display devices.*
Optilas B.V. Groenestein 67-69 Alphen A/D RIJN, 2403 JM Holland Tele: 01720-31234	*Laser display devices.*
Orwin Assoc. Inc. 88 Seabro Ave. Amityville, NY 11701	*CRT Vector Scan display devices.*
Panasonic Industrial Co. One Panasonic Way Secaucus, NJ 07094 Tele: 201-348-7000	*Electrofluorescent Incandescent LED Colored Plasma LCD CRT Projection Flat-Panel CRT Vector Scan display devices.*
Panelvision Corp. 265 Kappa Dr. Pittsburgh, PA 15238 Tele: 412-963-9635	*LCD display devices.*
Peritek Corp. 5550 Redwood Rd. Oakland, CA 94619 Tele: 415-531-6500	*CRT display devices.*
Perkin-Elmer/Applied Optics Div. 7421 Orangewood Ave., POB 3115 Garden Grove, CA 92642 Tele: 717-895-1667	*Projection display devices.*
Philips Research Laboratories Redhill, England	*FlatPanel CRT display devices.*

Philips Television Systems Inc. PO Box 618, 900 Corporate Dr. Mahwah, NJ 07430 Tele: 201-529-1550	*CRT FlatPanel display devices.*
Photonics Technology PO Box 423 Luckey, OH 43443 Tele: 419-666-0762 Attn: Donald K. Wedding Sr.	*Colored Plasma display devices.*
Pixel One Burtt Rd. Andover, MA 01810 Tele: 617-470-7190	*CRT display devices.*
Plasma Graphics PO Box 4903 Warren, NJ 07060 Tele: 201-757-5000	*Plasma DCGas display devices.*
Princeton Graphic System PGS 601 Ewing Street, Building A Princeton, NJ 08540 Tele: 800-221-1490	*RGB Sequential Scan CRT, HiResCRT display devices.*
Prior Data Sciences 39 Hwy. 7 Ottawa, Ontario K2H 8R2 Canada Tele: 613-820-7235	*CRT display devices.*
Projector Recorder Belt Corp. 200 E. Clay Whitewater, WI 53190 Tele: 414-473-2151	*LED SolidState display devices.*
PsiTech 16902 Von Karman Irvine, CA 92714 Tele: 714-863-0981	*CRT display devices.*

Qume Corp./ITT 2350 Qume Dr. San Jose, CA 95131 Tele: 800-223-2479	*CRT display devices.*
Ramtek Corp. 2211 Lawson Ln. Santa Clara, CA 95050 Tele: 408-988-2211 Attn: Tammy S. Palmer	*CRT display devices.*
Raster Graphics Inc. PO Box 23334 Tigard, OR 97223 Tele: 503-620-2241	*CRT display devices.*
Raytheon Co., Industrial Components Operation 465 Centre Street Quincy, MA 02169 Tele: 617-479-5300 Attn: Alvin S. Luftman	*CRT Storage Tubes CRT Vector Scan Projection display devices.*
Raytheon Data Systems 115 Norwood Park S. Norwood, MA 02062 Tele: 617-762-6700	*CRT display devices.*
RCA Electro Optics New Holland Ave. Lancaster, PA 17604 Tele: 717-295-6027 Attn: Carlton Lee Rintz	*FlatPanel LED Projection CRT display devices.*
RCA Laboratories Princeton, NJ 08540 Tele: 609-734-3128	*LCD display devices.*
REFAC Electronics Corp. PO Box 809 Winsted, CT 06098 Tele: 203-379-2731	*Incandescent LED LCD display devices.*
Relay Special Ties Inc. 1300 Plaza Rd. Fairlawn, NJ 07410 Tele: 201-797-3313	*LCD display devices.*

Robot Research Inc. 7591 Convoy Court San Diego, CA 92111 Tele: 619-279-9430	*CRT display devices.*
Rohm Corp. PO Box 19515 Irvine, CA 92713 Tele: 714-855-2131	*LED display devices.*
SAI Technology Corp. 4060 Sorrento Valley Blvd. San Diego, CA 92121 Tele: 619-450-2236 Attn: James H. Redman	*Plasma display devices.*
Sanders Associates Daniel Webster Hwy. S. Nashua, NH 03061 Tele: 603-885-4321	*CRT Vector Scan display devices.*
Schweber Electronics Jericho Turnpike Westbury, NY 11590 Tele: 516-334-7474	*LED LCD display devices.*
Scientific Systems Sales Corp. 333 Jericho Tpke. Jericho, NY 11753 Tele: 516-822-4880	*CRT Vector Scan display devices.*
Seiko Instruments USA, Graphics Div. 1623 Buckeye Dr. Milpitas, CA 95035 Tele: 408-943-9100	*CRT display devices.*
Seiler Instrument & Manufacturing Co. 170 E. Kirkham Ave. St. Louis, MO 63119 Tele: 314-968-2282	*Projection display devices.*

Selanar 437-A Aldo Ave. Santa Clara, CA 95054 Tele: 408-727-2811	*CRT Vector Scan display devices.*
Semiconductor Specialists Inc. 195 Spangler Ave. Elmhurst, IL 60126 Tele: 312-279-1005	*Electrofluorescent Incandescent LED LCD SolidState display devices.*
SGL Homalite 11 Brookside Dr. Wilmington, DE 19804 Tele: 302-652-3686	*? display devices.*
Sharp Nara, Japan	*LCD FlatPanel display devices.*
Shelly Assoc. Inc. 2942 Dow Ave. Tustin, CA 92680 Tele: 714-544-9970	*Electroluminescent Incandescent LCD display devices.*
Shogyo Intl. Corp. 287 Northern Blvd. Great Neck, NY 11021 Tele: 516-466-0911	*LED LCD display devices.*
Siemens Components Inc. Optoelectronics 19000 Homestead Rd. Cupertino,CA 95014 Tele: 406-257-3524	*LED display devices.*
Siliconix 2201 Laurelwood Road Santa Clara, CA 95054 Tele: 408-988-8000 Attn: Gayle Uchida	*ElectroluminescentDriver display devices.*
Simpson Electric Co. 853 Dundee Avenue Elgin, IL 60120	*Analog Meter display devices.*

Sinclair Research Ltd. 50 Staniford Street, Suite 800 Boston, MA 02114 Tele: 617-742-4826	*LCD display devices.*
Slatersville Div., Amperex Electronics Corp. Slatersville, RI 02876 Tele: 401-762-3800	*LCD display devices.*
SLR Systems Research Labs Inc. 2800 Indian Ripple Rd. Dayton, OH 45440 Tele: 513-426-6000	*CRT Vector Scan Projection display devices.*
Sony 9 W. 57th St. New York, NY 10019 Tele: 212-371-5800	*CRT Vector Scan display devices.*
Sony Component Products, Sony Corp. 15 Essex Rd. Paramus, NJ 07652 Tele: 201-368-5000	*CRT display devices.*
Sony Video Communications Sony Dr. Park Ridge, NJ 07656 Tele: 201-930-1000	*CRT FlatPanel Projection Semiconductor display devices.*
SORO 40 Pond Park Rd. Hingham, MA 02043 Tele: 617-740-1363	*Laser display devices.*
Spectragraphics Corp. 10260 Sorrento Valley Rd. San Diego, CA 92121 Tele: 619-450-0611 Attn: Anne L. Hutchison	*CRT display devices.*

Sperry Univac PO Box 500 Blue Bell, PA 19424 Tele: 215-542-4213 Attn: Michael M. Maynard	*CRT Vector Scan display devices.*
Sprague Electric Co. 41 Hampden Road Mansfield, MA 02048 Tele: 617-339-3701 Attn: Charles L. Welsch	*ElectroluminescentDrivers display devices.*
Standard Telecommunications Labs Essex, England	*LCD FlatPanel display devices.*
Stanley Electric Co. Ltd. 2-9-13 Nakameguro, Meguro-ku Tokyo, 153 Japan Tele: (03)711-3636	*LCD LED display devices.*
Stocker & Yale Inc. Post Electronics Div. Rt. 128 & Brimbal Ave. Beverly, MA 01915 Tele: 617-927-9340	*Electrofluorescent Projection display devices.*
Sunshine Scientific Instruments Inc. 1810 Grant Ave. Philadelphia, PA 19115 Tele: 215-673-5600	*LED LCD display devices.*
Supertex Inc. 1225 Bourdeaux Sunnyvale, CA 94089 Tele: 408-744-0100	*Plasma Electroluminescent LCD Semiconductor Solid-State display devices.*
Surrey Electro-Optics Ltd. Surrey House, London Rd. Staines, Middlesex TW18 4HW England Tele: (0784) 61393	*LCD display devices.*

Suwa Seikosha Nagano-Ken, Japan	*LCD FlatPanel display devices.*
Symbolics Inc. 9600 De Soto Ave. Chatsworth, CA 91311 Tele: 213-998-3600	*CRT display devices.*
Talbert Reflectors 442 Alcatraz Ave. Oakland, CA 94609 Tele: 415-839-6911	*Projection display devices.*
Technical Enterprises 1401 Bonnie Doone Corona del Mar, CA 92625 Tele: 714-644-9500	*Projection display devices.*
Technical Lighting Research PO Box D E. Aurora, NY 14052 Tele: 716-825-2803	*Electroluminescent SolidState Thin-Film Video display devices.*
Tektronix Inc. PO Box 4828 Portland, OR 97208 Tele: 800-547-1512	*CRT Vector Scan Electroluminescent Colored Plasma display devices.*
Tektronix, Inc. PO Box 500 Beaverton, OR 97007 Tele: 503-643-8354 Attn: Penny Jasso	*CRT display devices.*
Tele Measurements Inc. 145 Main Ave. Clifton, NJ 07014 Tele: 201-473-8822	*CRT Projection display devices.*
Teledyne Camera Systems 131 N. Fifth Ave. Arcadia, CA 91006 Tele: 213-359-6691	*Thin-Film Video display devices.*

Teledyne Industries,
Teledyne Semiconductor
1300 Terra Bella Ave.
Mountain View, CA 94043
Tele: 415-968-9214

LEDDrive Semiconductor display devices.

Telex Computer Products Inc.
6422 East 41st Street
Tulsa, OK 74135
Tele: 918-627-1111
Attn: John Hawkins

CRT display devices.

Telpar Inc.
PO Box 796
Addison, TX 75001
Tele: 214-233-6631

CRT display devices.

Temtron Electronics Ltd.
15 Main St.
E. Rockaway, NY 11518
Tele: 800-645-2300

Beam Tube ChromaTubes FlatPanel LED LCD display devices.

Texas Instruments Inc.
8360 LBJ Freeway, PO Box 225474
Dallas, TX 75227
Tele: 214-997-3406
Attn: Barbara L. Veal

LED Semiconductor SolidState LCD Electroluminescent Vacuum Fluorescent display devices.

Thomas Electronics Inc.
100 Riverview Drive
Wayne, NJ 07470
Tele: 201-696-5200
Attn: Ben Setticase

Beam Tubes CRT Vector Scan Projection display devices.

Thomson-CSF
101, BD Murat
Paris Cedex 16, 75781
France
Tele: (1) 743 96 40

Plasma CRT Vector Scan Electroluminescent Projection display devices.

Thomson-CSF Corp. 550 Pleasant Ave. Dover, NJ 07801 Tele: 201-328-1400	*Beam Tubes Chroma Tubes CRT Vector Scan display devices.*
Thor Electronics Corp. PO Box 707, 321 Penn. Ave. Linden, NJ 07036 Tele: 201-486-3300	*Beam Tubes FlatPanel Electrofluorescent Incandescent LED LCD display devices.*
TJS Laser Inc. 103 Rt. 46 Fairfield, NJ 07006	*Laser display devices.*
Trainer Co. Inc. 40 Freeman Pl. Needham, MA 02192 Tele: 617-449-2122	*Electrophoretic display devices.*
TRW, Electronics Components Group 14520 Aviation Blvd. Lawndale, CA 90260 Tele: 213-536-0888 Attn: Dan Faigenblat	*CRT display devices.*
TSD Display Products Inc. 35 Orville Dr. Bohemia, NY 11716 Tele: 516-589-6800	*CRT display devices.*
UCE Inc. 24 Fitch Street Norwalk, CT 06855 Tele: 203-838-7509	*Electroluminescent LCD display devices.*
Universal Photonics 495 W. John St. Hicksville, NY 11801 Tele: 516-935-4000	*Semiconductor display devices.*

Vector General Inc., Sunnyvale/CPS Prod.
110 Wolfe Rd.
Sunnyvale, CA 94086
Tele: 408-738-0530

Beam Tubes CRT Vector Scan display devices.

VG Systems Inc.
21300 Oxnard St.
Woodland Hills, CA 91367
Tele: 818-346-3410
Attn: Creighton Van Horn

CRTRaster display devices.

Vidco Inc.
2400 West 10 Place, #4
Tempe, AZ 85281
Tele: 602-966-2221
Attn: James P. Hoy

Projection CRT display devices.

Video Monitors Inc.
3833 N. White Ave.
Eau Claire, WI 54703
Tele: 715-834-7785

CRT display devices.

Visual Communications Co.
PO Box 986
El Segundo, CA 90245
Tele: 213-822-4727
Attn: John Savage

Incandescent LED display devices.

Visual Technology Inc.
1703 Middlesex Street
Lowell, MA 01851
Tele: 617-459-4903
Attn: Dave Berndtson

CRT display devices.

Voice & Video Inc.
5038 Ruffner St.
San Diego, CA 92111
Tele: 619-560-1166

CRT Projection display devices.

Wamco Technical Sales Inc.
11555-A Coley River Circle
Fountain Valley, CA 92708
Tele: 714-545-5560

Incandescent display devices.

Westinghouse Electric Corp., IGTD Westinghouse Circle Horseheads, NY 14845 Tele: 607-796-3211	*Projection Storage Tubes display devices.*
Woodson Consulting Engineer Co. 1661 N. Ridgewood Ln. St. Paul, MN 55113 Tele: 612-631-1661	*Laser Projection display devices.*
World Video Inc. PO Box 117, 23 S. Reading Ave. Boyertown, PA 19512 Tele: 215-367-6055	*CRT Projection display devices.*
Wycat Systems Inc. PO Box 539, 1875 State St. Orem, UT 84057 Tele: 801-224-6400	*CRT Vector Scan display devices.*
XKD Corp. 101 Cooper Court Los Gatos, CA 95030 Tele: 408-395-3700 Attn: Robert S. Anderson	*CRT Vector Scan CRT display devices.*
Zenith Data Systems 1000 Milwaukee Ave. Glenview, IL 60025 Tele: 312-391-8860	*CRT display devices.*

Appendix B

Photometry

Photometry is the science of measuring light. Its measurements are made only in the visible portion of the electromagnetic spectrum. Photometry should not be confused with radiometry, which measures the entire electromagnetic spectrum. The measurement of light is so important to us that a special science has been formed just to study it.

Photometry bases its measurements in spherical geometry. Light is a 360 degree radiator in all directions and most measurements are made in three dimensions. In plane geometry, the angle whose arc is equal to the radius is called a radian. The radian is a unit of angular measurement in plane figures and is equal to about 52.27 degrees. In solid geometry a steradian is a unit of three dimensional angular measurement. One steradian is the solid angle subtended at a sphere's center by the area on the sphere's surface equal to the square of the sphere's radius. The abbreviation for steradian is STER.

Practical photometry concerns itself with three basic quantities—luminous flux, luminous intensity, and illumination. Let's look at luminous flux first. Luminous flux is that part of the total energy radiated per unit time from a luminous source which is capable of producing the sensation of sight. Luminous flux measurements take into account the bias of human vision. This bias is clearly shown in Fig. 1-5, which is the standard CIE observer sensitivity curve.

The unit of luminous flux is the lumen. A lumen is defined as the flux emitted per unit solid angle by a point source of 1 candle of luminous intensity. Thus, a uniform point light source of 1 candle luminous intensity emits 4Π lumens in three dimensions. Luminous flux is abbreviated by the symbol "F." In practical terms, a 40-watt incandescent lightbulb is rated at about 450 lumens.

Luminous intensity is the ratio of the luminous flux of a point light source to the solid angle formed by the area of detection and the point source. The unit of luminous intensity is the candle. It is abbreviated as the letter "l." One candle is equal to one lumen per steradian. A physical definition of the candle is the intensity of the light emitted through an opening 1/60 of a square centimeter in area from a hollow platinum enclosure maintained at a temperature of 1773° C. In terms of general experience, a 40-watt incandescent lightbulb has a luminous intensity of about 35 candles, while a 100-watt lightbulb puts out about 130 candles.

Illumination is defined as the density of the luminous flux on a surface. This is a measurement of light received rather than light transmitted. Illuminance is the total luminous flux received on a unit area of a given real or imaginary surface. It is abbreviated by the letter "E", and has units of lumens per square unit of area. Illuminance units include one lumen per one square meter (lux), one lumen per one square centimeter (phot), and one lumen per one square foot (foot-Candle).

The following mathematical relationships hold for the three types of photometric measurement:

$$F = 4\Pi l$$ **Equation B-1.**

F = luminous flux expressed in lumens
l = luminous intensity expressed in candles

$$E = \frac{F}{A}$$ **Equation B-2.**

E = illuminance expressed in lumens per square meter
F = luminous flux expressed in lumens
A = area expressed in square meters

Not all light sources are points, some are light emitting areas. Photometry has evolved a system of measurement specifically for light emitting areas. Two basic units are involved. The first is luminous emittance (symbol is the letter L) which is defined as the ratio of the luminous flux emitted by the source to the radiating area of that source. Luminous emittance is expressed in the same units as illuminance, lumens per square meter. The second unit of area photometry is luminance (symbol is the letter *B*), and is sometimes called photometric brightness. Luminance is applied to light emitting areas of appreciable size. Mathematically if the area of an emitter has a diameter or diagonal dimension greater than 1⁄10 the distance to the detector, it should be considered as an area source. Luminance is defined as the ratio of the luminous emittance to the solid angle formed by the center of the source and the detection area; this quantity multiplied by the cosine of the angle between the perpendicular to the source at its center and the perpendicular to the detection area at its center.

$$B = \frac{L\ (\cos\theta)}{\omega}$$ **Equation B-3.**

B = luminance expressed in candles per square meter
L = luminous emittance expressed in lumens per square meter
Ω = solid angle expressed in steradians
θ = plane angle expressed in radians

Glossary

Glossary

angle of incidence—The angle at which a light ray strikes a surface, measured between the incoming ray and a perpendicular to the surface.
angle of reflection—The angle at which a light ray is reflected from a surface, measured between the ray and a perpendicular to the surface.
annunciator—A word, picture or symbol that is displayed as a unit by an LCD.
anode—The positive terminal of an LED's junction.

backplane—A conductive area held electrically in common by all segments of an LCD display.
brightness—A subjective description of light intensity.

CAD—Computer Aided Design
candela—A modern unit of luminous intensity, roughly approximate to the older unit, candle.
capacitor—A device for storing an electrical charge.
catastrophic failure—The complete failure of a display device, the cessation of operation and light output.
cathode—The negative terminal of an LED junction.
cell—The single basic unit of an LCD display. The cell consists of all the electrical connections, and other hardware in addition to the liquid crystal medium.
chrominance—The quality of a color compared to a chosen reference color of the same luminous intensity.

clearing point—The temperature at which a nematic liquid changes into an isotropic fluid. The clearing point is the upper temperature limit of operation for an LCD.

cones—Photoreceptor cells within the retina responsible for color sensitivity and detail.

contrast ratio—The ratio of the luminance of the active segments to the inactive segments of an LCD.

CPU—Central Processing Unit, the microprocessor within a computer, its brain.

CRT—An acronym for Cathode Ray Tube.

deflection—The process of moving the high-energy electron beam around a CRT's screen by either electromagnetic or electrostatic forces.

delay time—The time interval between the end of an LCD's ''on'' pulse to when the display ceases to show the information.

dichroism—A property of certain crystalline substances in which one polarized component of incident light is absorbed and the other is transmitted.

dielectric—A material having a relatively low electrical conductivity.

dielectric anisotropy—The property of certain liquid crystals to twist when in the presence of an electric field.

dominant wavelength—The mean wavelength of an LED's light output.

dot matrix—A rectilinear grid made up of dots (pixels).

dot-pitch—The diagonal distance between two adjacent pixels on a CRT screen.

ELD—Electroluminescent Display

electromagnetic waves—Transverse waves in space having an electric component and a magnetic component, each being perpendicular to the other, and both perpendicular to the direction of propagation.

electromagnetism—The branch of the physical science that deals with the relations between electricity and magnetism.

EX-OR gate—An Exclusive OR electronic logic gate.

field—An image generated by a single complete horizontal set of raster scans in a CRT. A field may or may not constitute a complete picture or frame.

film deposition—A method of making thin films for semiconductor junctions by vapor deposition.

filter—Any device that is frequency sensitive to the passage of light.

font—The style of an alphabetical character or digit.

fovea—A small area in the central part of the retina which contains only cones.

frame—A frame is a complete video image reproduced on a CRT. A frame may consist of one or more fields.

gallium—A chemical element used in semiconductor manufacture, notably in LED junctions.

ghosting—The condition in which display areas that should be off are partially activated or on.

guest-host dicronic—A type of colored LCD where the liquid crystal medium acts as host, while the colored dye material acts as guest.

HDTV—High Definition Television

IC—An Integrated Circuit

interlaced scanning—Raster scanning of a CRT requiring more than one field to complete a frame.

ion implantation—A method of semiconductor manufacture that uses electrostatic fields to place dopant ions into a substrate.

ITO—Indium Tin Oxide is a transparent conducting material used in display manufacture.

LC—LC is an acronym for liquid crystal.

LCD—Liquid Crystal Display

LED—Light Emitting Diode

Lumen—Unit of luminous flux. See Appendix B.

LUT—An acronym for Look Up Table. A look up table is a section of computer memory reserved for the storage of image parameters.

mask—A metallic grid used to shadow portions of a CRT's screen.

MIM—Metal Insulator Metal. A form of transistor junction.

misconvergence—The inability of a multi-gun CRT to focus all guns on the same point on the screen. Misconvergence is usually less than 0.75 mm in modern CRTs.

MTBF—An acronym for Mean Time Before Failure.

multiplex (MUX)—A method of driving complex displays by a matrix scheme. MUX techniques save interconnection at the expense of drive electronics complexity.

nanometer—A nanometer is one billionth of a meter.

neck—The narrow area of a CRT that contains the active electrodes that control the electron beam(s).

neutral density filter—An optical filter that attenuates all colors equally.

noninterlaced—A system of raster scanning a CRT requiring only a single field to complete a frame.

NTSC—An acronym for National Television Standards Committee. This body established the video encoding parameters for U.S. television in 1943.

oscillator—An electronic device or circuit which generates an alternating current at a specified frequency.

PAL—A system of video information encoding for CRTs used in Europe.

parallax—The difference in the apparent direction or position of an object when viewed from different angles.

parametric—Relating to the intercepts made by a plane on a crystallographic axis.

parametric failure—The partial failure of a display device, such as a weakening of light output, but not the complete failure of light output.

phosphors—The material coating the inside of a CRT's screen. Phosphors give off light when struck by high energy electrons.

photolithography—The process of printing using photographic images.

photometer—A device for measuring the intensity of light.

pixel—The smallest unit it is possible to display on an electronic display device.

PLA—A Programmable Logic Array

polarization—The property of light which vibrates only in a single plane perpendicular to the direction of the ray's propagation.

primary colors—Any set of three colors whose mixture, in various proportions, will produce white. The most commonly used primary colors are red, green, and blue.

RAM—Random Access Memory, computer memory that is electronic in nature and can be either read or written.

raster—The systematic horizontal scanning of a CRT.

retina—The innermost layer of the eye where light sensitive rods and cones are located.

RGB—An acronym for Red, Green, and Blue, the primary colors used by many displays to make all colors.

rods—Photoreceptors in the retina which respond to low light levels and give only black & white information.

ROM—Read Only Memory, a form of electronic memory that can only be read and not rewritten.

scrambler—A plastic lens used to diffuse the light output of LEDs.

segment—An active area, usually linear, in an electronic display. This term is most commonly used in relation to LEDs and LCDs.

semiconductor—A solid state electronic conductor with resistivity between conductors and insulators.

slit photometer—A type of photometer that uses a very thin linear aperture.

spectral line halfwidth—A measure of an LED's color purity corresponding to the output wavelength's half intensity levels.

static drive—A method of wiring an LCD where each segment has its own individual electrical connections. Static drive is the opposite of multiplexed drive.

T-1—A standardized LED package.

T-1 ¾—A standardized LED package.

TFT—Thin-Film Transistor

transflective—The property of a material to reflect light from one side while transmitting it from the other side. A one way mirror is an example of a transflective device.

twisted nematic (TN)—A type of liquid crystal whose molecular alignment is a spiral. At rest, such a crystal has all its molecules parallel within a plane.

VFD—Vacuum Fluorescent Display

visibility curve—A graph illustrating the eye's sensitivity to light of different colors.

wavelength—The distance between one particle in a wave and a corresponding particle in the next wave.

yoke—The coils of wire, located on the CRT's neck, used to electromagnetically deflect the CRT's electron beam.

zener—A diode whose reverse bias breakdown voltage is constant.

Index

Index